Shojo Beat

yona of the Dawn

30

Story & Art by

Mizuho Kusanagi

YONA OF THE DAWN

Story Thus Far

Hak

Yona

One of the greatest heroes in the nation, known as the "Thunder Beast." He'd obeyed King Il's orders and became bodyguard to his childhood friend, Yona. He walks away from his position as general in order to protect his tribe.

Princess of the Kingdom of **Kohka**. While on the run from her deceased father's political enemies, she comes to the realization that she's spent her life being protected by other people. She gathers the Four Dragons in order to protect herself and the people who are most important to her.

Su-won

Ying Kuelbo

A young scion of the royal bloodline and king of Kohka. To keep Kohka safe from invasion by the Kai Empire to the north or the nations of Xing and Sei to the south, he is trying to create a powerful nation by uniting and ruling over the Five Tribes.

King of the Tuuli Tribe in North Kai. He control Sen Province in the Kai Empire. He wants the powe of the Four Dragon Warriors so that he can tak possession of Kohka and gain control of the entir Kai Empire.

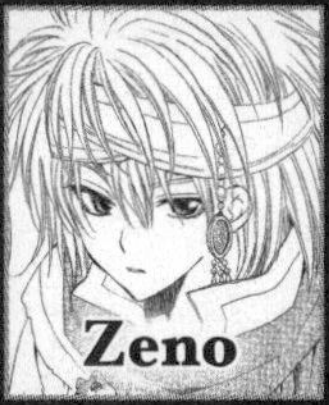
Zeno

The Yellow Dragon of the Four Dragon Warriors. He has the power of a dragon in his body—the power of immortality! He is one of the first Dragons who served the Crimson Dragon King, and he finally met Yona after many years of waiting.

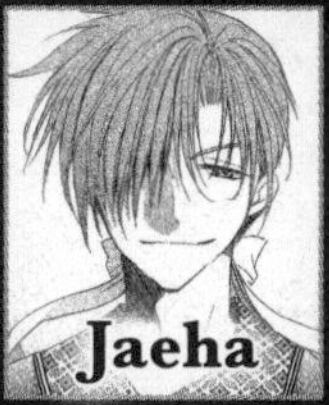
Jaeha

The Green Dragon of the Four Dragon Warriors. With the power of a dragon in his right leg, he can leap to tremendous heights. He loves freedom and hates the idea of being tied down to duty as one of the Four Legendary Dragons.

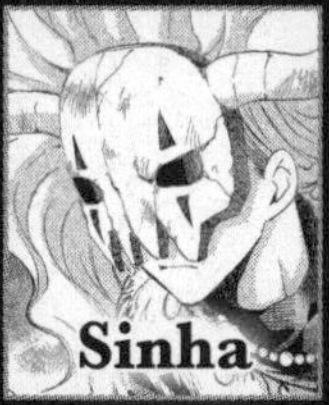
Sinha

The Blue Dragon of the Four Dragon Warriors. With the power of a dragon in his eyes, he can paralyze anyone he looks at. He grew up being hated and feared for his incredible power.

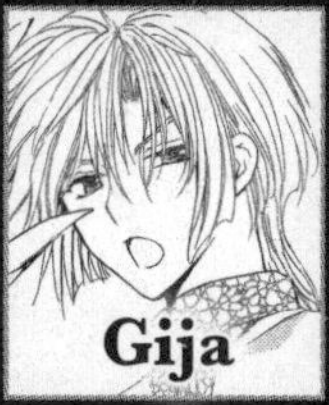
Gija

The White Dragon, one of the Four Dragon Warriors. His right hand contains a dragon's might and is more powerful than ten men. He adores Yona and finds fulfillment in his role as one of the Four Legendary Dragons.

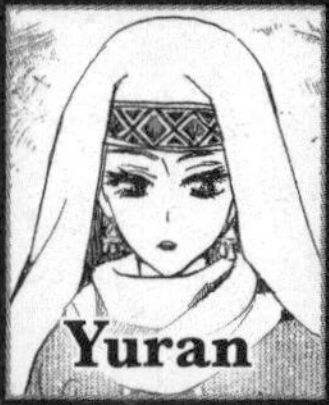
Yuran

Kuelbo's wife. Her husband ordered her to look after Yona.

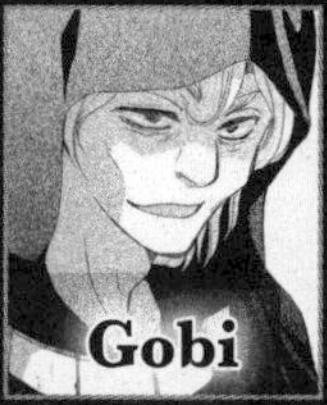
Gobi

A priest from Xing. He went to the Kai Empire after being driven out of Xing. He's trying to gain control of Yona and the Four Dragon Warriors.

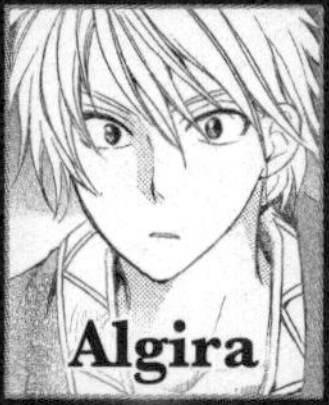
Algira

One of a group of warriors in Xing known as the Five Stars. He and Voldo, another of the Five Stars, have come to assist Hak and the others.

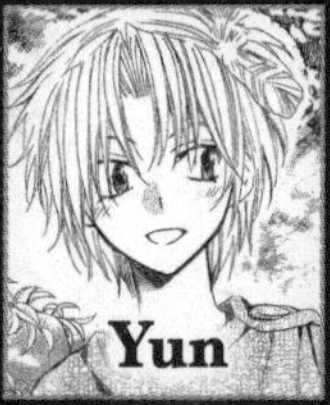
Yun

A mouthy pretty boy, he has a lot of practical knowledge and takes good care of others. He is like a mother to Yona and her friends.

The Four Dragon Warriors… In the Age of Myths, a dragon god took on human form and founded a nation. As the Crimson Dragon King, he was the first ruler of the Kingdom of Kohka. Four other dragons shared their blood with humans so that they could protect him. Those warriors became known as the Four Legendary Dragons, or the Four Dragon Warriors, and their power has been passed down for generations.

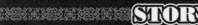

STORY

Yona, the princess of the Kingdom of Kohka, was raised by her kind, loving father, King Il. She has deep feelings for her cousin Su-won, a companion since childhood. On her 16th birthday, she sees her father being stabbed to death—by Su-won!

Driven from the palace, Yona and Hak meet a priest named Ik-su who tells Yona a prophecy that leads her to gather the Four Dragon Warriors together. Yona then decides to take up arms and defend her nation with the Four Dragon Warriors at her side.

War between Xing and Kohka is narrowly averted thanks to Yona and her friends. After this tension lifts, Hak tells Yona the truth about his feelings for her.

Ying Kuelbo of the Kai Empire wants the power of the Dragon Warriors, and to that end, he's taken Yona, Jaeha, Zeno and Yun captive! Kuelbo forces Jaeha and Zeno to fight for the Kai army by threatening Yona. Meanwhile, Hak, Gija and Sinha have joined the Kohka army, leading to a battlefield showdown between the Dragons! As the Kai Empire overpowers the disadvantaged Kohka army, Hak, despite his injuries, comes up with a plan to turn the tide!

*The Kingdom of Kohka is a coalition of five tribes: Fire, Water, Wind, Earth and Sky. The throne is held by the tribe with the greatest influence, so the current royal family are of the Sky Tribe. The royal capital is Kuuto. Each tribe's chief also holds the rank of general, and the Meeting of the Five Tribes is the nation's most powerful decision-making body.

yona of the Dawn
Volume 30

CONTENTS

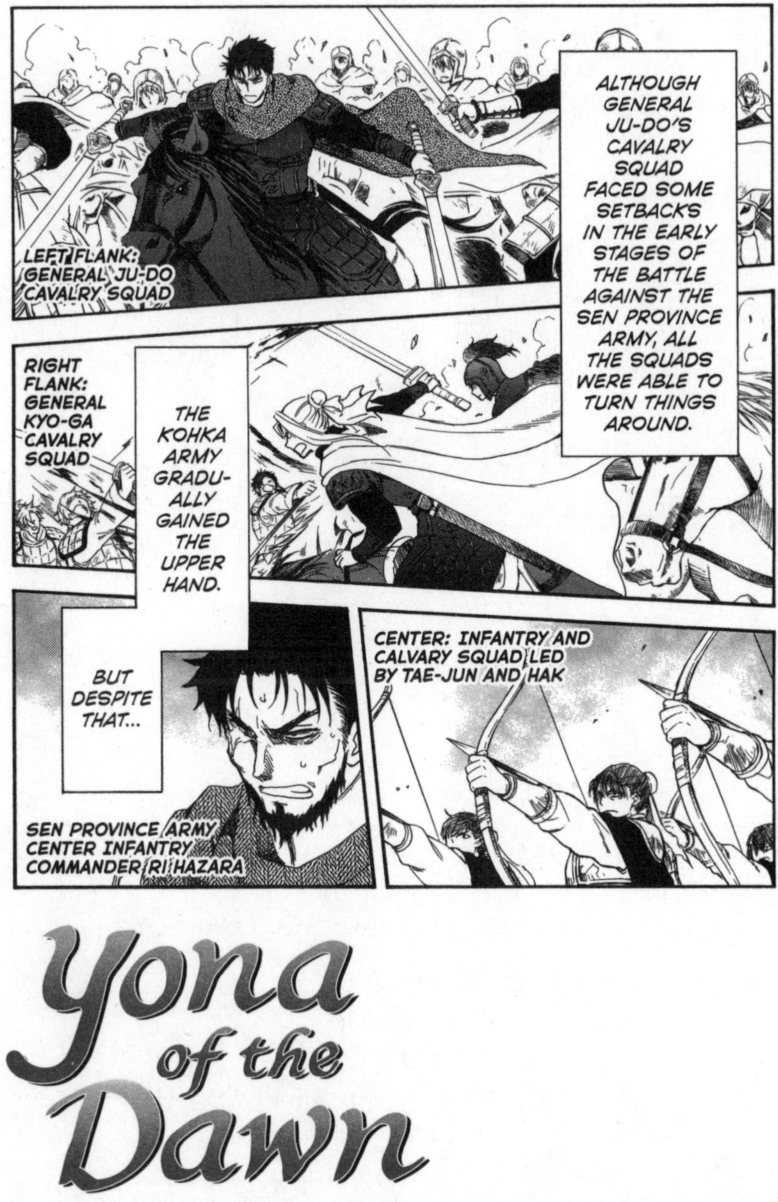
ALTHOUGH GENERAL JU-DO'S CAVALRY SQUAD FACED SOME SETBACKS IN THE EARLY STAGES OF THE BATTLE AGAINST THE SEN PROVINCE ARMY, ALL THE SQUADS WERE ABLE TO TURN THINGS AROUND.
LEFT FLANK: GENERAL JU-DO CAVALRY SQUAD
RIGHT FLANK: GENERAL KYO-GA CAVALRY SQUAD
THE KOHKA ARMY GRADUALLY GAINED THE UPPER HAND.
CENTER: INFANTRY AND CALVARY SQUAD LED BY TAE-JUN AND HAK
BUT DESPITE THAT...
SEN PROVINCE ARMY CENTER INFANTRY COMMANDER RI HAZARA

Yona of the Dawn

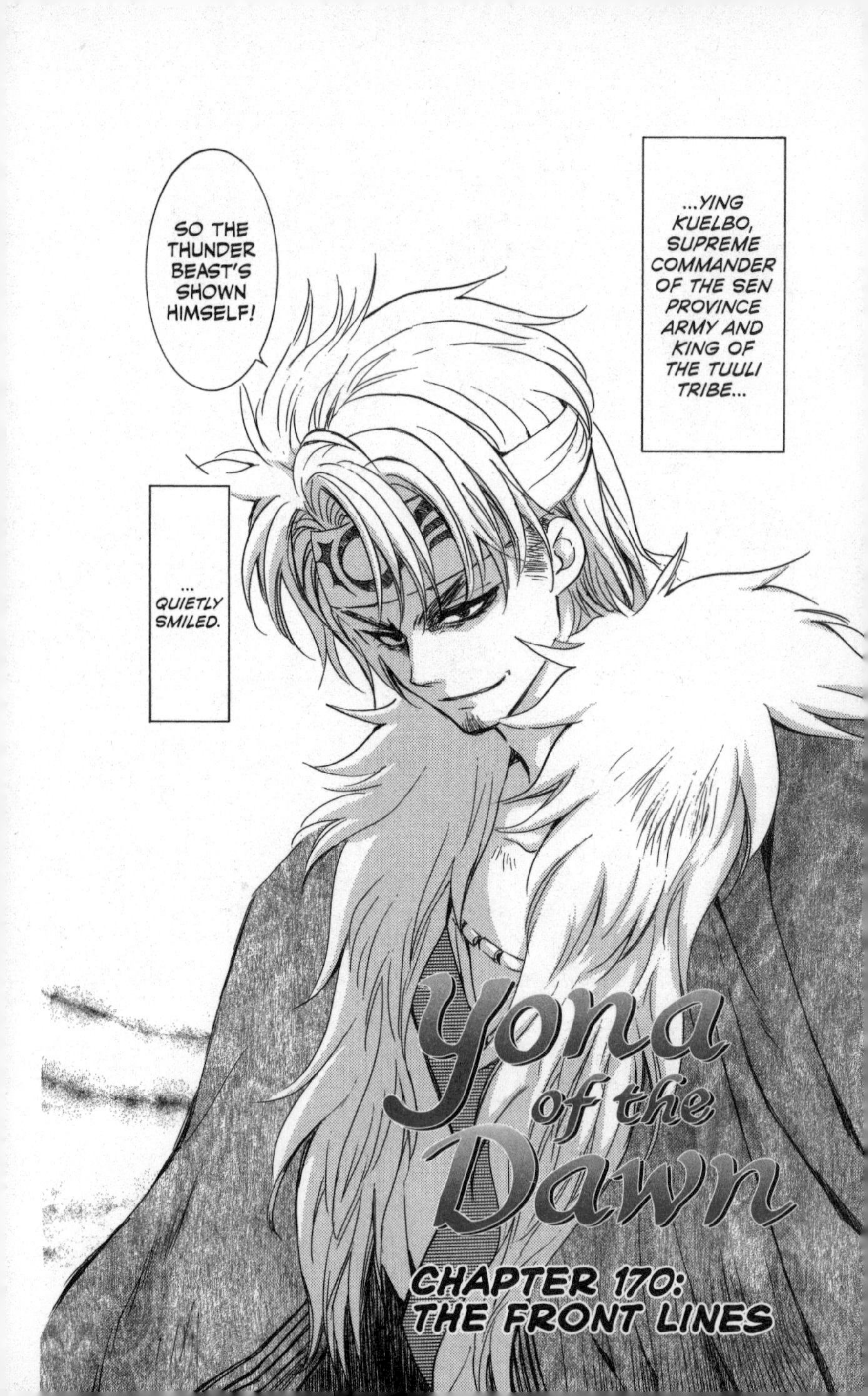
...YING KUELBO, SUPREME COMMANDER OF THE SEN PROVINCE ARMY AND KING OF THE TUULI TRIBE...
SO THE THUNDER BEAST'S SHOWN HIMSELF!
... QUIETLY SMILED.
Yona of the Dawn
CHAPTER 170: THE FRONT LINES

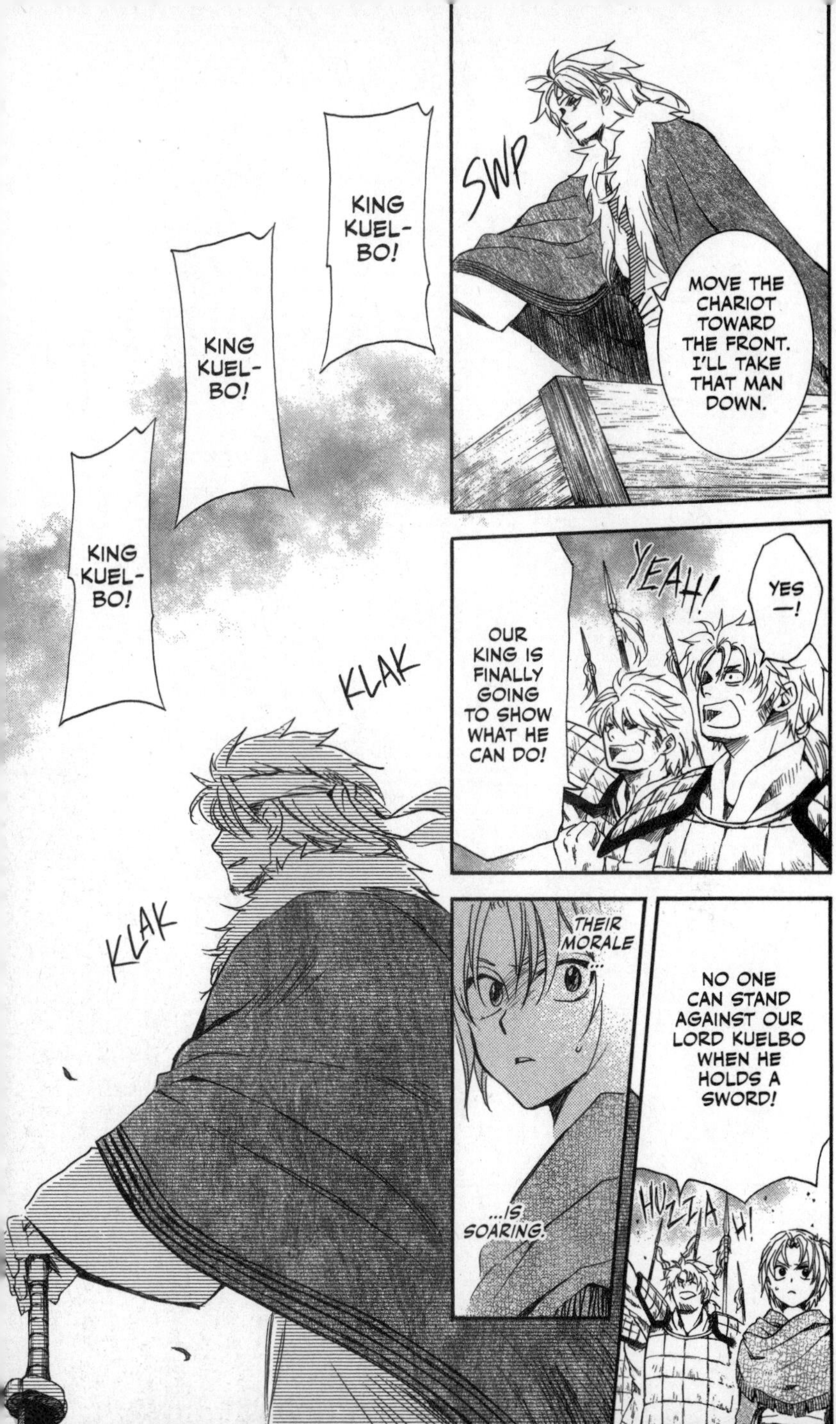
SWP
MOVE THE CHARIOT TOWARD THE FRONT. I'LL TAKE THAT MAN DOWN.
YES—!
YEAH!
OUR KING IS FINALLY GOING TO SHOW WHAT HE CAN DO!
NO ONE CAN STAND AGAINST OUR LORD KUELBO WHEN HE HOLDS A SWORD!
HUZZAH!
THEIR MORALE...
...IS SOARING.
KING KUEL-BO!
KING KUEL-BO!
KING KUEL-BO!
KLAK
KLAK

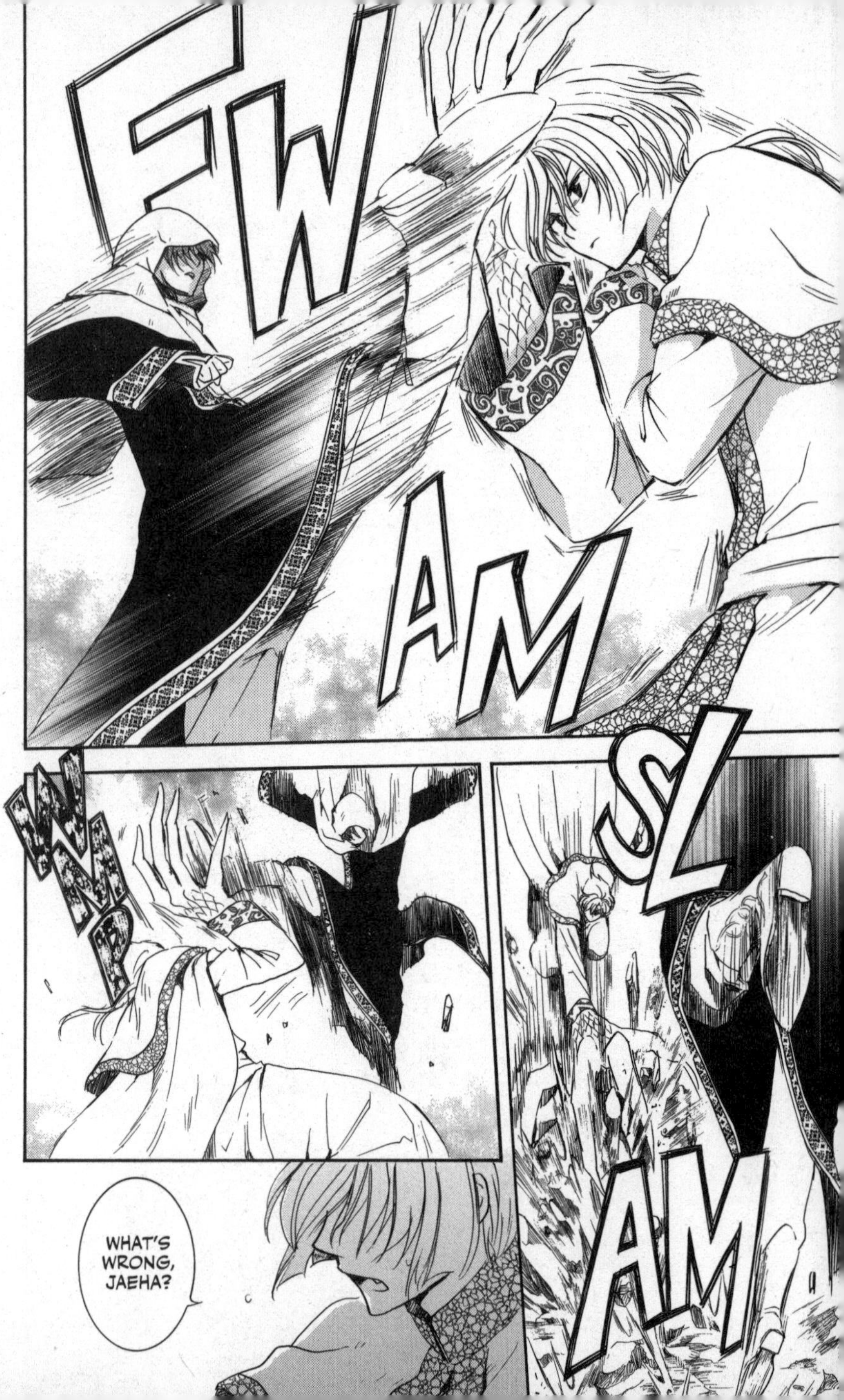
FWAM
SLAM
WMP
WHAT'S WRONG, JAEHA?

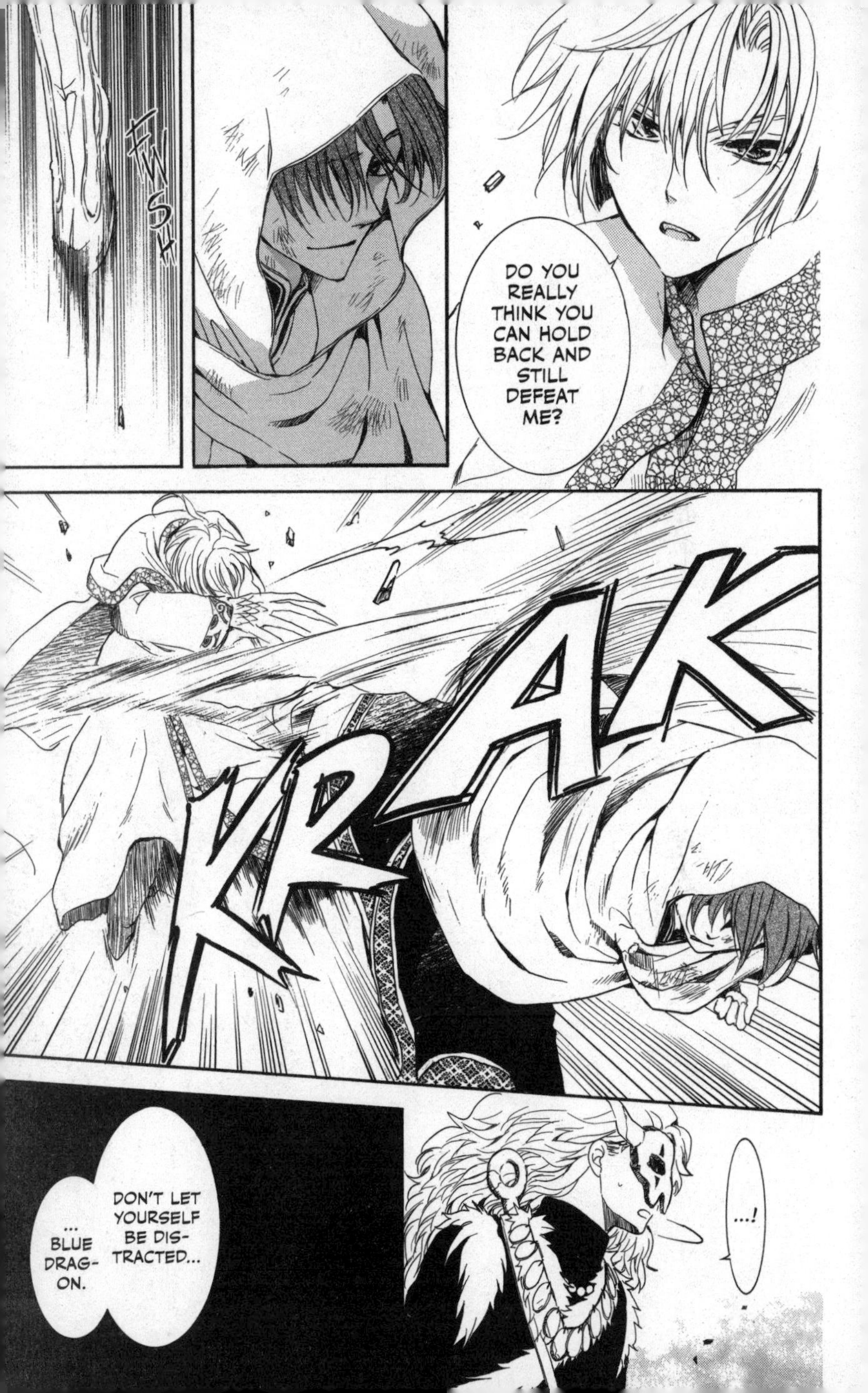
DO YOU REALLY THINK YOU CAN HOLD BACK AND STILL DEFEAT ME?
FWSH
KRAK
...!
DON'T LET YOURSELF BE DIS-TRACTED...
... BLUE DRAG-ON.

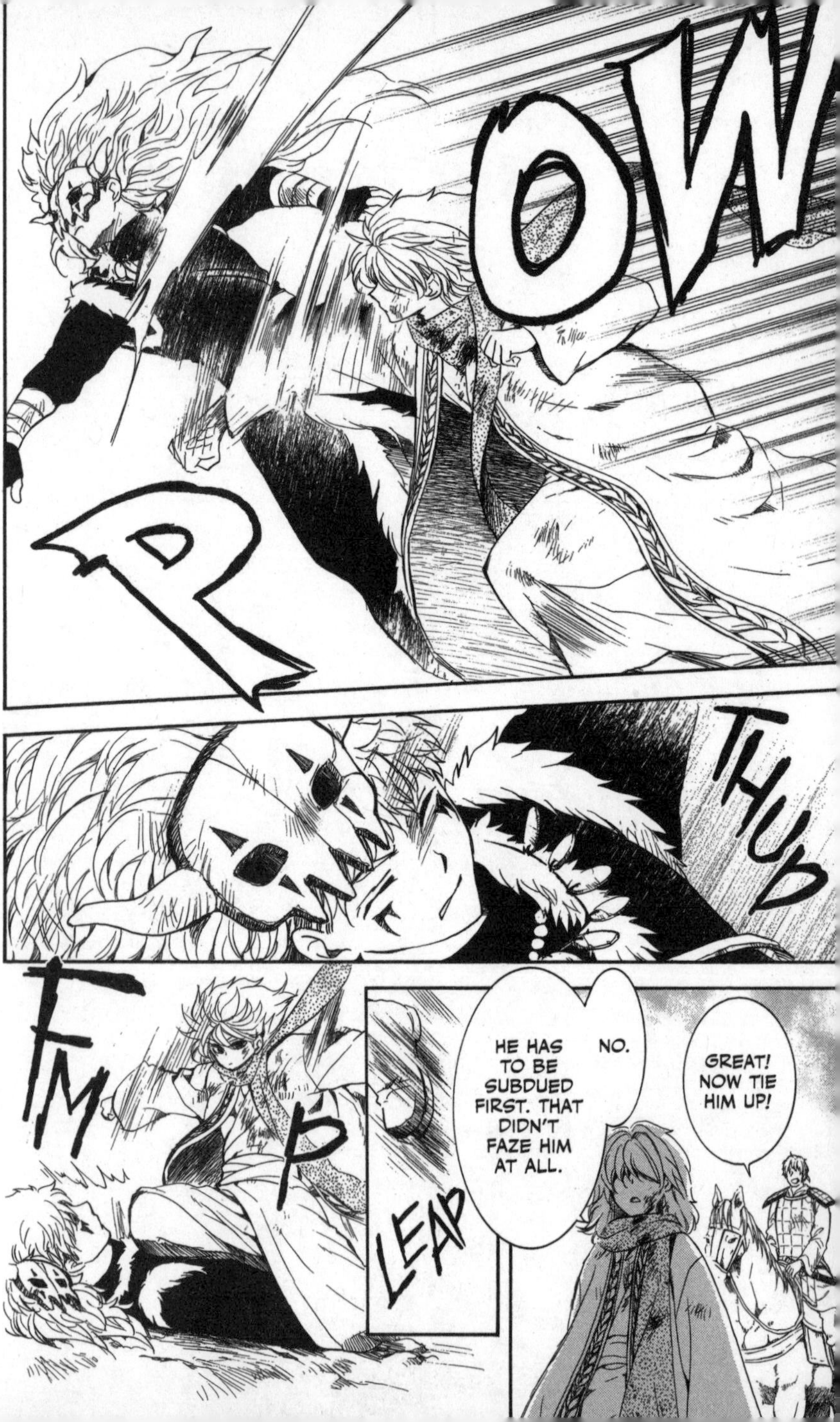
POW
THUD
GREAT! NOW TIE HIM UP!
NO.
HE HAS TO BE SUBDUED FIRST. THAT DIDN'T FAZE HIM AT ALL.
LEAP
FMP

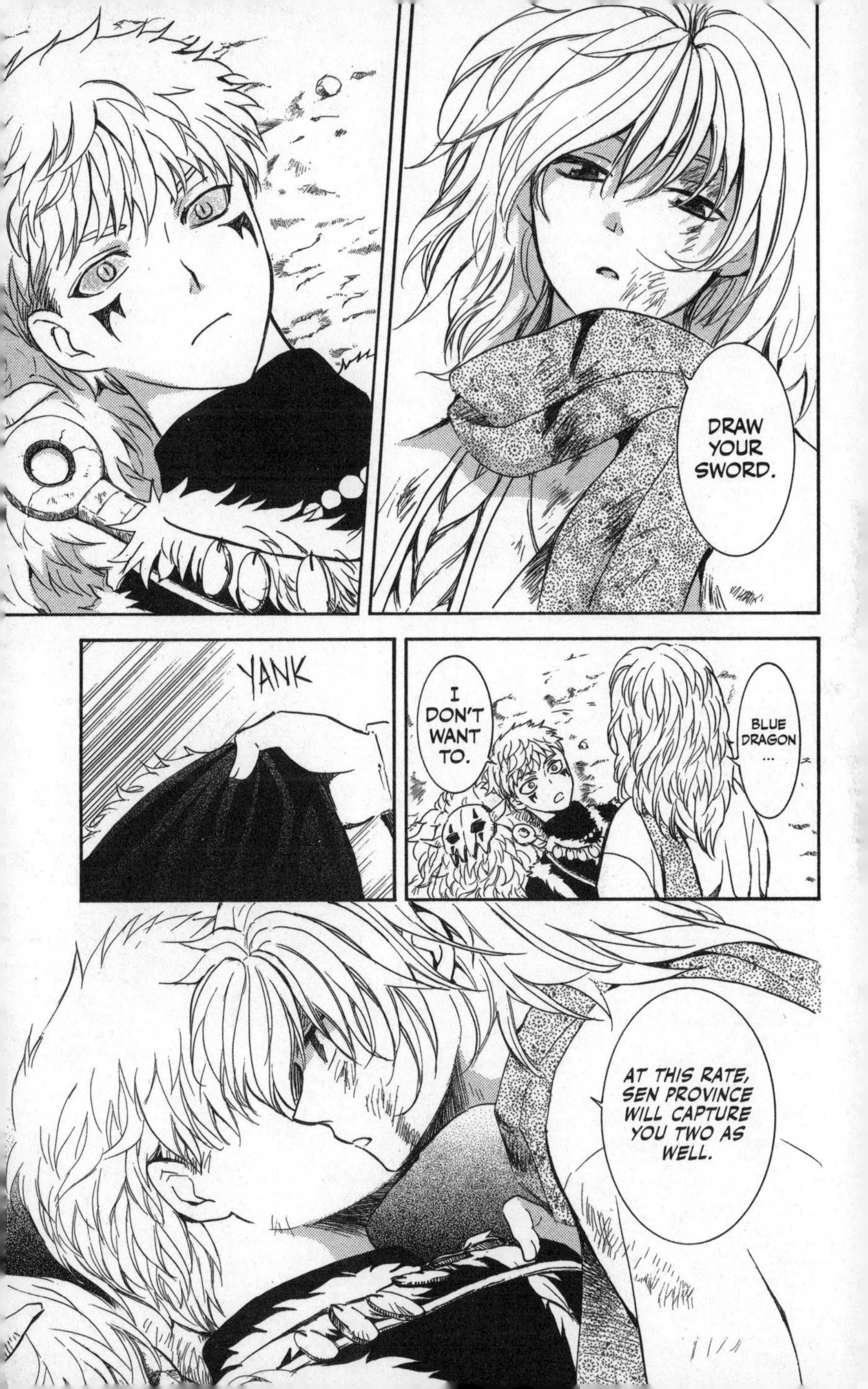
DRAW YOUR SWORD.
BLUE DRAGON ...
I DON'T WANT TO.
YANK
AT THIS RATE, SEN PROVINCE WILL CAPTURE YOU TWO AS WELL.

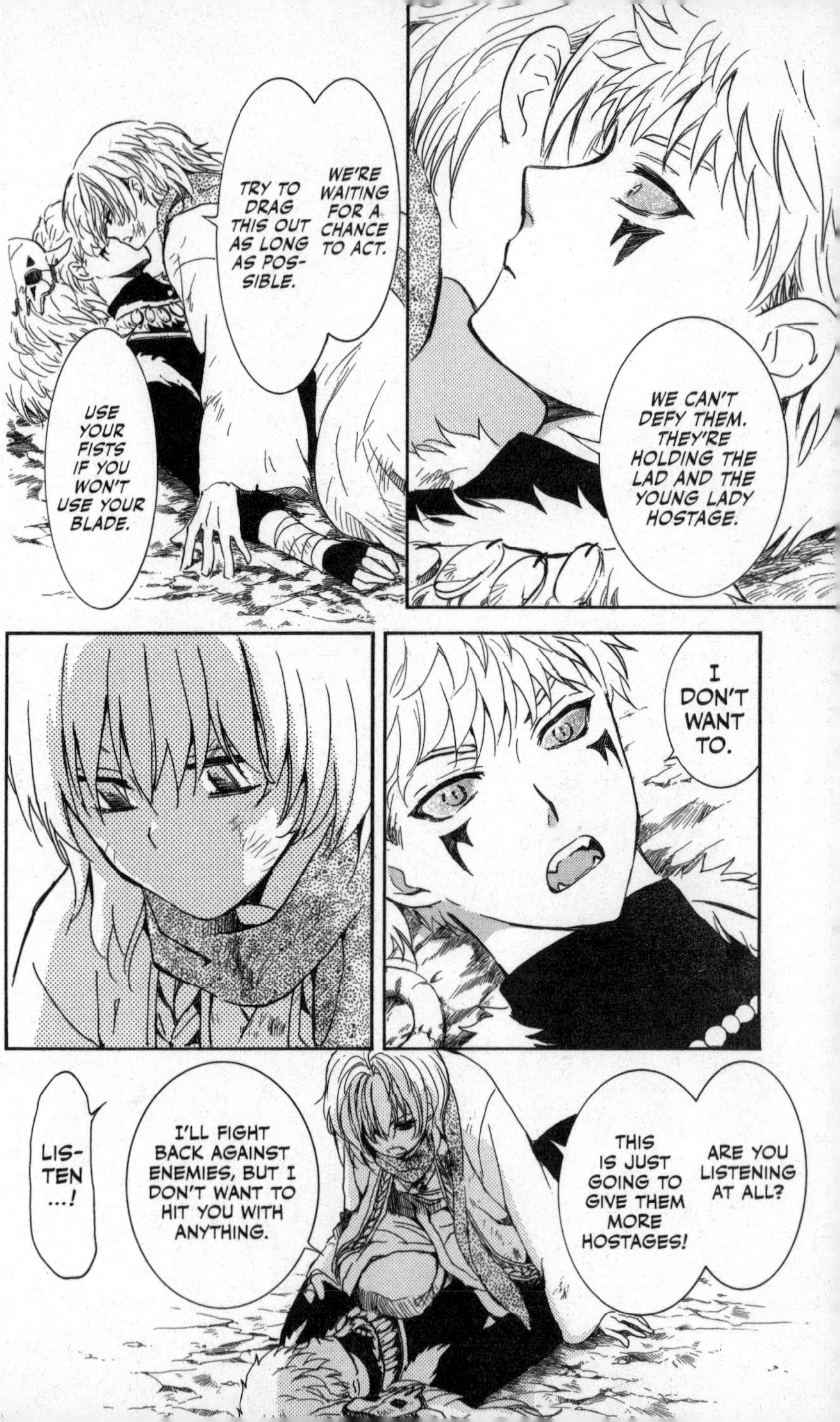
WE CAN'T DEFY THEM. THEY'RE HOLDING THE LAD AND THE YOUNG LADY HOSTAGE.
WE'RE WAITING FOR A CHANCE TO ACT.
TRY TO DRAG THIS OUT AS LONG AS POS-SIBLE.
USE YOUR FISTS IF YOU WON'T USE YOUR BLADE.
I DON'T WANT TO.
ARE YOU LISTENING AT ALL?
THIS IS JUST GOING TO GIVE THEM MORE HOSTAGES!
I'LL FIGHT BACK AGAINST ENEMIES, BUT I DON'T WANT TO HIT YOU WITH ANYTHING.
LIS-TEN ...!

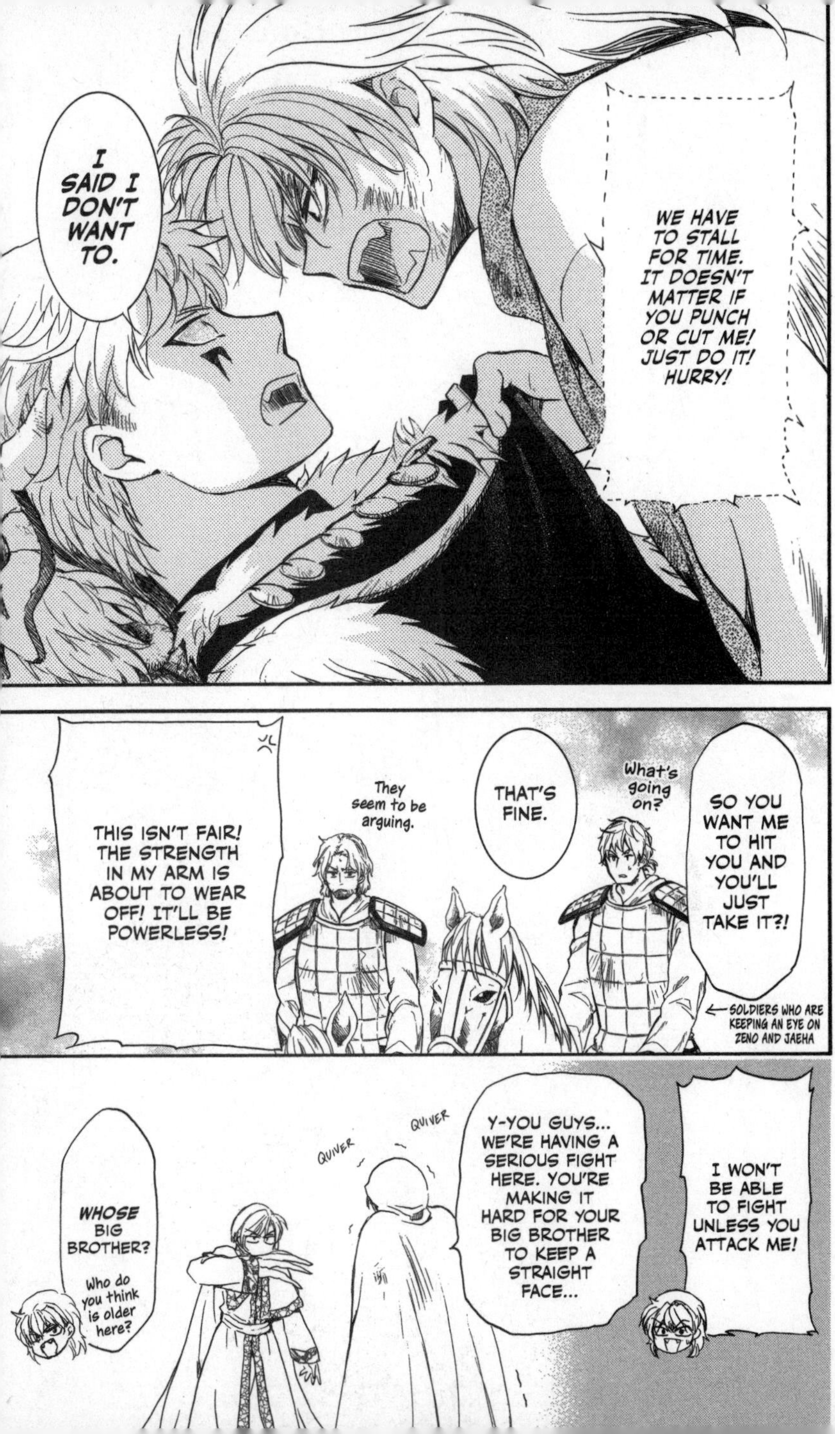
WE HAVE TO STALL FOR TIME. IT DOESN'T MATTER IF YOU PUNCH OR CUT ME! JUST DO IT! HURRY!
I SAID I DON'T WANT TO.
SO YOU WANT ME TO HIT YOU AND YOU'LL JUST TAKE IT?!
What's going on?
THAT'S FINE.
They seem to be arguing.
THIS ISN'T FAIR! THE STRENGTH IN MY ARM IS ABOUT TO WEAR OFF! IT'LL BE POWERLESS!
← SOLDIERS WHO ARE KEEPING AN EYE ON ZENO AND JAEHA
I WON'T BE ABLE TO FIGHT UNLESS YOU ATTACK ME!
Y-YOU GUYS... WE'RE HAVING A SERIOUS FIGHT HERE. YOU'RE MAKING IT HARD FOR YOUR BIG BROTHER TO KEEP A STRAIGHT FACE...
QUIVER
QUIVER
WHOSE BIG BROTHER?
Who do you think is older here?

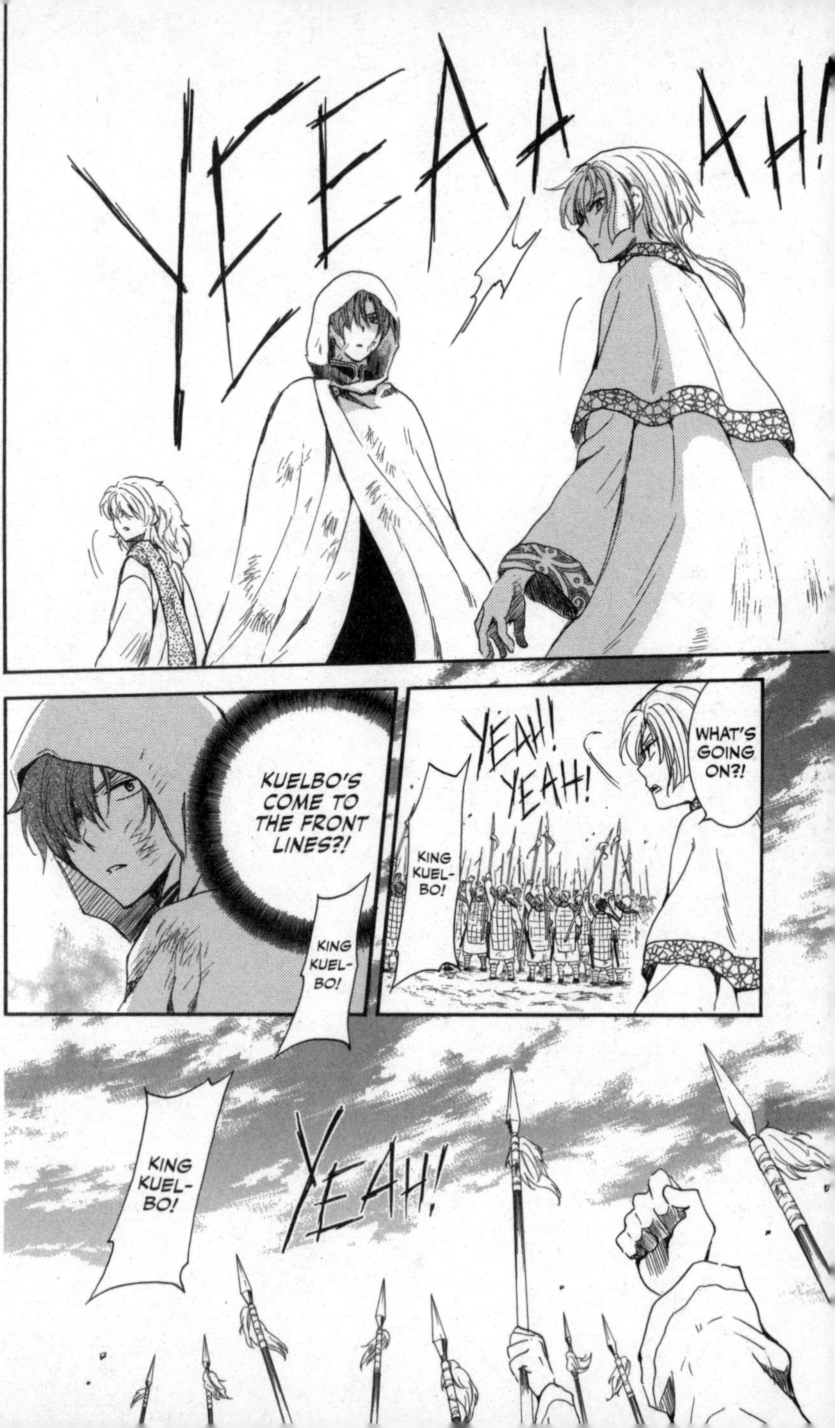
YEEAA AH!
WHAT'S GOING ON?!
YEAH! YEAH!
KING KUEL-BO!
KUELBO'S COME TO THE FRONT LINES?!
KING KUEL-BO!
YEAH!
KING KUEL-BO!

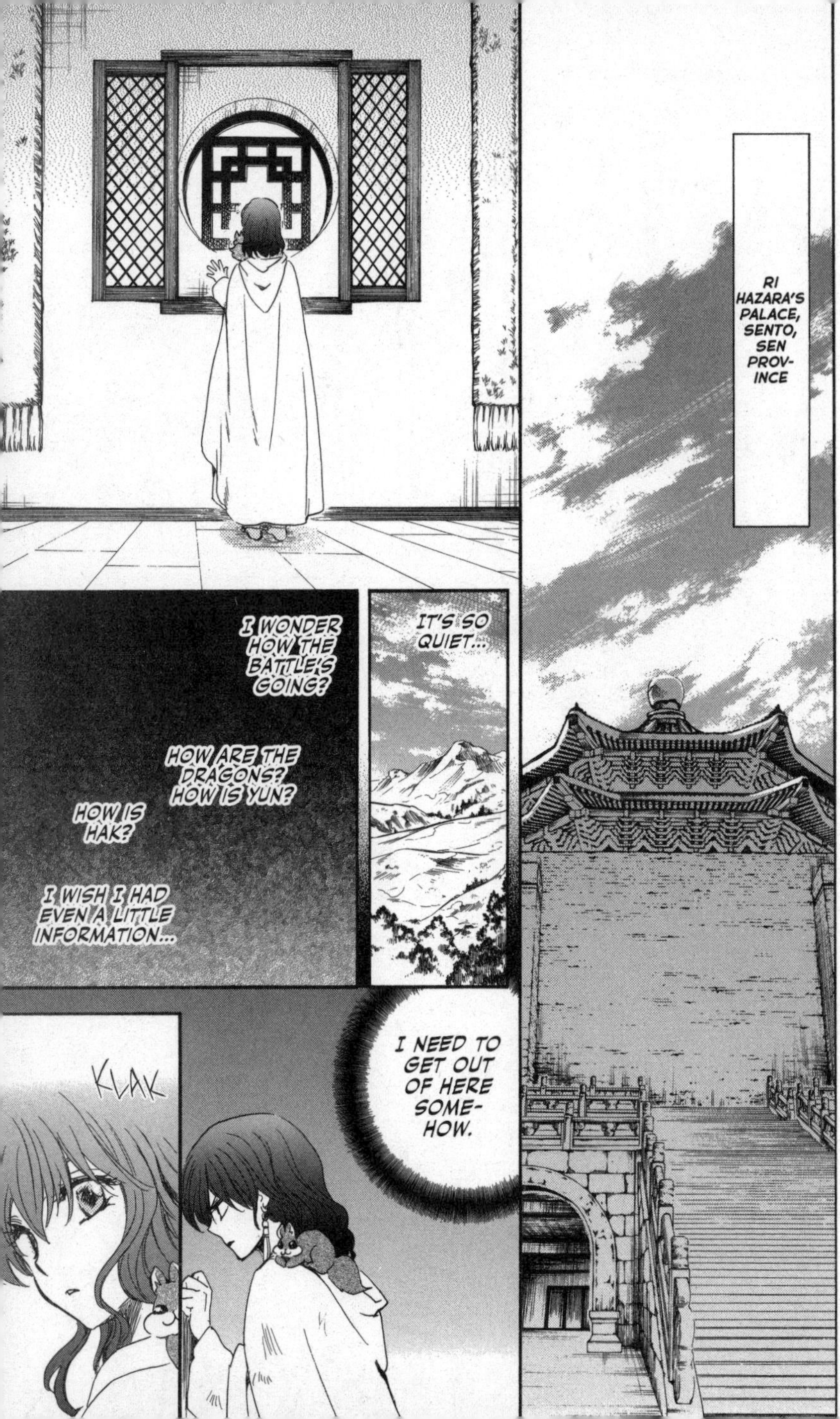
RI HAZARA'S PALACE, SENTO, SEN PROVINCE
IT'S SO QUIET...
I WONDER HOW THE BATTLE'S GOING?
HOW ARE THE DRAGONS? HOW IS YUN?
HOW IS HAK?
I WISH I HAD EVEN A LITTLE INFORMATION...
I NEED TO GET OUT OF HERE SOME-HOW.
KLAK

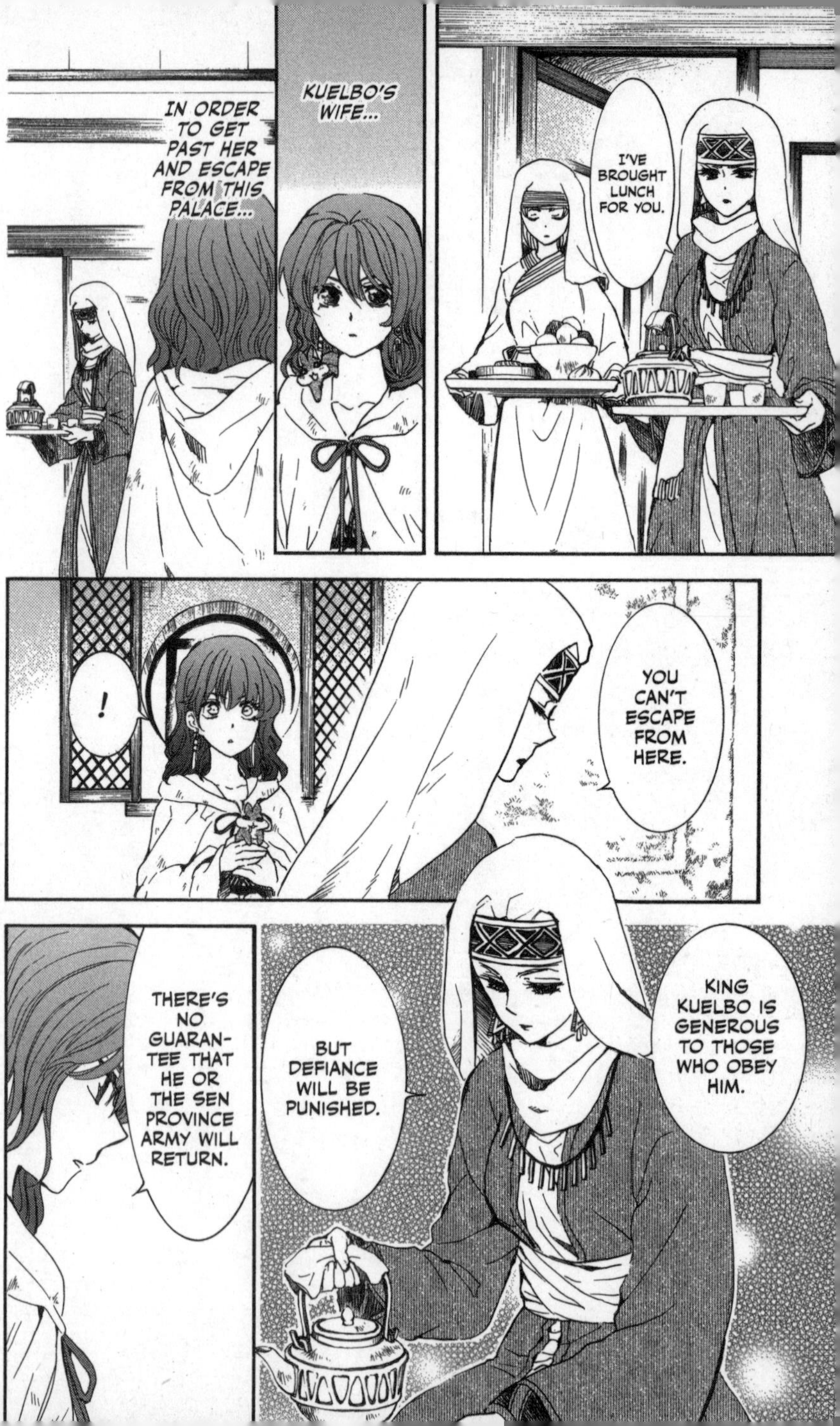
I'VE BROUGHT LUNCH FOR YOU.
KUELBO'S WIFE...
IN ORDER TO GET PAST HER AND ESCAPE FROM THIS PALACE...
YOU CAN'T ESCAPE FROM HERE.
!
KING KUELBO IS GENEROUS TO THOSE WHO OBEY HIM.
BUT DEFIANCE WILL BE PUNISHED.
THERE'S NO GUARANTEE THAT HE OR THE SEN PROVINCE ARMY WILL RETURN.

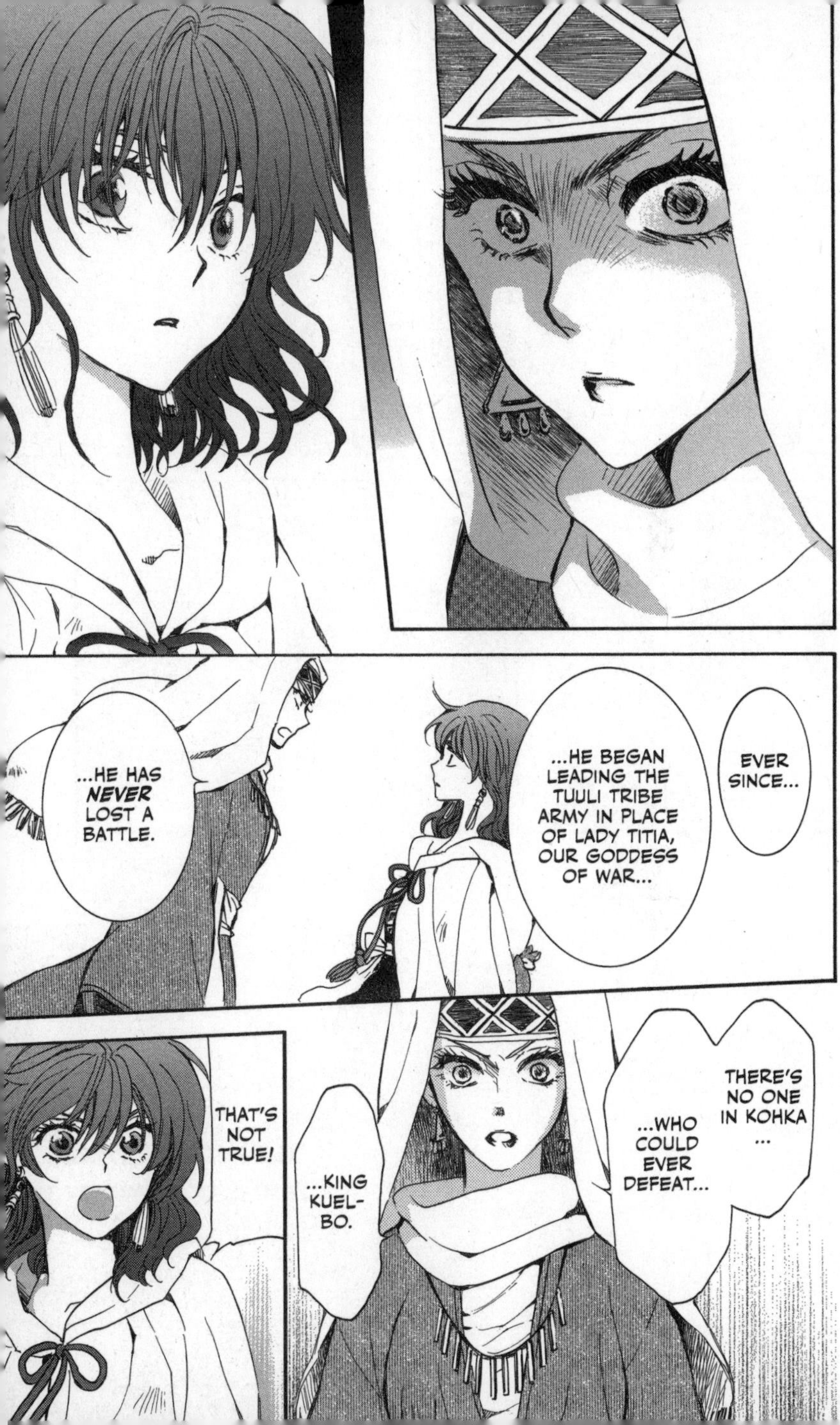
EVER SINCE...
...HE BEGAN LEADING THE TUULI TRIBE ARMY IN PLACE OF LADY TITIA, OUR GODDESS OF WAR...
...HE HAS *NEVER* LOST A BATTLE.
THERE'S NO ONE IN KOHKA ...
...WHO COULD EVER DEFEAT...
...KING KUEL-BO.
THAT'S NOT TRUE!

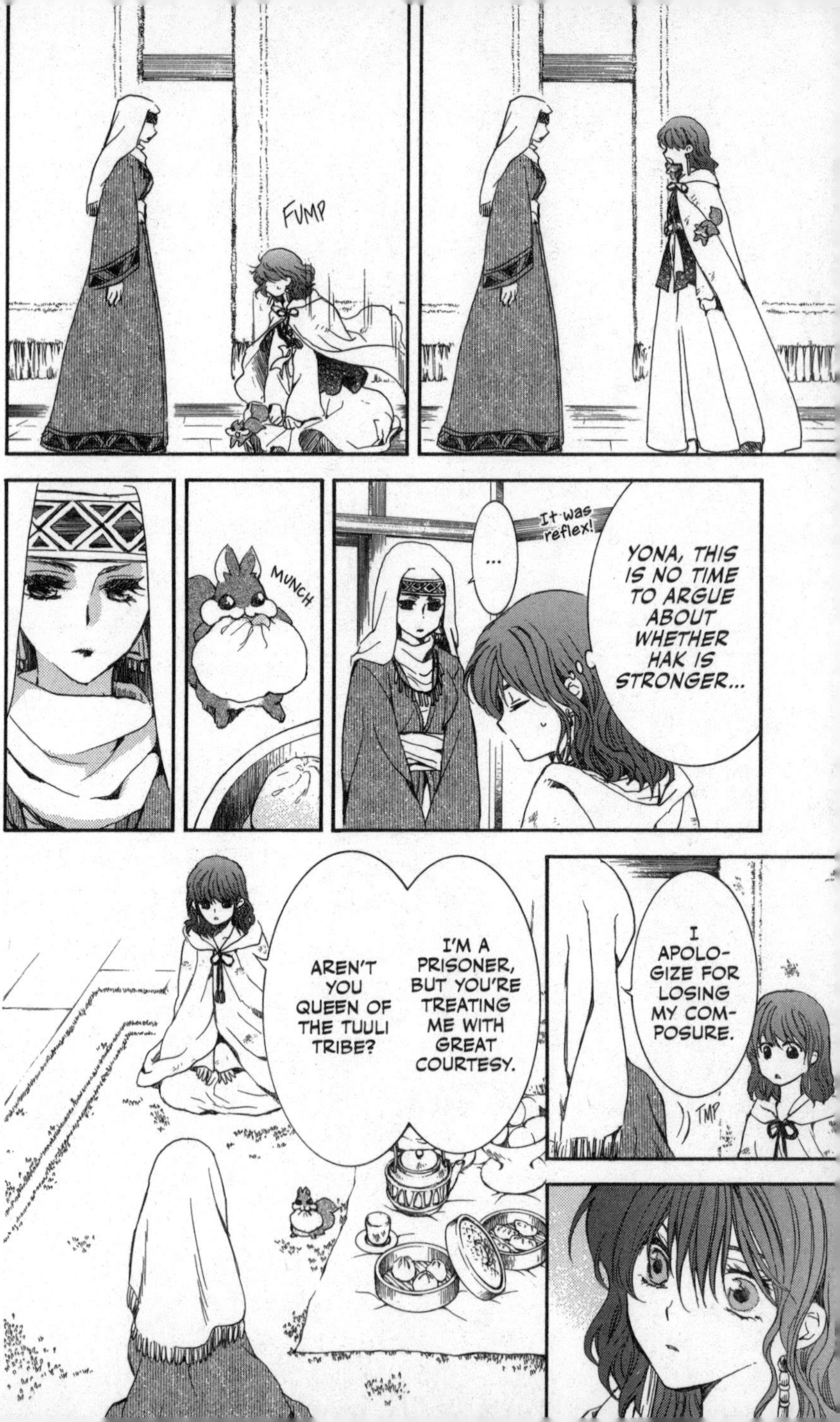
FUMP
YONA, THIS IS NO TIME TO ARGUE ABOUT WHETHER HAK IS STRONGER...
It was reflex!
...
MUNCH
I APOLOGIZE FOR LOSING MY COMPOSURE.
TMP
I'M A PRISONER, BUT YOU'RE TREATING ME WITH GREAT COURTESY.
AREN'T YOU QUEEN OF THE TUULI TRIBE?

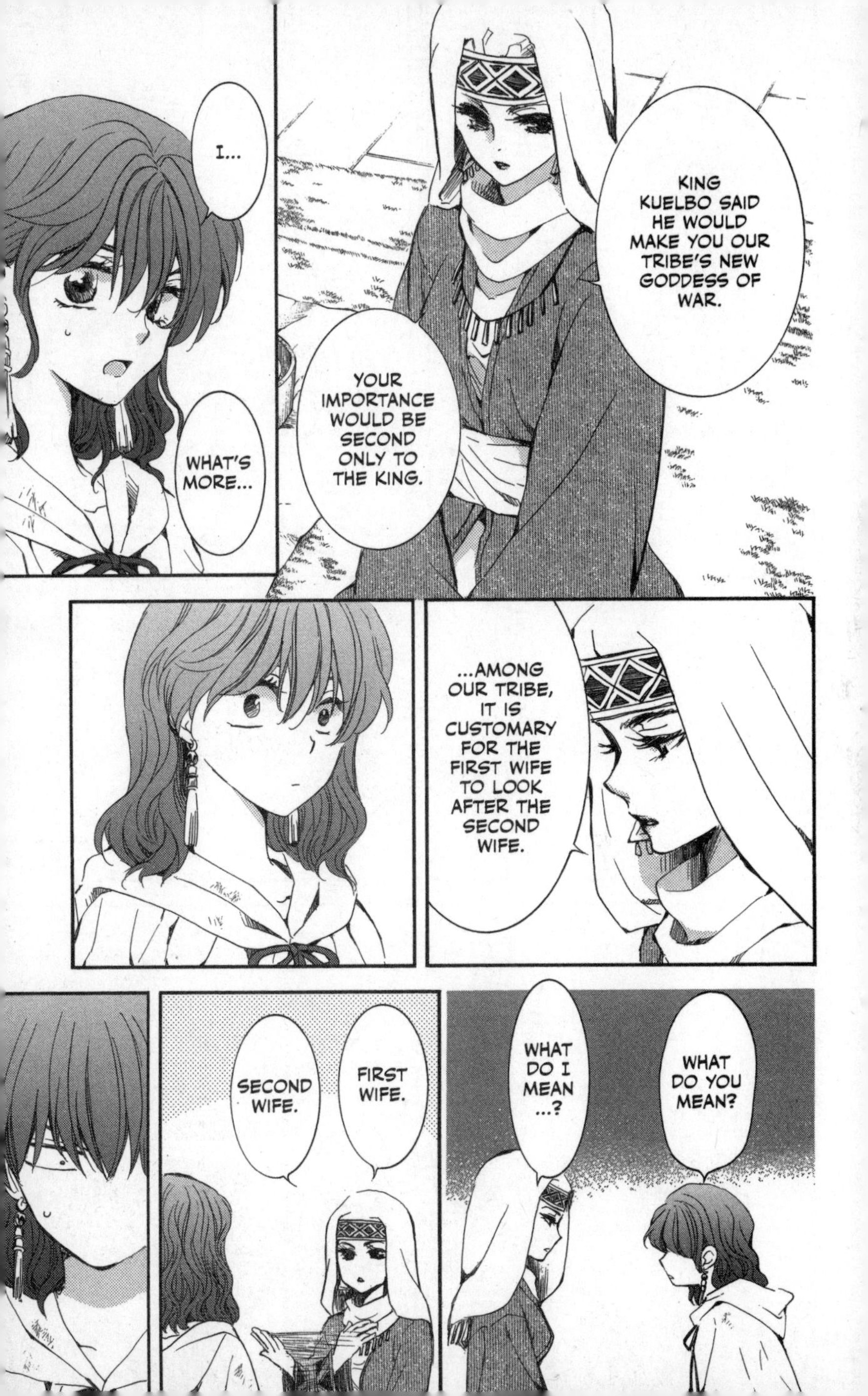
KING KUELBO SAID HE WOULD MAKE YOU OUR TRIBE'S NEW GODDESS OF WAR.
YOUR IMPORTANCE WOULD BE SECOND ONLY TO THE KING.
I...
WHAT'S MORE...
...AMONG OUR TRIBE, IT IS CUSTOMARY FOR THE FIRST WIFE TO LOOK AFTER THE SECOND WIFE.
WHAT DO YOU MEAN?
WHAT DO I MEAN ...?
FIRST WIFE.
SECOND WIFE.

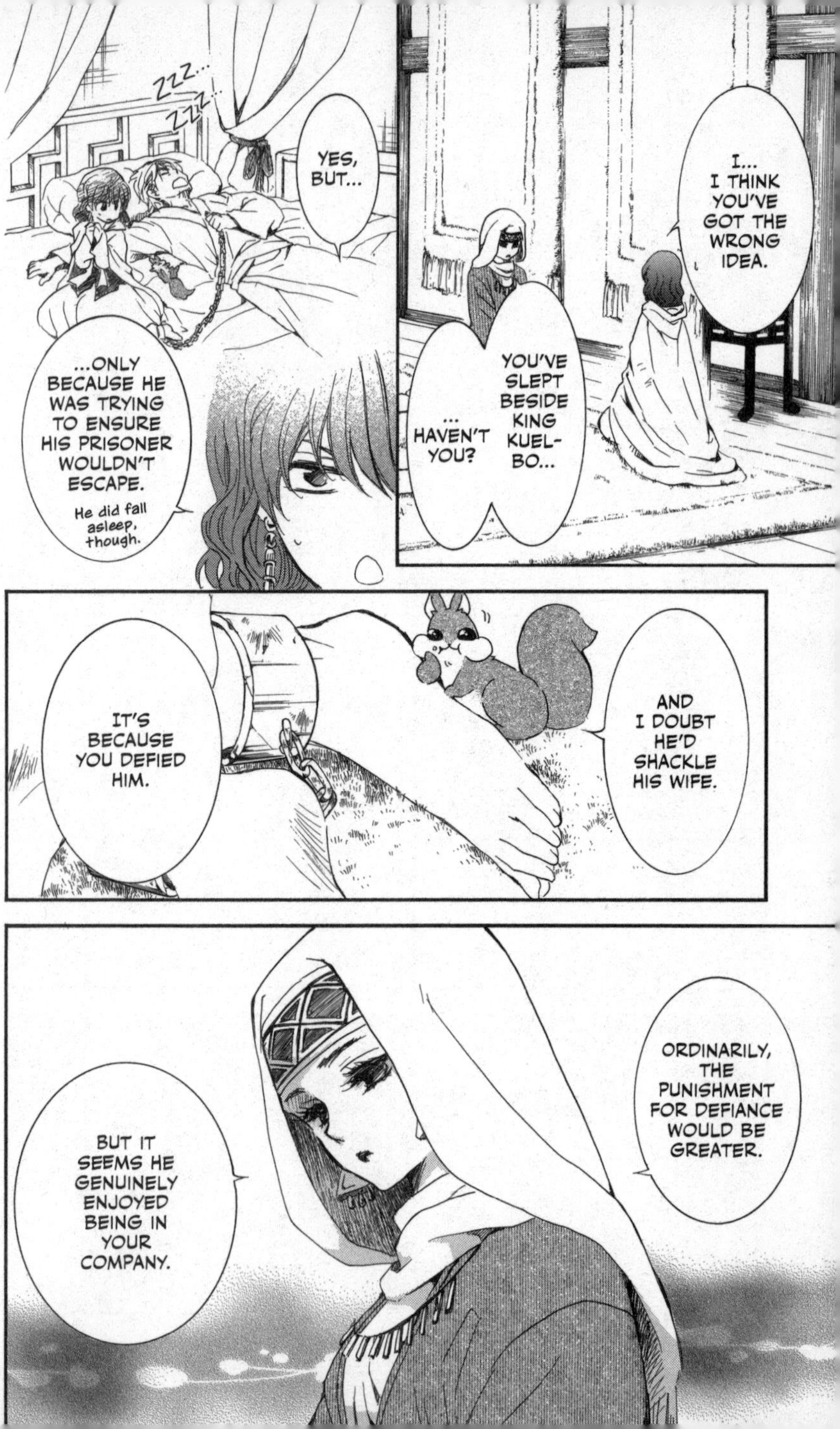
I... I THINK YOU'VE GOT THE WRONG IDEA.
YOU'VE SLEPT BESIDE KING KUEL-BO...
... HAVEN'T YOU?
ZZZ... ZZZ...
YES, BUT...
...ONLY BECAUSE HE WAS TRYING TO ENSURE HIS PRISONER WOULDN'T ESCAPE.
He did fall asleep, though.
AND I DOUBT HE'D SHACKLE HIS WIFE.
IT'S BECAUSE YOU DEFIED HIM.
ORDINARILY, THE PUNISHMENT FOR DEFIANCE WOULD BE GREATER.
BUT IT SEEMS HE GENUINELY ENJOYED BEING IN YOUR COMPANY.

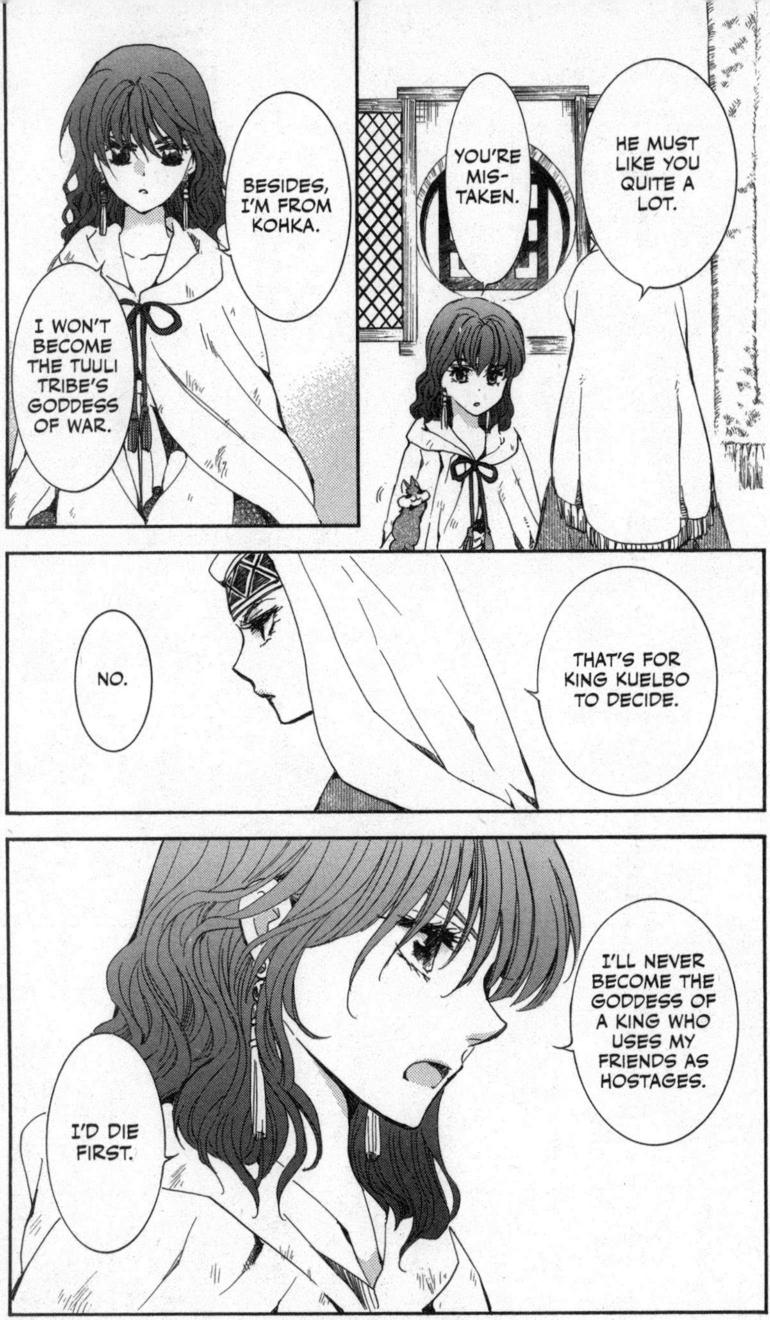
HE MUST LIKE YOU QUITE A LOT.
YOU'RE MIS-TAKEN.
BESIDES, I'M FROM KOHKA.
I WON'T BECOME THE TUULI TRIBE'S GODDESS OF WAR.
THAT'S FOR KING KUELBO TO DECIDE.
NO.
I'LL NEVER BECOME THE GODDESS OF A KING WHO USES MY FRIENDS AS HOSTAGES.
I'D DIE FIRST.

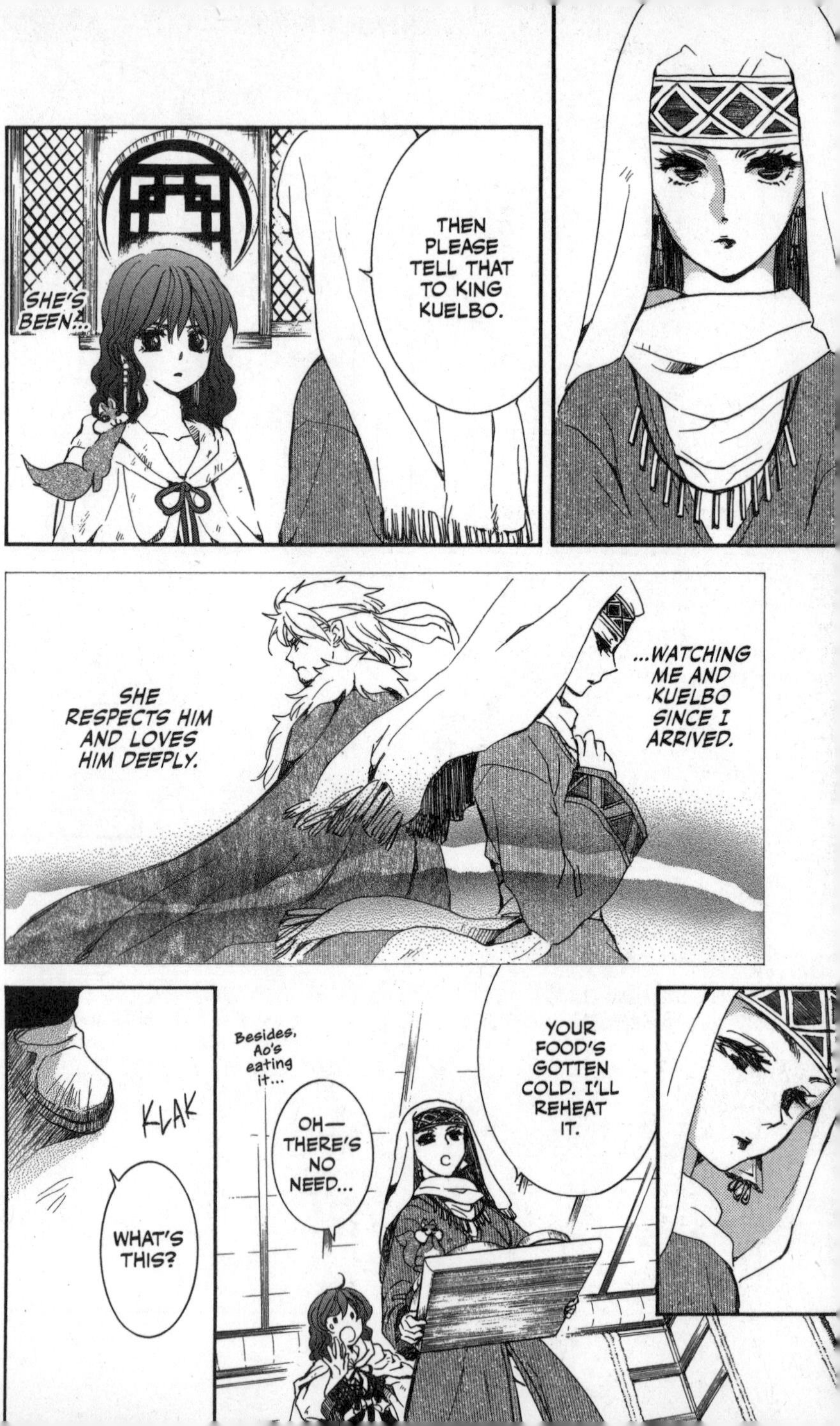
THEN PLEASE TELL THAT TO KING KUELBO.
SHE'S BEEN...
...WATCHING ME AND KUELBO SINCE I ARRIVED.
SHE RESPECTS HIM AND LOVES HIM DEEPLY.
YOUR FOOD'S GOTTEN COLD. I'LL REHEAT IT.
OH— THERE'S NO NEED...
Besides, Ao's eating it...
KLAK
WHAT'S THIS?

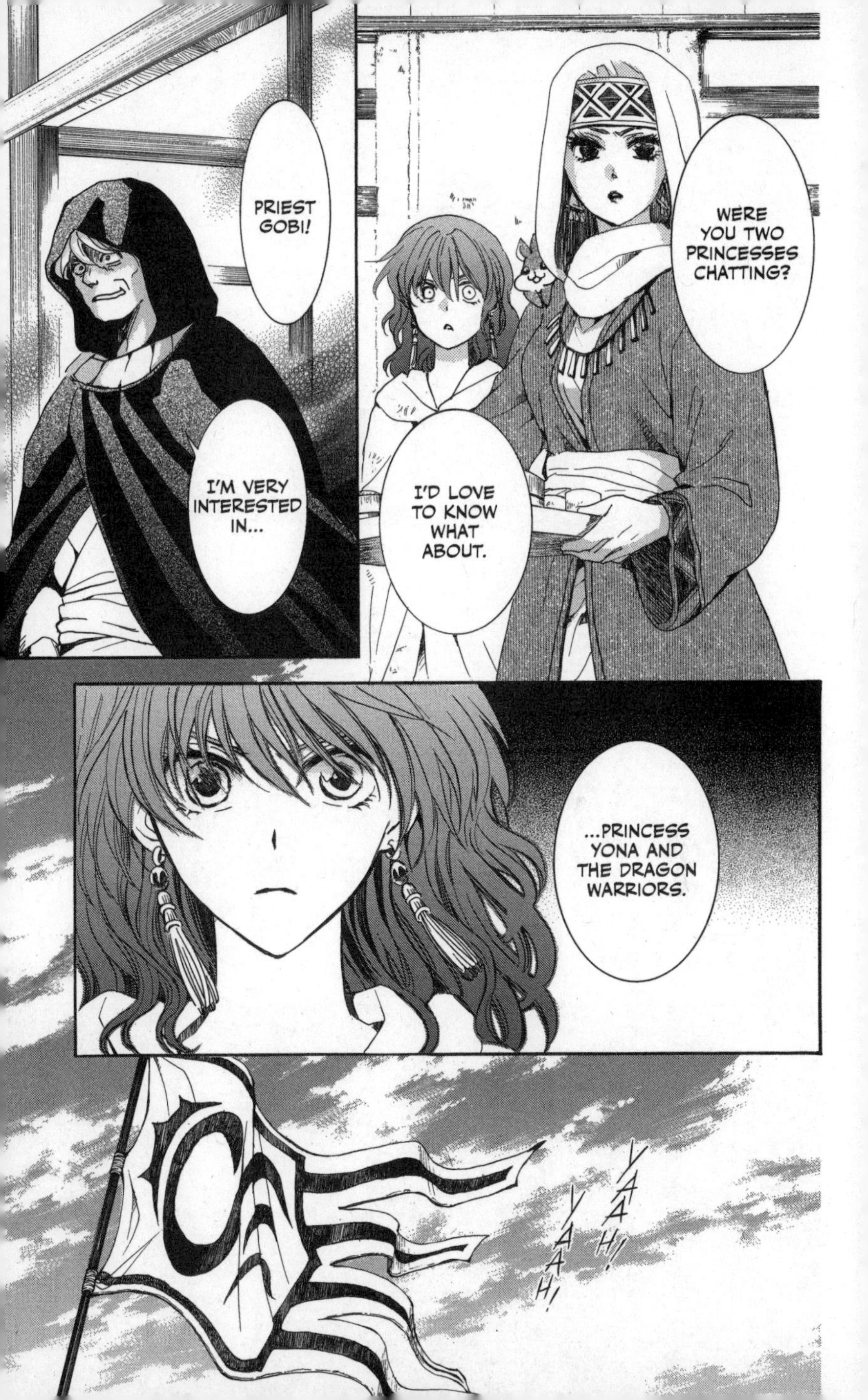
WERE YOU TWO PRINCESSES CHATTING?
I'D LOVE TO KNOW WHAT ABOUT.
PRIEST GOBI!
I'M VERY INTERESTED IN...
...PRINCESS YONA AND THE DRAGON WARRIORS.
YAAH!
YAAH!

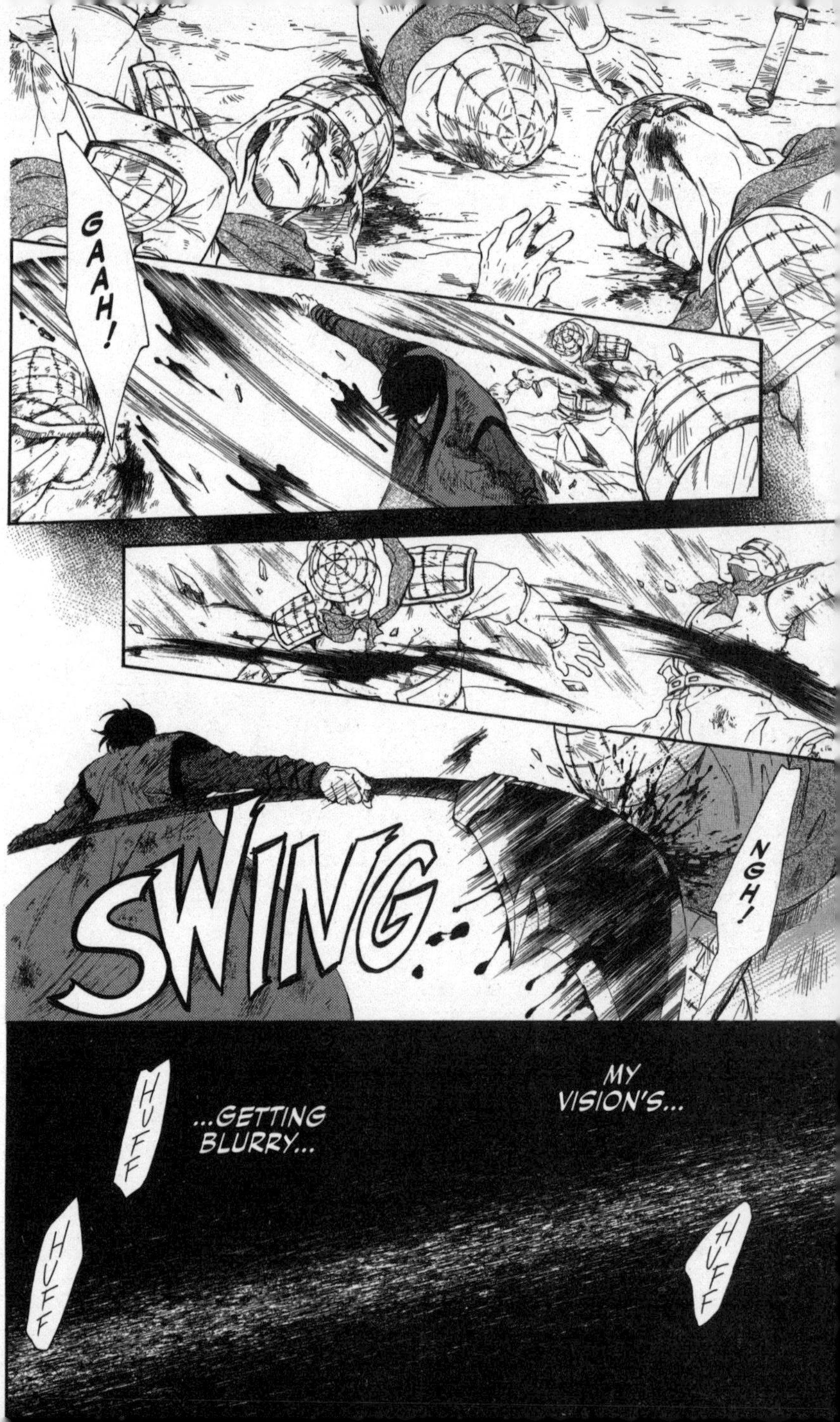
GAAH!
NGH!
SWING
MY VISION'S...
HUFF
...GETTING BLURRY...
HUFF
HUFF

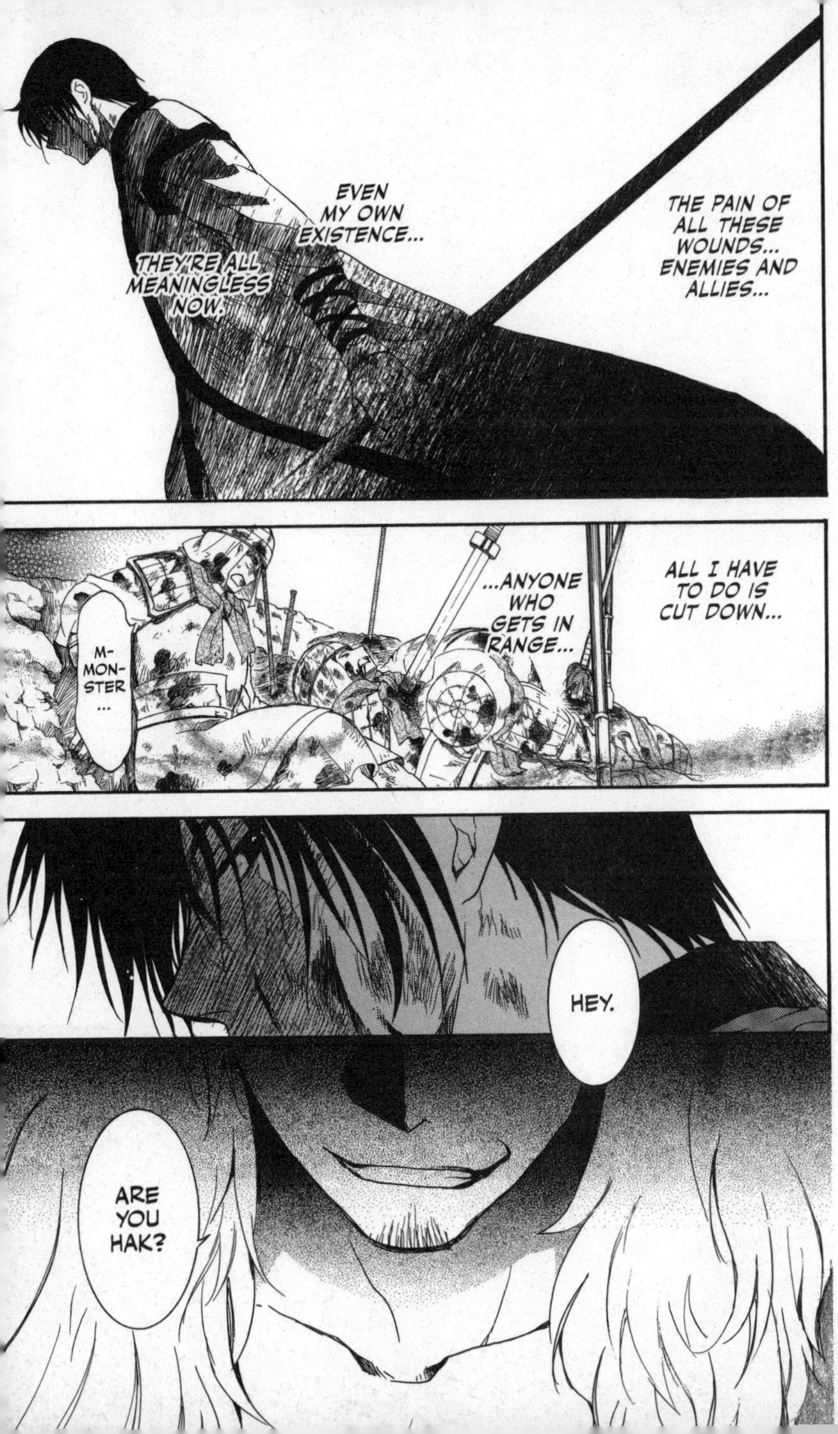
THE PAIN OF ALL THESE WOUNDS... ENEMIES AND ALLIES...
EVEN MY OWN EXISTENCE...
THEY'RE ALL MEANINGLESS NOW.
ALL I HAVE TO DO IS CUT DOWN...
...ANYONE WHO GETS IN RANGE...
M-MONSTER...
HEY.
ARE YOU HAK?

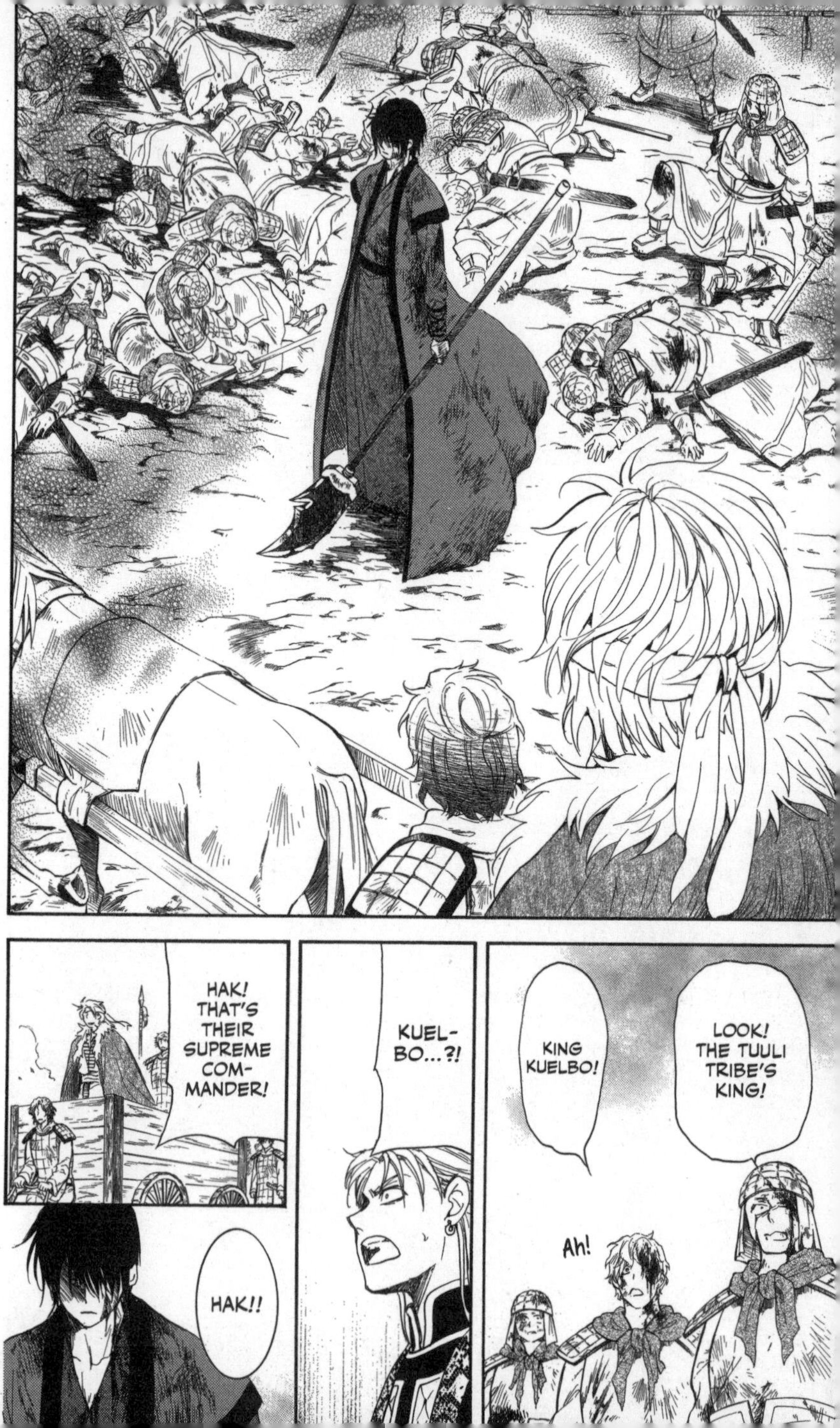
LOOK! THE TUULI TRIBE'S KING!
KING KUELBO!
Ah!
KUEL-BO...?!
HAK! THAT'S THEIR SUPREME COM-MANDER!
HAK!!

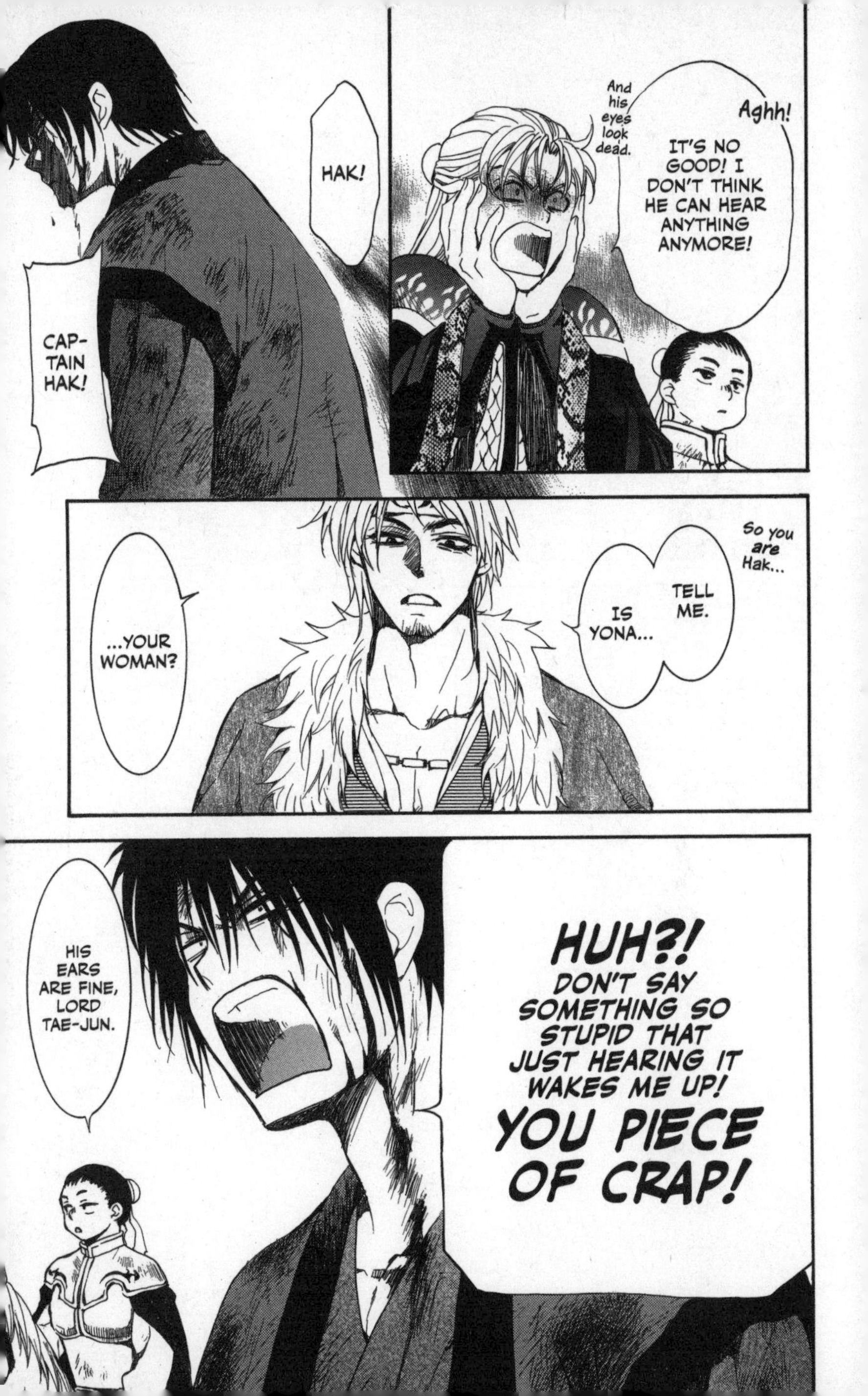
Aghh!
IT'S NO GOOD! I DON'T THINK HE CAN HEAR ANYTHING ANYMORE!
And his eyes look dead.
HAK!
CAP-TAIN HAK!
So you are Hak...
TELL ME.
IS YONA...
...YOUR WOMAN?
HUH?! DON'T SAY SOMETHING SO STUPID THAT JUST HEARING IT WAKES ME UP! YOU PIECE OF CRAP!
HIS EARS ARE FINE, LORD TAE-JUN.

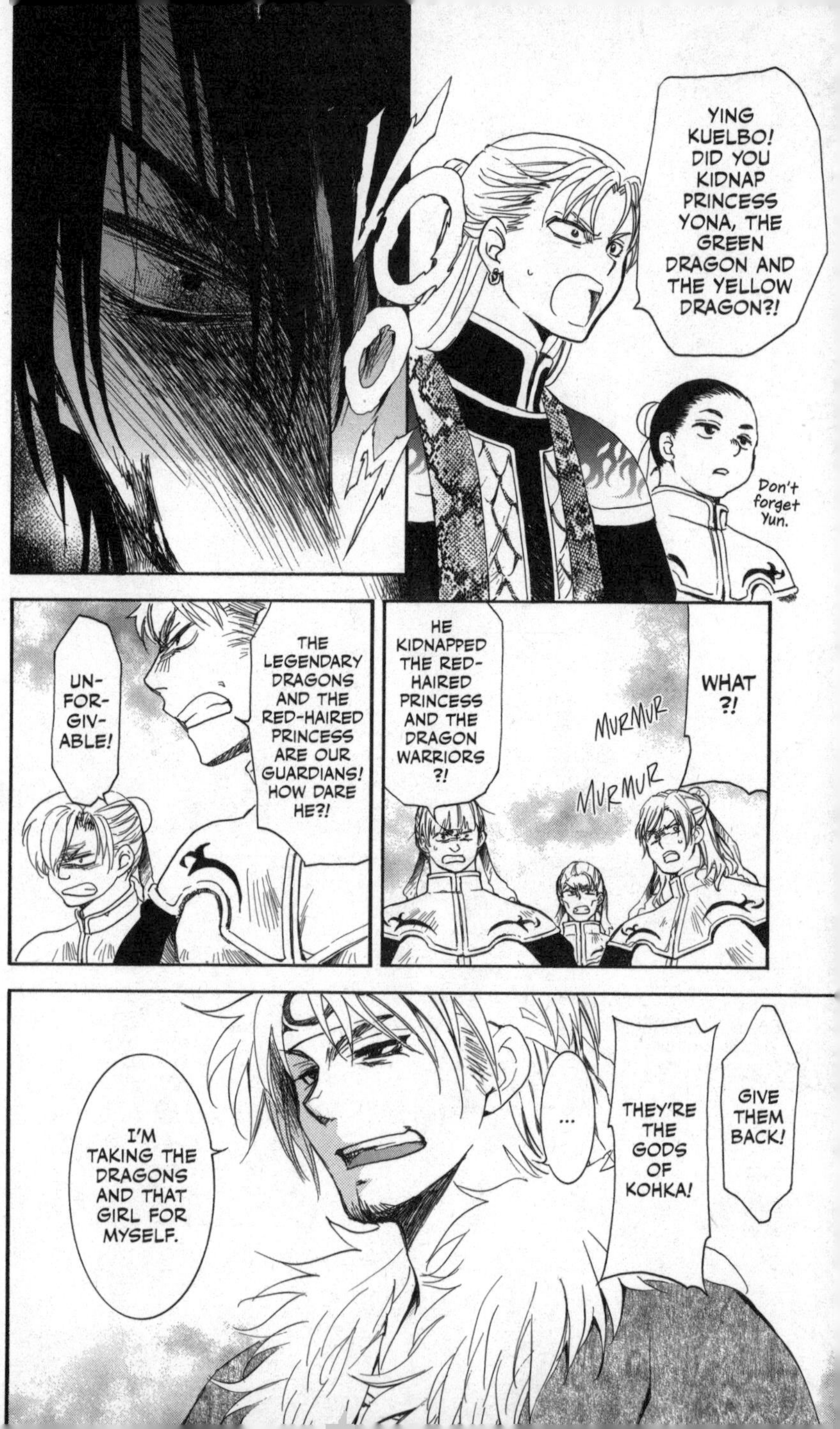
YING KUELBO! DID YOU KIDNAP PRINCESS YONA, THE GREEN DRAGON AND THE YELLOW DRAGON?!
Don't forget Yun.
WHAT?!
MURMUR
HE KIDNAPPED THE RED-HAIRED PRINCESS AND THE DRAGON WARRIORS?!
MURMUR
THE LEGENDARY DRAGONS AND THE RED-HAIRED PRINCESS ARE OUR GUARDIANS! HOW DARE HE?!
UN-FOR-GIV-ABLE!
GIVE THEM BACK!
THEY'RE THE GODS OF KOHKA!
...
I'M TAKING THE DRAGONS AND THAT GIRL FOR MYSELF.

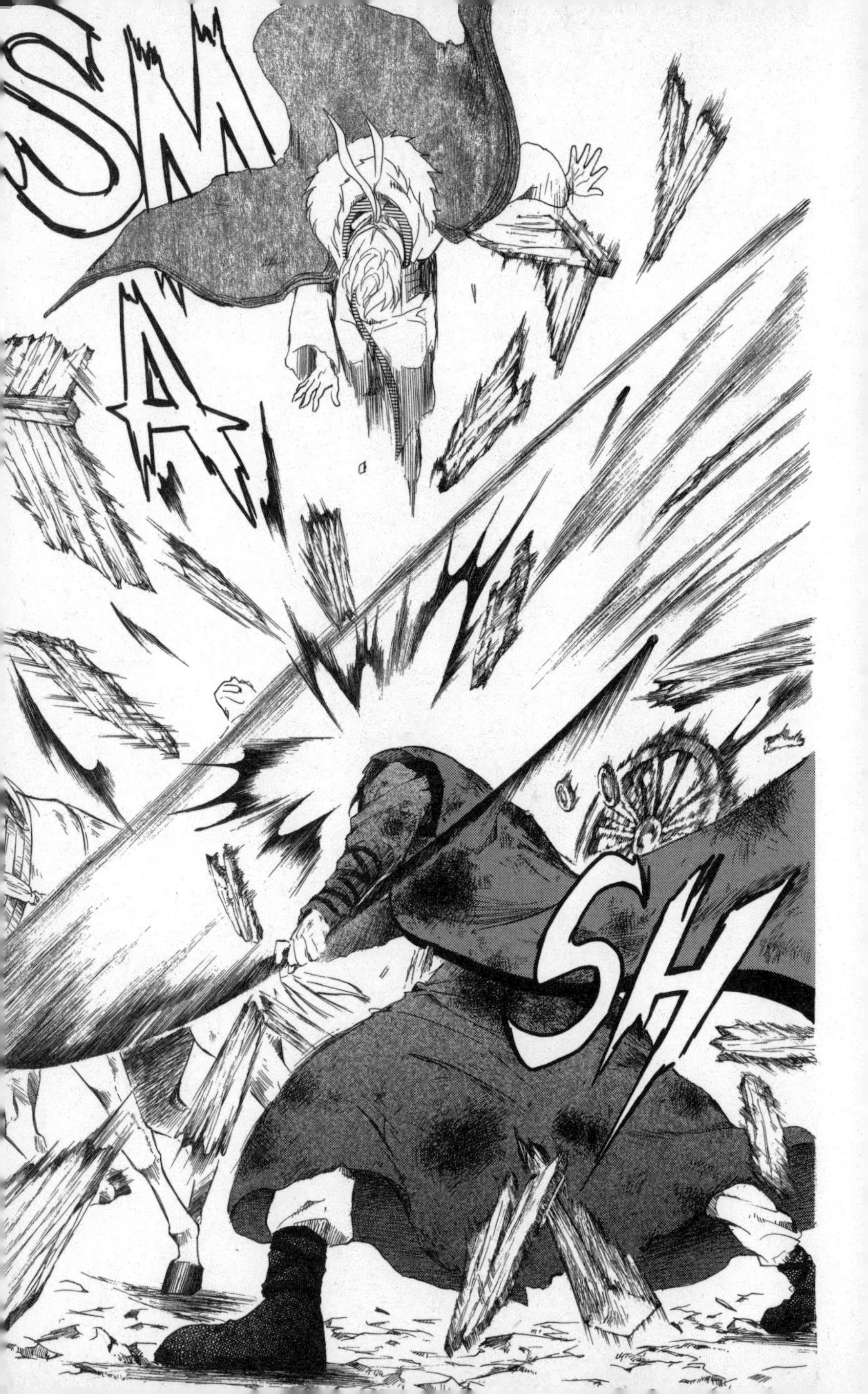
SMASH

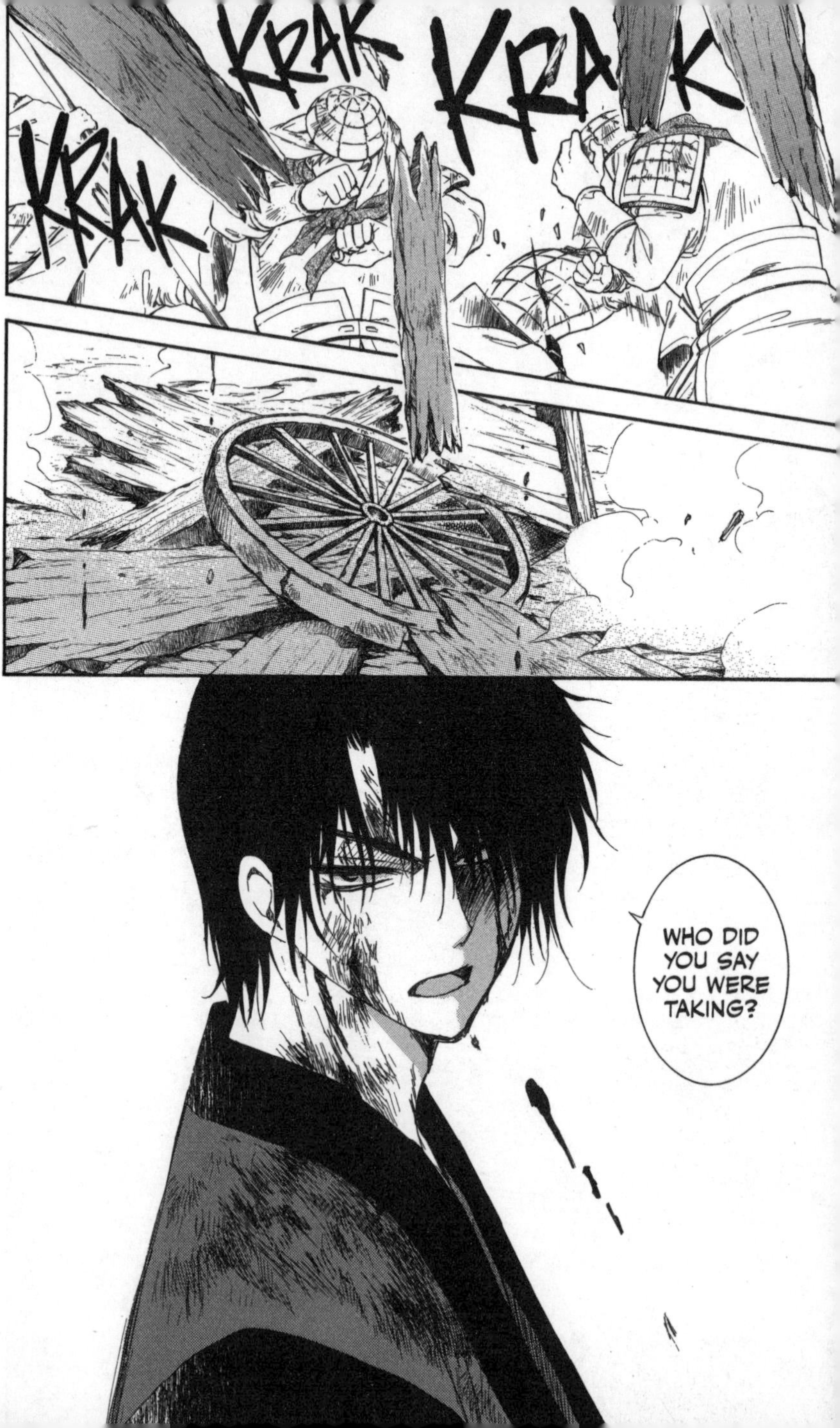
KRA K
KRAK
KRAK
WHO DID YOU SAY YOU WERE TAKING?

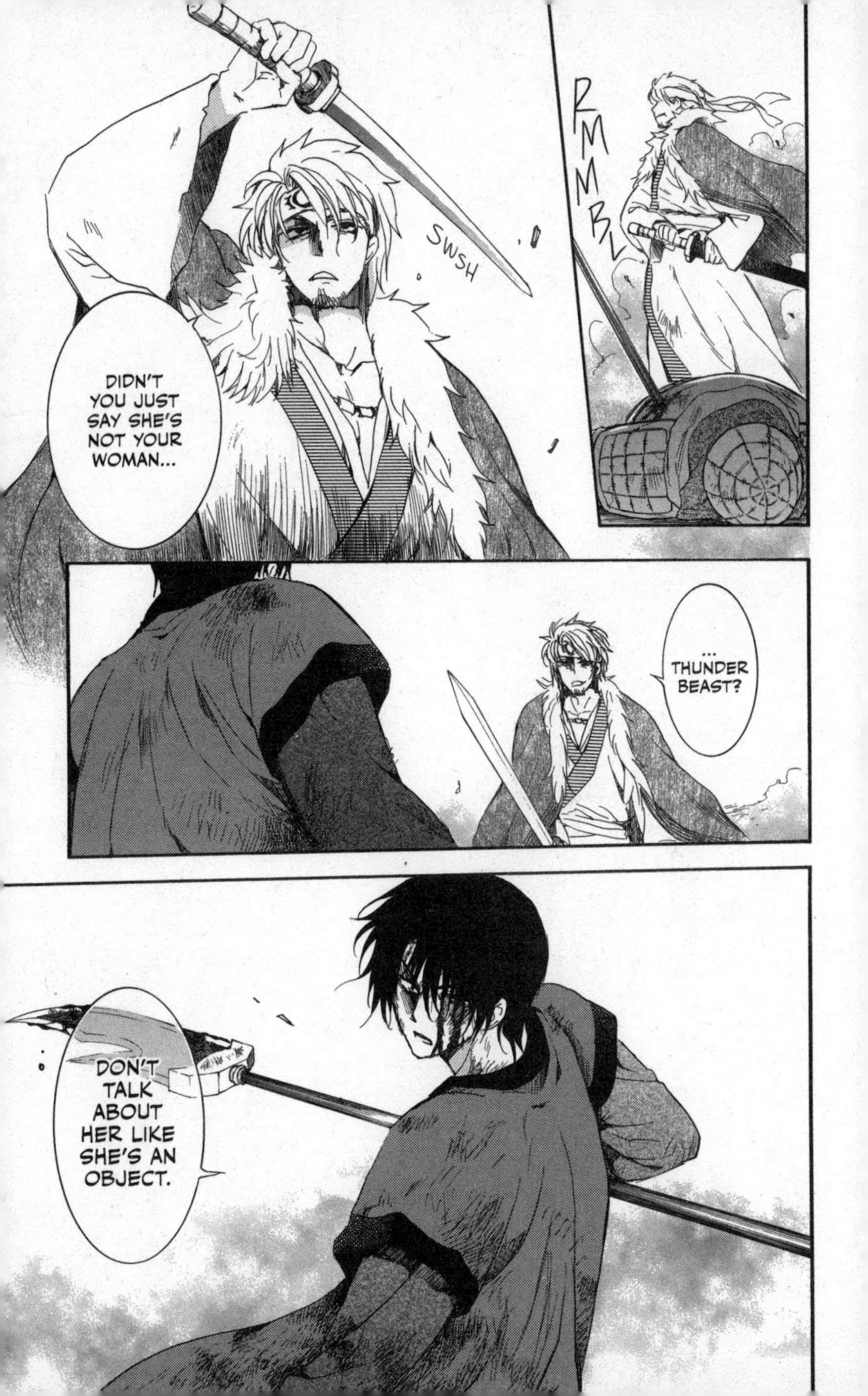
RMMBL
SWSH
DIDN'T YOU JUST SAY SHE'S NOT YOUR WOMAN...
...THUNDER BEAST?
DON'T TALK ABOUT HER LIKE SHE'S AN OBJECT.

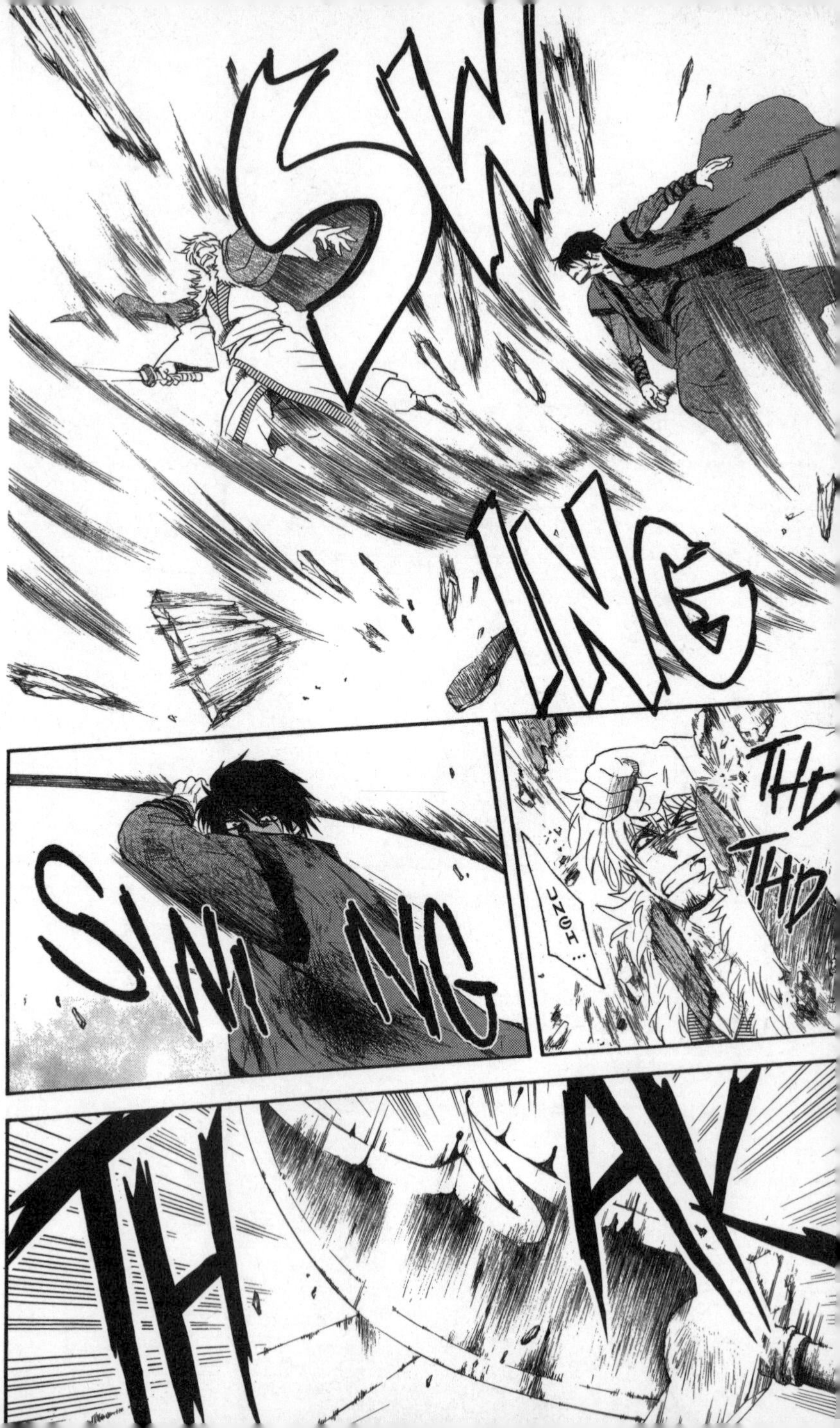
SWING
THD
THD
UNGH...
SWING
THAK

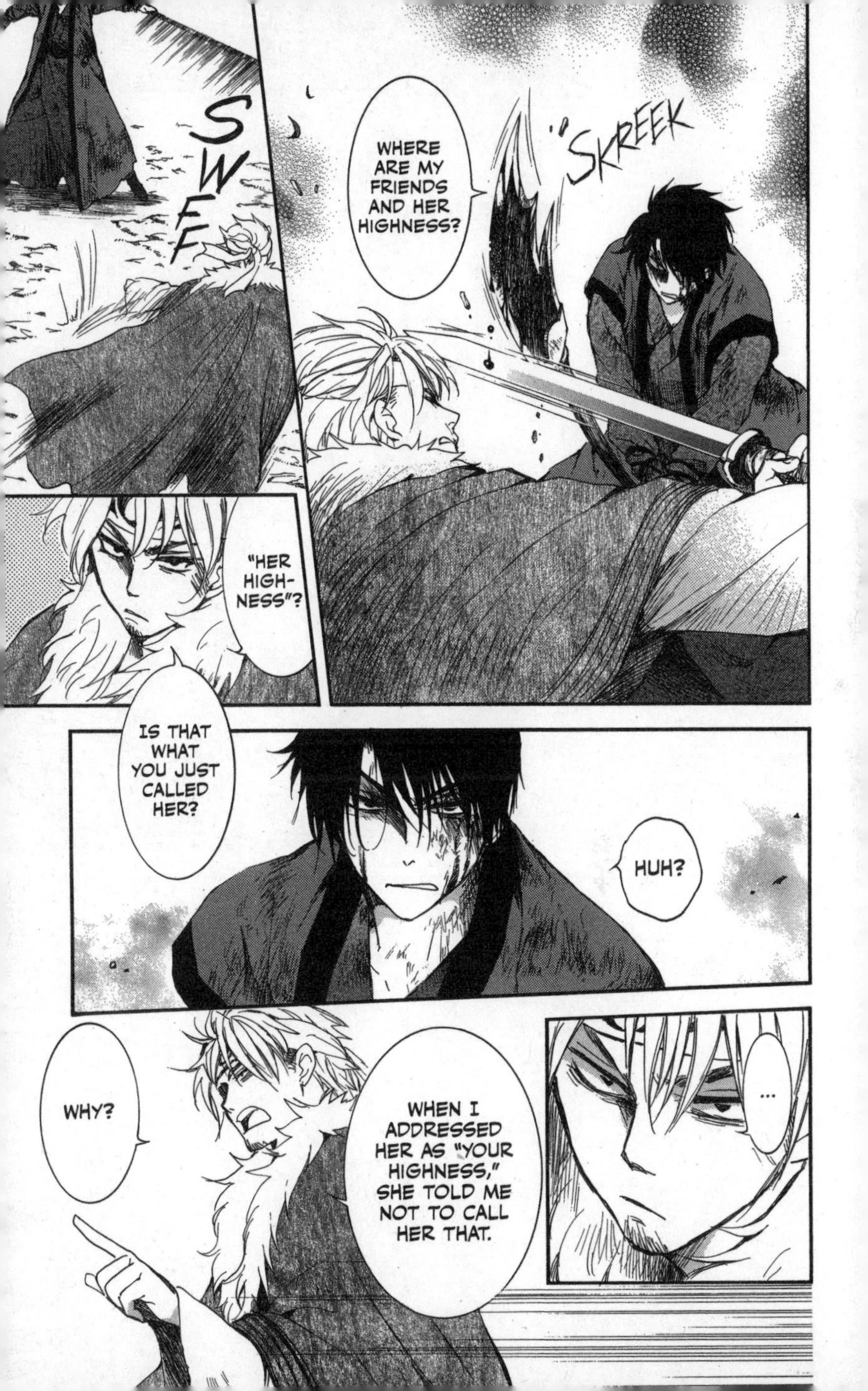
SKREEK
WHERE ARE MY FRIENDS AND HER HIGHNESS?
SWEFF
"HER HIGHNESS"?
IS THAT WHAT YOU JUST CALLED HER?
HUH?
...
WHEN I ADDRESSED HER AS "YOUR HIGHNESS," SHE TOLD ME NOT TO CALL HER THAT.
WHY?

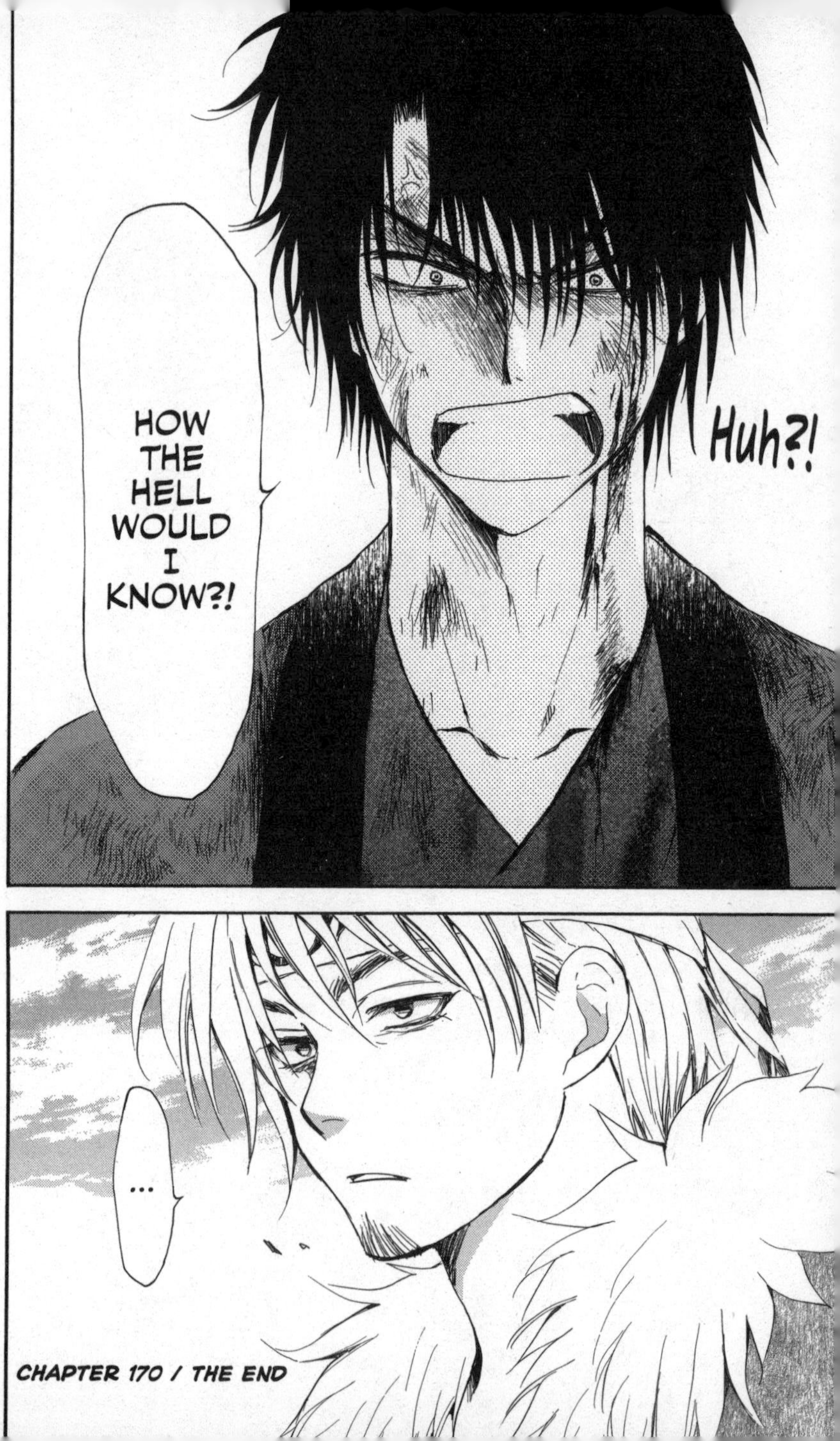
Huh?!
HOW THE HELL WOULD I KNOW?!
...
CHAPTER 170 / THE END

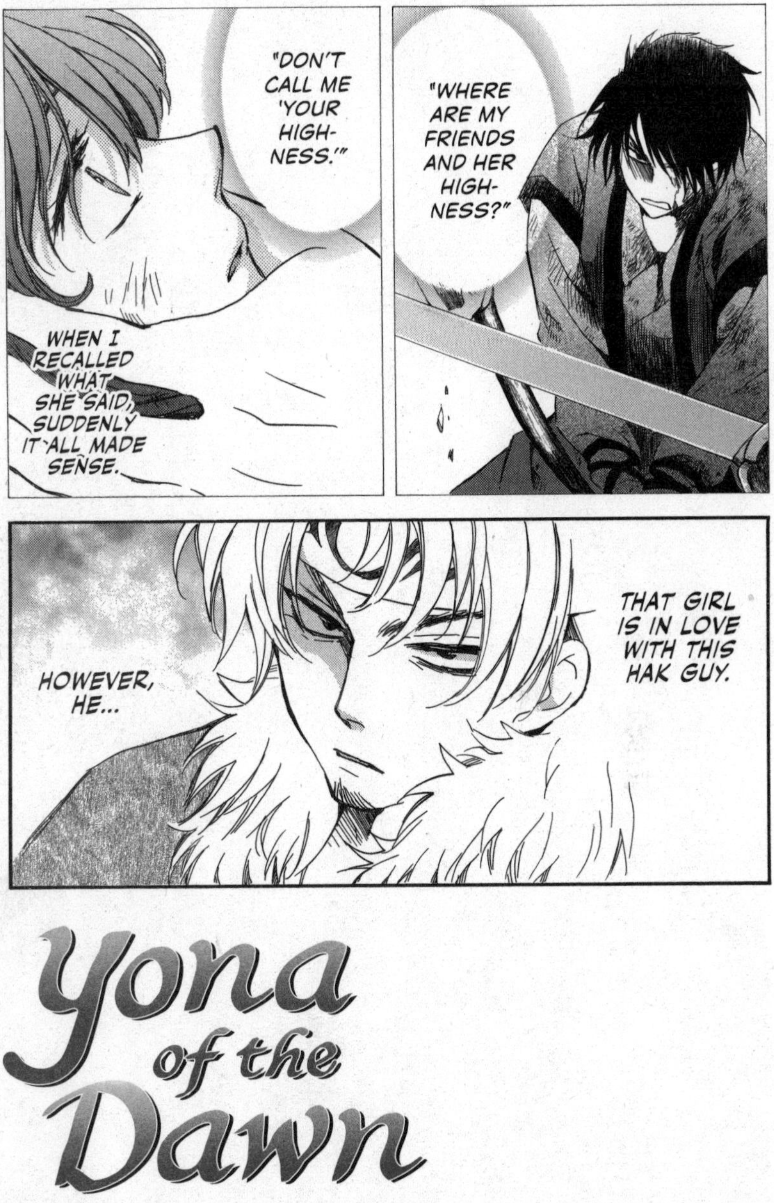
"WHERE ARE MY FRIENDS AND HER HIGH-NESS?"
"DON'T CALL ME 'YOUR HIGH-NESS.'"
WHEN I RECALLED WHAT SHE SAID, SUDDENLY IT ALL MADE SENSE.
THAT GIRL IS IN LOVE WITH THIS HAK GUY.
HOWEVER, HE...

Yona of the Dawn

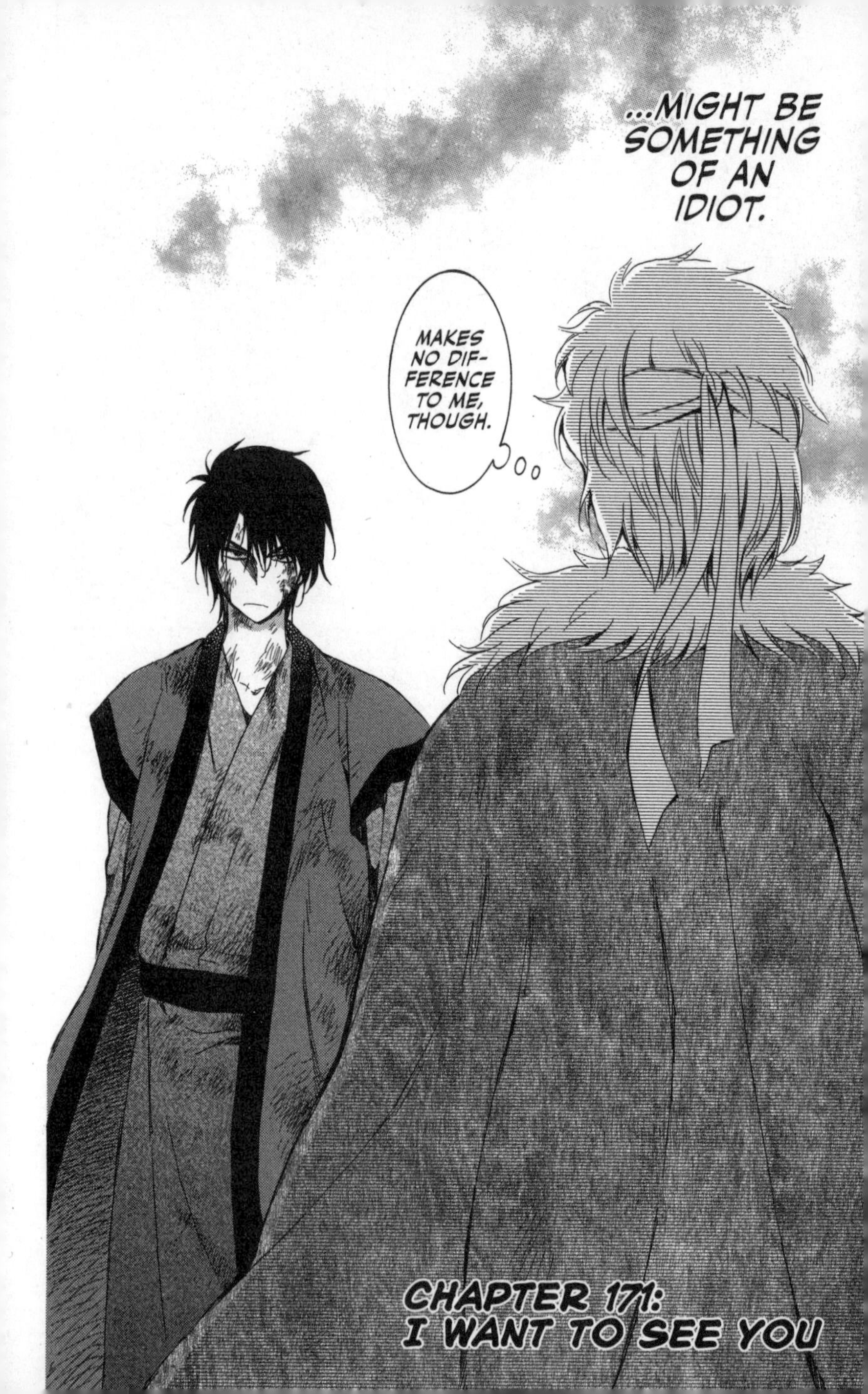
...MIGHT BE SOMETHING OF AN IDIOT.
MAKES NO DIFFERENCE TO ME, THOUGH.
CHAPTER 171: I WANT TO SEE YOU

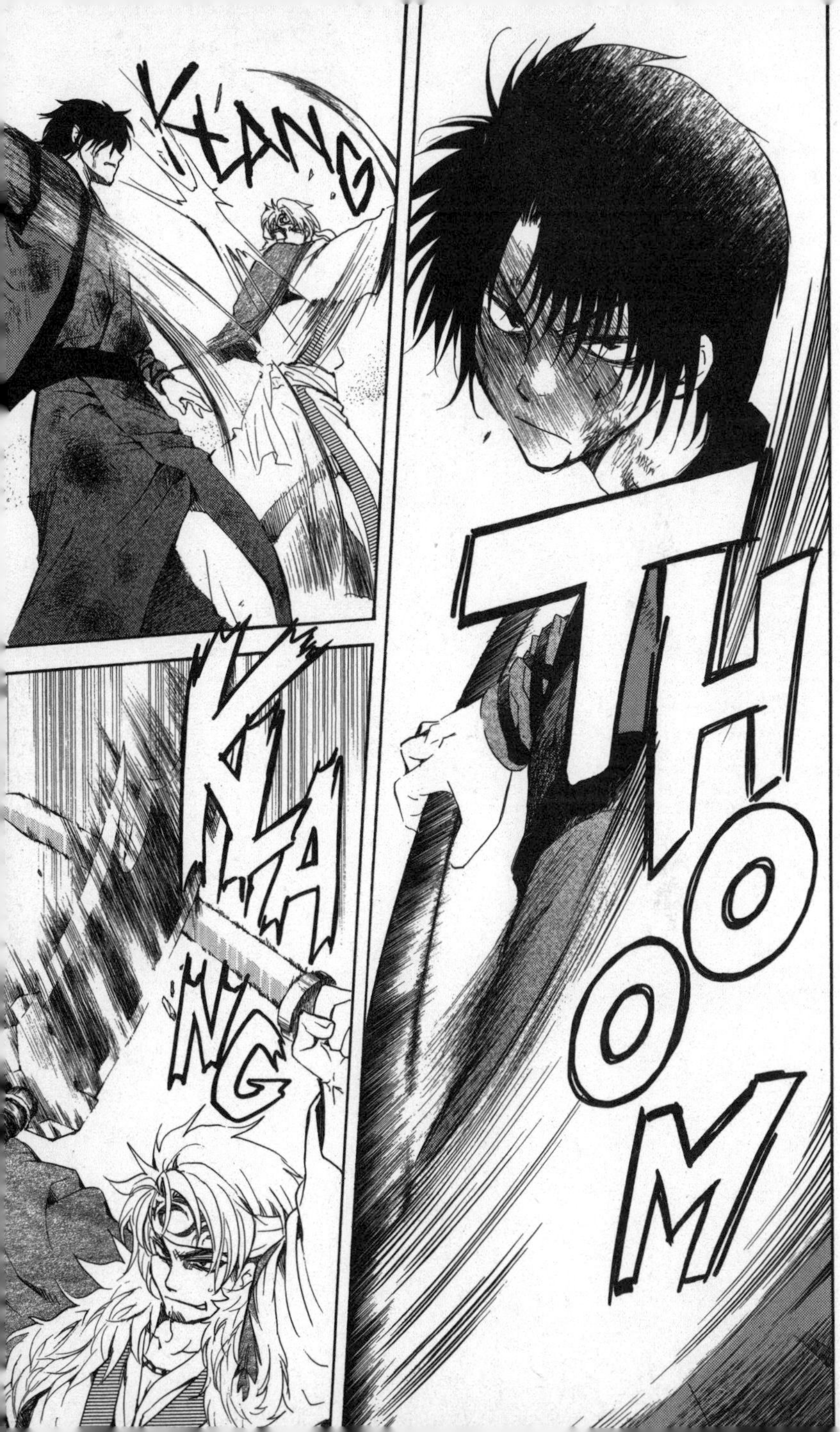
THOOOOM
KLANG
KLANNG

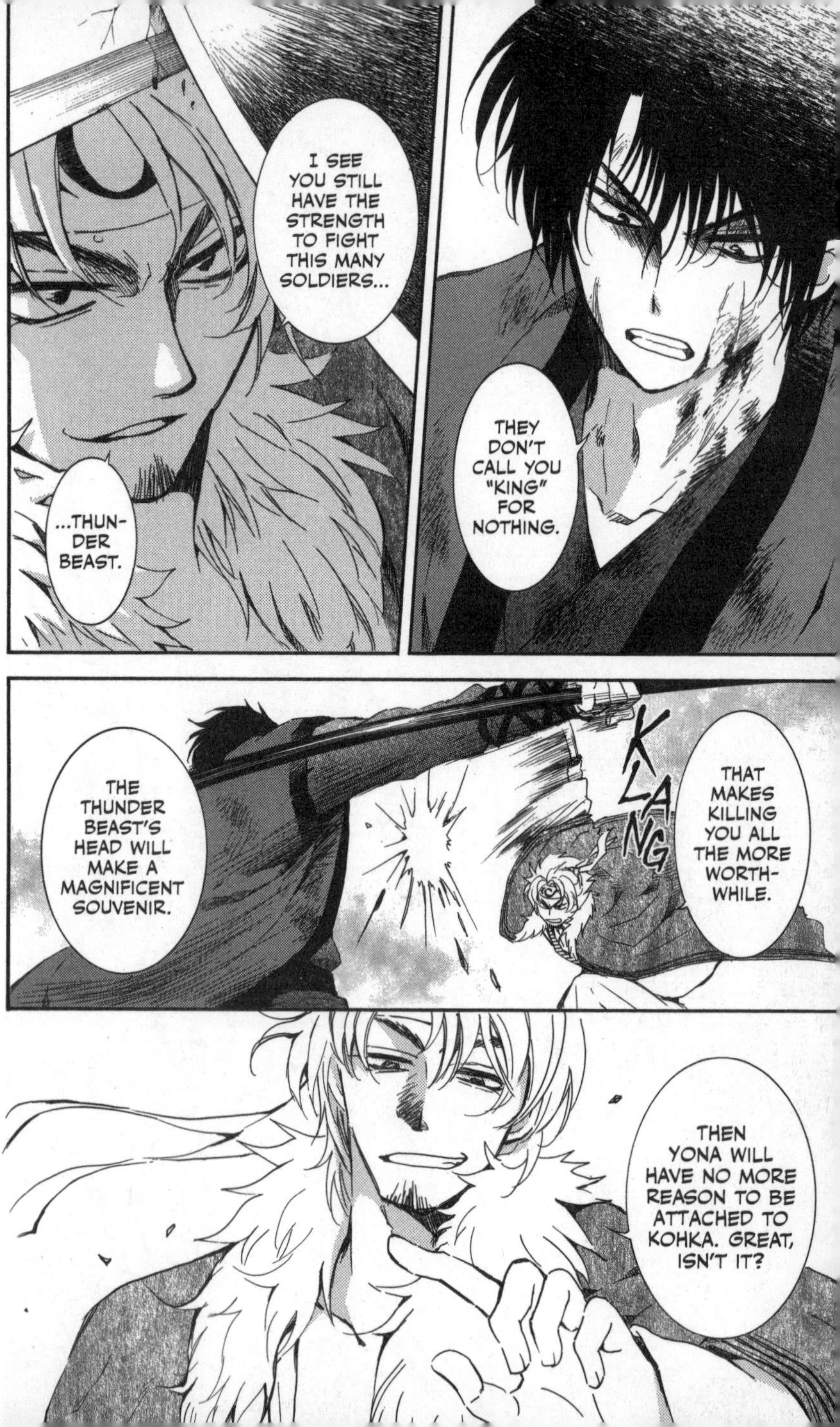
THEY DON'T CALL YOU "KING" FOR NOTHING.
I SEE YOU STILL HAVE THE STRENGTH TO FIGHT THIS MANY SOLDIERS...
...THUNDER BEAST.
THAT MAKES KILLING YOU ALL THE MORE WORTHWHILE.
KLANG
THE THUNDER BEAST'S HEAD WILL MAKE A MAGNIFICENT SOUVENIR.
THEN YONA WILL HAVE NO MORE REASON TO BE ATTACHED TO KOHKA. GREAT, ISN'T IT?

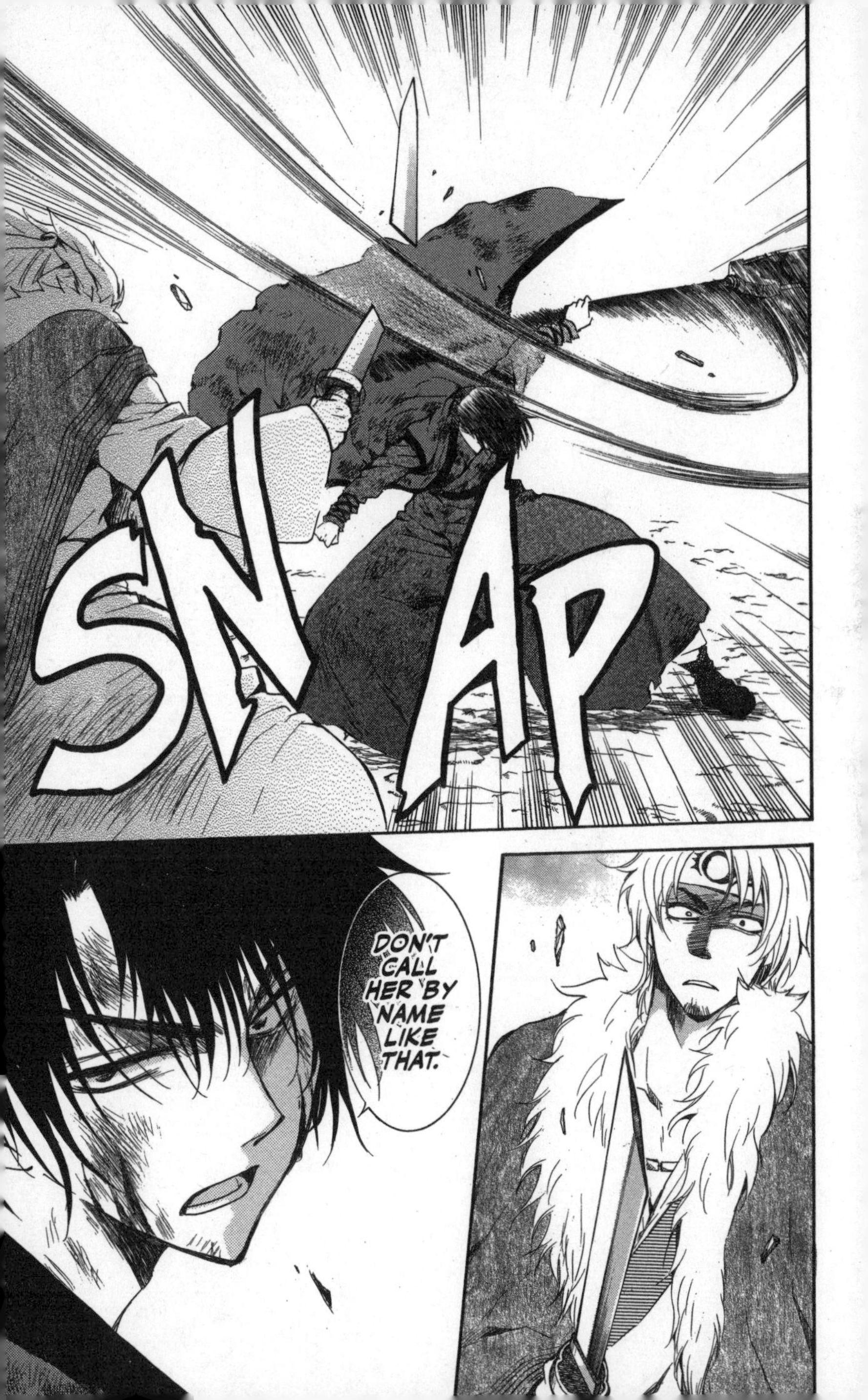
SNAP
DON'T CALL HER BY NAME LIKE THAT.

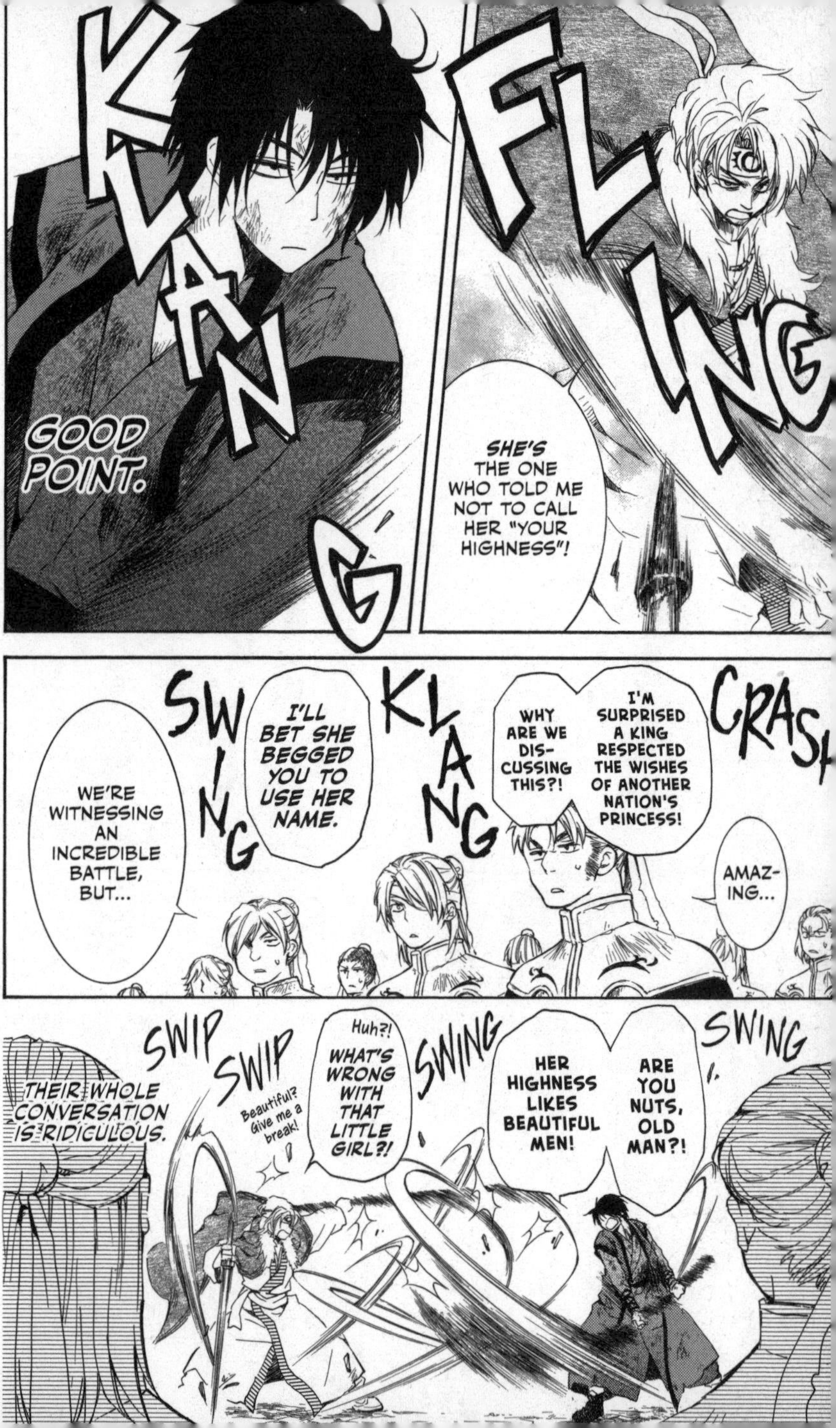
FLING
SHE'S THE ONE WHO TOLD ME NOT TO CALL HER "YOUR HIGHNESS"!
KLANG
GOOD POINT.
CRASH
AMAZ-ING...
I'M SURPRISED A KING RESPECTED THE WISHES OF ANOTHER NATION'S PRINCESS!
WHY ARE WE DIS-CUSSING THIS?!
KLANG
I'LL BET SHE BEGGED YOU TO USE HER NAME.
SWING
WE'RE WITNESSING AN INCREDIBLE BATTLE, BUT...
SWING
ARE YOU NUTS, OLD MAN?!
HER HIGHNESS LIKES BEAUTIFUL MEN!
SWING
Huh?! WHAT'S WRONG WITH THAT LITTLE GIRL?!
Beautiful? Give me a break!
SWIP
SWIP
THEIR WHOLE CONVERSATION IS RIDICULOUS.

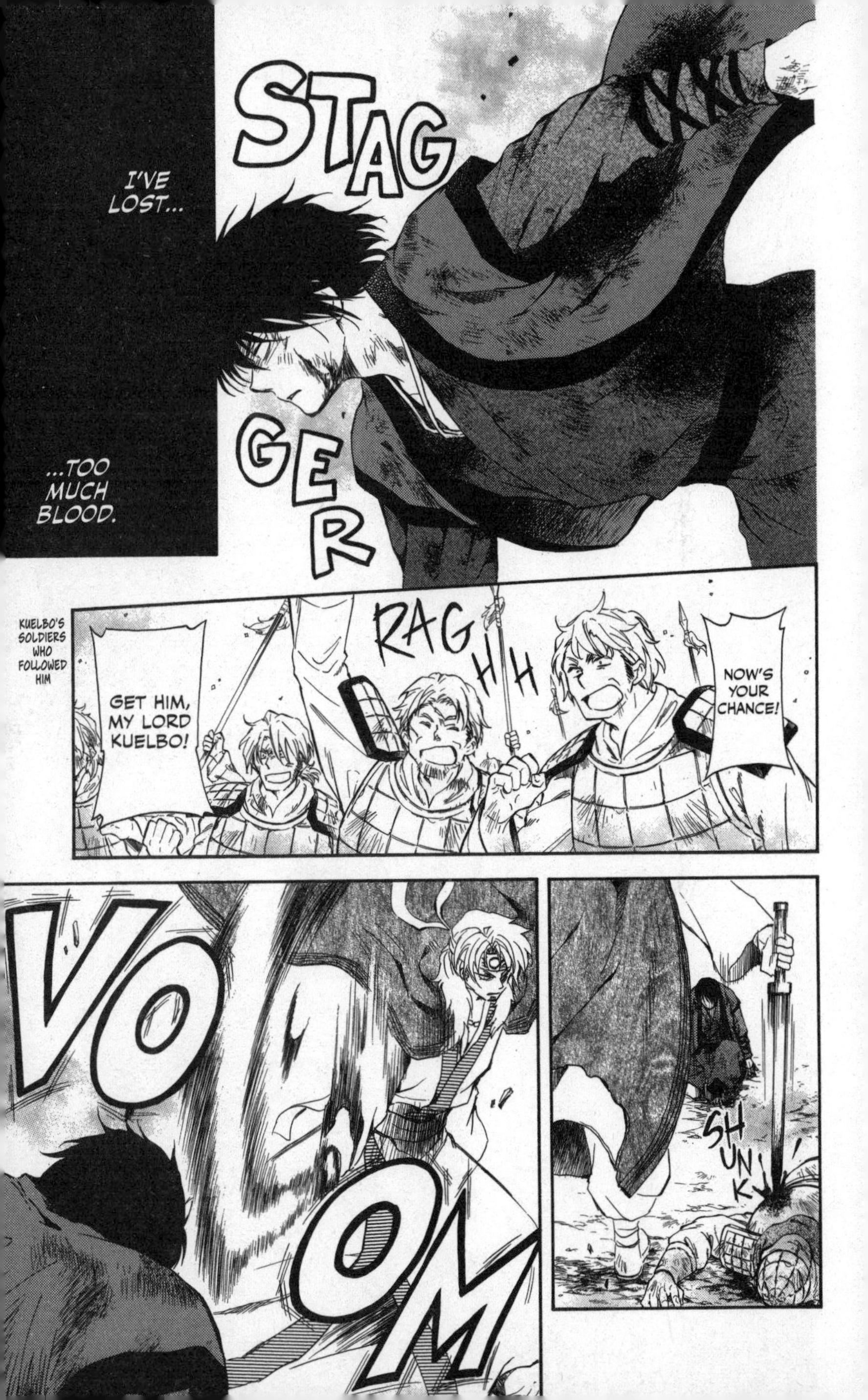
STAGGER
I'VE LOST...
...TOO MUCH BLOOD.
NOW'S YOUR CHANCE!
RAGHHH
GET HIM, MY LORD KUELBO!
KUELBO'S SOLDIERS WHO FOLLOWED HIM
SHUNK
VOOM

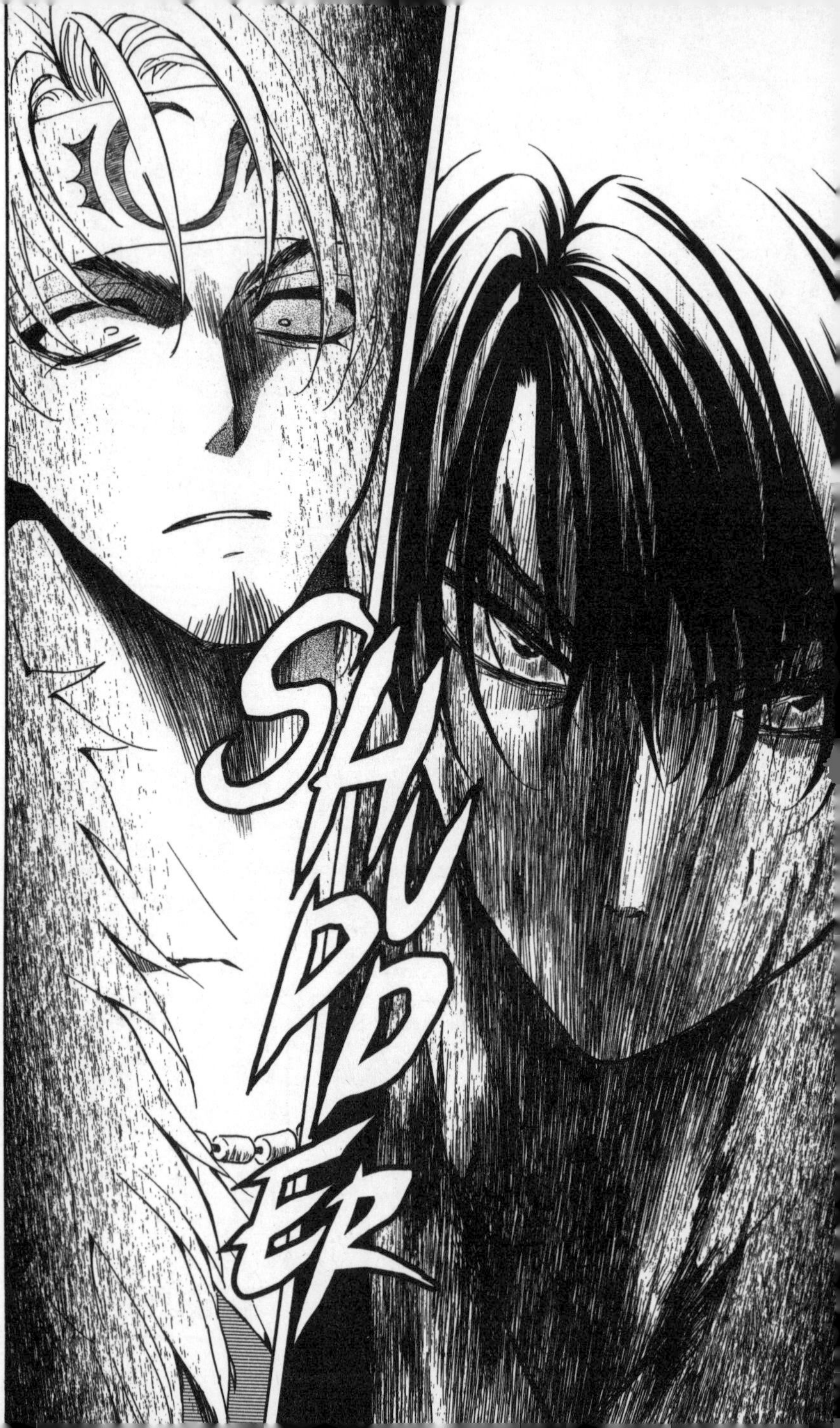
SHUDDER

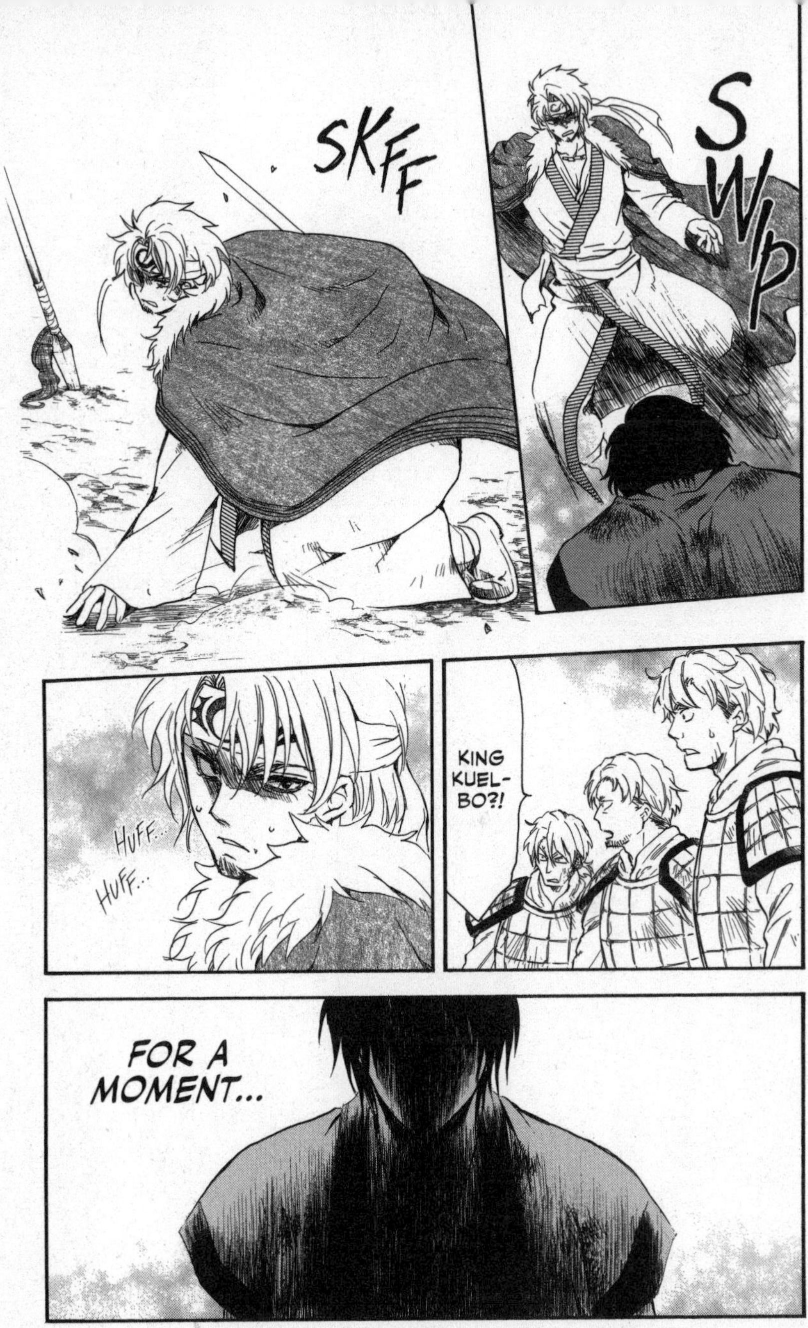
SWP
SKFF
KING KUEL-BO?!
HUFF...
HUFF...
FOR A MOMENT...

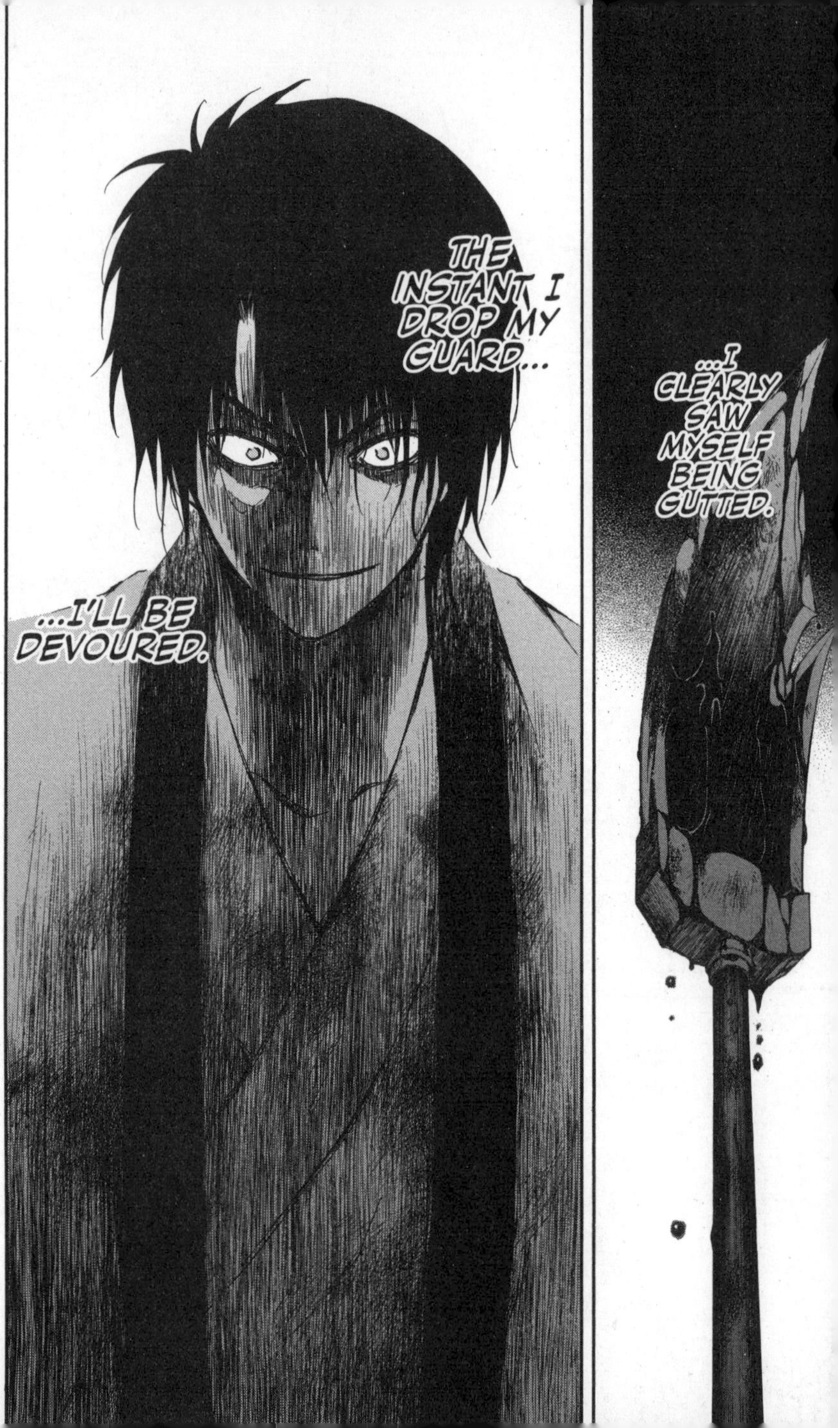
...I CLEARLY SAW MYSELF BEING GUTTED.
THE INSTANT I DROP MY GUARD...
...I'LL BE DEVOURED.

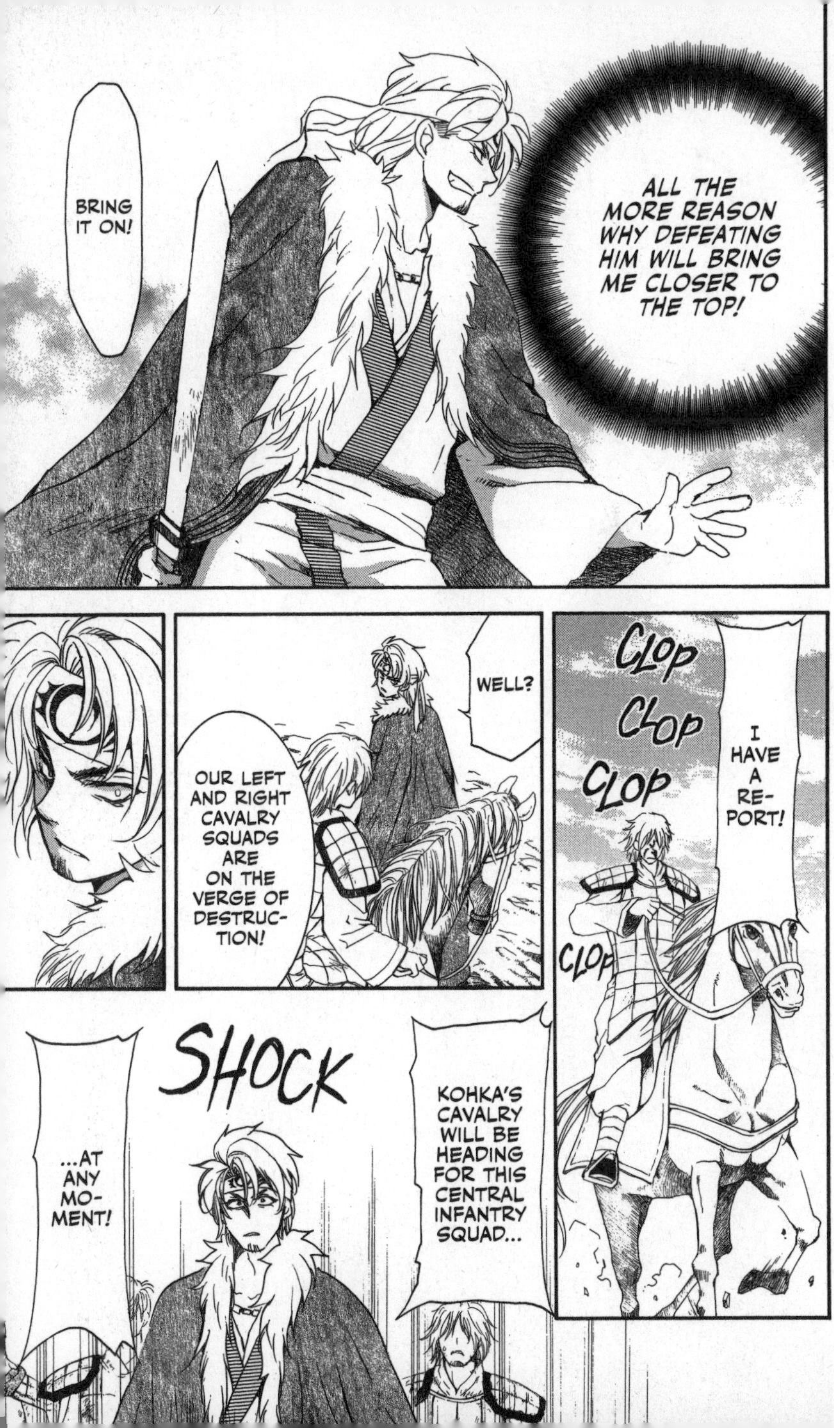
ALL THE MORE REASON WHY DEFEATING HIM WILL BRING ME CLOSER TO THE TOP!
BRING IT ON!
CLOP
CLOP
CLOP
I HAVE A RE-PORT!
CLOP
WELL?
OUR LEFT AND RIGHT CAVALRY SQUADS ARE ON THE VERGE OF DESTRUC-TION!
SHOCK
KOHKA'S CAVALRY WILL BE HEADING FOR THIS CENTRAL INFANTRY SQUAD...
...AT ANY MO-MENT!

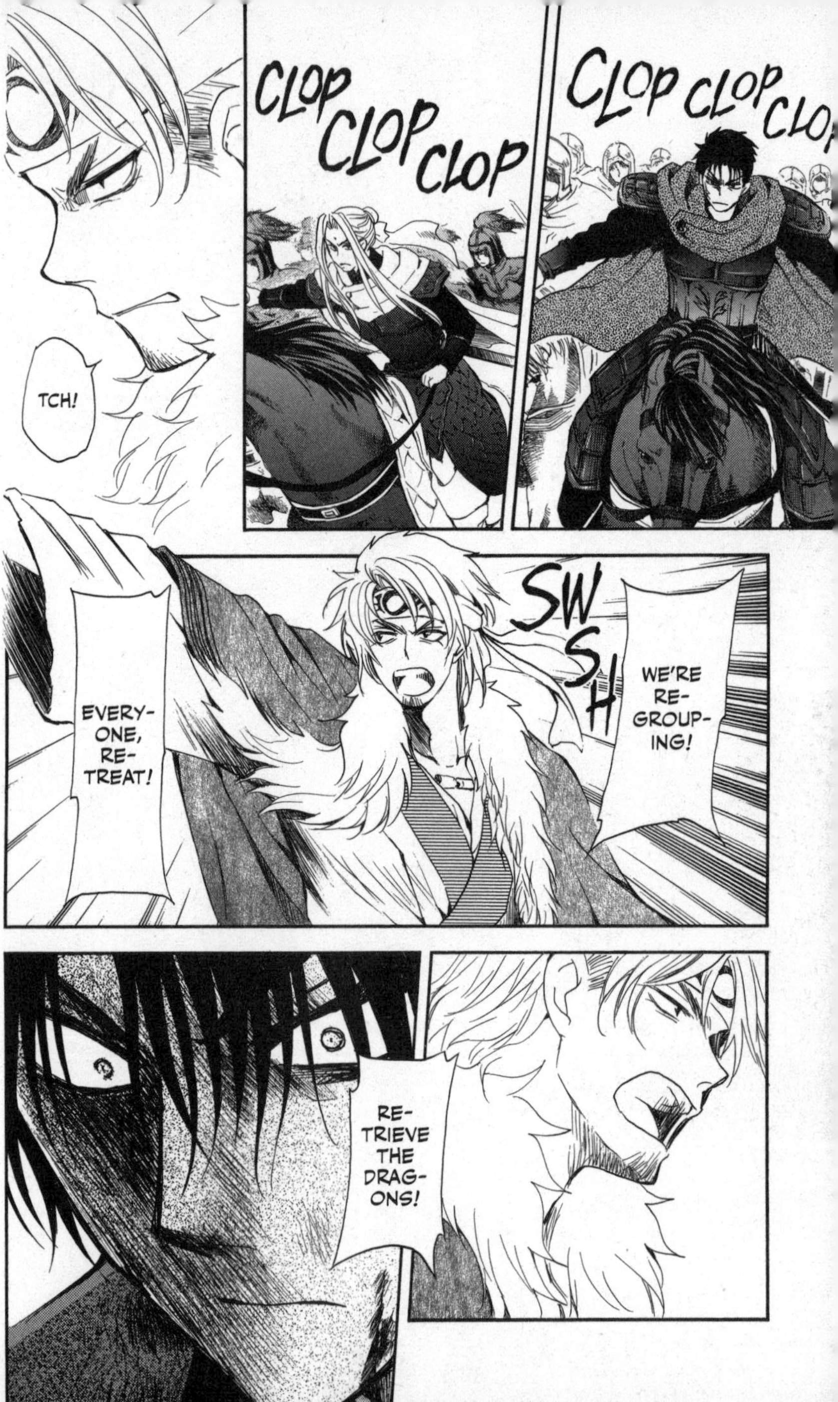
CLOP CLOP CLO
CLOP CLOP CLOP
TCH!
WE'RE RE-GROUP-ING!
SWSH
EVERY-ONE, RE-TREAT!
RE-TRIEVE THE DRAG-ONS!

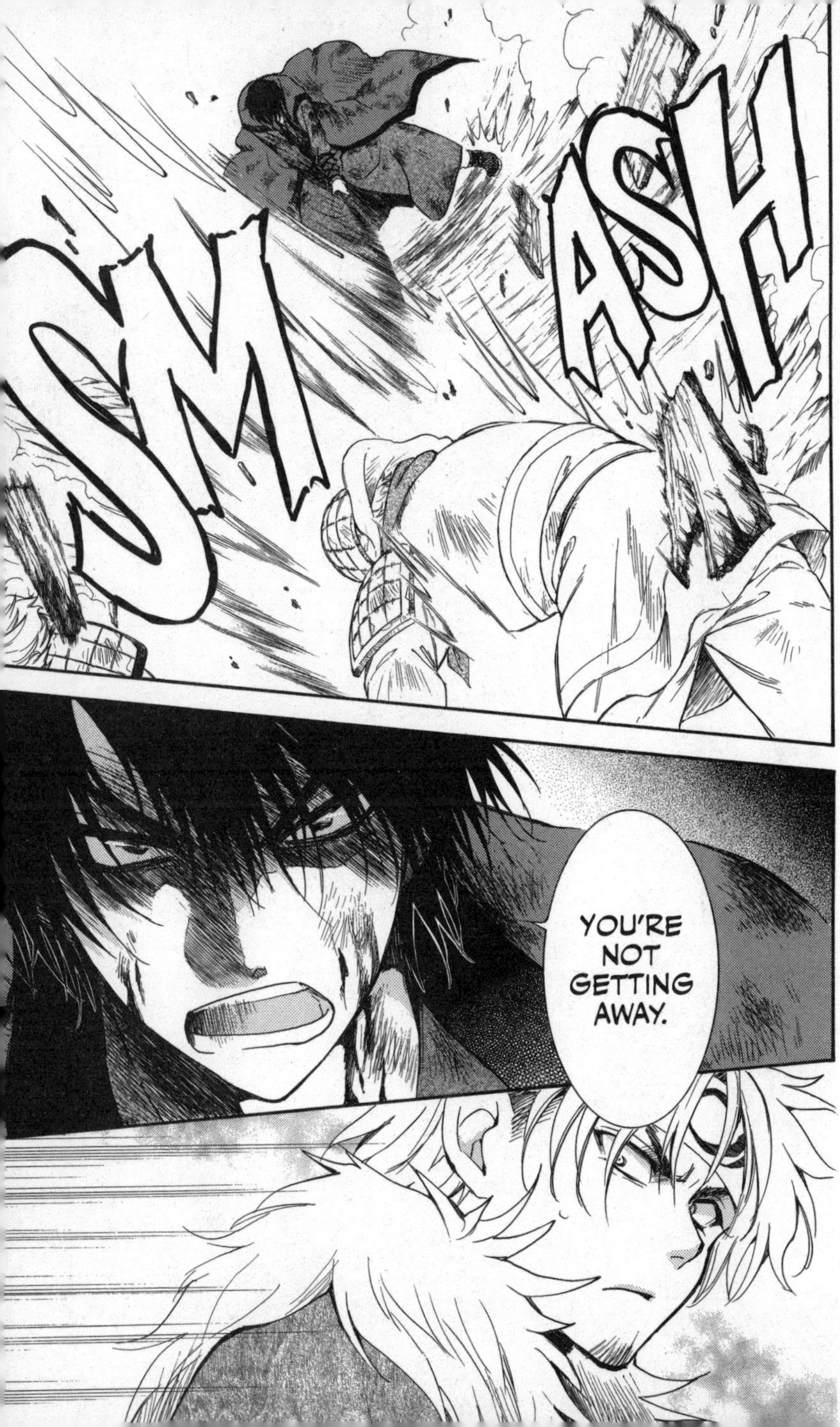
SMASH
YOU'RE NOT GETTING AWAY.

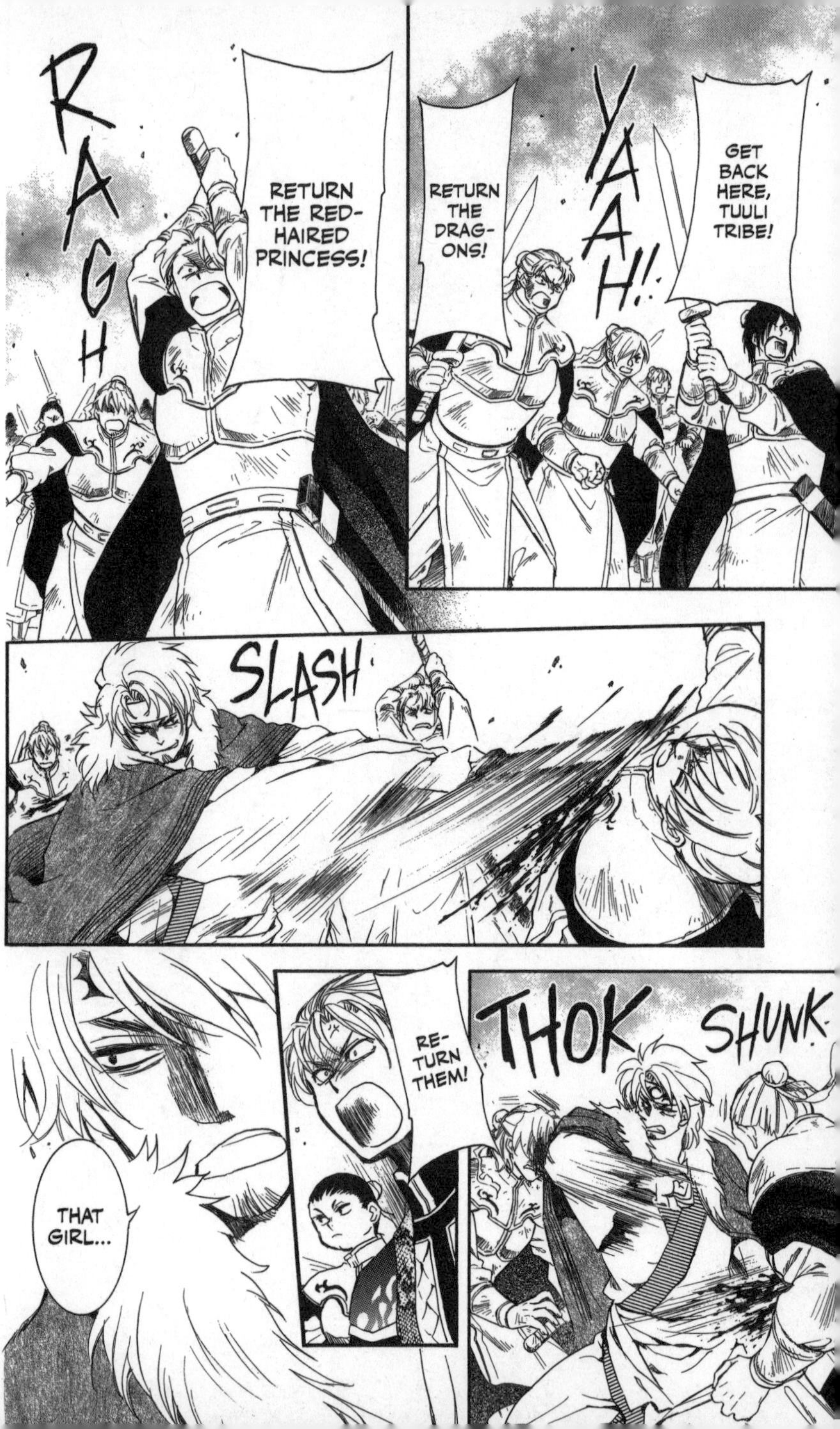
GET BACK HERE, TUULI TRIBE!
YAAH!!
RETURN THE DRAG-ONS!
RETURN THE RED-HAIRED PRINCESS!
RAGH
SLASH
SHUNK
THOK
RE-TURN THEM!
THAT GIRL...

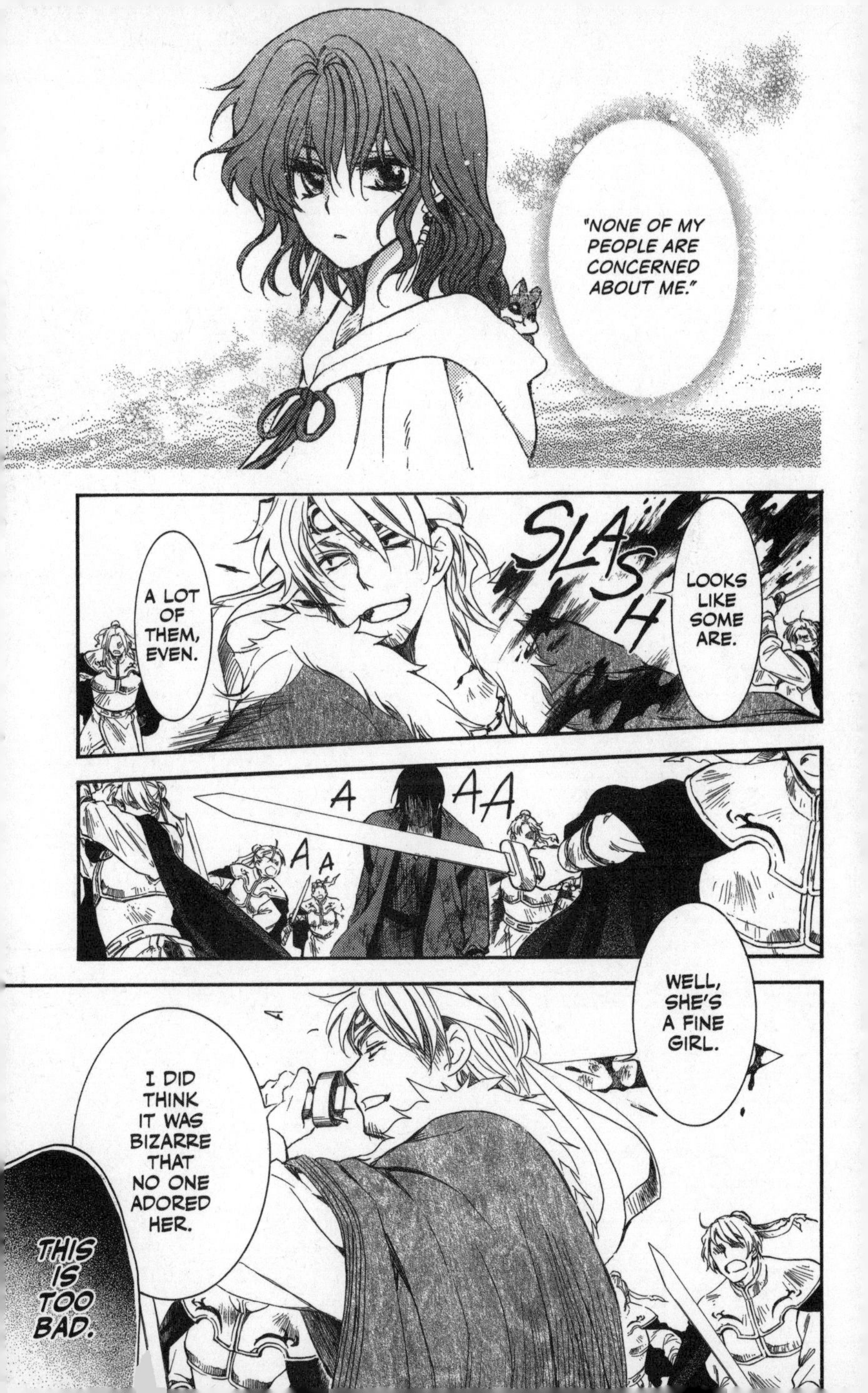
"NONE OF MY PEOPLE ARE CONCERNED ABOUT ME."
LOOKS LIKE SOME ARE.
SLASH
A LOT OF THEM, EVEN.
A AA
A A
WELL, SHE'S A FINE GIRL.
I DID THINK IT WAS BIZARRE THAT NO ONE ADORED HER.
THIS IS TOO BAD.

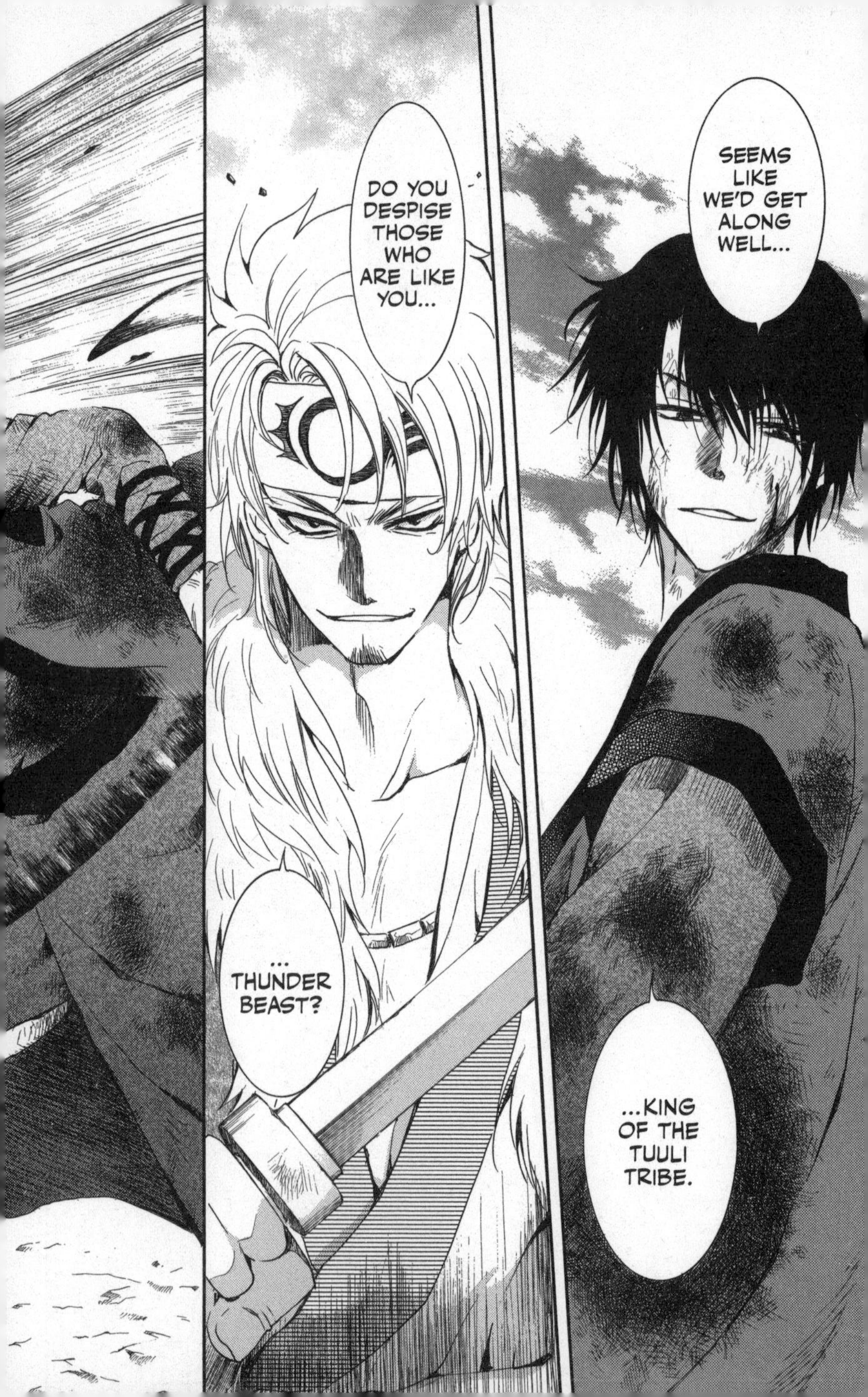
SEEMS LIKE WE'D GET ALONG WELL...
...KING OF THE TUULI TRIBE.
DO YOU DESPISE THOSE WHO ARE LIKE YOU...
...THUNDER BEAST?

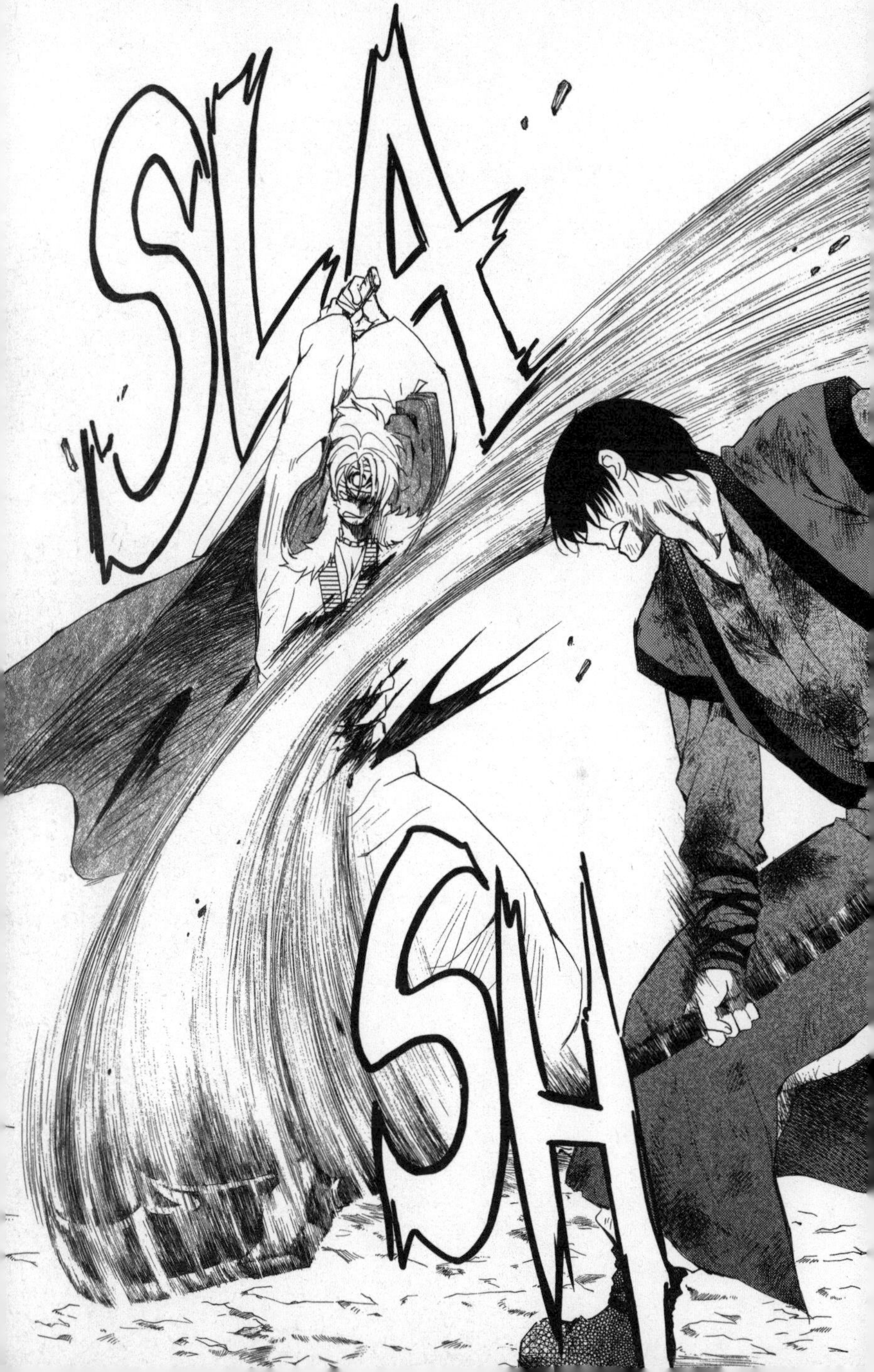
SLA
SH

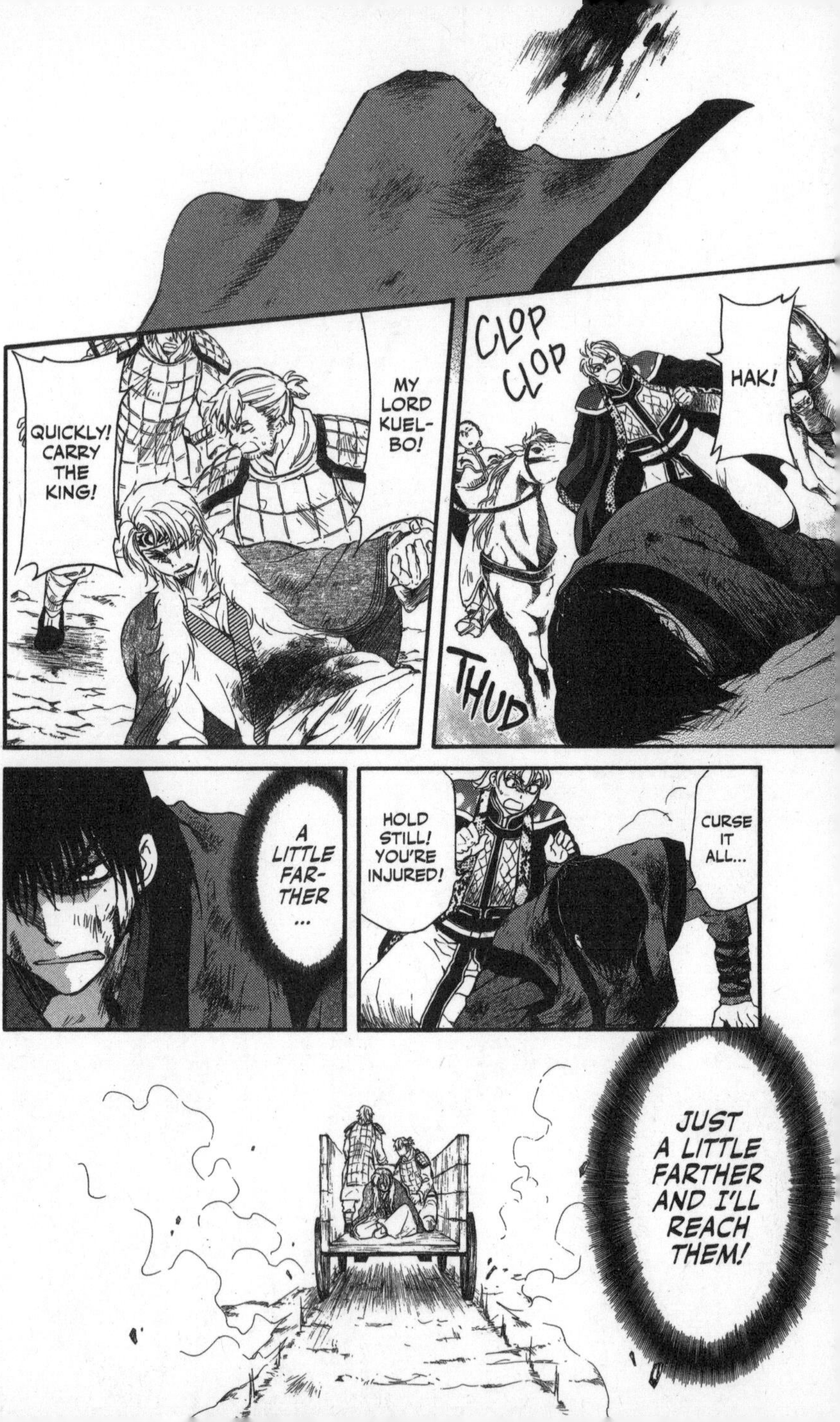
HAK!
CLOP CLOP
THUD
MY LORD KUEL-BO!
QUICKLY! CARRY THE KING!
CURSE IT ALL...
HOLD STILL! YOU'RE INJURED!
A LITTLE FAR-THER...
JUST A LITTLE FARTHER AND I'LL REACH THEM!

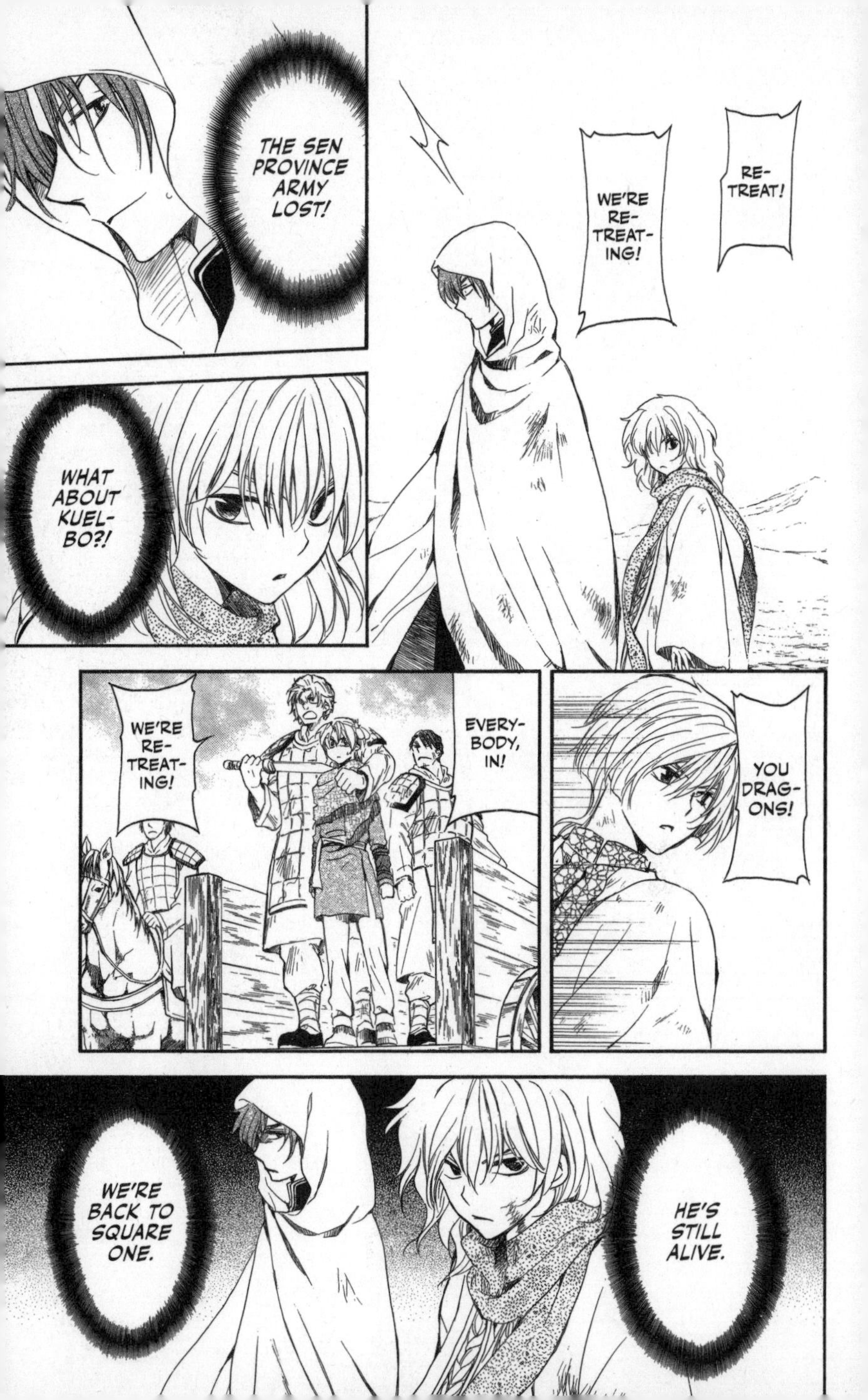
RE-TREAT!
WE'RE RE-TREAT-ING!
THE SEN PROVINCE ARMY LOST!
WHAT ABOUT KUEL-BO?!
YOU DRAG-ONS!
EVERY-BODY, IN!
WE'RE RE-TREAT-ING!
HE'S STILL ALIVE.
WE'RE BACK TO SQUARE ONE.

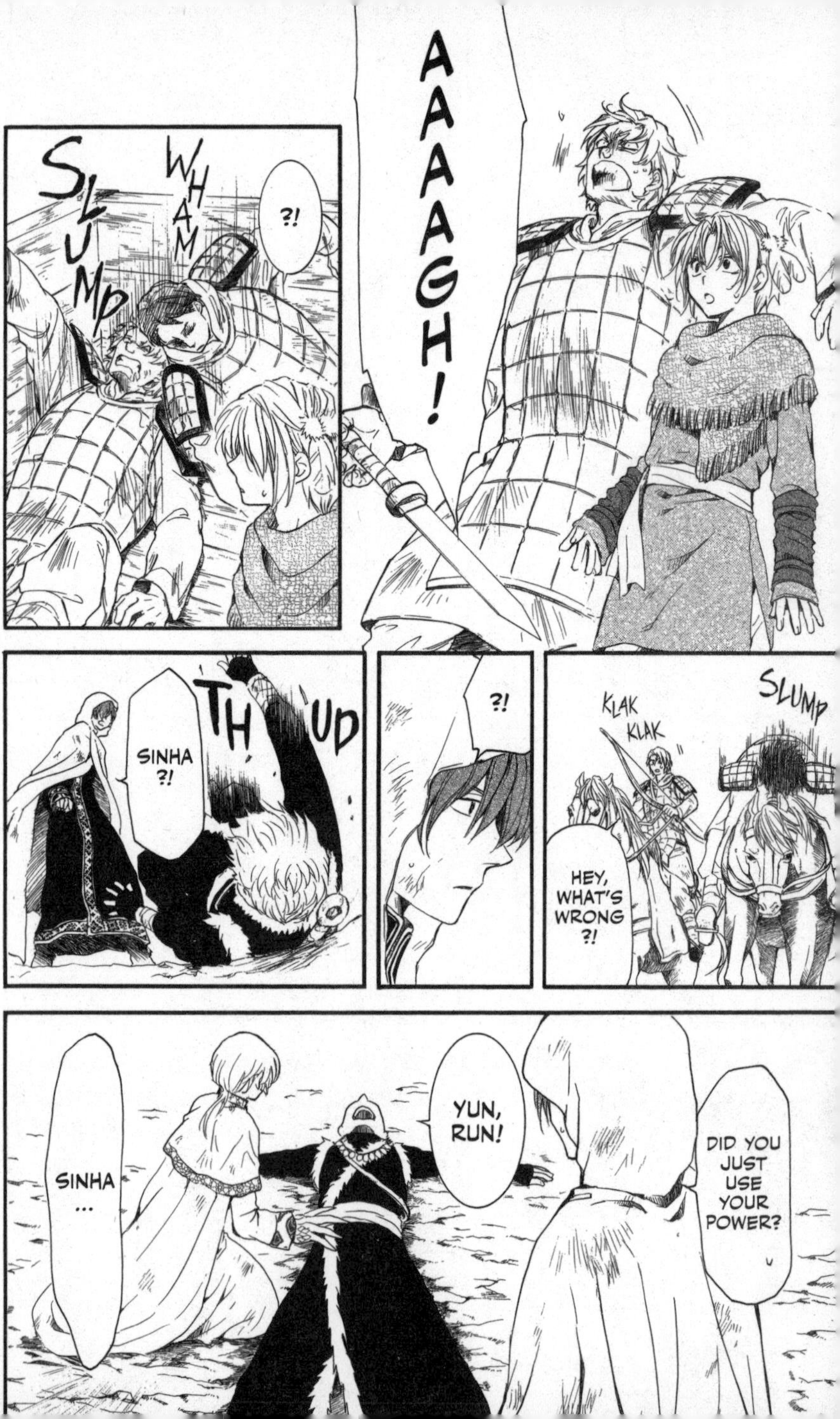
AAAAAGH!
?!
WHAM
SLUMP
SLUMP
KLAK KLAK
HEY, WHAT'S WRONG ?!
?!
THUD
SINHA ?!
DID YOU JUST USE YOUR POWER?
YUN, RUN!
SINHA ...

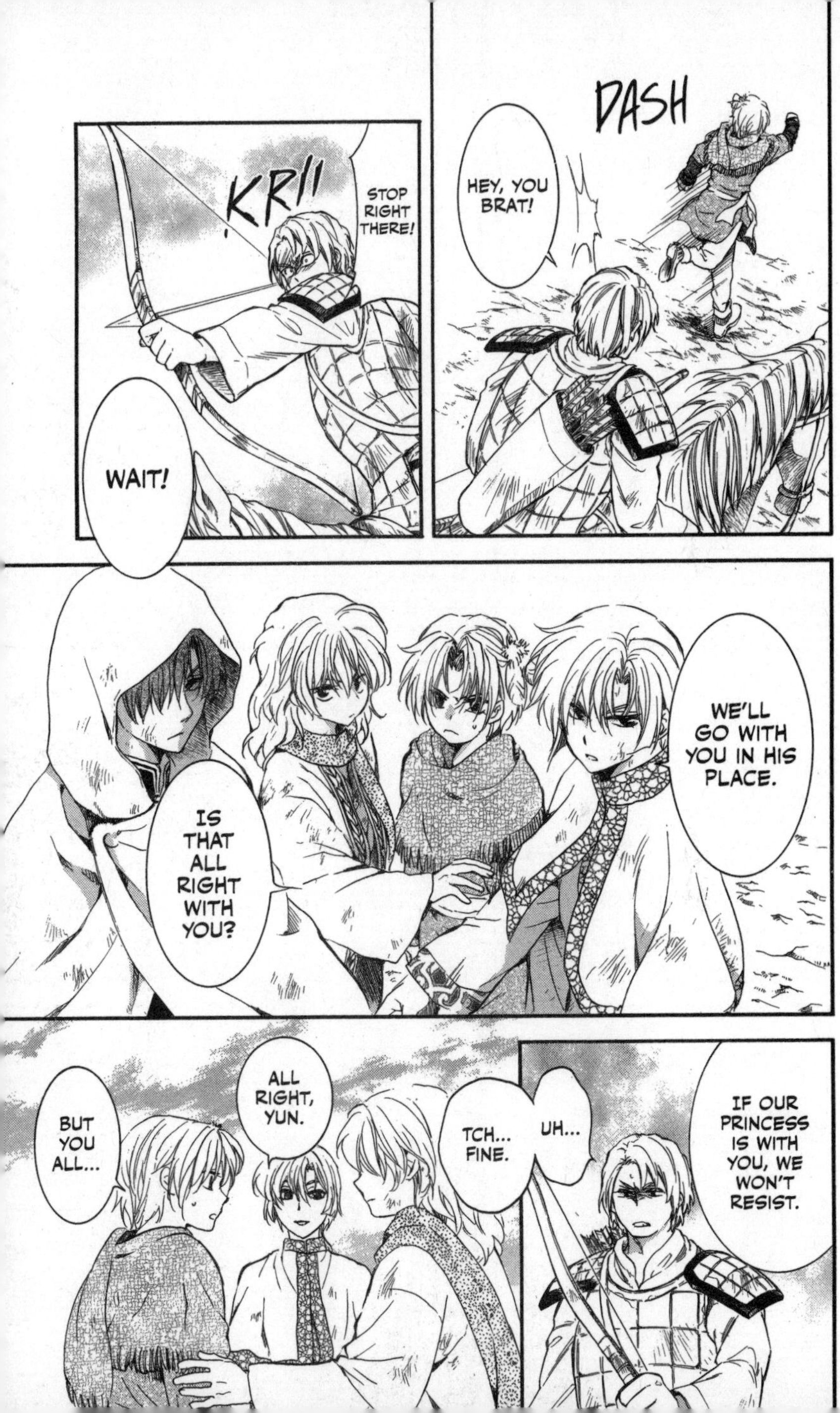
DASH
HEY, YOU BRAT!
KRII
STOP RIGHT THERE!
WAIT!
WE'LL GO WITH YOU IN HIS PLACE.
IS THAT ALL RIGHT WITH YOU?
IF OUR PRINCESS IS WITH YOU, WE WON'T RESIST.
UH...
TCH... FINE.
ALL RIGHT, YUN.
BUT YOU ALL...

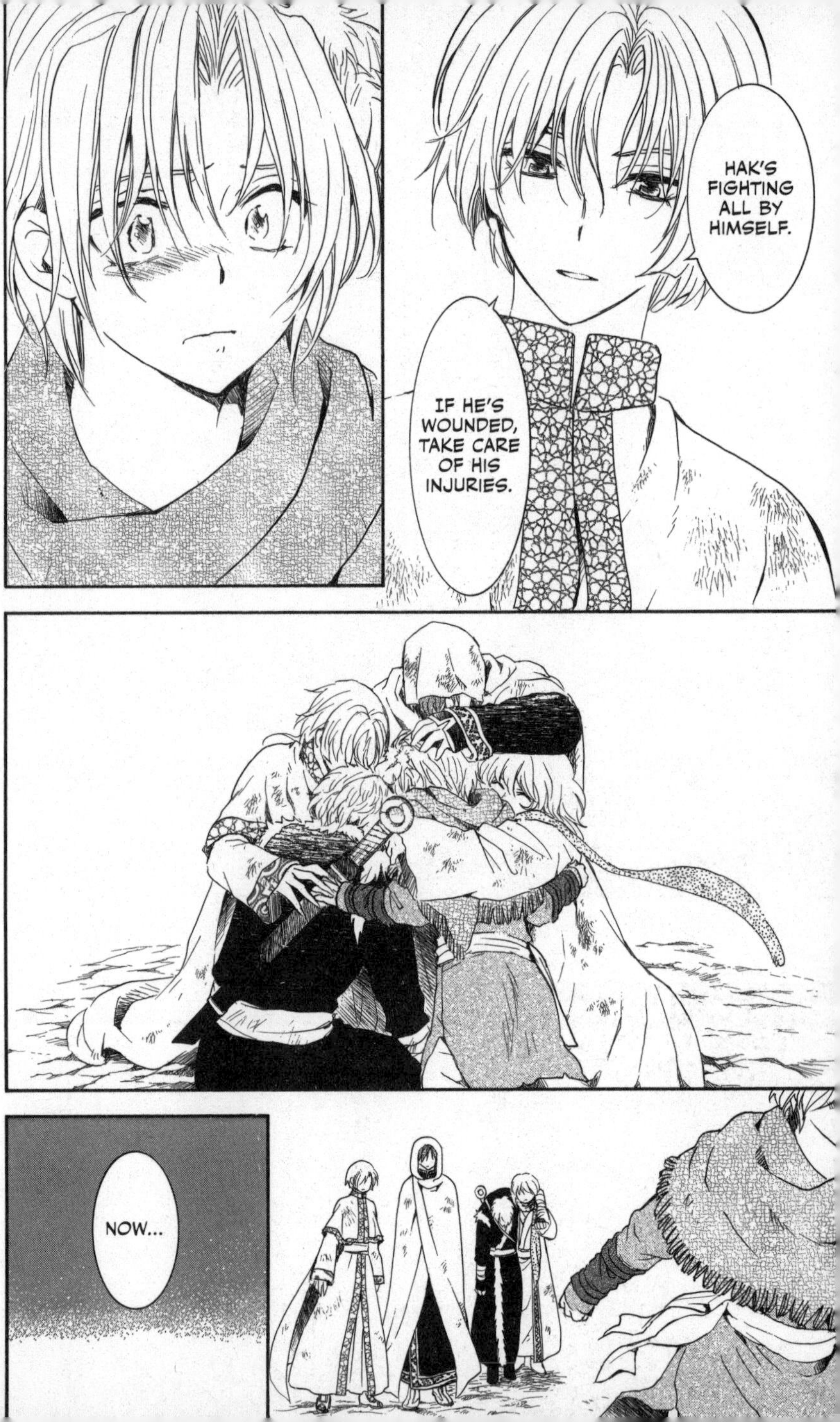
HAK'S FIGHTING ALL BY HIMSELF.
IF HE'S WOUNDED, TAKE CARE OF HIS INJURIES.
NOW...

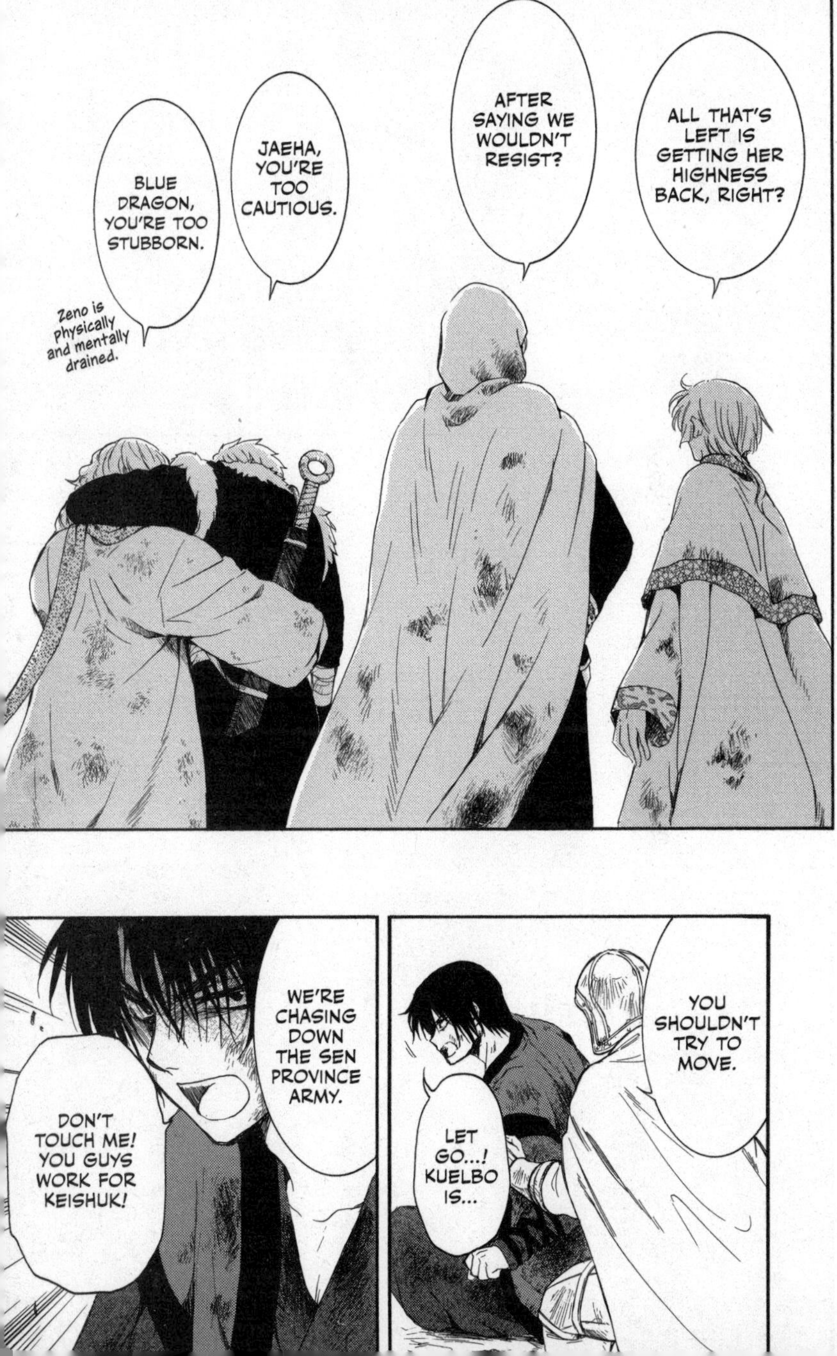
ALL THAT'S LEFT IS GETTING HER HIGHNESS BACK, RIGHT?
AFTER SAYING WE WOULDN'T RESIST?
JAEHA, YOU'RE TOO CAUTIOUS.
BLUE DRAGON, YOU'RE TOO STUBBORN.
Zeno is physically and mentally drained.
YOU SHOULDN'T TRY TO MOVE.
LET GO...! KUELBO IS...
WE'RE CHASING DOWN THE SEN PROVINCE ARMY.
DON'T TOUCH ME! YOU GUYS WORK FOR KEISHUK!

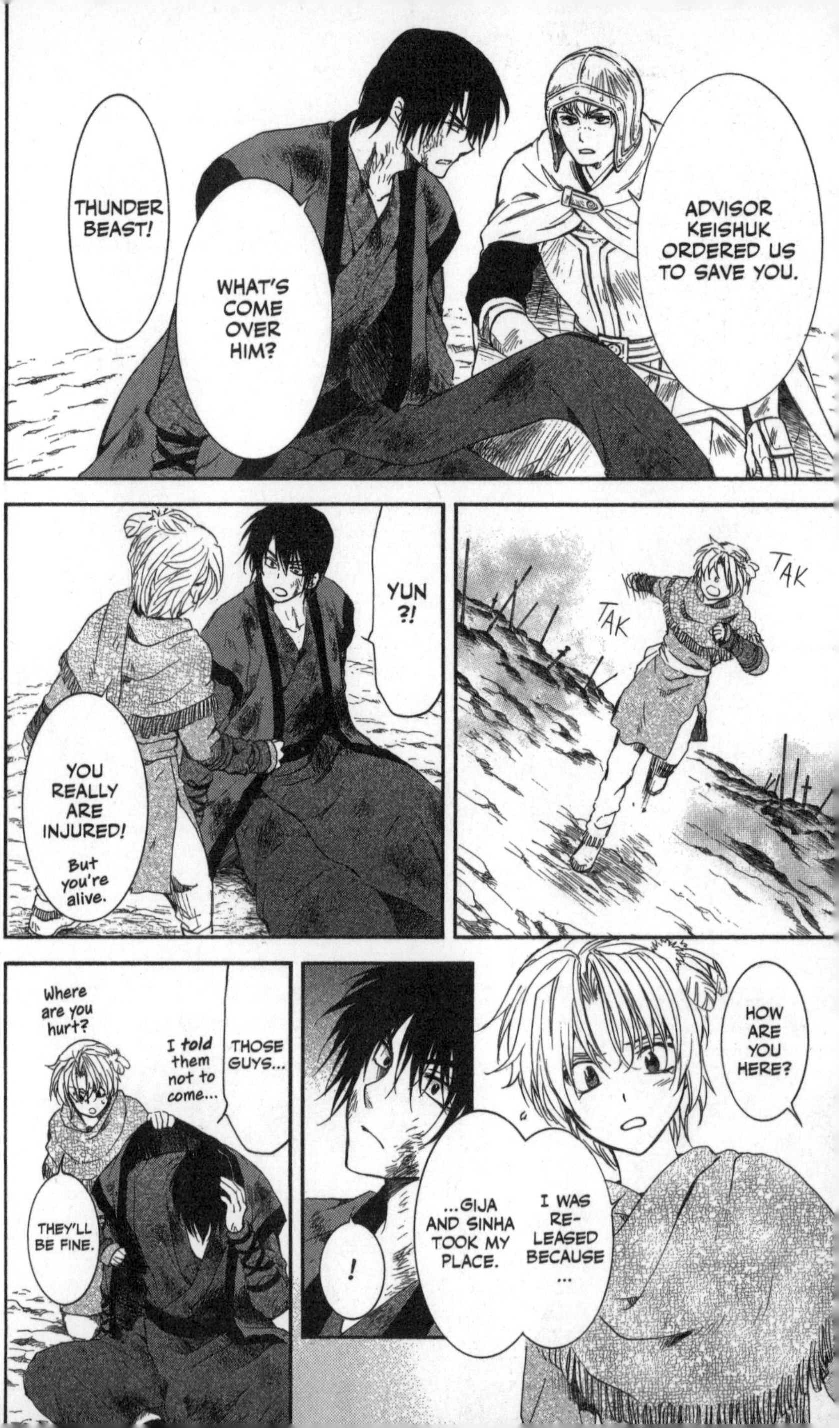
ADVISOR KEISHUK ORDERED US TO SAVE YOU.
THUNDER BEAST!
WHAT'S COME OVER HIM?
TAK
TAK
YUN ?!
YOU REALLY ARE INJURED!
But you're alive.
HOW ARE YOU HERE?
I WAS RE-LEASED BECAUSE ...
...GIJA AND SINHA TOOK MY PLACE.
!
THOSE GUYS...
I told them not to come...
Where are you hurt?
THEY'LL BE FINE.

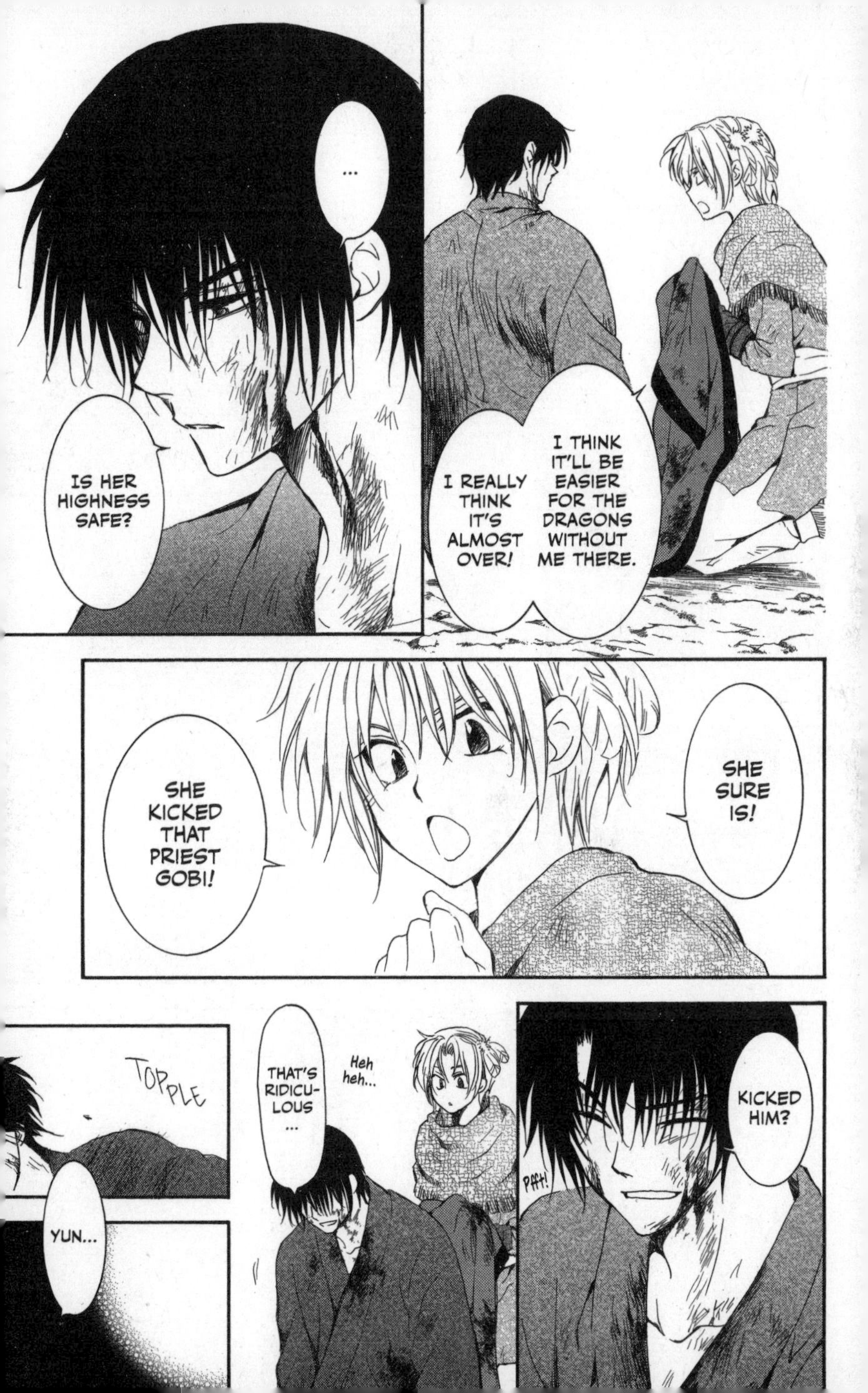
I THINK IT'LL BE EASIER FOR THE DRAGONS WITHOUT ME THERE.
I REALLY THINK IT'S ALMOST OVER!
...
IS HER HIGHNESS SAFE?
SHE SURE IS!
SHE KICKED THAT PRIEST GOBI!
KICKED HIM?
Pfft!
Heh heh...
THAT'S RIDICULOUS...
TOPPLE
YUN...

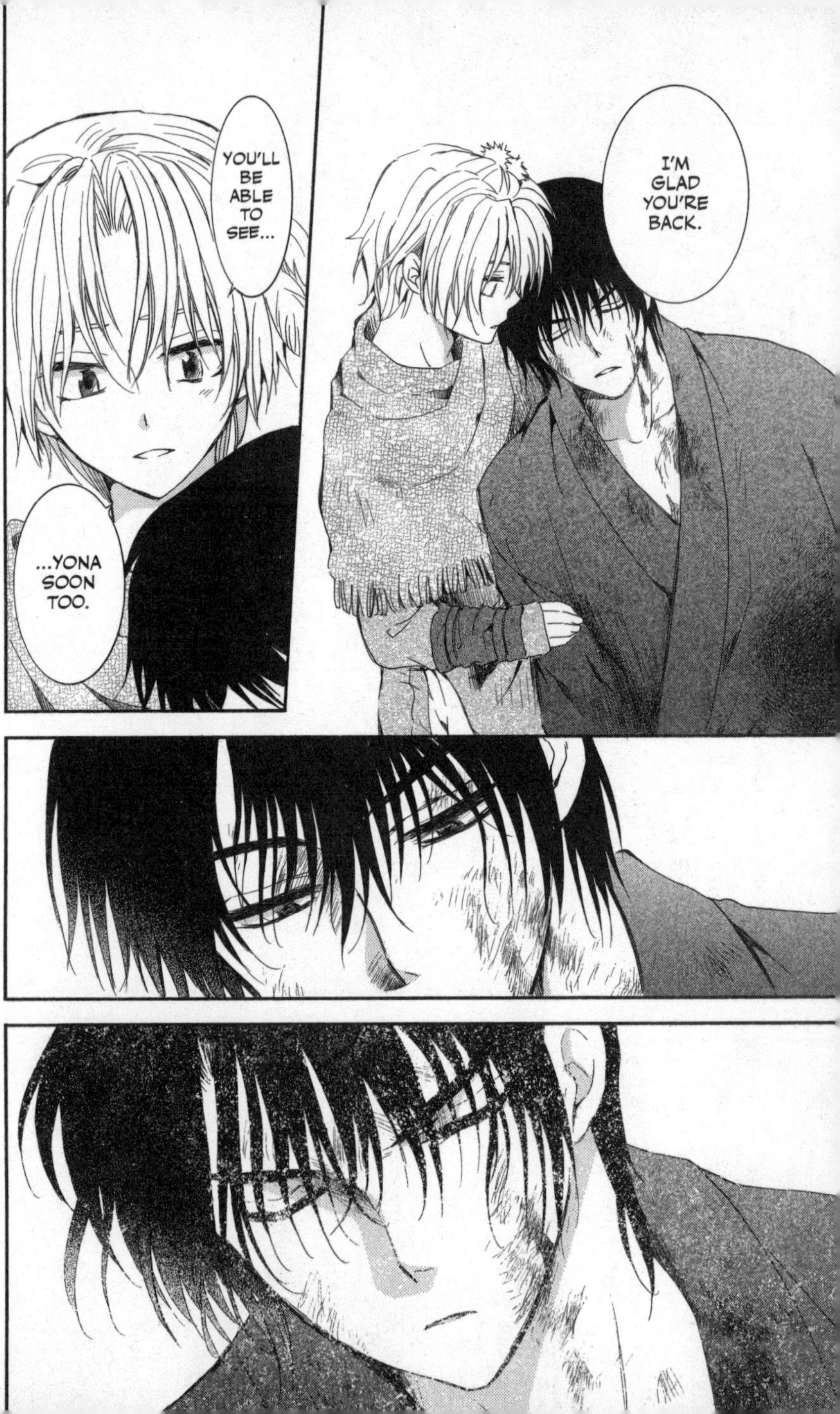
I'M GLAD YOU'RE BACK.
YOU'LL BE ABLE TO SEE...
...YONA SOON TOO.

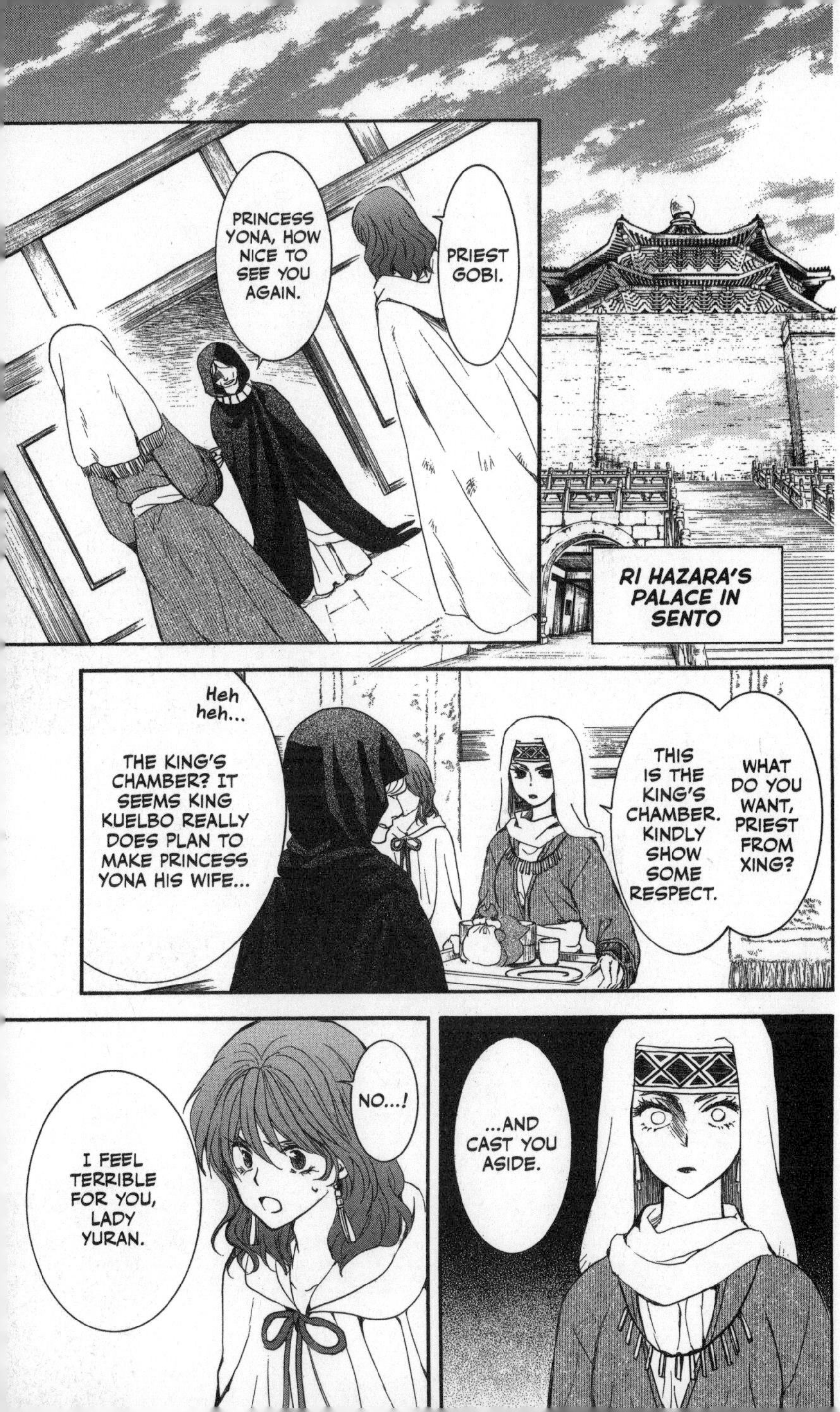
RI HAZARA'S PALACE IN SENTO
PRIEST GOBI.
PRINCESS YONA, HOW NICE TO SEE YOU AGAIN.
WHAT DO YOU WANT, PRIEST FROM XING?
THIS IS THE KING'S CHAMBER. KINDLY SHOW SOME RESPECT.
Heh heh...
THE KING'S CHAMBER? IT SEEMS KING KUELBO REALLY DOES PLAN TO MAKE PRINCESS YONA HIS WIFE...
...AND CAST YOU ASIDE.
NO...!
I FEEL TERRIBLE FOR YOU, LADY YURAN.

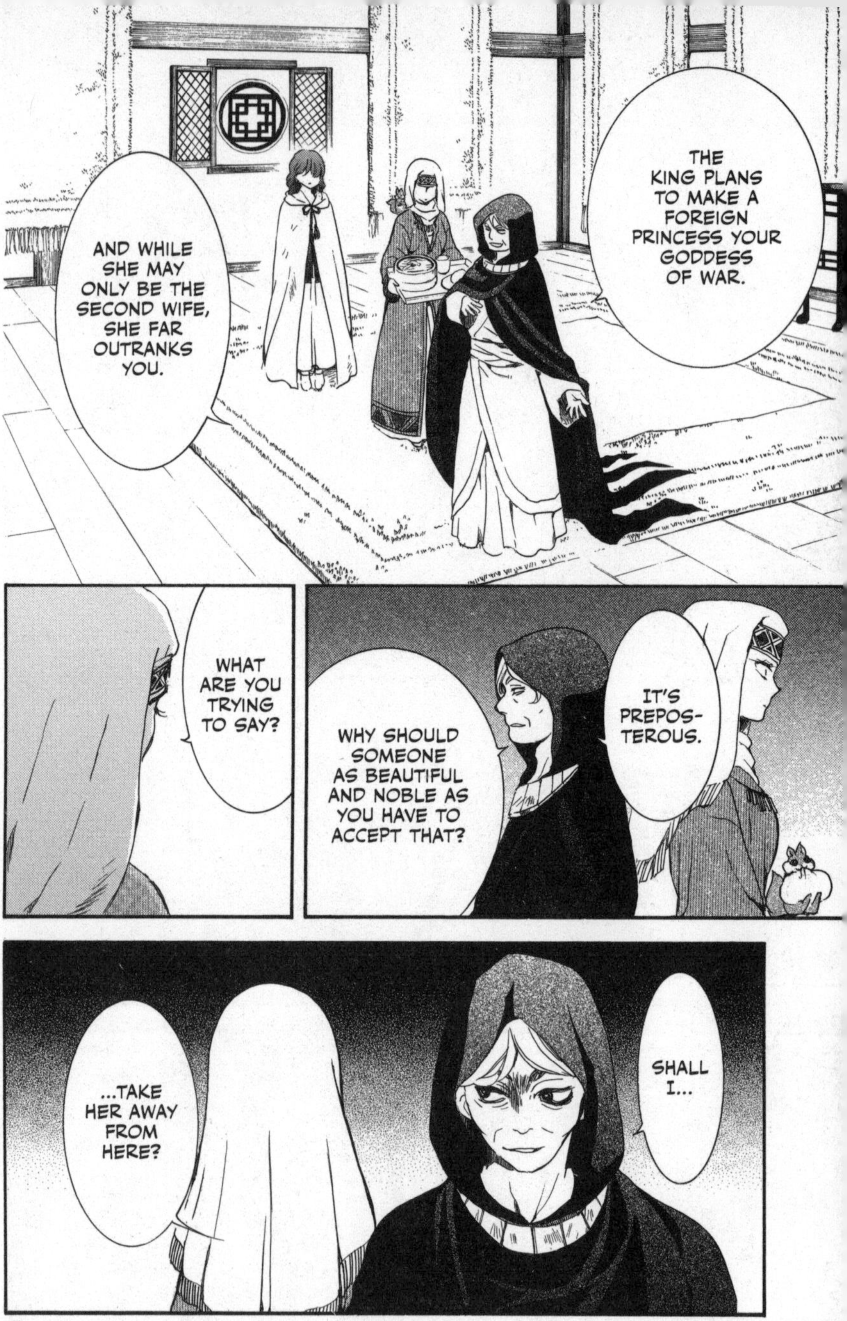
THE KING PLANS TO MAKE A FOREIGN PRINCESS YOUR GODDESS OF WAR.
AND WHILE SHE MAY ONLY BE THE SECOND WIFE, SHE FAR OUTRANKS YOU.
IT'S PREPOS-TEROUS.
WHY SHOULD SOMEONE AS BEAUTIFUL AND NOBLE AS YOU HAVE TO ACCEPT THAT?
WHAT ARE YOU TRYING TO SAY?
SHALL I...
...TAKE HER AWAY FROM HERE?

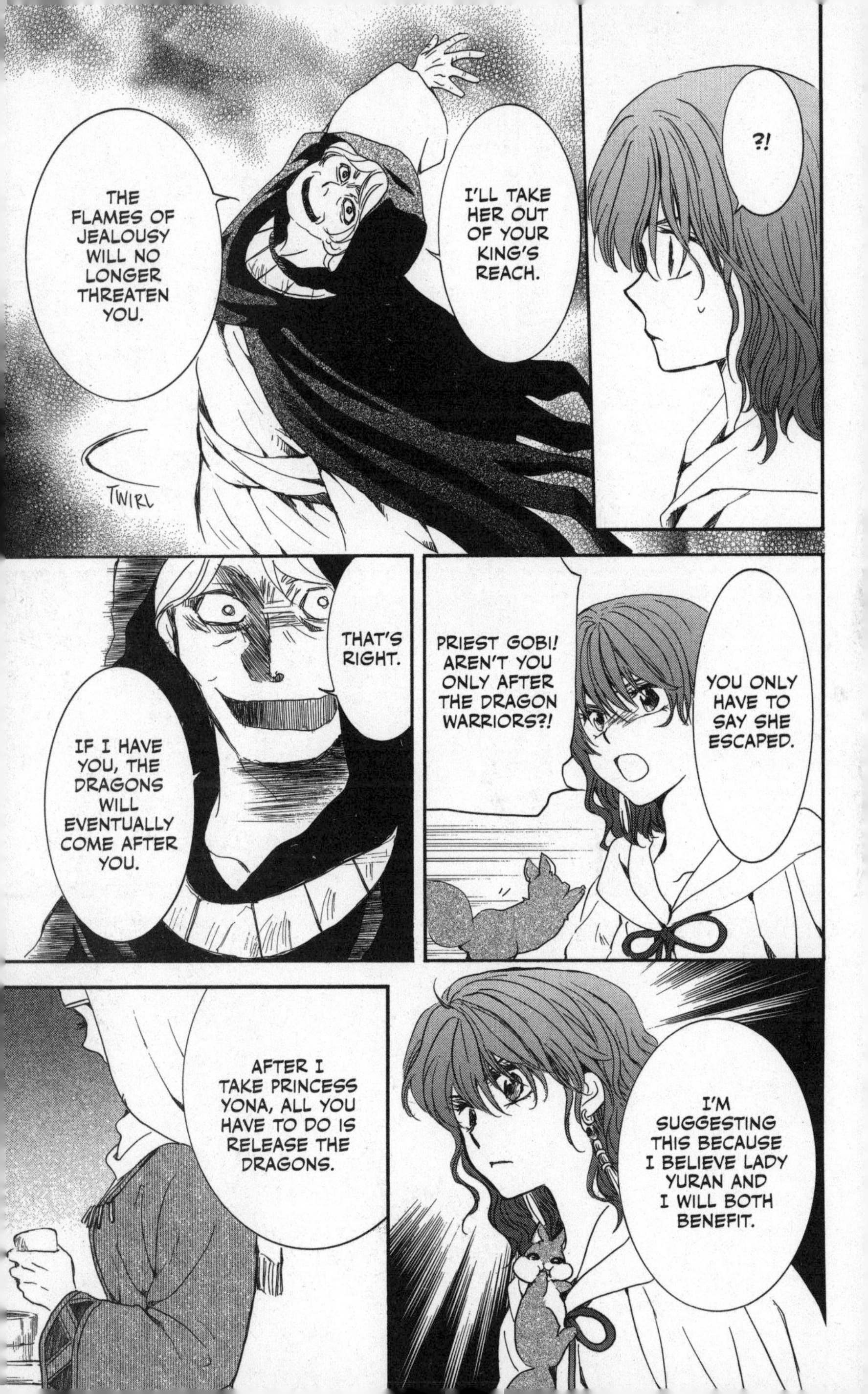
?!
I'LL TAKE HER OUT OF YOUR KING'S REACH.
THE FLAMES OF JEALOUSY WILL NO LONGER THREATEN YOU.
TWIRL
YOU ONLY HAVE TO SAY SHE ESCAPED.
PRIEST GOBI! AREN'T YOU ONLY AFTER THE DRAGON WARRIORS?!
THAT'S RIGHT.
IF I HAVE YOU, THE DRAGONS WILL EVENTUALLY COME AFTER YOU.
I'M SUGGESTING THIS BECAUSE I BELIEVE LADY YURAN AND I WILL BOTH BENEFIT.
AFTER I TAKE PRINCESS YONA, ALL YOU HAVE TO DO IS RELEASE THE DRAGONS.

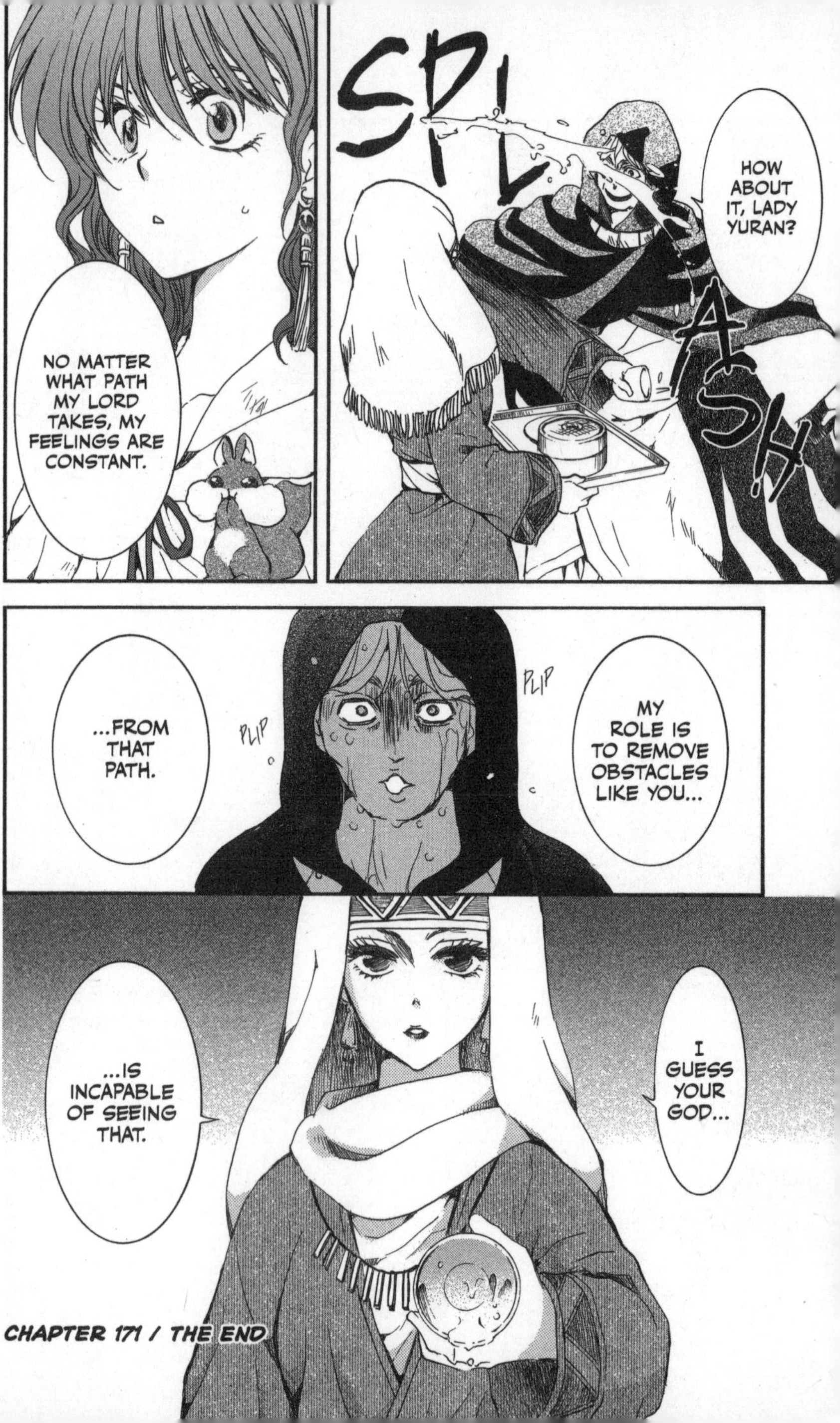
SPLASH
HOW ABOUT IT, LADY YURAN?
NO MATTER WHAT PATH MY LORD TAKES, MY FEELINGS ARE CONSTANT.
PLIP
PLIP
MY ROLE IS TO REMOVE OBSTACLES LIKE YOU...
...FROM THAT PATH.
I GUESS YOUR GOD...
...IS INCAPABLE OF SEEING THAT.
CHAPTER 171 / THE END

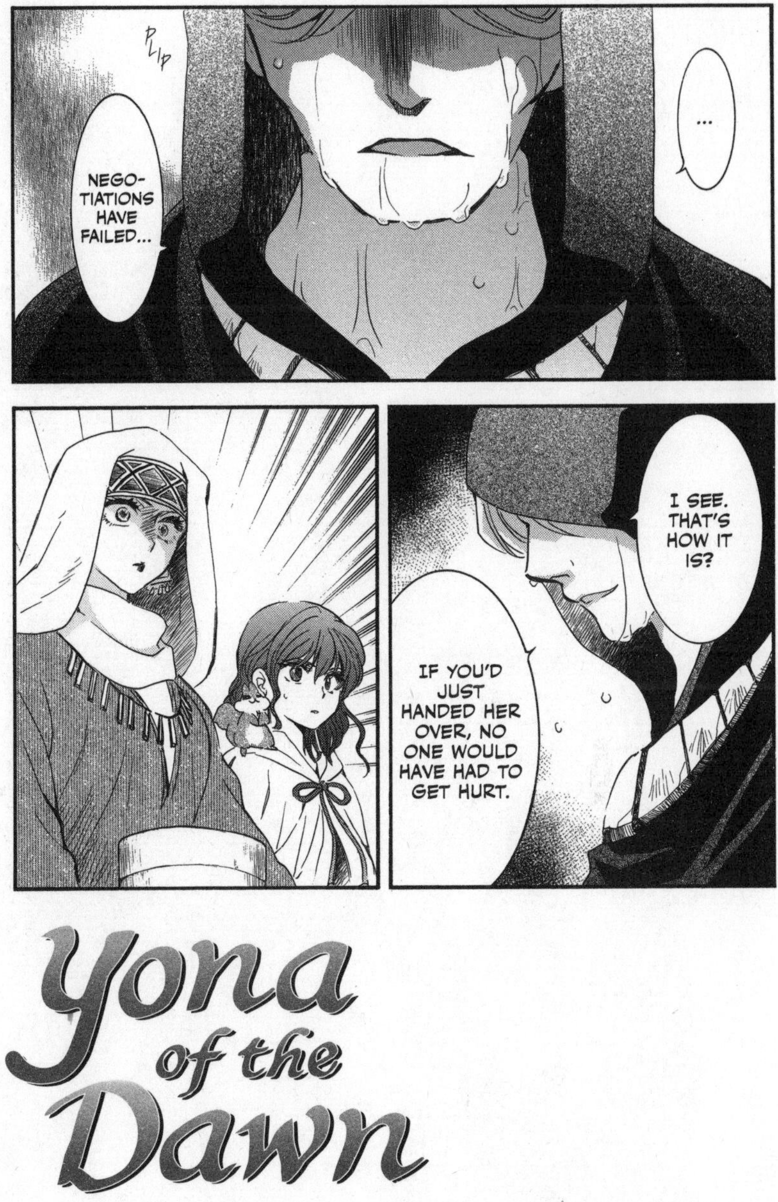
...
PLIP
NEGO-TIATIONS HAVE FAILED...
I SEE. THAT'S HOW IT IS?
IF YOU'D JUST HANDED HER OVER, NO ONE WOULD HAVE HAD TO GET HURT.

Yona of the Dawn

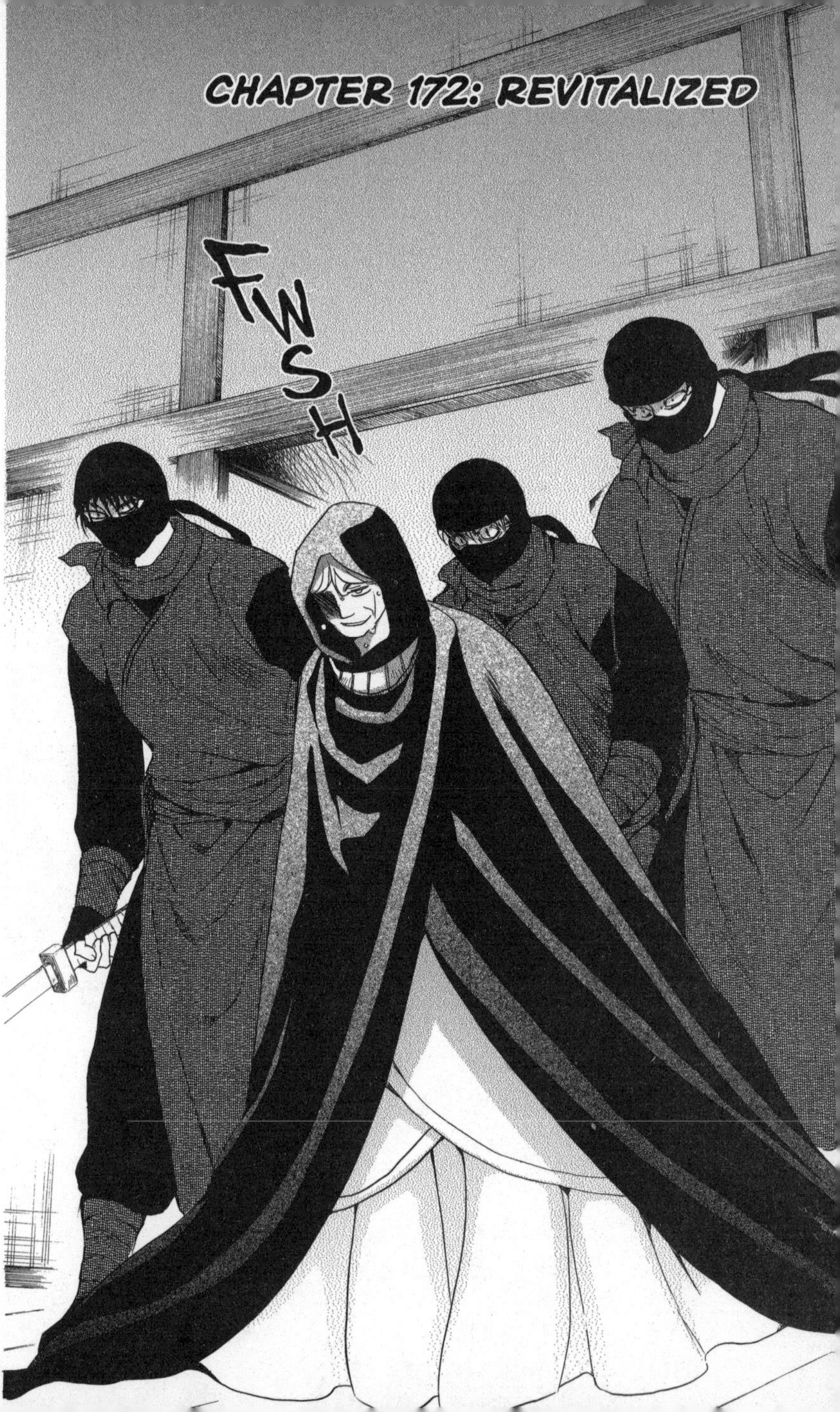
CHAPTER 172: REVITALIZED
FWSH

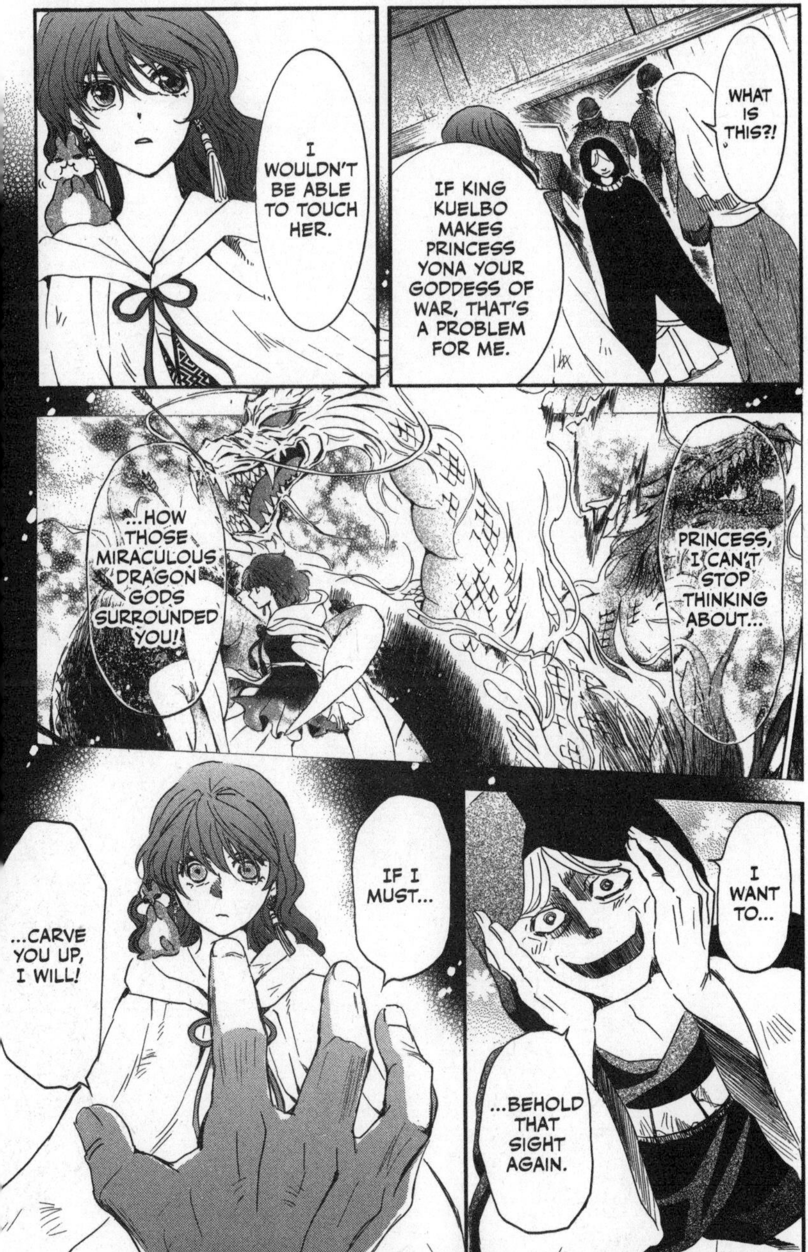
WHAT IS THIS?!
IF KING KUELBO MAKES PRINCESS YONA YOUR GODDESS OF WAR, THAT'S A PROBLEM FOR ME.
I WOULDN'T BE ABLE TO TOUCH HER.
PRINCESS, I CAN'T STOP THINKING ABOUT...
...HOW THOSE MIRACULOUS DRAGON GODS SURROUNDED YOU!
I WANT TO...
...BEHOLD THAT SIGHT AGAIN.
IF I MUST...
...CARVE YOU UP, I WILL!

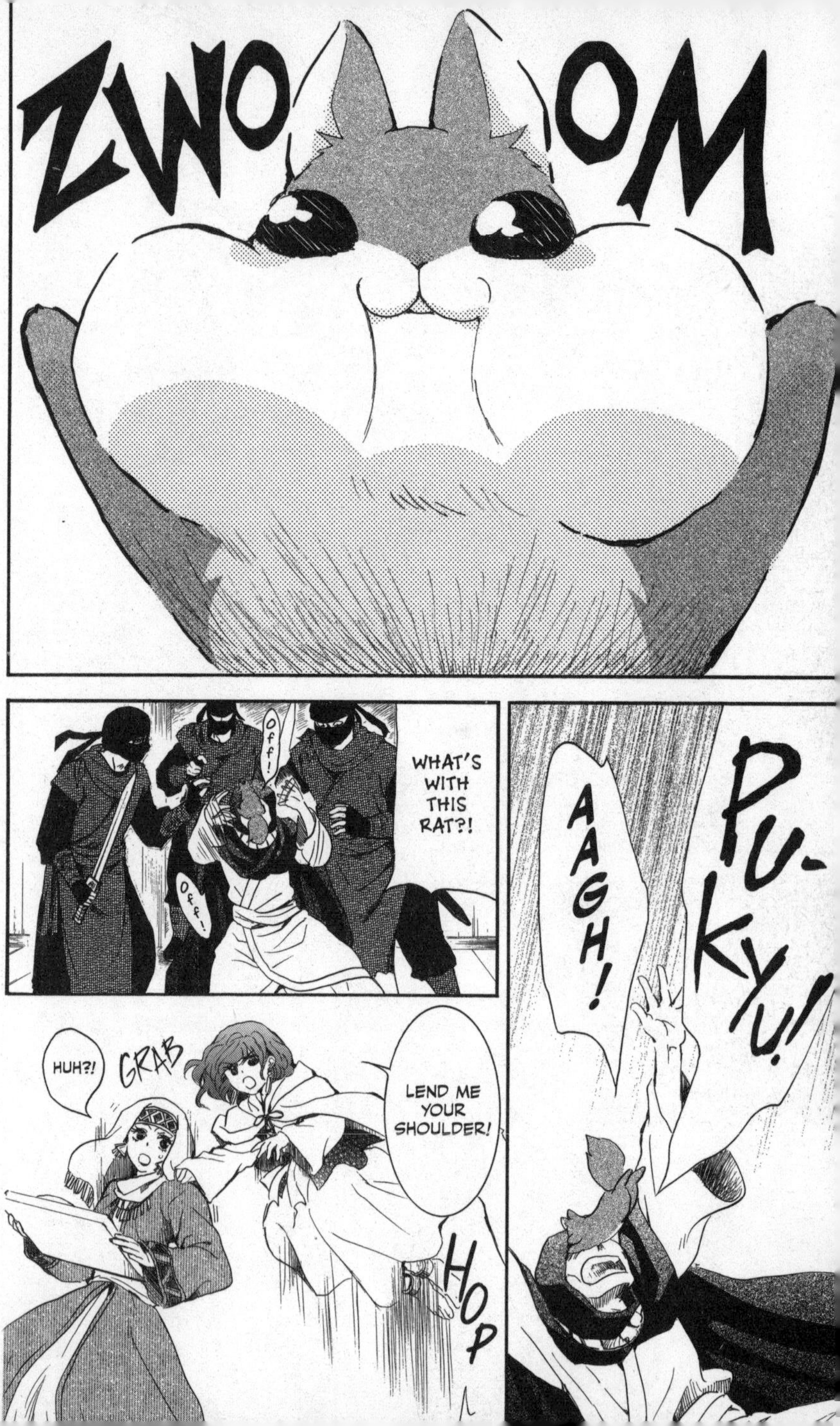
ZWOOOM
PU-KYU!
AAGH!
WHAT'S WITH THIS RAT?!
Off!
Off!
LEND ME YOUR SHOULDER!
GRAB
HUH?!
HOP

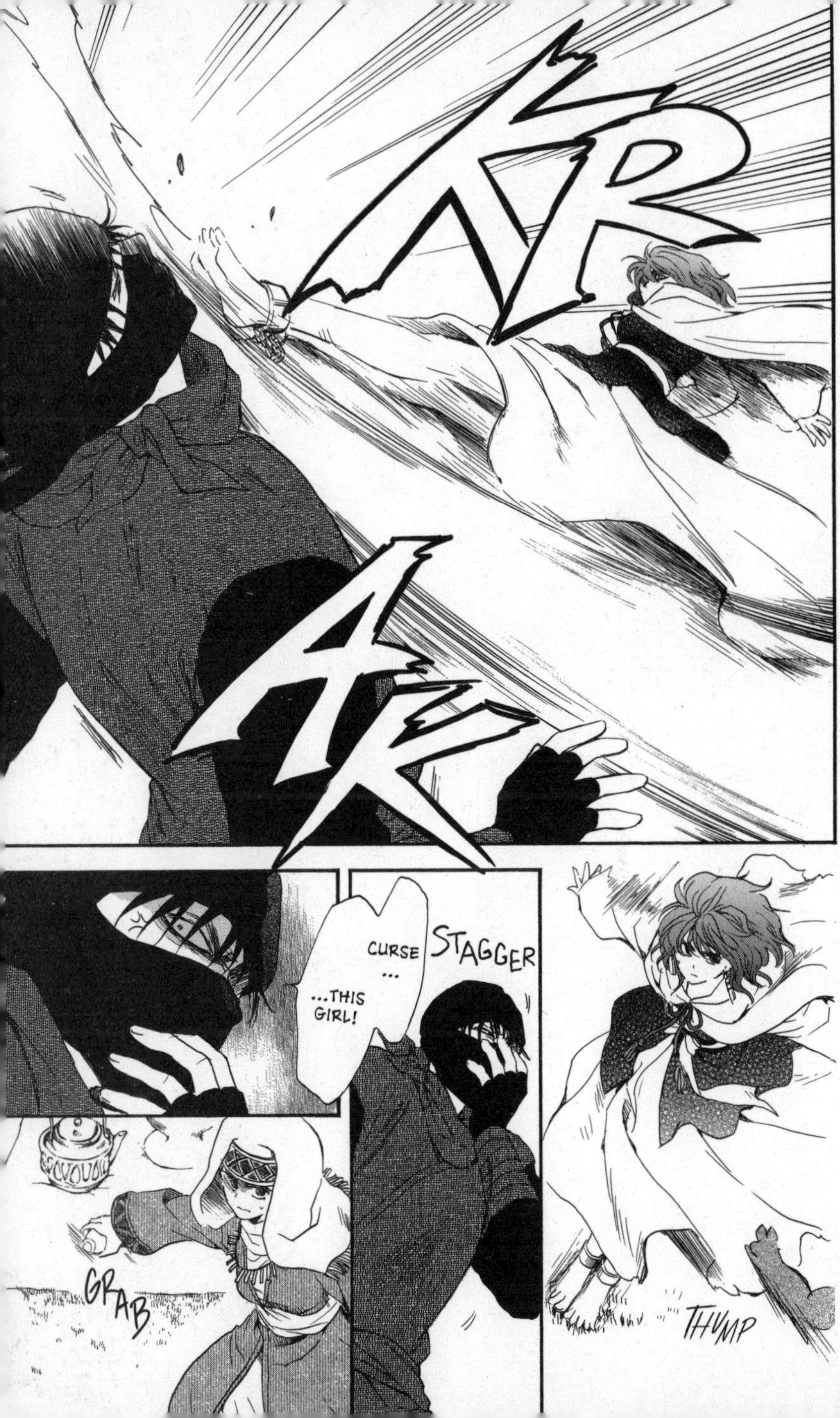
THUMP
STAGGER
CURSE ...
...THIS GIRL!
GRAB

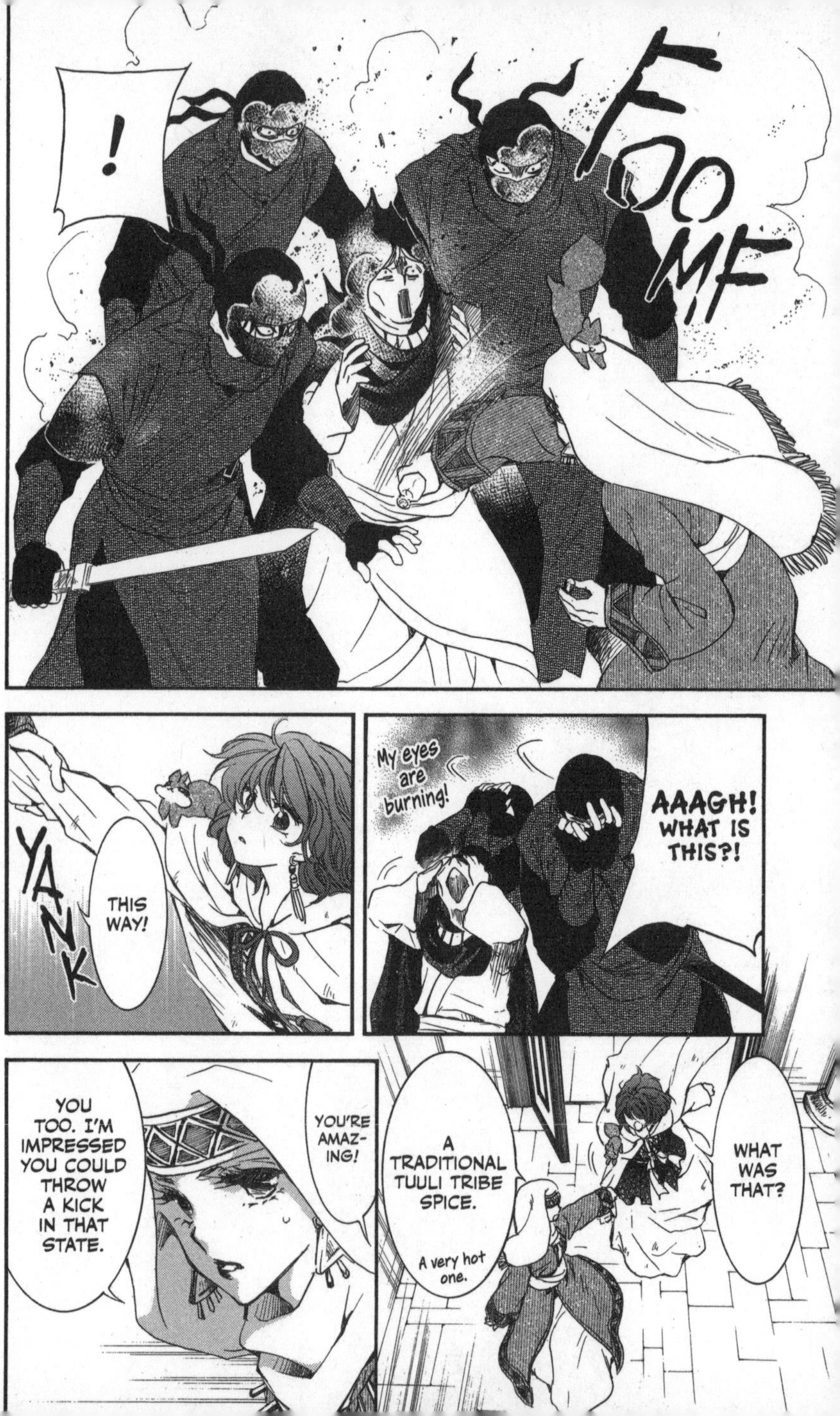
FOOMF
!
AAAGH! WHAT IS THIS?!
My eyes are burning!
YANK
THIS WAY!
WHAT WAS THAT?
A TRADITIONAL TUULI TRIBE SPICE.
A very hot one.
YOU'RE AMAZING!
YOU TOO. I'M IMPRESSED YOU COULD THROW A KICK IN THAT STATE.

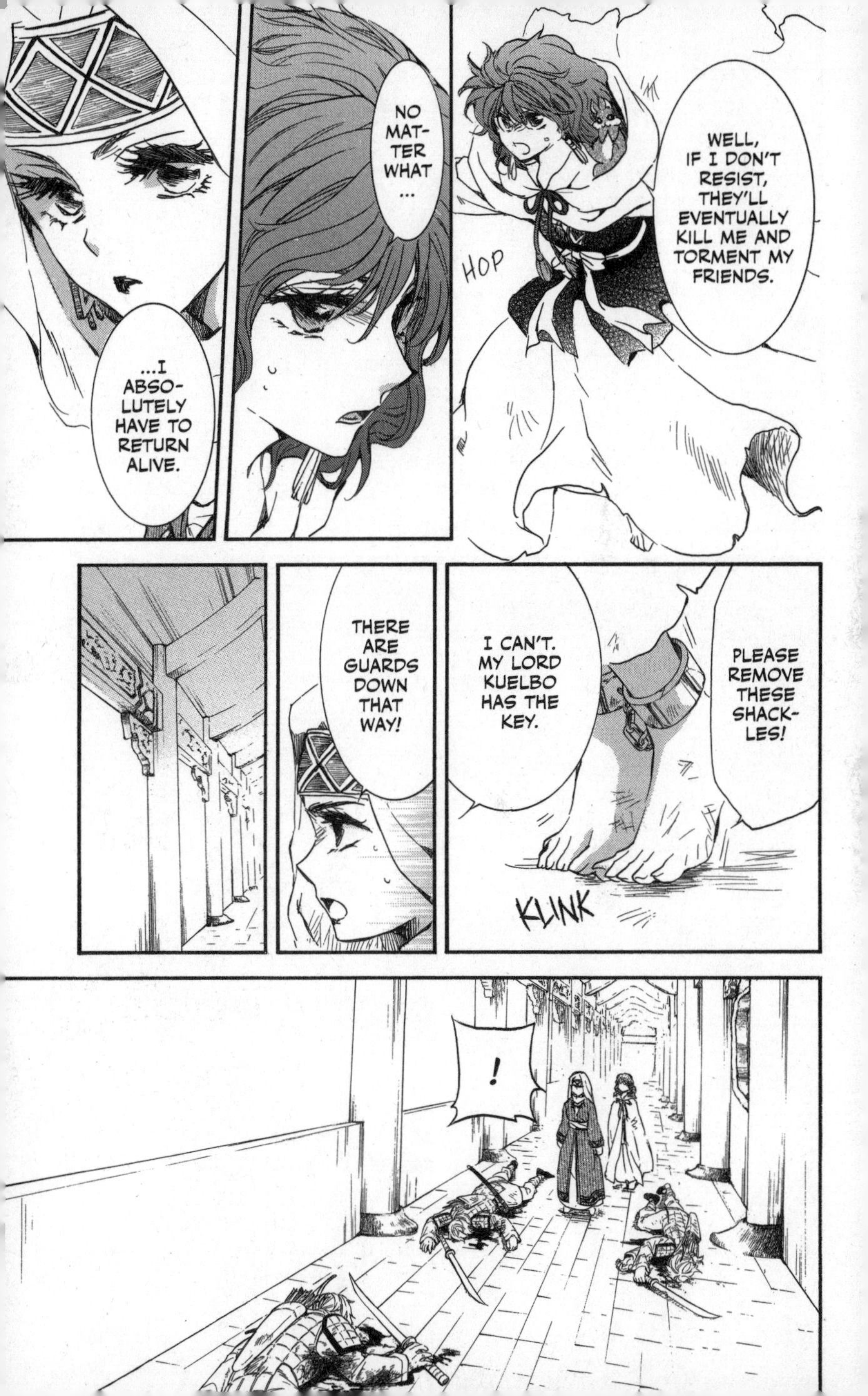

WELL, IF I DON'T RESIST, THEY'LL EVENTUALLY KILL ME AND TORMENT MY FRIENDS.
HOP
NO MATTER WHAT...
...I ABSOLUTELY HAVE TO RETURN ALIVE.
PLEASE REMOVE THESE SHACKLES!
I CAN'T. MY LORD KUELBO HAS THE KEY.
KLINK
THERE ARE GUARDS DOWN THAT WAY!
!

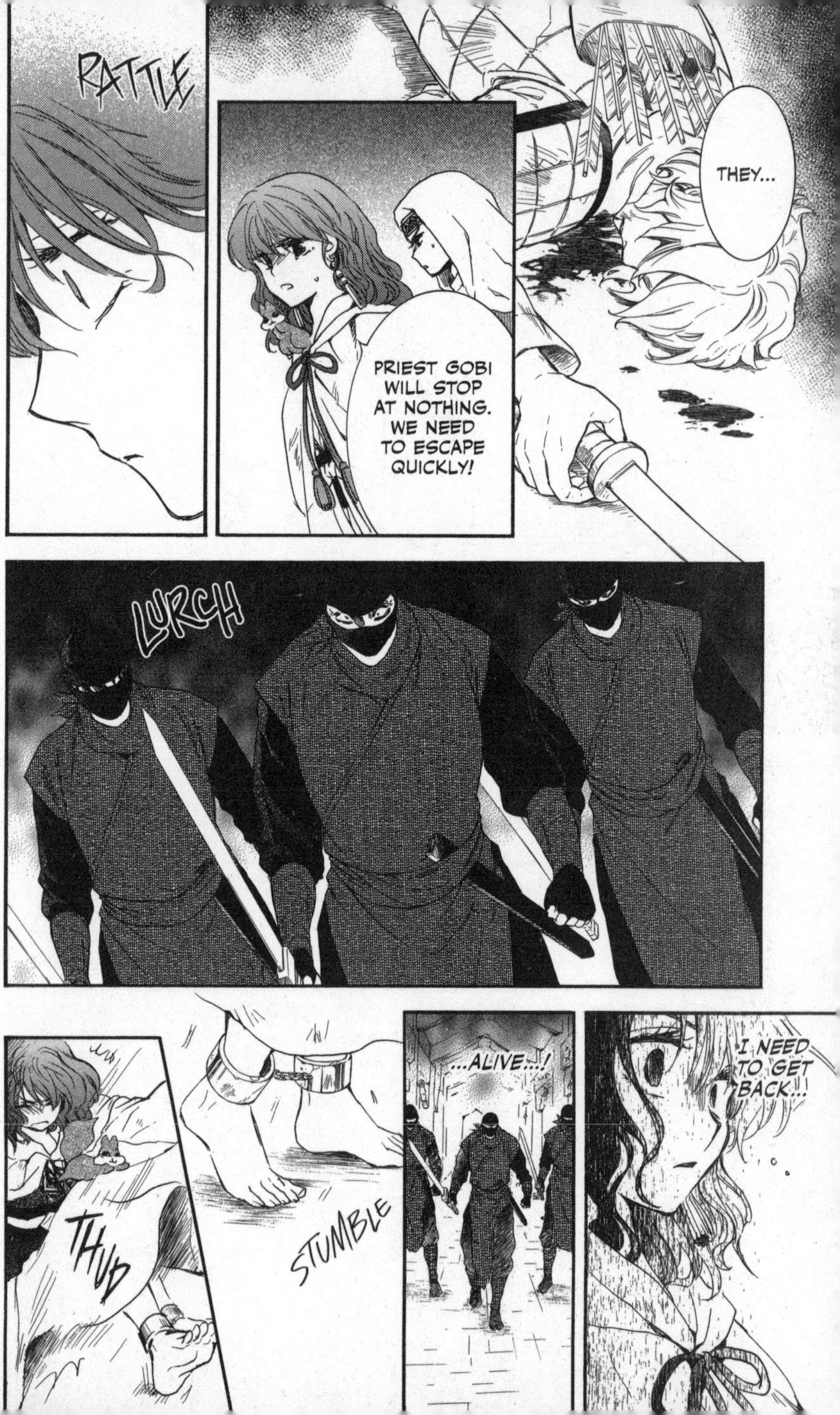
THEY...
PRIEST GOBI WILL STOP AT NOTHING. WE NEED TO ESCAPE QUICKLY!
RATTLE
LURCH
I NEED TO GET BACK...
...ALIVE...!
STUMBLE
THUD

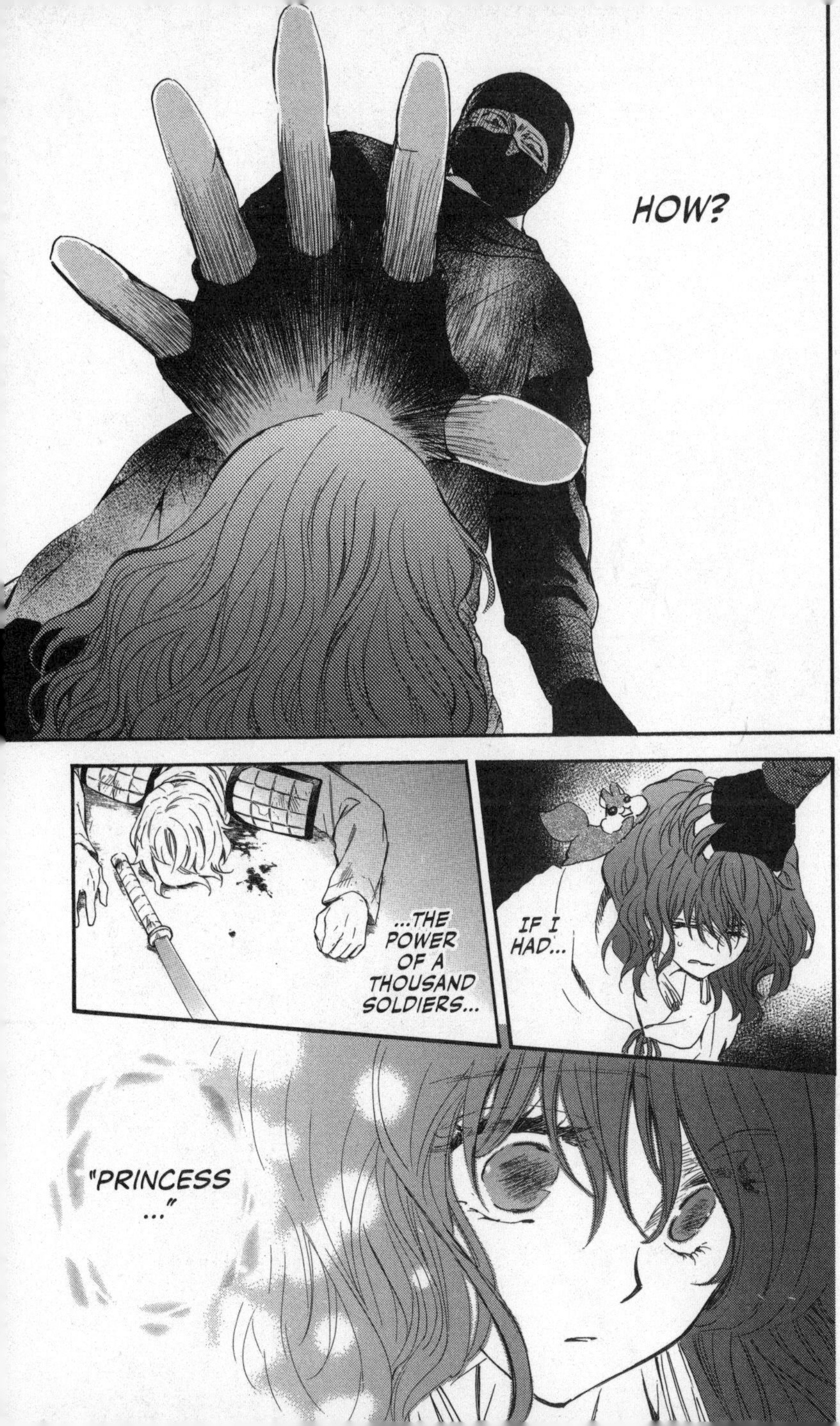
HOW?
IF I HAD...
...THE POWER OF A THOUSAND SOLDIERS...
"PRINCESS ..."

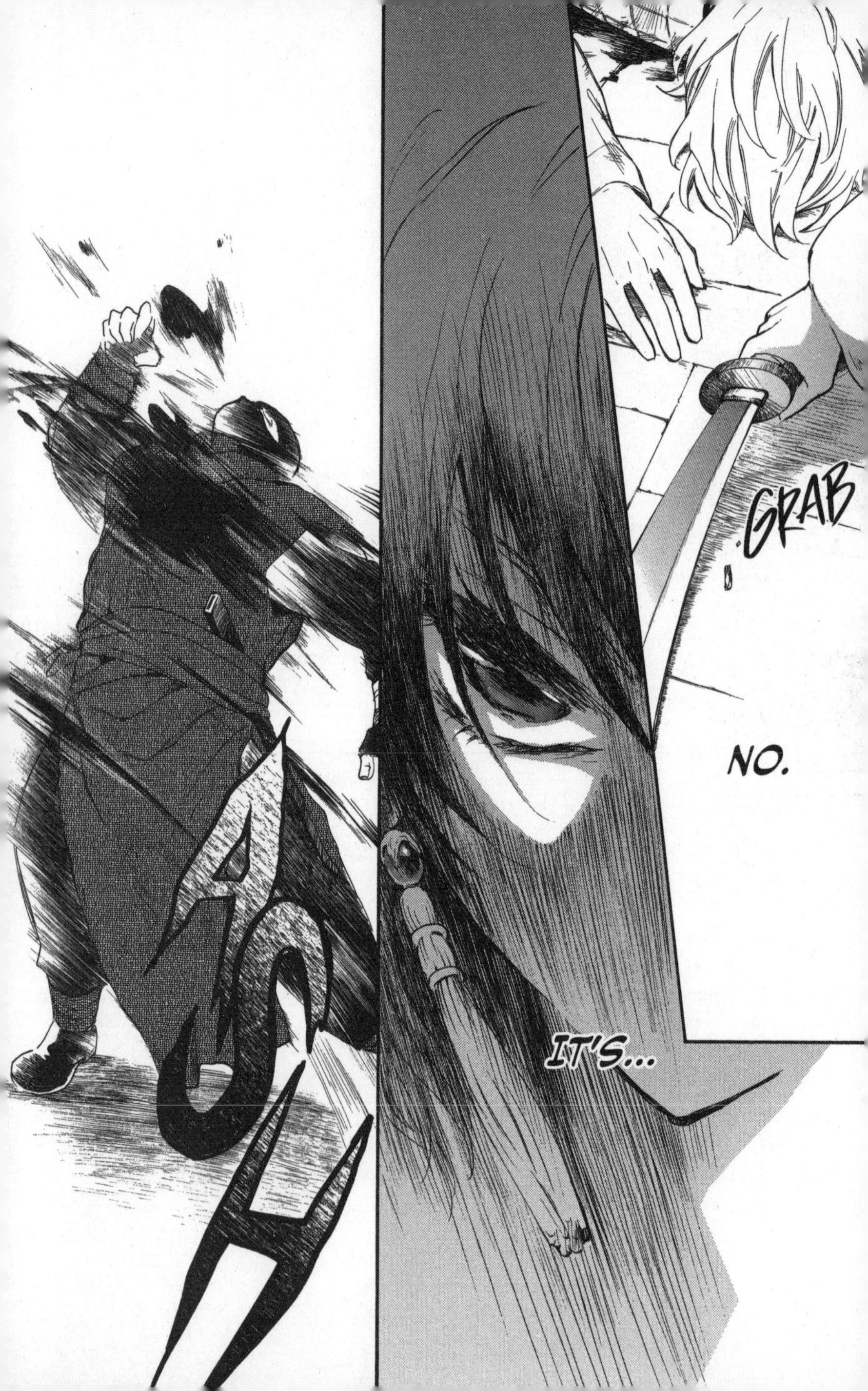
GRAB
NO.
IT'S...

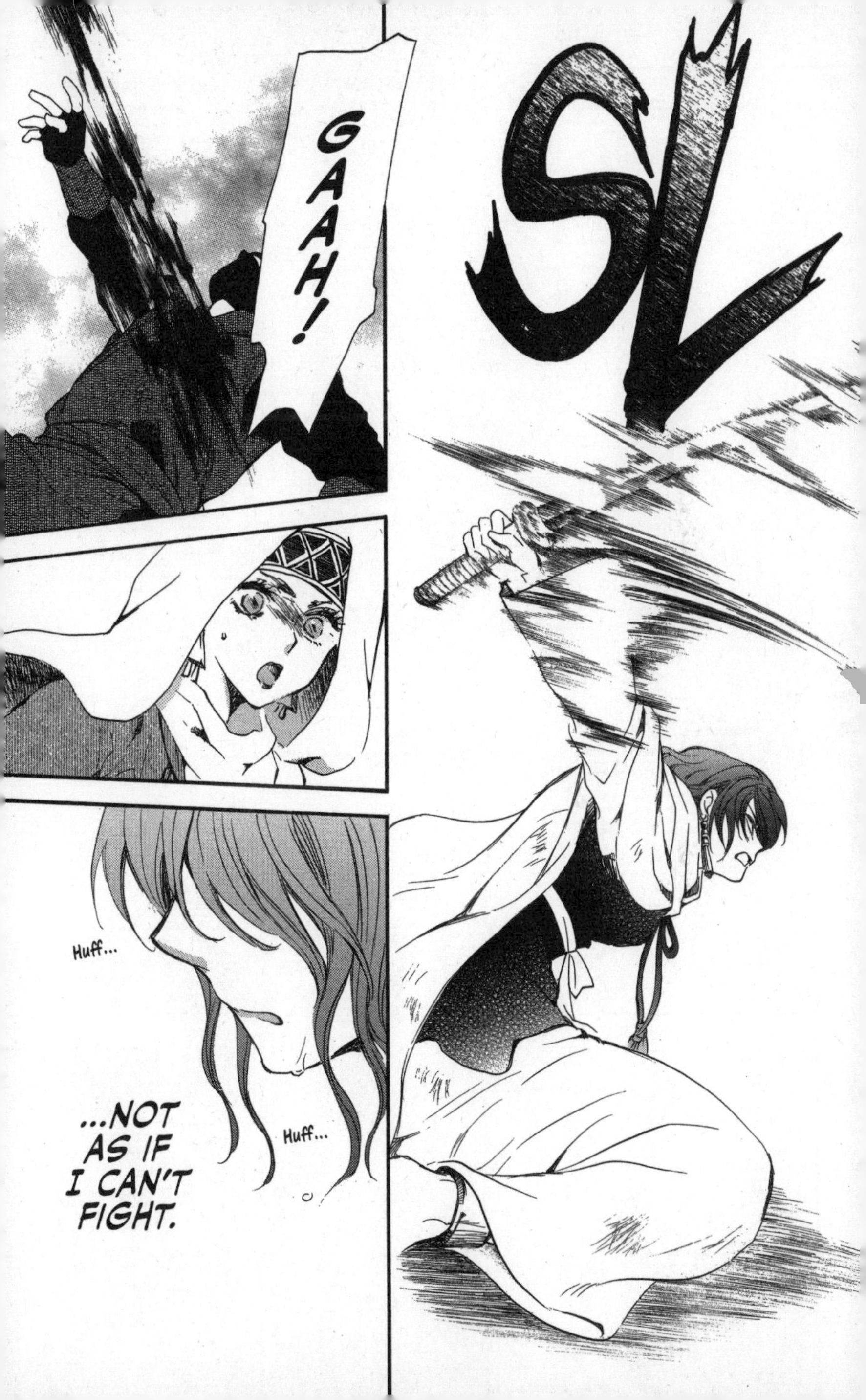
SL
GAAH!
Huff...
Huff...
...NOT AS IF I CAN'T FIGHT.

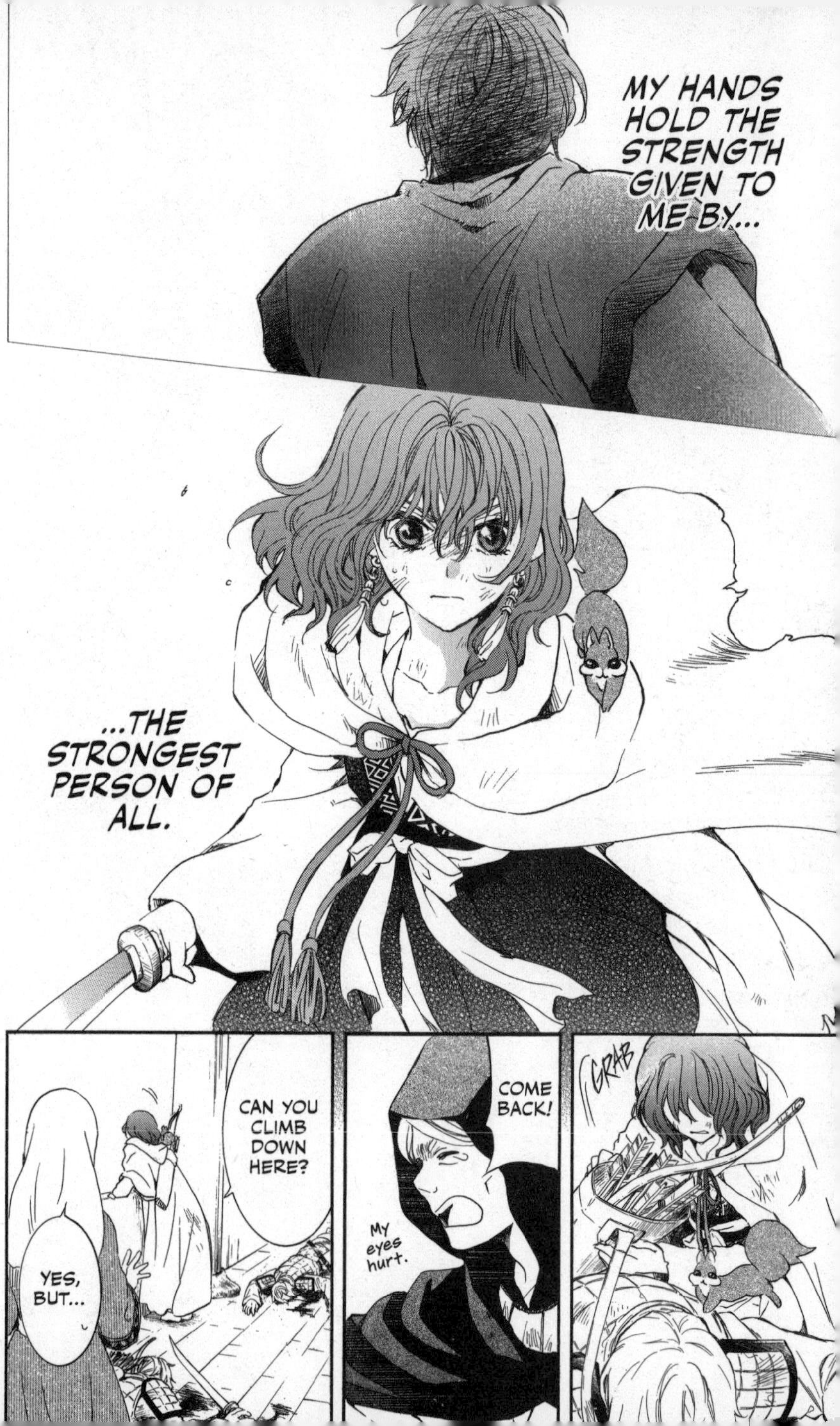
MY HANDS HOLD THE STRENGTH GIVEN TO ME BY...
...THE STRONGEST PERSON OF ALL.
GRAB
COME BACK!
My eyes hurt.
CAN YOU CLIMB DOWN HERE?
YES, BUT...

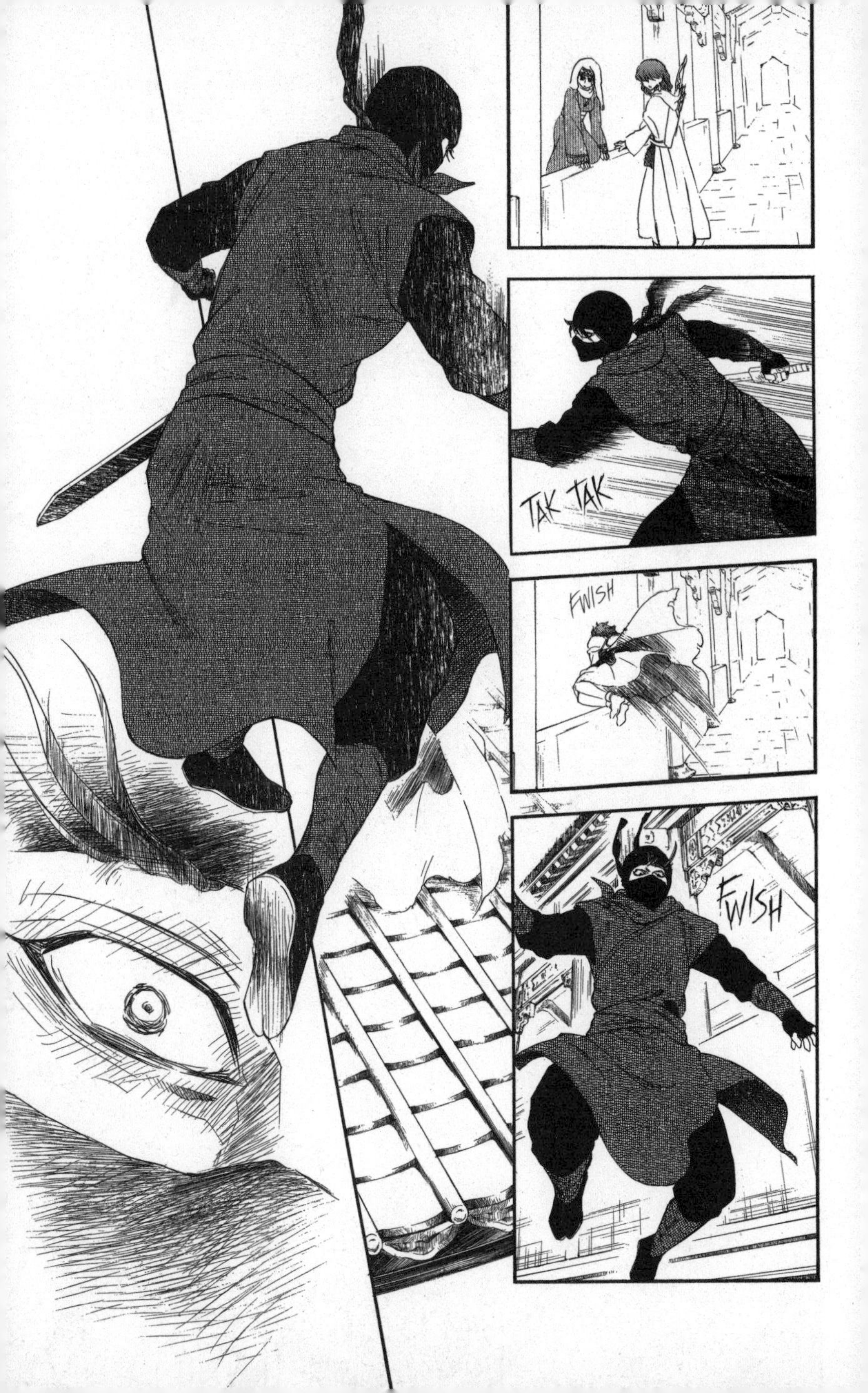
TAK TAK
FWISH
FWISH

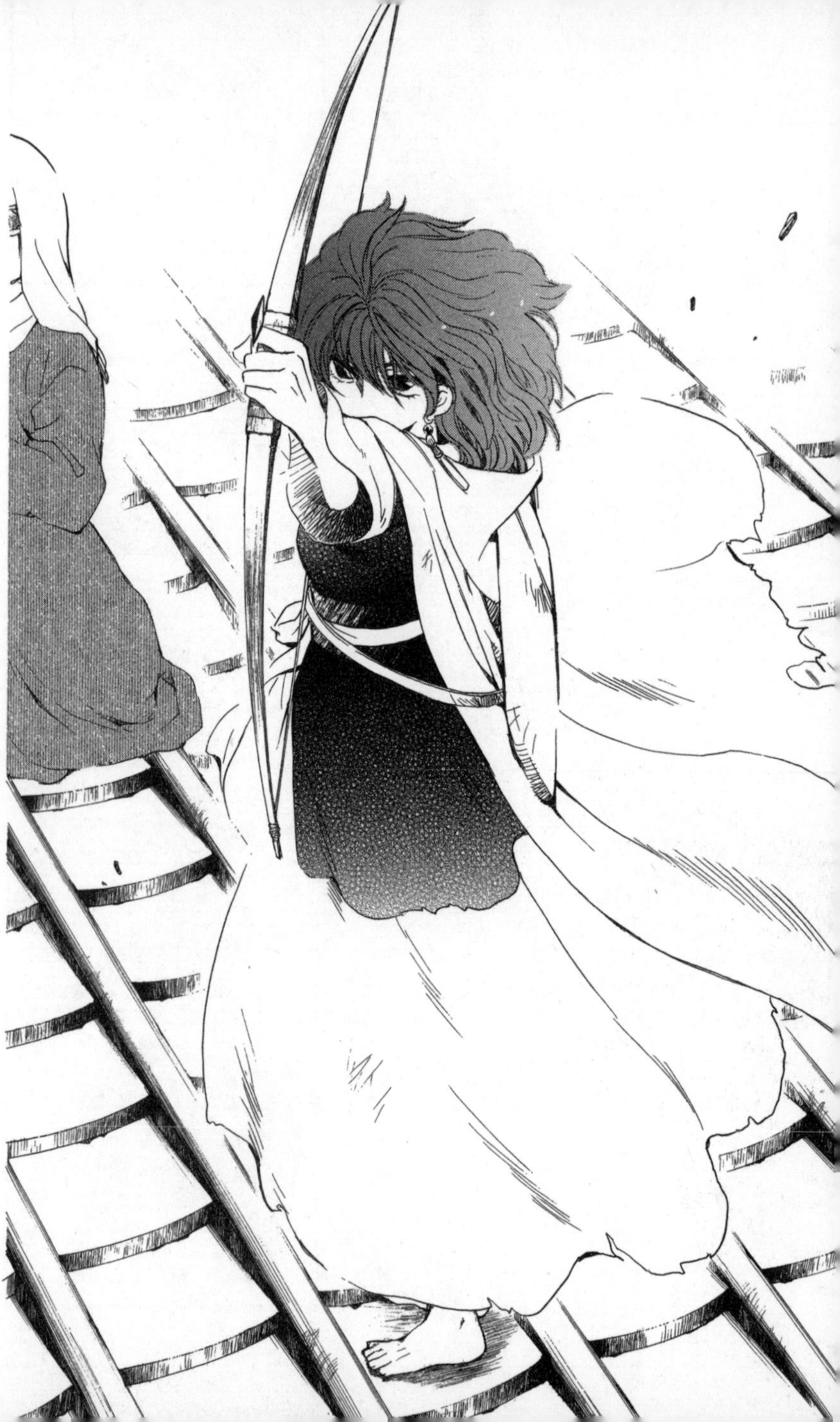

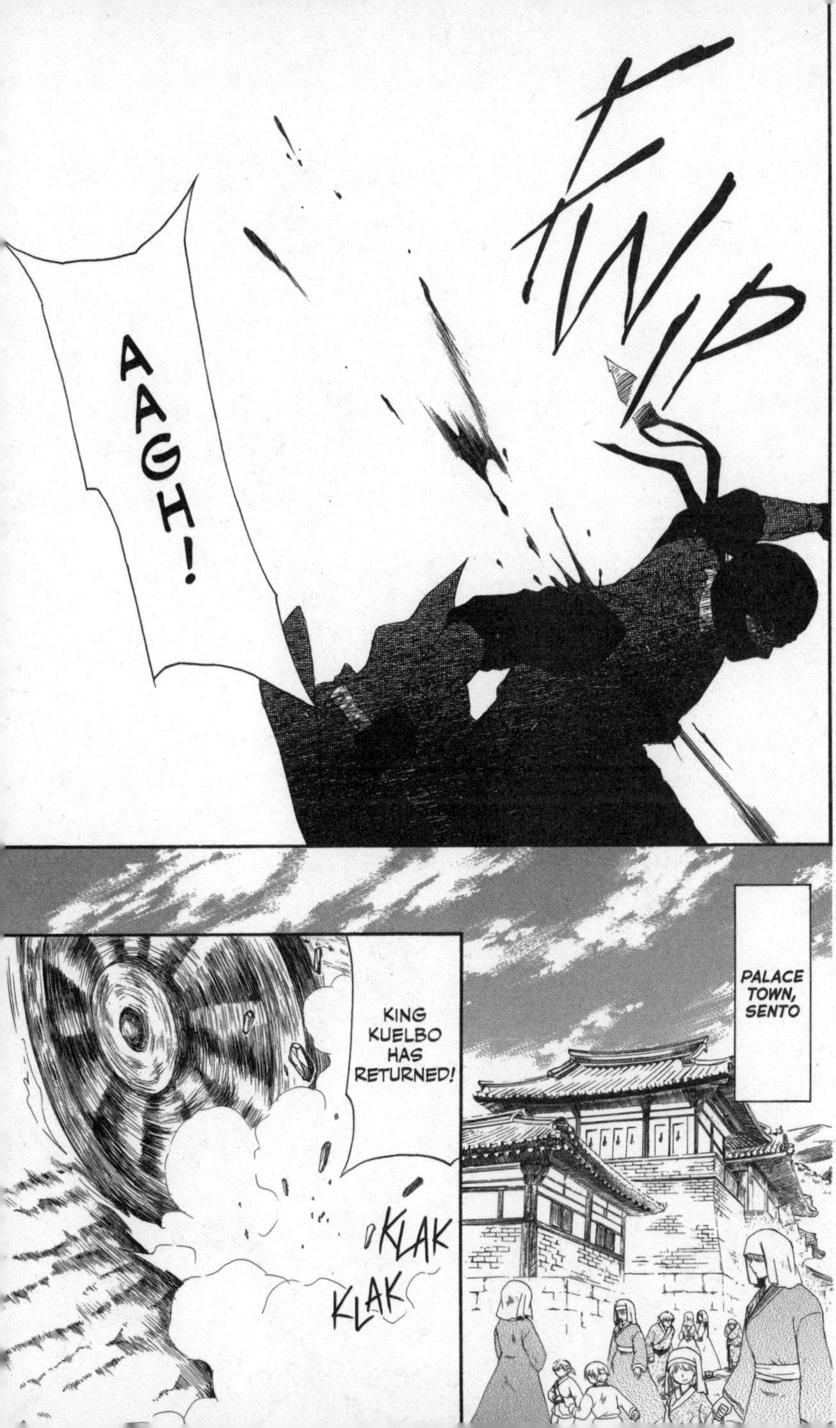
TWIP
AAGH!
PALACE TOWN, SENTO
KING KUELBO HAS RETURNED!
KLAK
KLAK

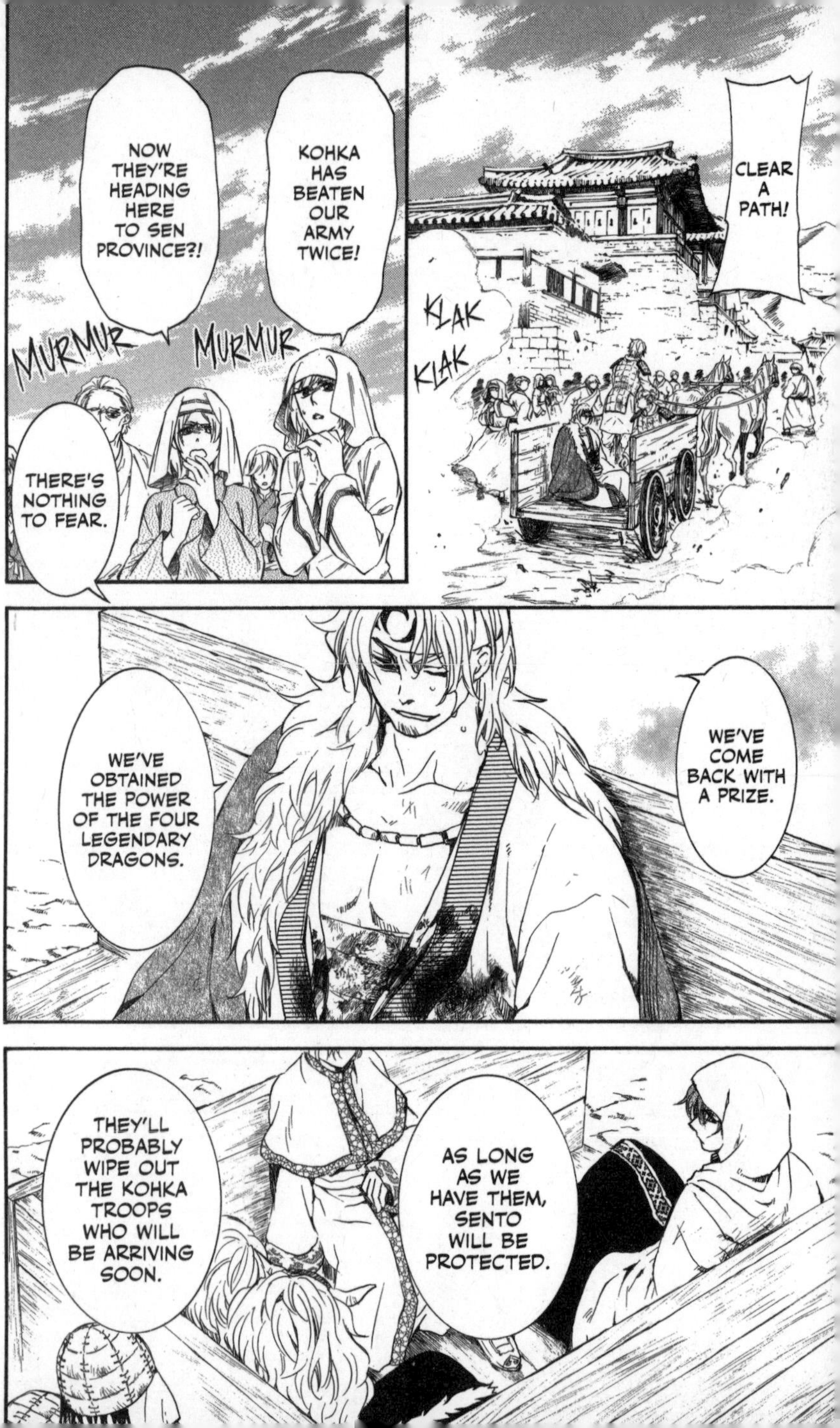
CLEAR A PATH!
KLAK
KLAK
KOHKA HAS BEATEN OUR ARMY TWICE!
NOW THEY'RE HEADING HERE TO SEN PROVINCE?!
MURMUR
MURMUR
THERE'S NOTHING TO FEAR.
WE'VE COME BACK WITH A PRIZE.
WE'VE OBTAINED THE POWER OF THE FOUR LEGENDARY DRAGONS.
AS LONG AS WE HAVE THEM, SENTO WILL BE PROTECTED.
THEY'LL PROBABLY WIPE OUT THE KOHKA TROOPS WHO WILL BE ARRIVING SOON.

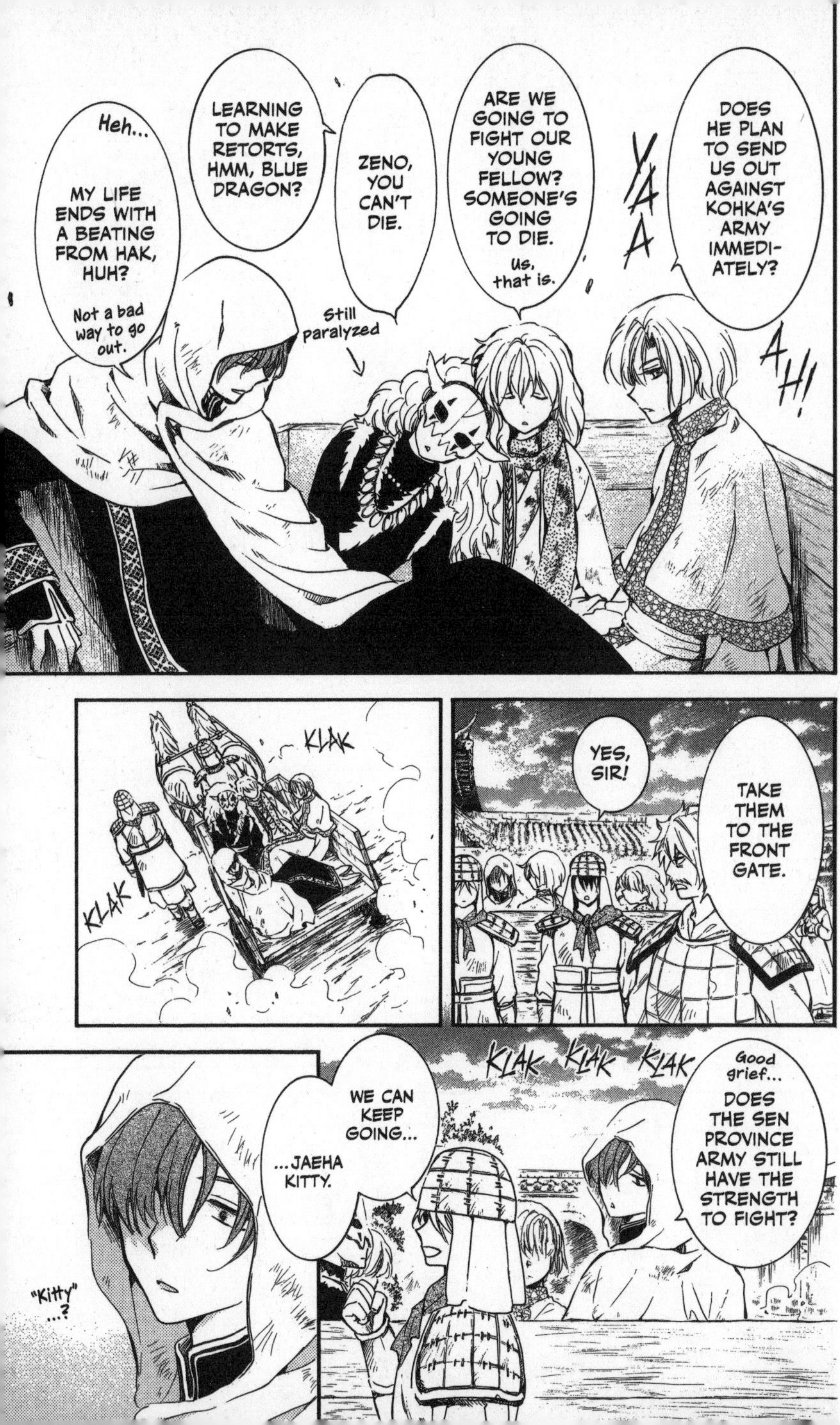
DOES HE PLAN TO SEND US OUT AGAINST KOHKA'S ARMY IMMEDIATELY?
AH!
YAA
ARE WE GOING TO FIGHT OUR YOUNG FELLOW? SOMEONE'S GOING TO DIE.
Us, that is.
ZENO, YOU CAN'T DIE.
Still paralyzed
LEARNING TO MAKE RETORTS, HMM, BLUE DRAGON?
Heh...
MY LIFE ENDS WITH A BEATING FROM HAK, HUH?
Not a bad way to go out.
TAKE THEM TO THE FRONT GATE.
YES, SIR!
KLAK
KLAK
KLAK KLAK KLAK
Good grief...
DOES THE SEN PROVINCE ARMY STILL HAVE THE STRENGTH TO FIGHT?
WE CAN KEEP GOING...
...JAEHA KITTY.
"Kitty" ...?

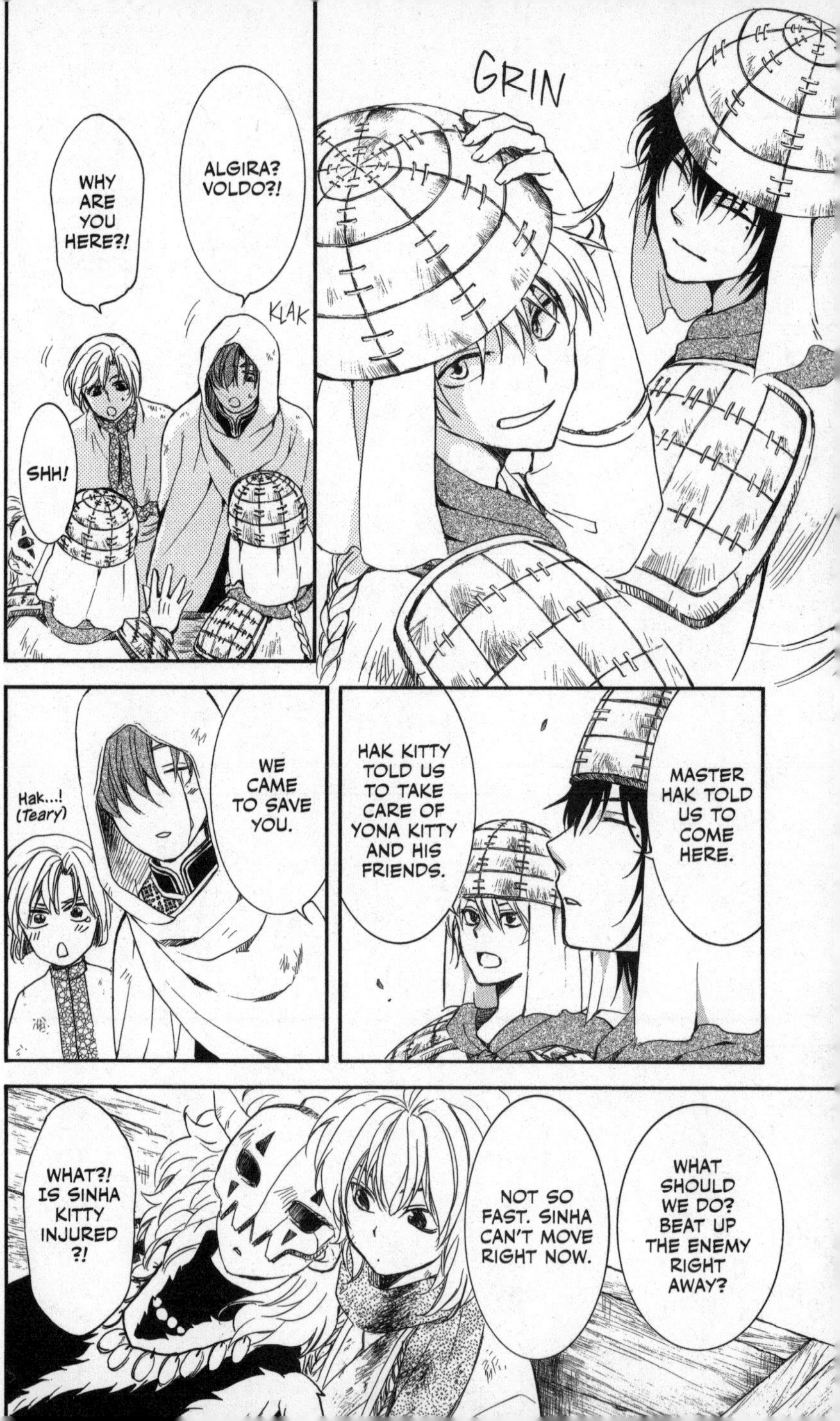

GRIN
ALGIRA? VOLDO?!
WHY ARE YOU HERE?!
KLAK
SHH!
MASTER HAK TOLD US TO COME HERE.
HAK KITTY TOLD US TO TAKE CARE OF YONA KITTY AND HIS FRIENDS.
WE CAME TO SAVE YOU.
Hak...! (Teary)
WHAT SHOULD WE DO? BEAT UP THE ENEMY RIGHT AWAY?
NOT SO FAST. SINHA CAN'T MOVE RIGHT NOW.
WHAT?! IS SINHA KITTY INJURED?!

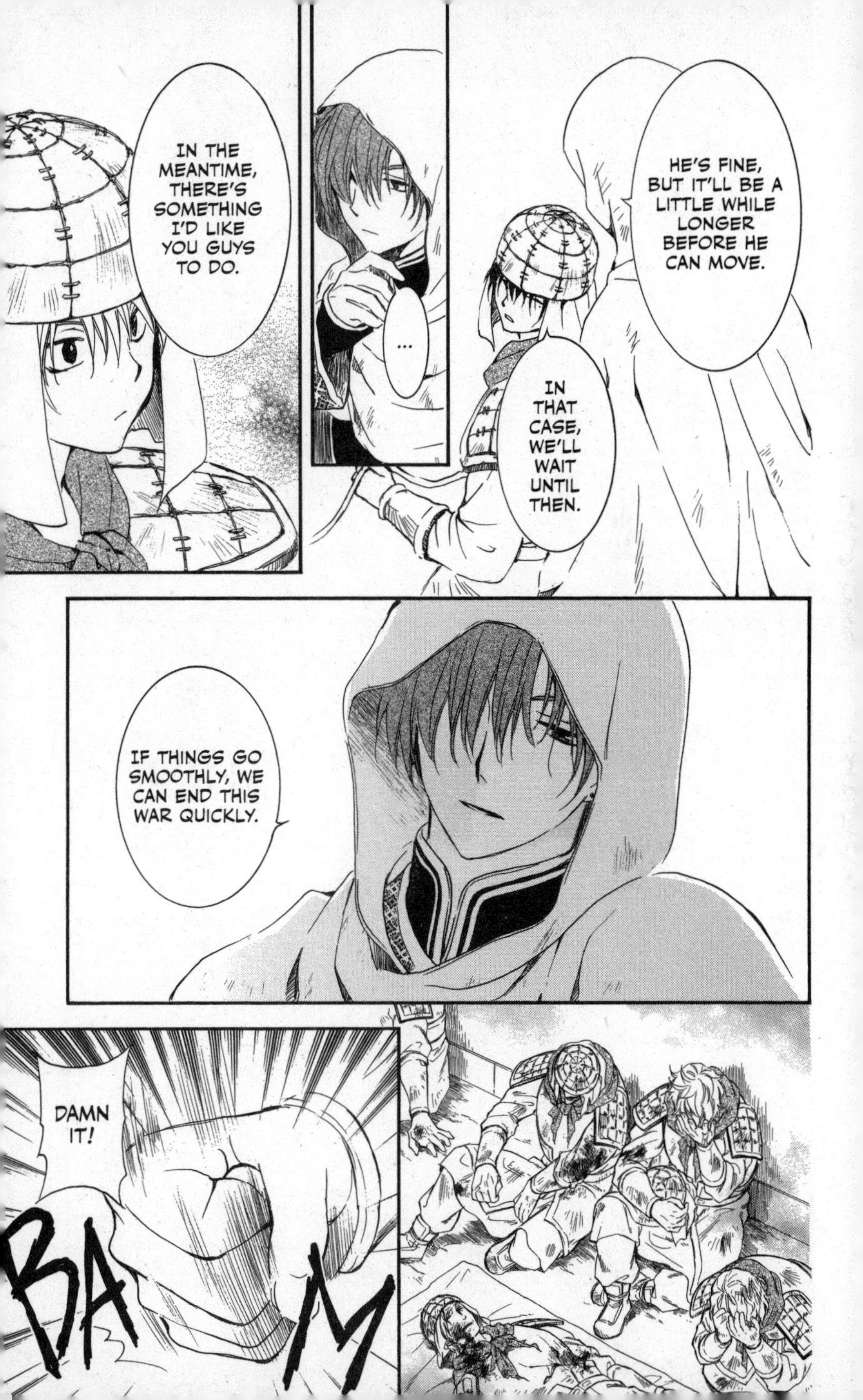
HE'S FINE, BUT IT'LL BE A LITTLE WHILE LONGER BEFORE HE CAN MOVE.
IN THAT CASE, WE'LL WAIT UNTIL THEN.
...
IN THE MEANTIME, THERE'S SOMETHING I'D LIKE YOU GUYS TO DO.
IF THINGS GO SMOOTHLY, WE CAN END THIS WAR QUICKLY.
DAMN IT!
BAM

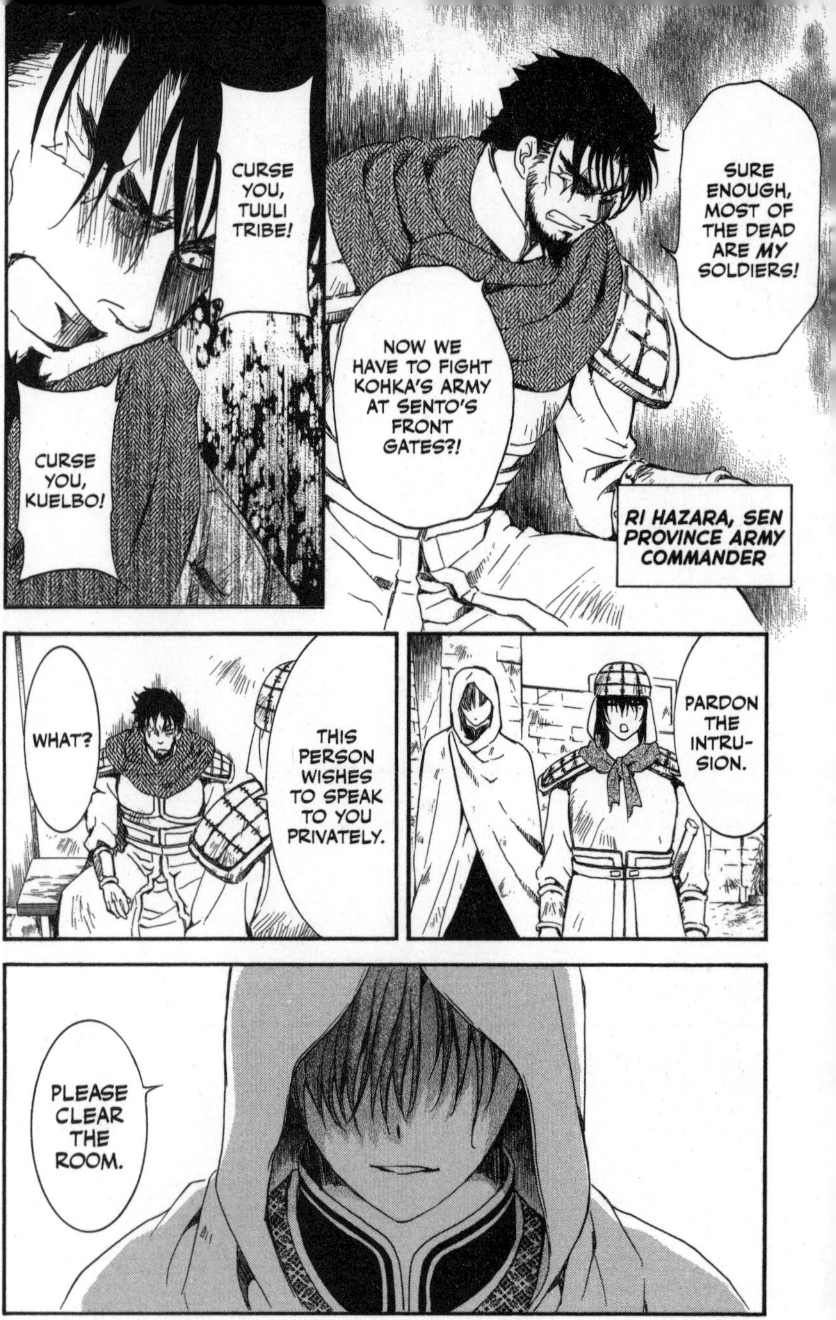
SURE ENOUGH, MOST OF THE DEAD ARE *MY* SOLDIERS!
NOW WE HAVE TO FIGHT KOHKA'S ARMY AT SENTO'S FRONT GATES?!
RI HAZARA, SEN PROVINCE ARMY COMMANDER
CURSE YOU, TUULI TRIBE!
CURSE YOU, KUELBO!
PARDON THE INTRU-SION.
THIS PERSON WISHES TO SPEAK TO YOU PRIVATELY.
WHAT?
PLEASE CLEAR THE ROOM.

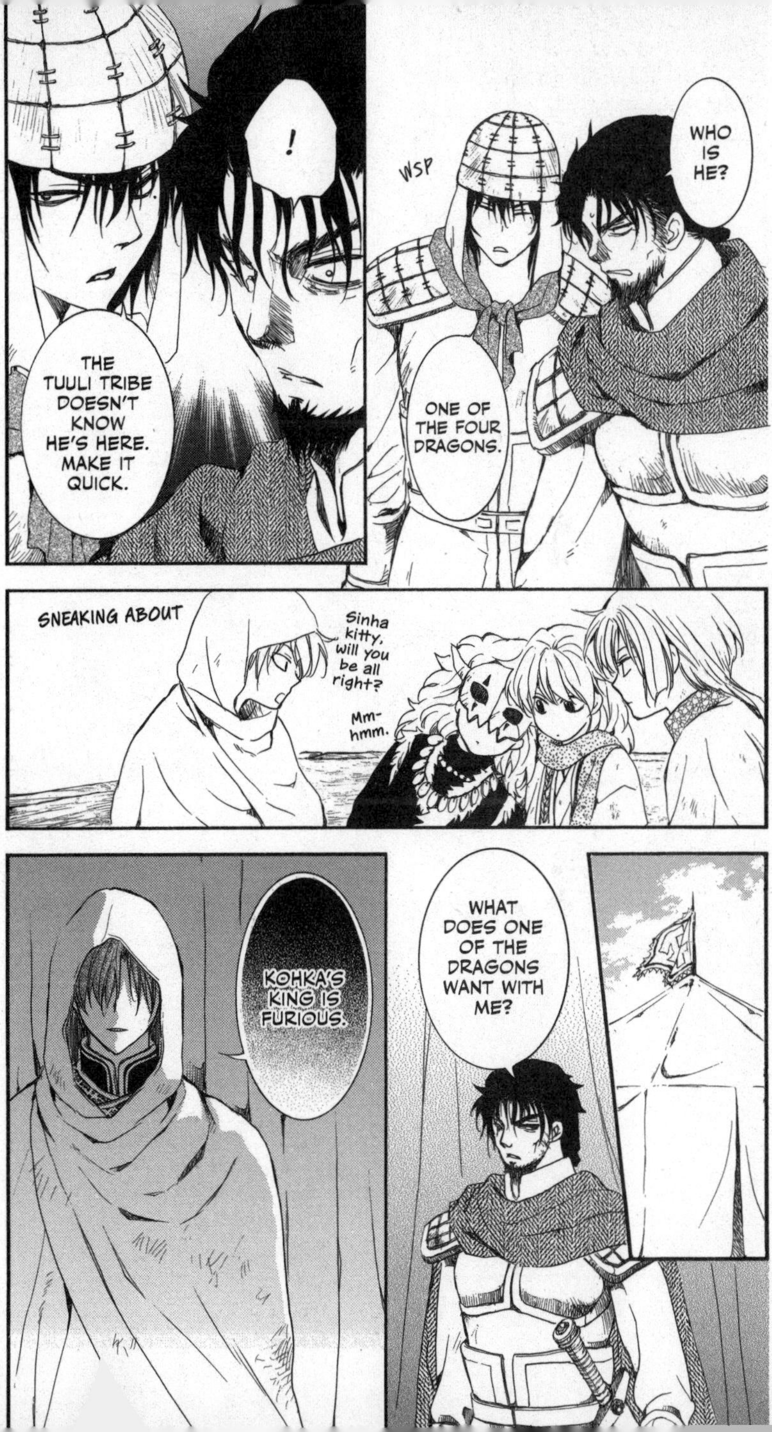
WHO IS HE?
WSP
ONE OF THE FOUR DRAGONS.
!
THE TUULI TRIBE DOESN'T KNOW HE'S HERE. MAKE IT QUICK.
SNEAKING ABOUT
Sinha kitty, will you be all right?
Mm-hmm.
WHAT DOES ONE OF THE DRAGONS WANT WITH ME?
KOHKA'S KING IS FURIOUS.

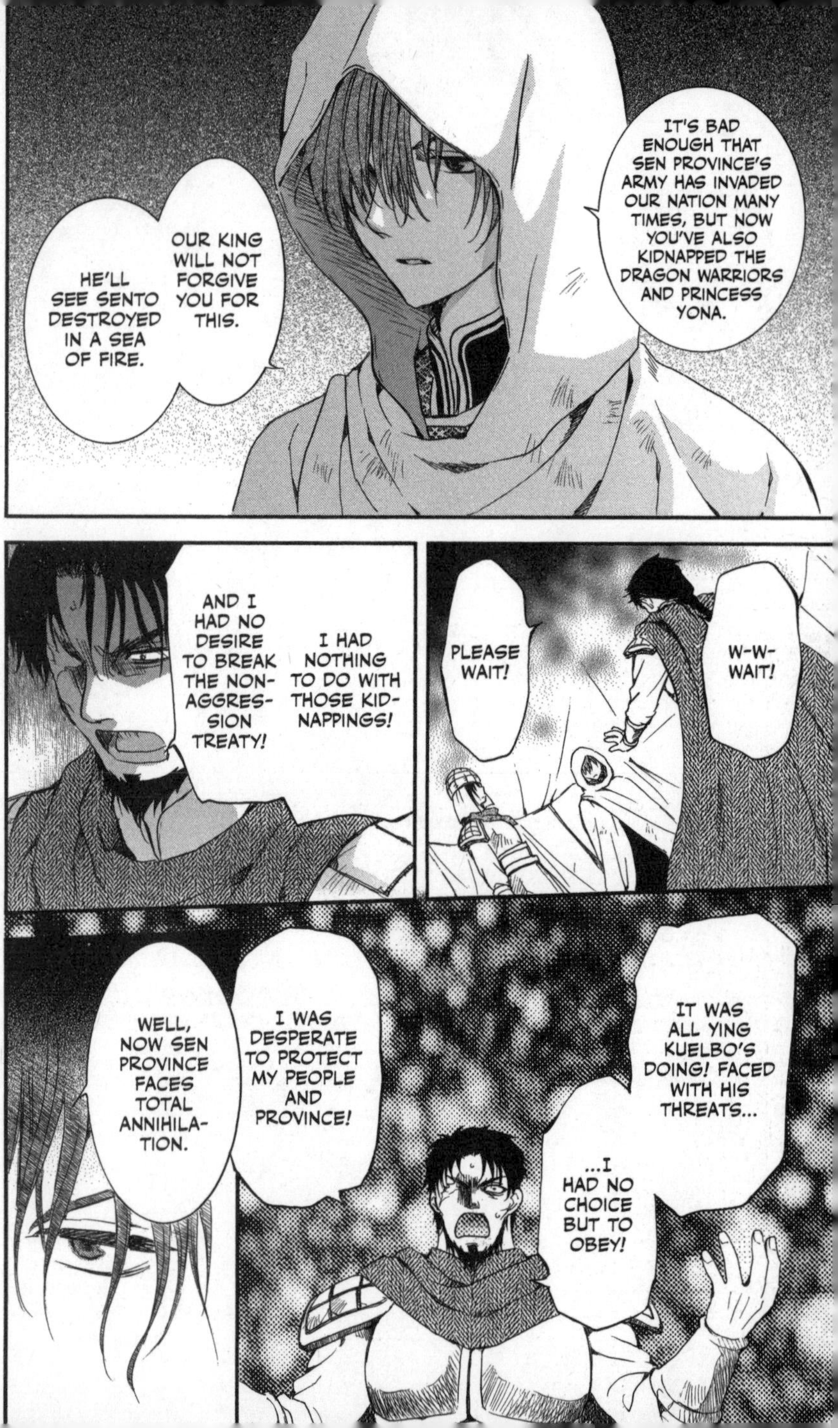
IT'S BAD ENOUGH THAT SEN PROVINCE'S ARMY HAS INVADED OUR NATION MANY TIMES, BUT NOW YOU'VE ALSO KIDNAPPED THE DRAGON WARRIORS AND PRINCESS YONA.
OUR KING WILL NOT FORGIVE YOU FOR THIS.
HE'LL SEE SENTO DESTROYED IN A SEA OF FIRE.
W-W-WAIT!
PLEASE WAIT!
I HAD NOTHING TO DO WITH THOSE KID-NAPPINGS!
AND I HAD NO DESIRE TO BREAK THE NON-AGGRES-SION TREATY!
IT WAS ALL YING KUELBO'S DOING! FACED WITH HIS THREATS...
...I HAD NO CHOICE BUT TO OBEY!
I WAS DESPERATE TO PROTECT MY PEOPLE AND PROVINCE!
WELL, NOW SEN PROVINCE FACES TOTAL ANNIHILA-TION.

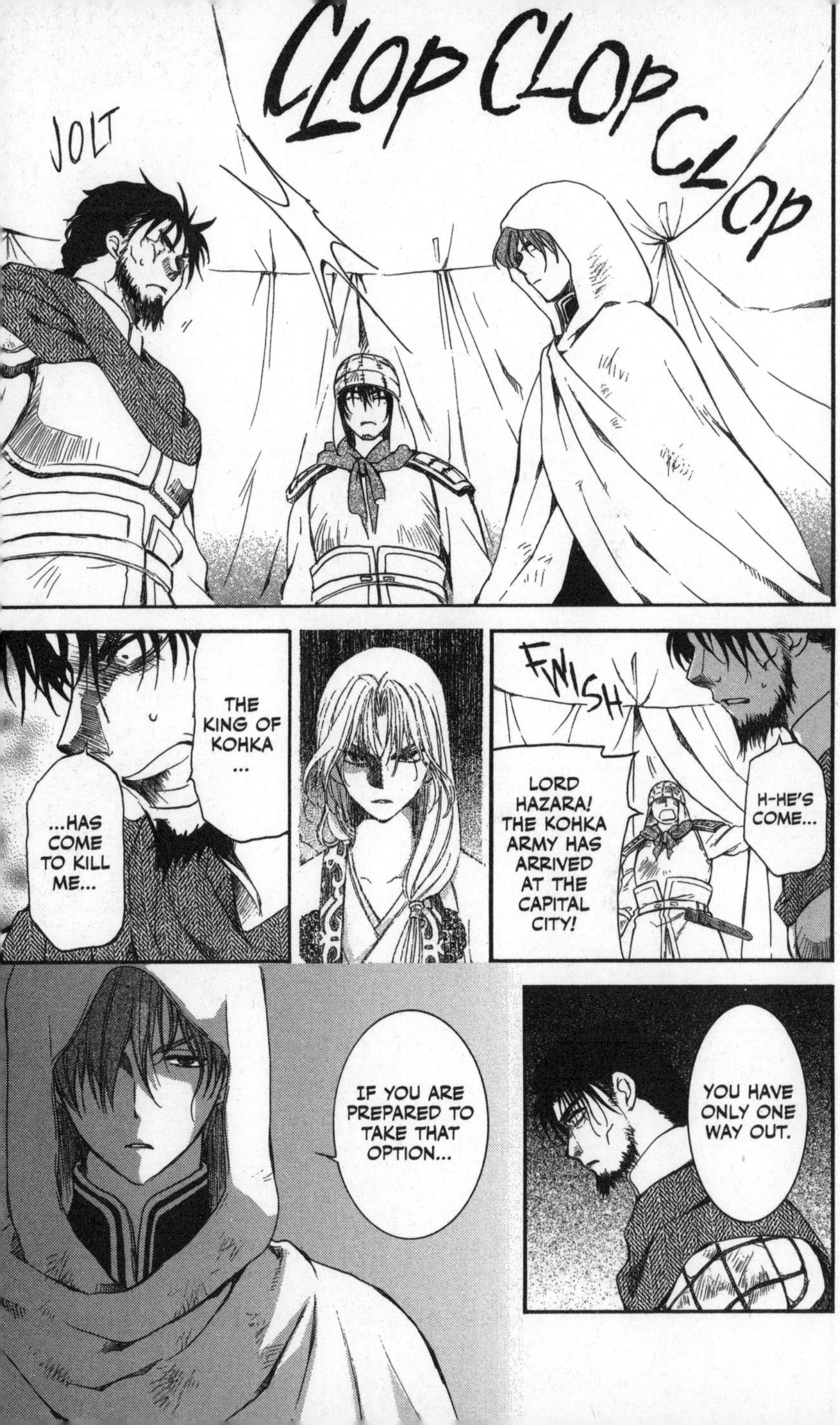
CLOP CLOP CLOP CLOP
JOLT
FWISH
LORD HAZARA! THE KOHKA ARMY HAS ARRIVED AT THE CAPITAL CITY!
H-HE'S COME...
THE KING OF KOHKA ...
...HAS COME TO KILL ME...
YOU HAVE ONLY ONE WAY OUT.
IF YOU ARE PREPARED TO TAKE THAT OPTION...

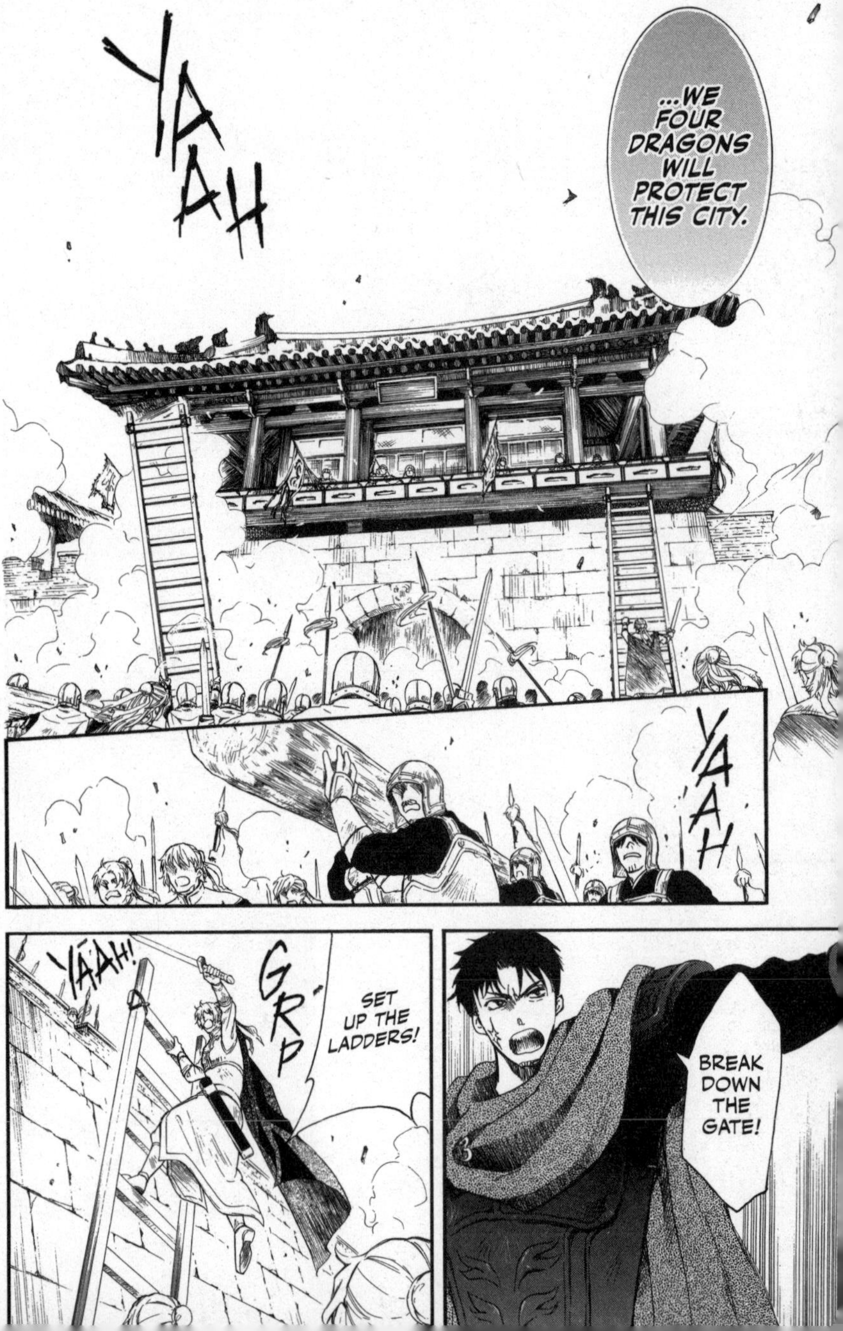
...WE FOUR DRAGONS WILL PROTECT THIS CITY.
YAAH
YAAH
BREAK DOWN THE GATE!
SET UP THE LADDERS!
GRP
YAAH!

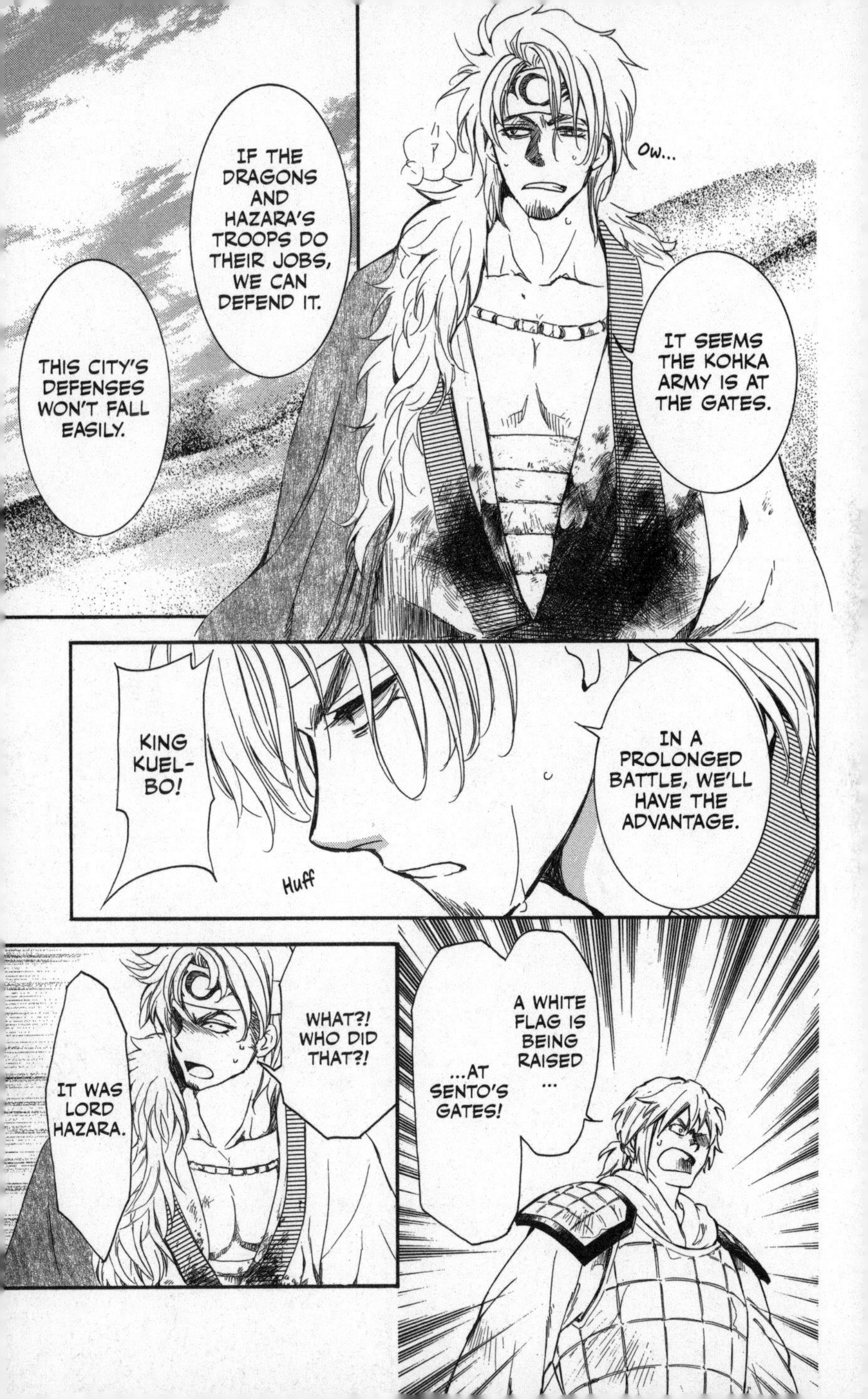
OW...
IT SEEMS THE KOHKA ARMY IS AT THE GATES.
IF THE DRAGONS AND HAZARA'S TROOPS DO THEIR JOBS, WE CAN DEFEND IT.
THIS CITY'S DEFENSES WON'T FALL EASILY.
IN A PROLONGED BATTLE, WE'LL HAVE THE ADVANTAGE.
Huff
KING KUEL-BO!
A WHITE FLAG IS BEING RAISED ...
...AT SENTO'S GATES!
WHAT?! WHO DID THAT?!
IT WAS LORD HAZARA.

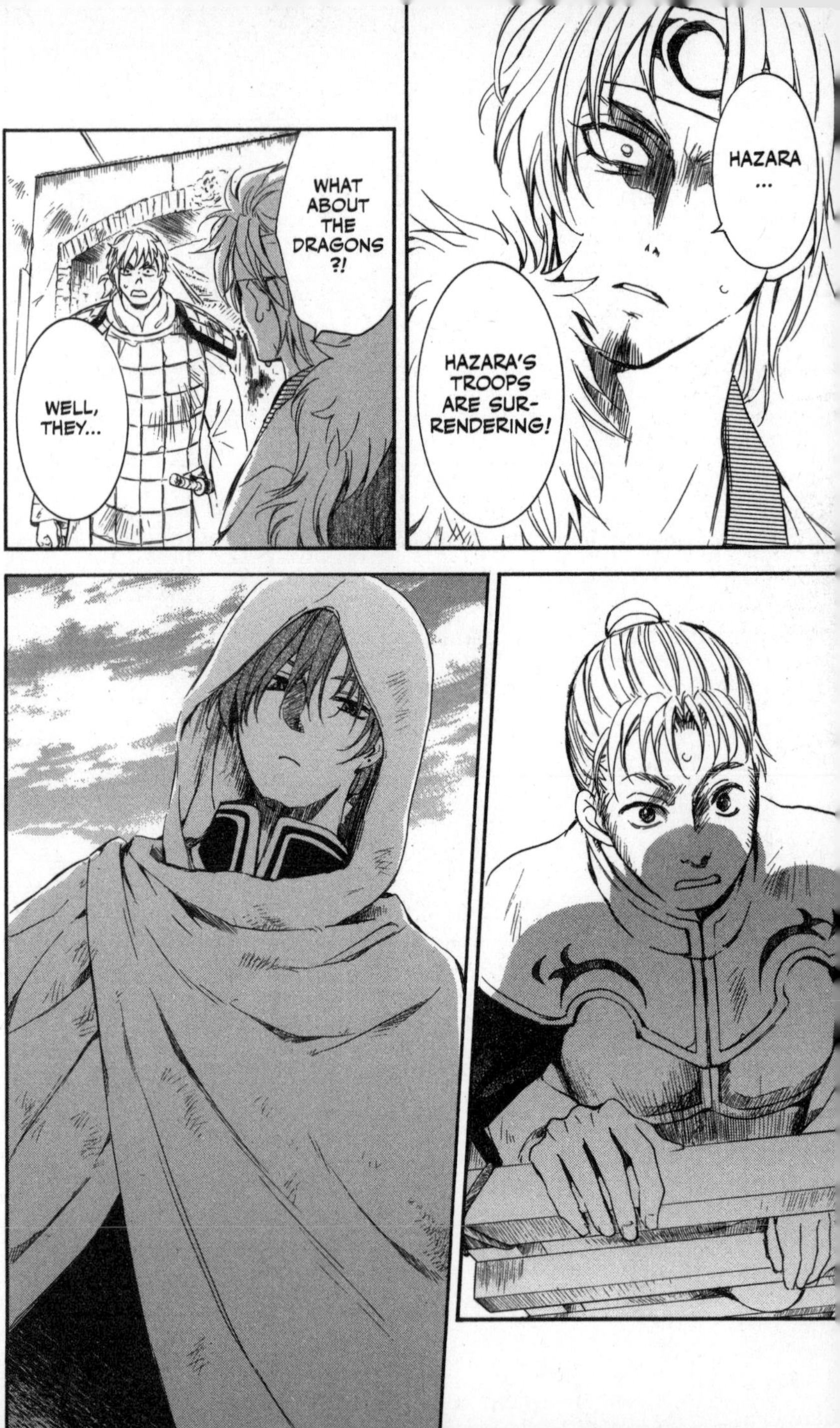
HAZARA ...
HAZARA'S TROOPS ARE SUR- RENDERING!
WHAT ABOUT THE DRAGONS ?!
WELL, THEY...

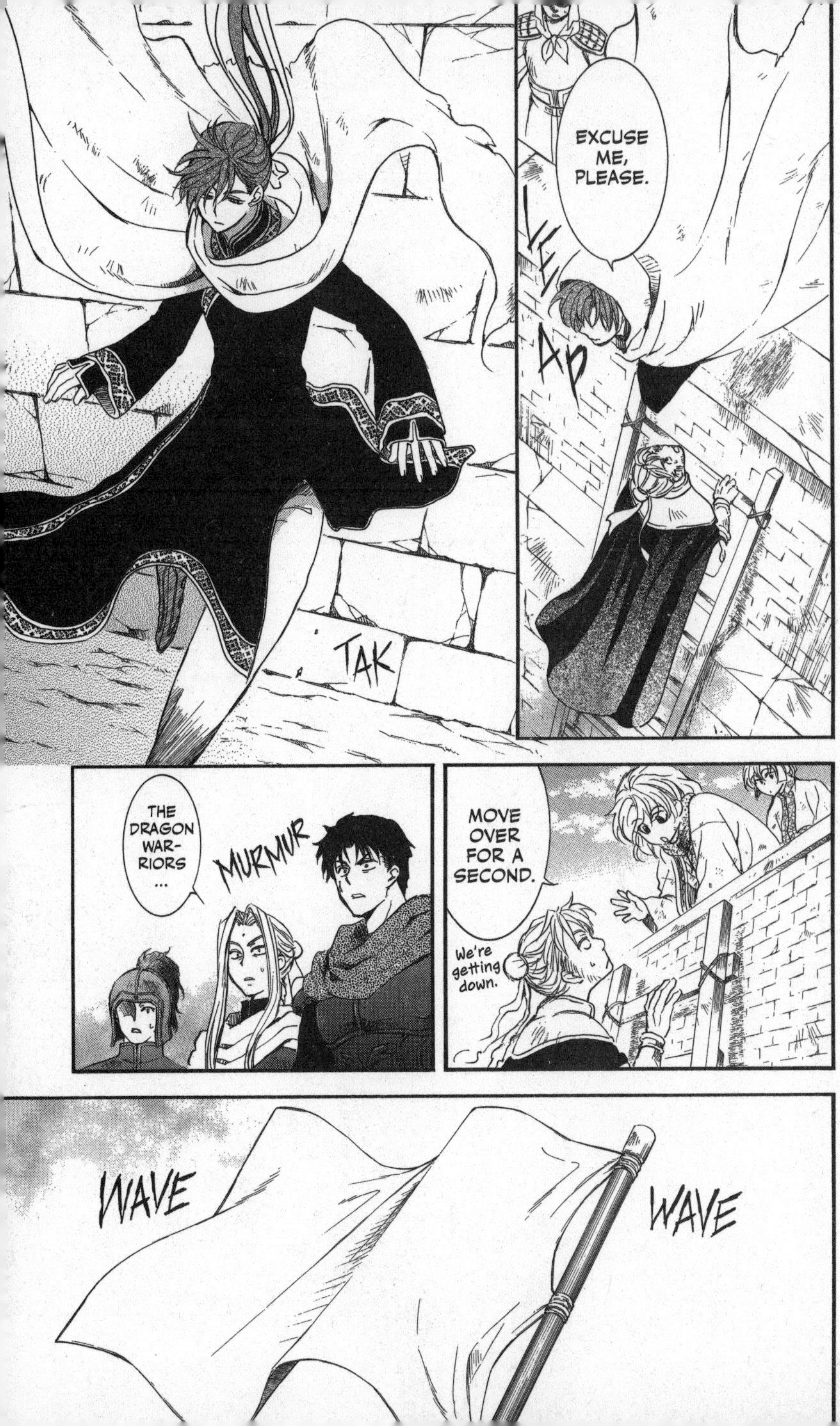
EXCUSE ME, PLEASE.
LEAP
TAK
MOVE OVER FOR A SECOND.
We're getting down.
THE DRAGON WAR-RIORS ...
MURMUR
WAVE
WAVE

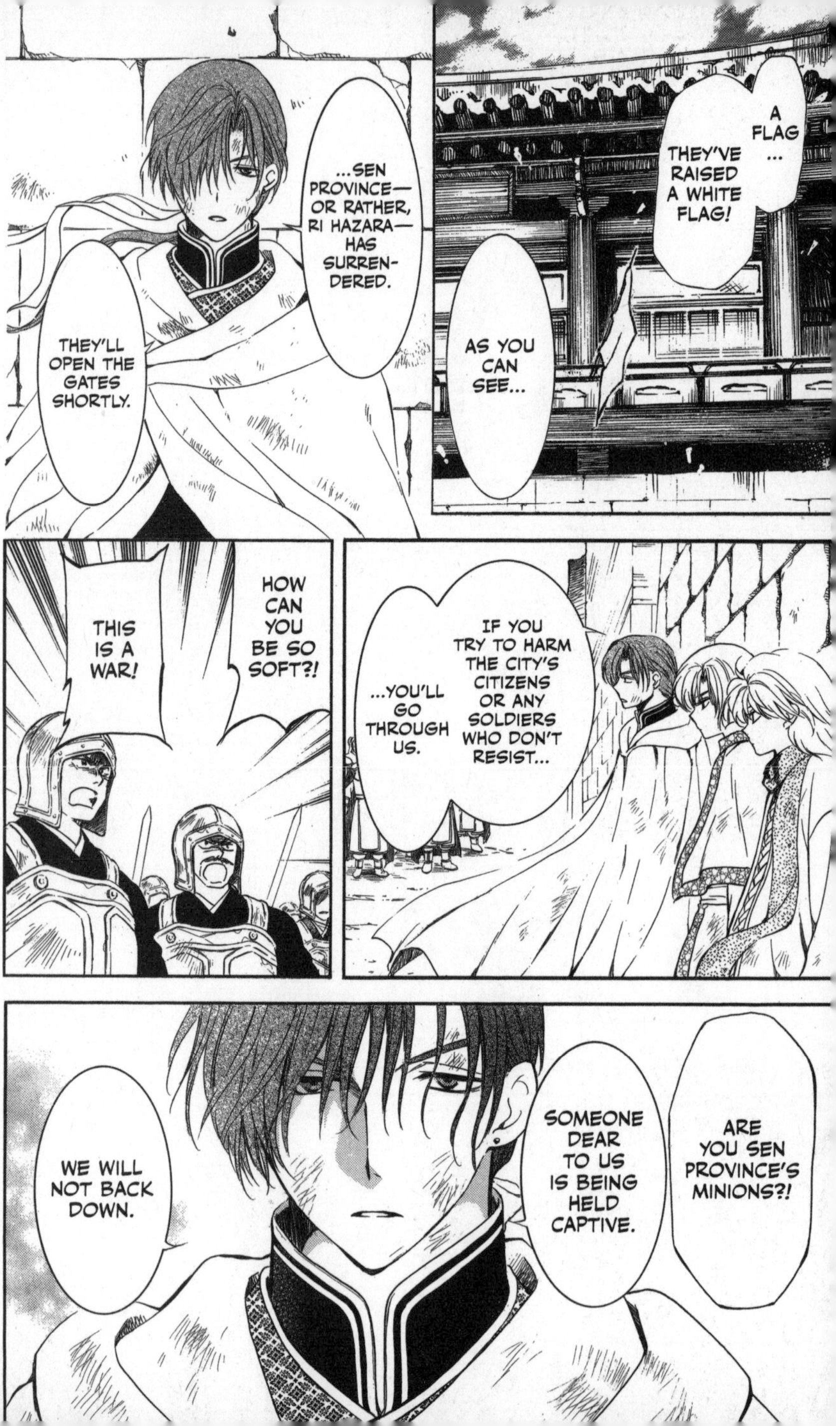
A FLAG...
THEY'VE RAISED A WHITE FLAG!
AS YOU CAN SEE...
...SEN PROVINCE—OR RATHER, RI HAZARA—HAS SURREN-DERED.
THEY'LL OPEN THE GATES SHORTLY.
IF YOU TRY TO HARM THE CITY'S CITIZENS OR ANY SOLDIERS WHO DON'T RESIST...
...YOU'LL GO THROUGH US.
HOW CAN YOU BE SO SOFT?!
THIS IS A WAR!
ARE YOU SEN PROVINCE'S MINIONS?!
SOMEONE DEAR TO US IS BEING HELD CAPTIVE.
WE WILL NOT BACK DOWN.

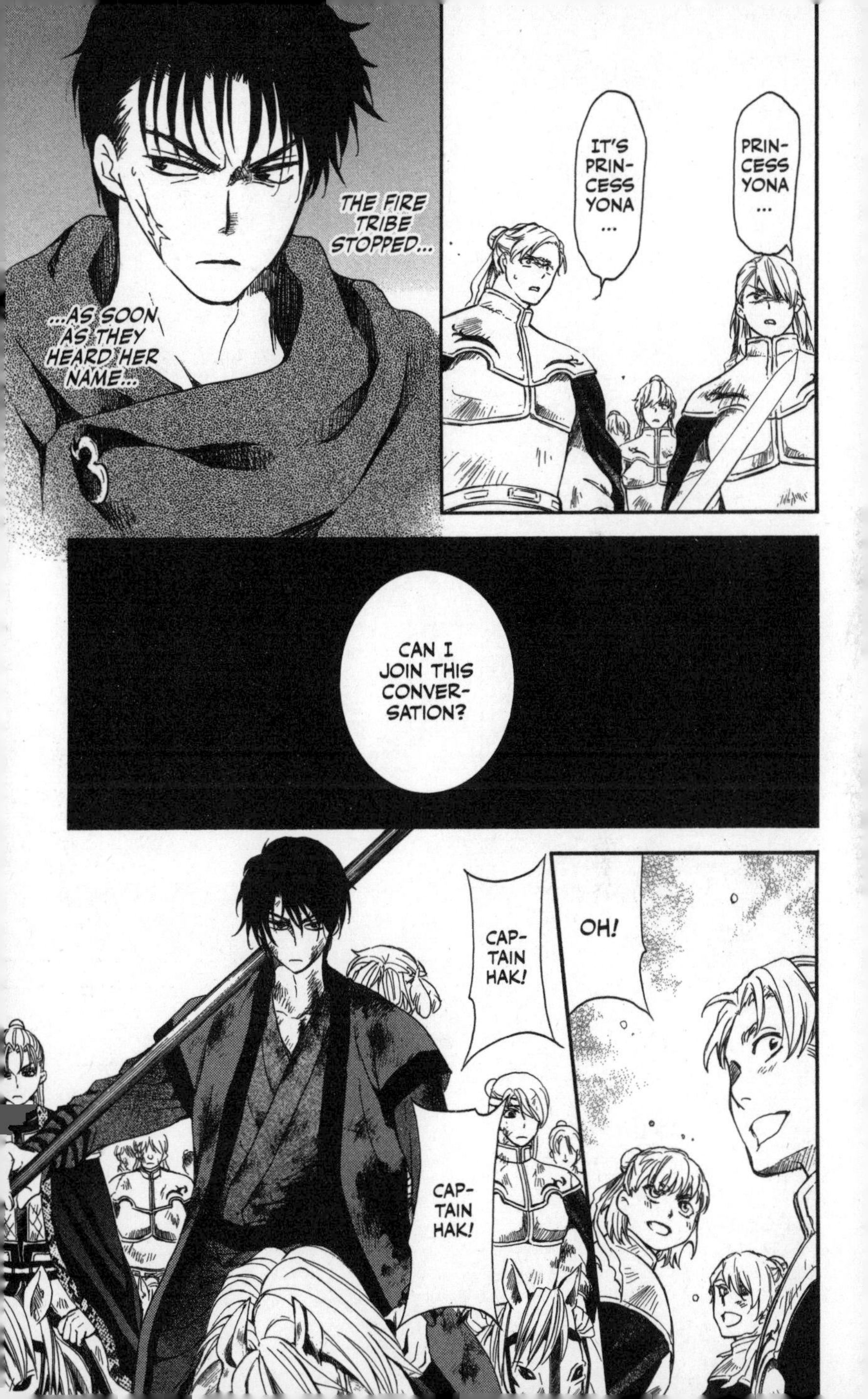
PRINCESS YONA...
IT'S PRINCESS YONA...
THE FIRE TRIBE STOPPED...
...AS SOON AS THEY HEARD HER NAME...
CAN I JOIN THIS CONVERSATION?
OH!
CAPTAIN HAK!
CAPTAIN HAK!

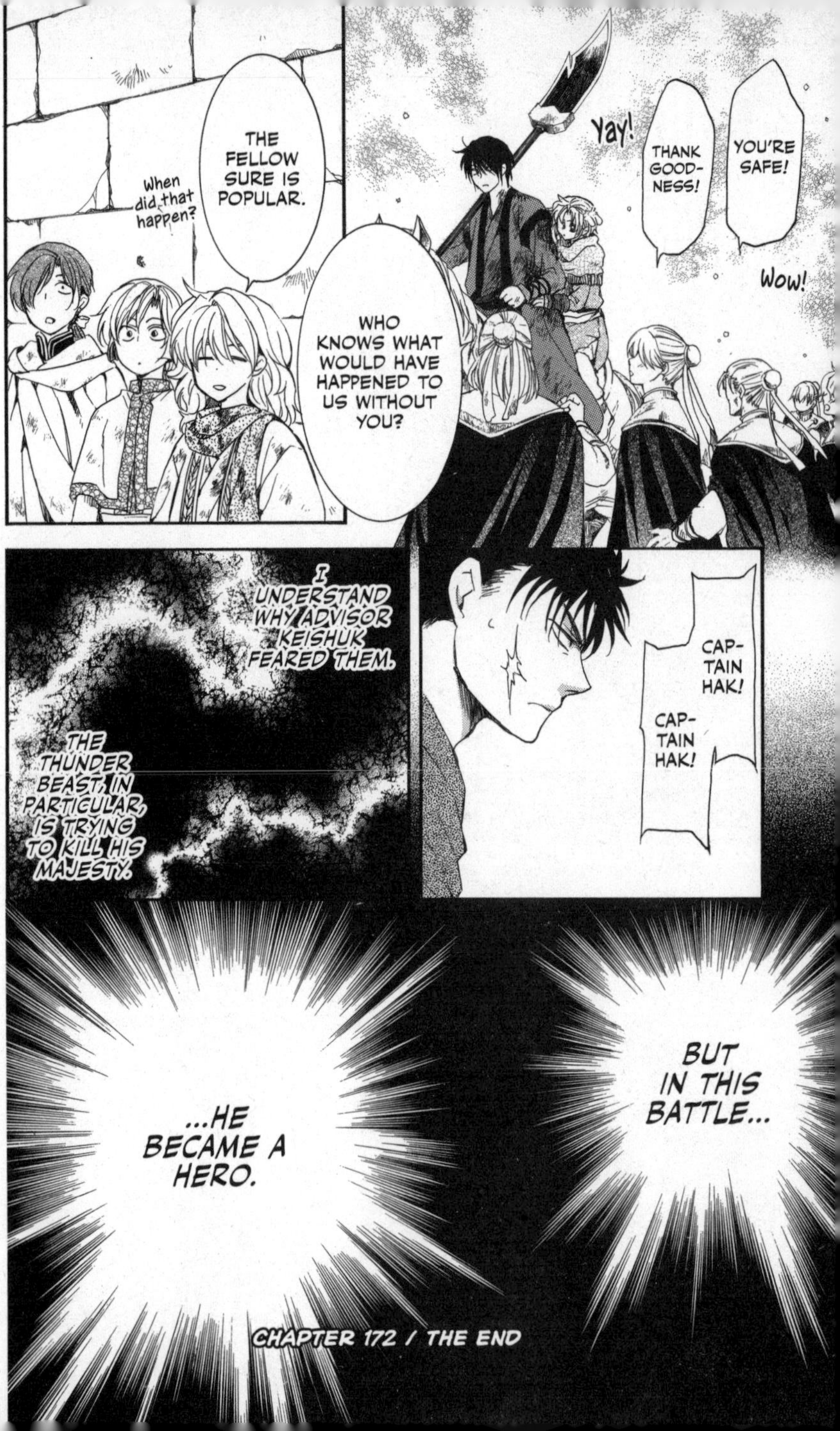
YOU'RE SAFE!
THANK GOODNESS!
Yay!
Wow!
THE FELLOW SURE IS POPULAR.
When did that happen?
WHO KNOWS WHAT WOULD HAVE HAPPENED TO US WITHOUT YOU?
CAPTAIN HAK!
CAPTAIN HAK!
I UNDERSTAND WHY ADVISOR KEISHUK FEARED THEM.
THE THUNDER BEAST, IN PARTICULAR, IS TRYING TO KILL HIS MAJESTY.
BUT IN THIS BATTLE...
...HE BECAME A HERO.
CHAPTER 172 / THE END

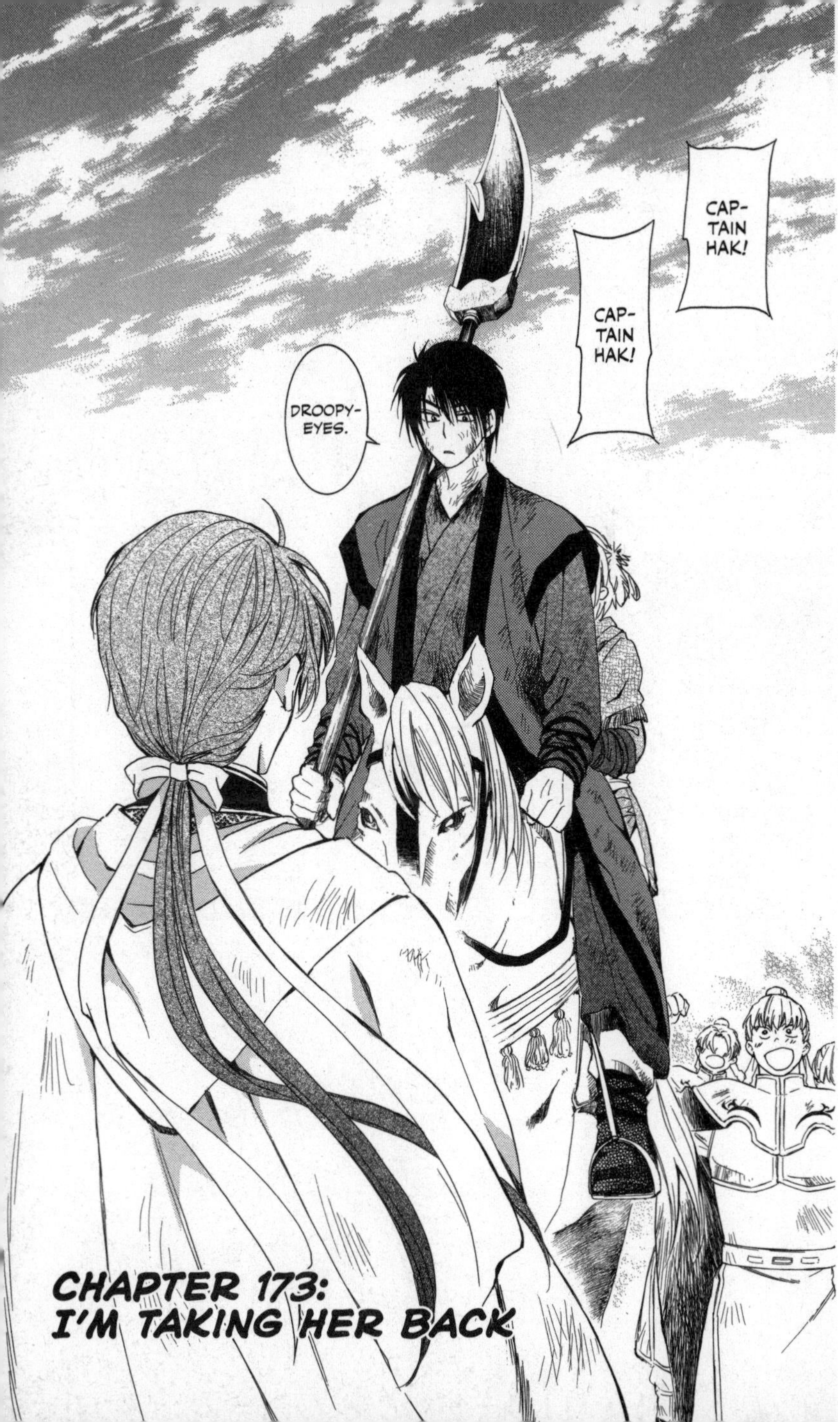
CAP-TAIN HAK!
CAP-TAIN HAK!
DROOPY-EYES.
CHAPTER 173: I'M TAKING HER BACK

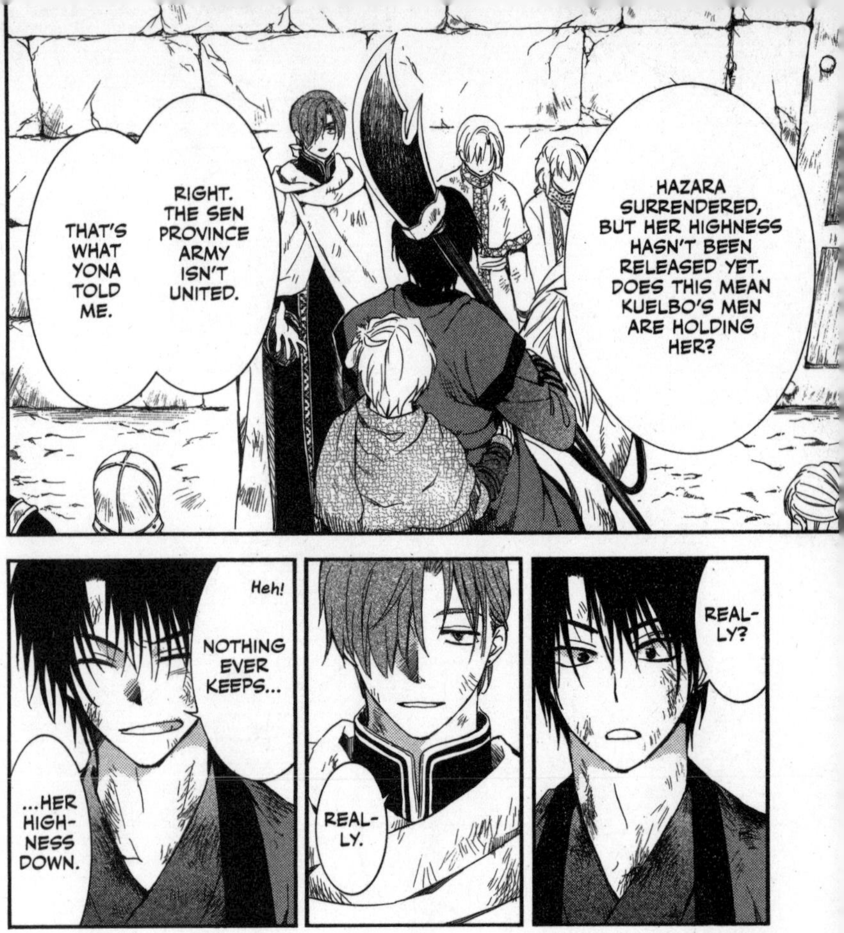
HAZARA SURRENDERED, BUT HER HIGHNESS HASN'T BEEN RELEASED YET. DOES THIS MEAN KUELBO'S MEN ARE HOLDING HER?
RIGHT. THE SEN PROVINCE ARMY ISN'T UNITED.
THAT'S WHAT YONA TOLD ME.
REAL-LY?
REAL-LY.
Heh!
NOTHING EVER KEEPS...
...HER HIGH-NESS DOWN.

Yona of the Dawn

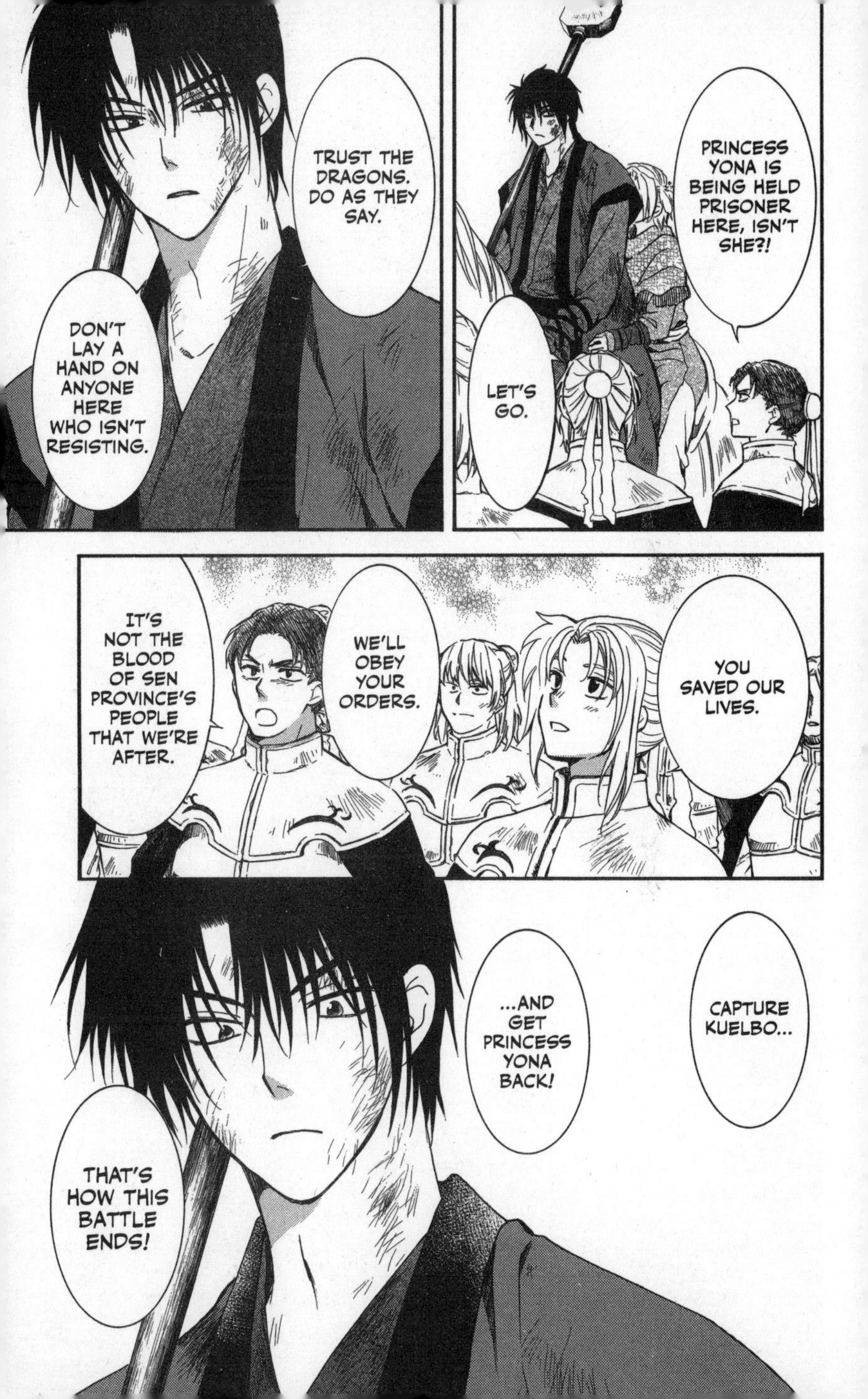
PRINCESS YONA IS BEING HELD PRISONER HERE, ISN'T SHE?!
LET'S GO.
TRUST THE DRAGONS. DO AS THEY SAY.
DON'T LAY A HAND ON ANYONE HERE WHO ISN'T RESISTING.
YOU SAVED OUR LIVES.
WE'LL OBEY YOUR ORDERS.
IT'S NOT THE BLOOD OF SEN PROVINCE'S PEOPLE THAT WE'RE AFTER.
CAPTURE KUELBO...
...AND GET PRINCESS YONA BACK!
THAT'S HOW THIS BATTLE ENDS!

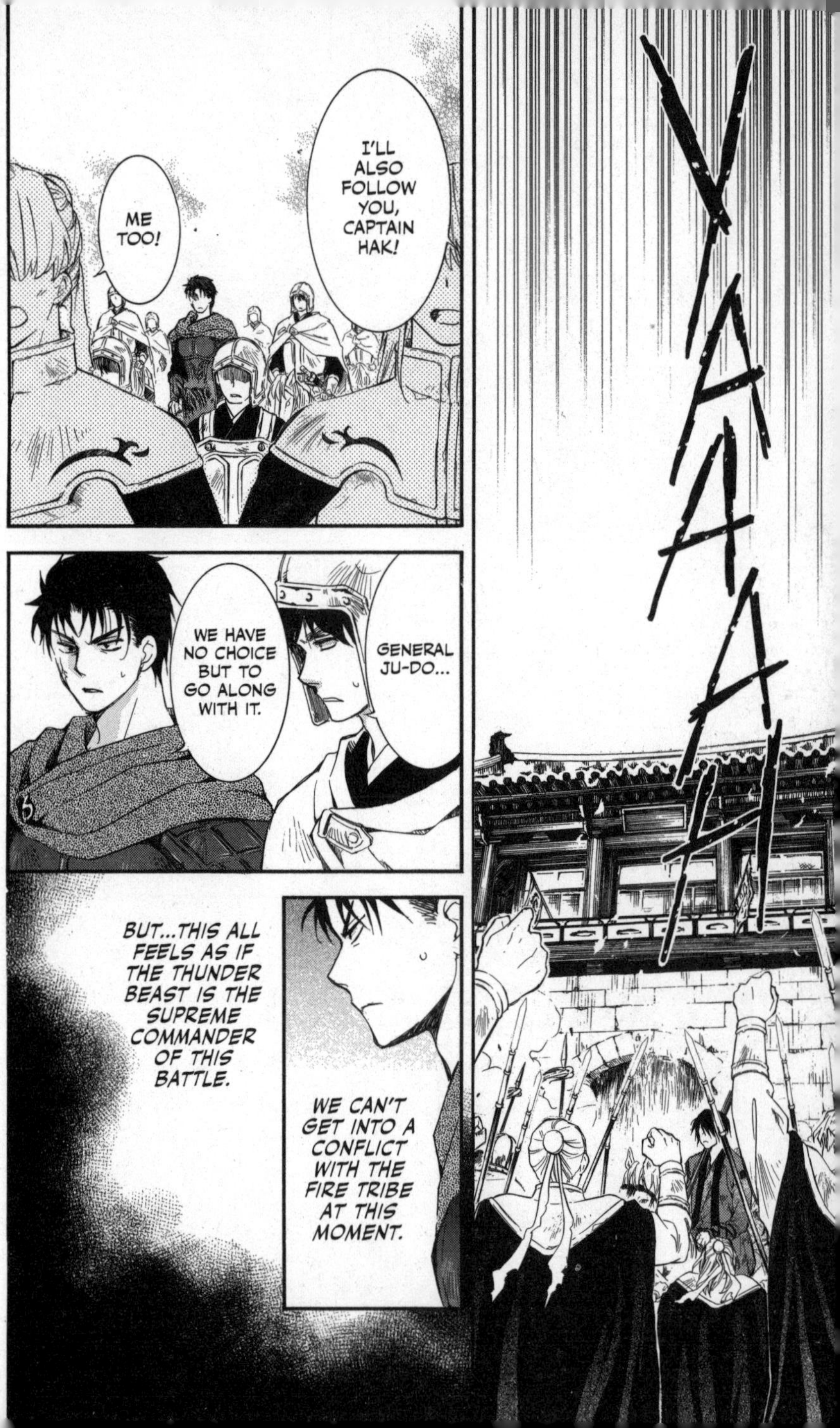
YAAAAH
I'LL ALSO FOLLOW YOU, CAPTAIN HAK!
ME TOO!
GENERAL JU-DO...
WE HAVE NO CHOICE BUT TO GO ALONG WITH IT.
BUT...THIS ALL FEELS AS IF THE THUNDER BEAST IS THE SUPREME COMMANDER OF THIS BATTLE.
WE CAN'T GET INTO A CONFLICT WITH THE FIRE TRIBE AT THIS MOMENT.

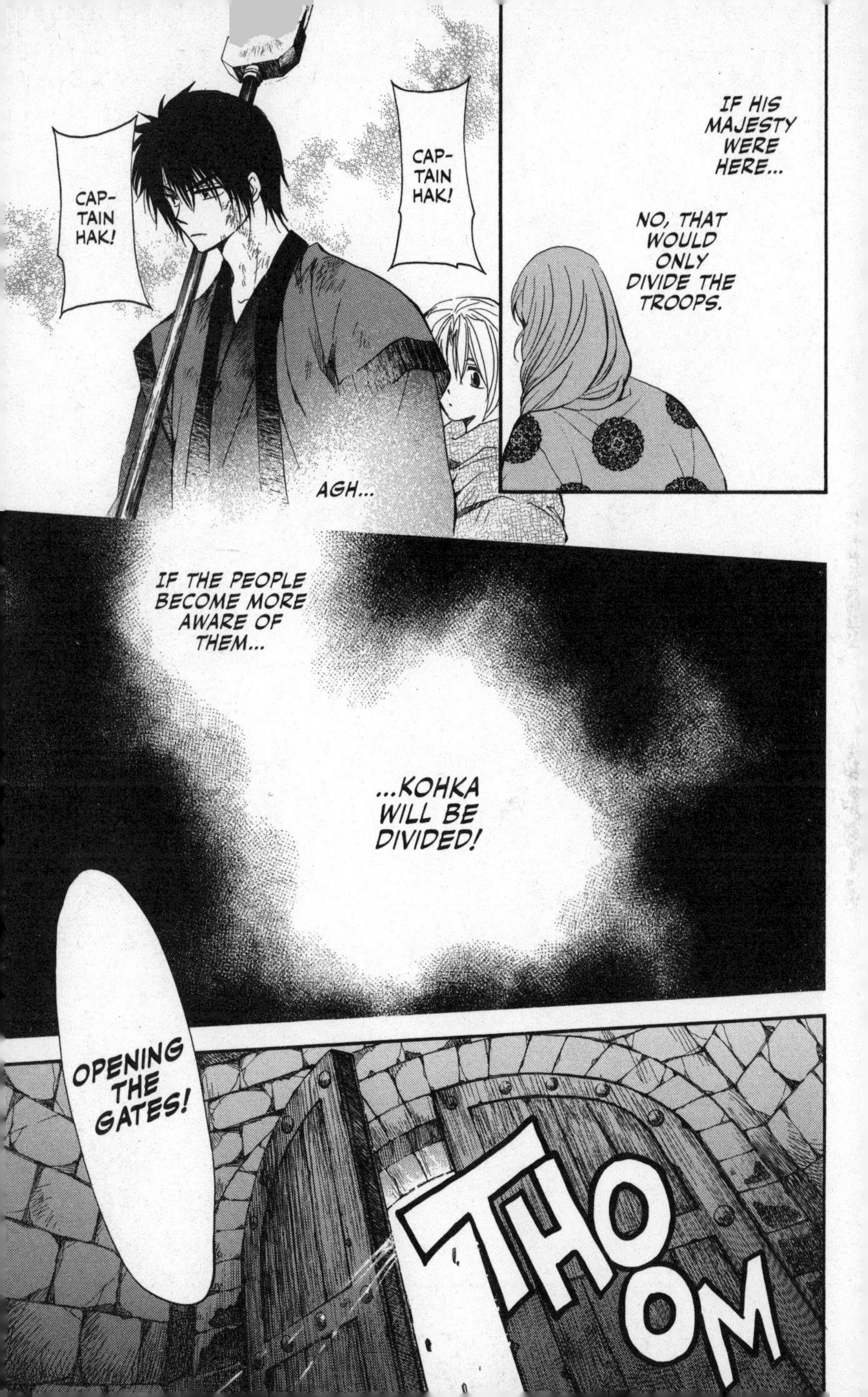
IF HIS MAJESTY WERE HERE...
NO, THAT WOULD ONLY DIVIDE THE TROOPS.
CAP-TAIN HAK!
CAP-TAIN HAK!
AGH...
IF THE PEOPLE BECOME MORE AWARE OF THEM...
...KOHKA WILL BE DIVIDED!
OPENING THE GATES!
THOOM

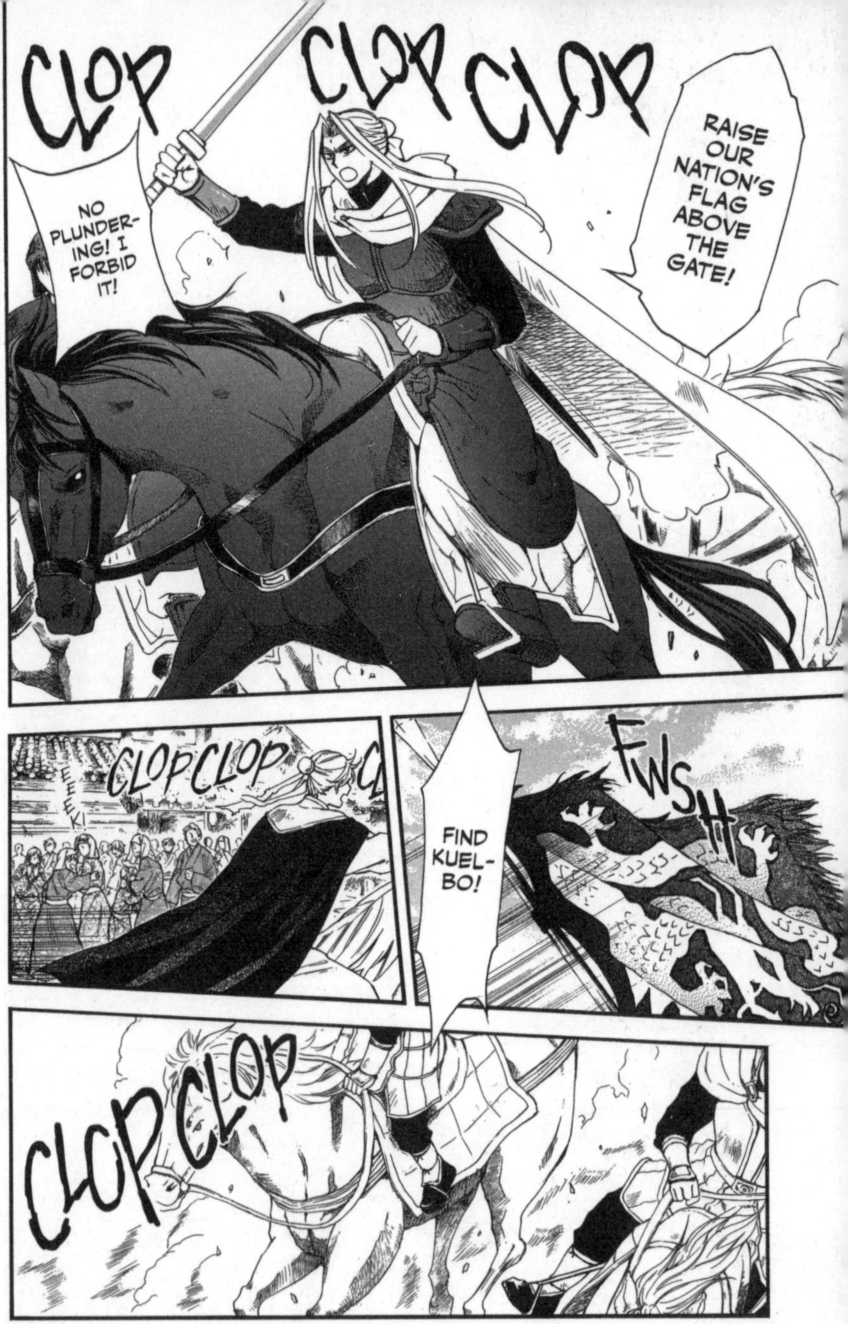
CLOP CLOP CLOP
RAISE OUR NATION'S FLAG ABOVE THE GATE!
CLOP
NO PLUNDER-ING! I FORBID IT!
FWSH
FIND KUEL-BO!
CLOP CLOP
EEEEK!
CLOP CLOP

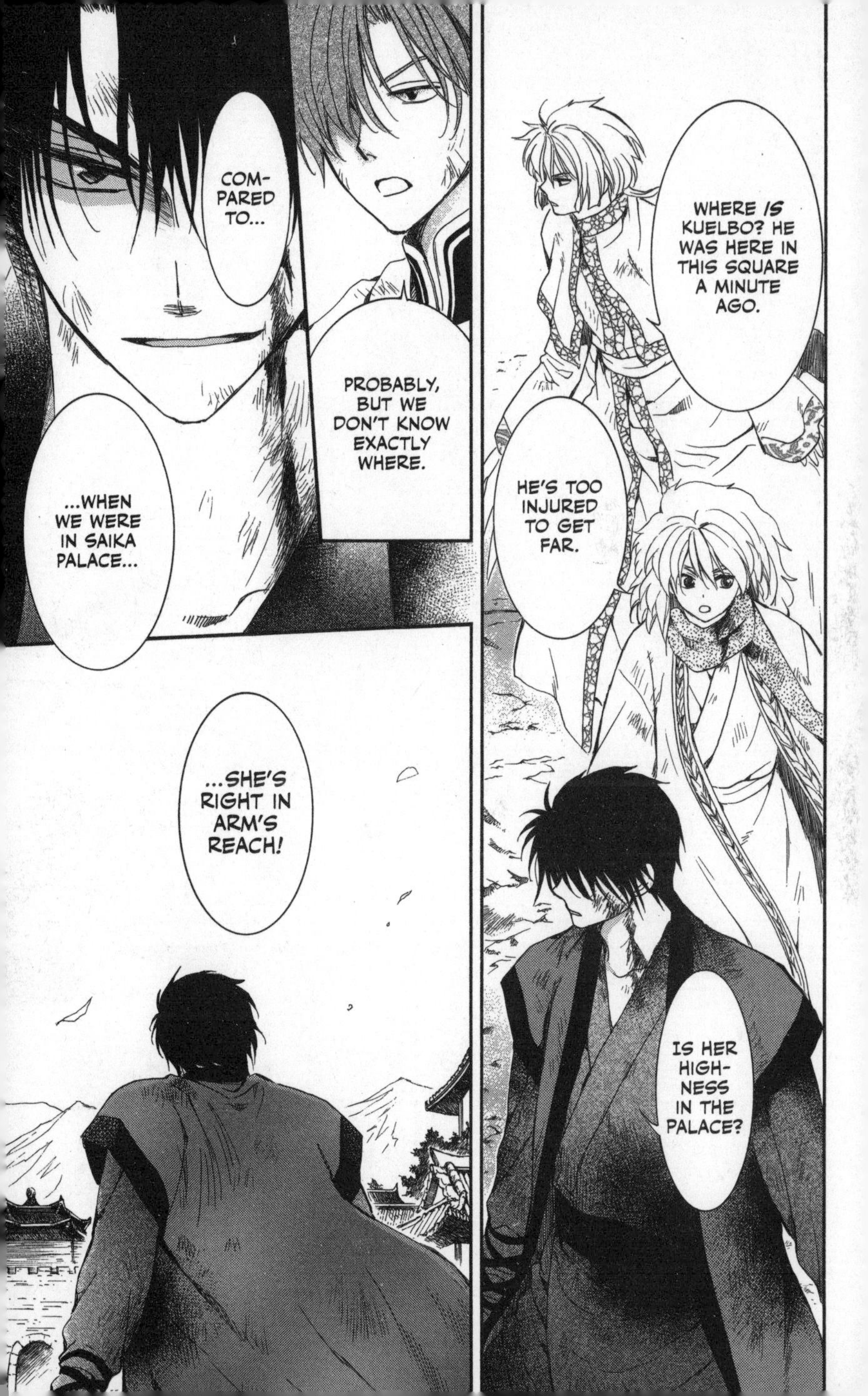
WHERE *IS* KUELBO? HE WAS HERE IN THIS SQUARE A MINUTE AGO.
HE'S TOO INJURED TO GET FAR.
IS HER HIGHNESS IN THE PALACE?
PROBABLY, BUT WE DON'T KNOW EXACTLY WHERE.
COMPARED TO...
...WHEN WE WERE IN SAIKA PALACE...
...SHE'S RIGHT IN ARM'S REACH!

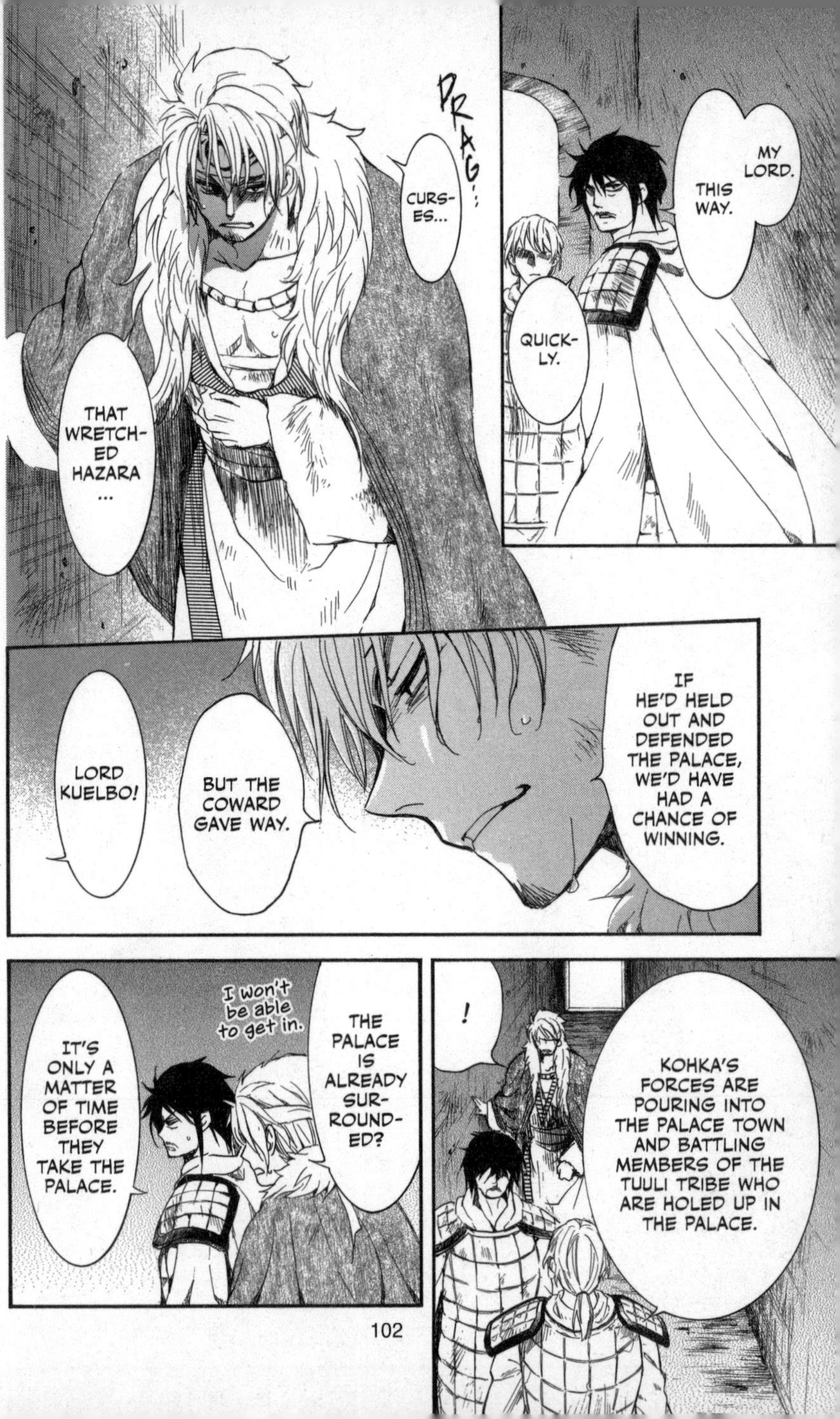
MY LORD.
THIS WAY.
QUICKLY.
DRAG
CURSES...
THAT WRETCHED HAZARA...
IF HE'D HELD OUT AND DEFENDED THE PALACE, WE'D HAVE HAD A CHANCE OF WINNING.
BUT THE COWARD GAVE WAY.
LORD KUELBO!
!
KOHKA'S FORCES ARE POURING INTO THE PALACE TOWN AND BATTLING MEMBERS OF THE TUULI TRIBE WHO ARE HOLED UP IN THE PALACE.
THE PALACE IS ALREADY SURROUNDED?
I won't be able to get in.
IT'S ONLY A MATTER OF TIME BEFORE THEY TAKE THE PALACE.

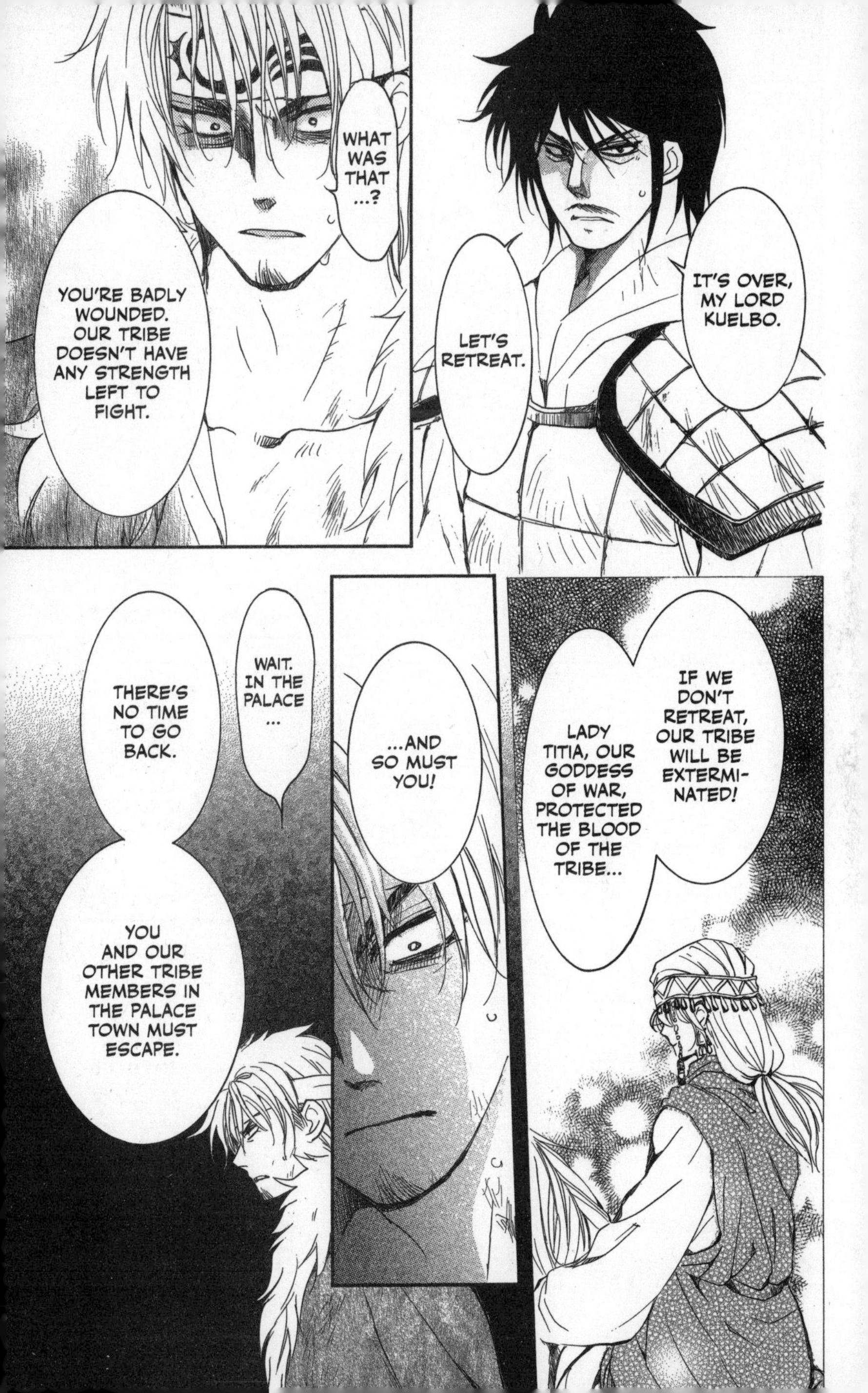
IT'S OVER, MY LORD KUELBO.
LET'S RETREAT.
WHAT WAS THAT ...?
YOU'RE BADLY WOUNDED. OUR TRIBE DOESN'T HAVE ANY STRENGTH LEFT TO FIGHT.
IF WE DON'T RETREAT, OUR TRIBE WILL BE EXTERMINATED!
LADY TITIA, OUR GODDESS OF WAR, PROTECTED THE BLOOD OF THE TRIBE...
...AND SO MUST YOU!
WAIT. IN THE PALACE ...
THERE'S NO TIME TO GO BACK.
YOU AND OUR OTHER TRIBE MEMBERS IN THE PALACE TOWN MUST ESCAPE.

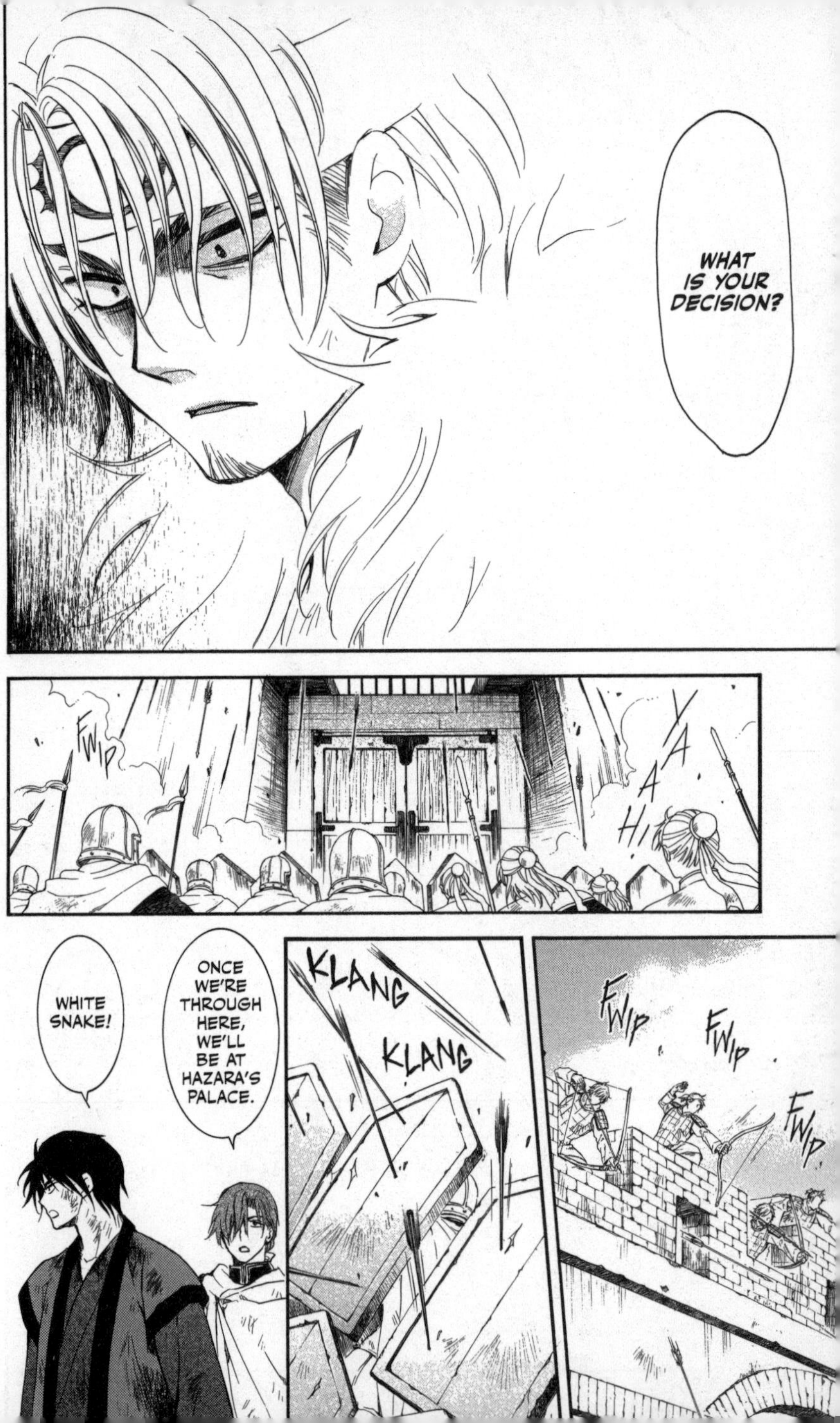
WHAT IS YOUR DECISION?
YAAAH
FWIP
FWIP
FWIP
FWIP
KLANG
KLANG
ONCE WE'RE THROUGH HERE, WE'LL BE AT HAZARA'S PALACE.
WHITE SNAKE!

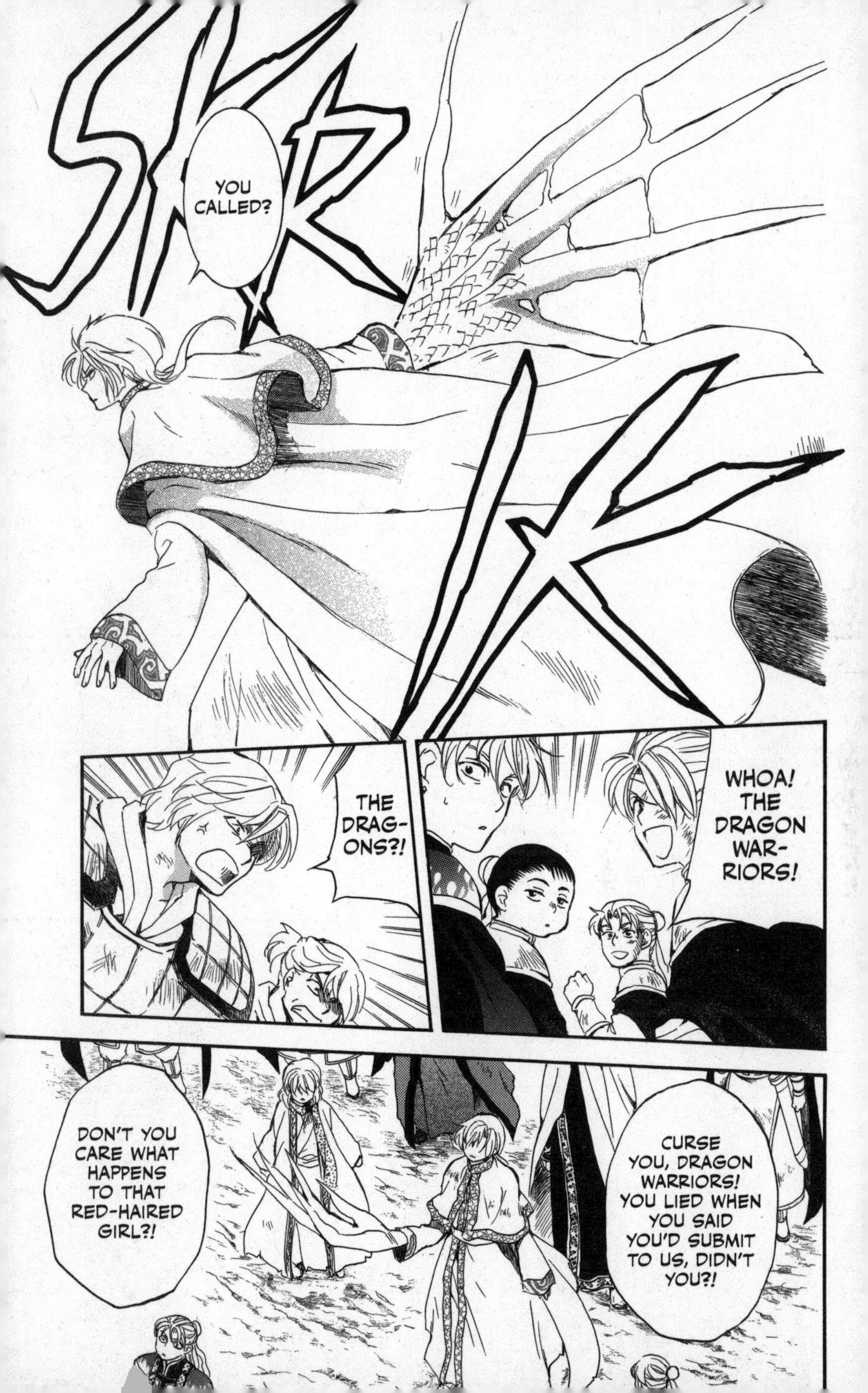
YOU CALLED?
WHOA! THE DRAGON WARRIORS!
THE DRAGONS?!
CURSE YOU, DRAGON WARRIORS! YOU LIED WHEN YOU SAID YOU'D SUBMIT TO US, DIDN'T YOU?!
DON'T YOU CARE WHAT HAPPENS TO THAT RED-HAIRED GIRL?!

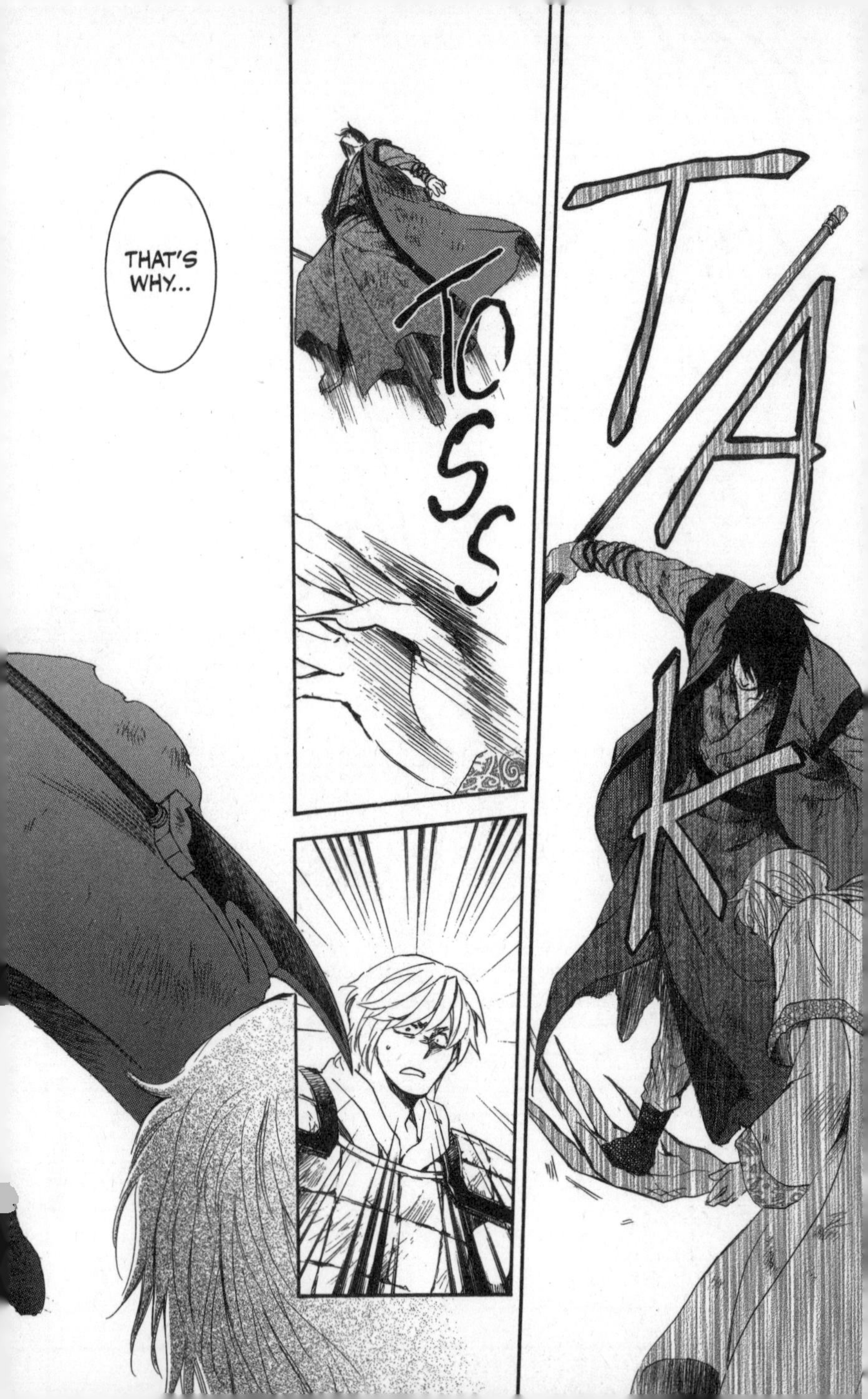
TAK
TOSS
THAT'S WHY...

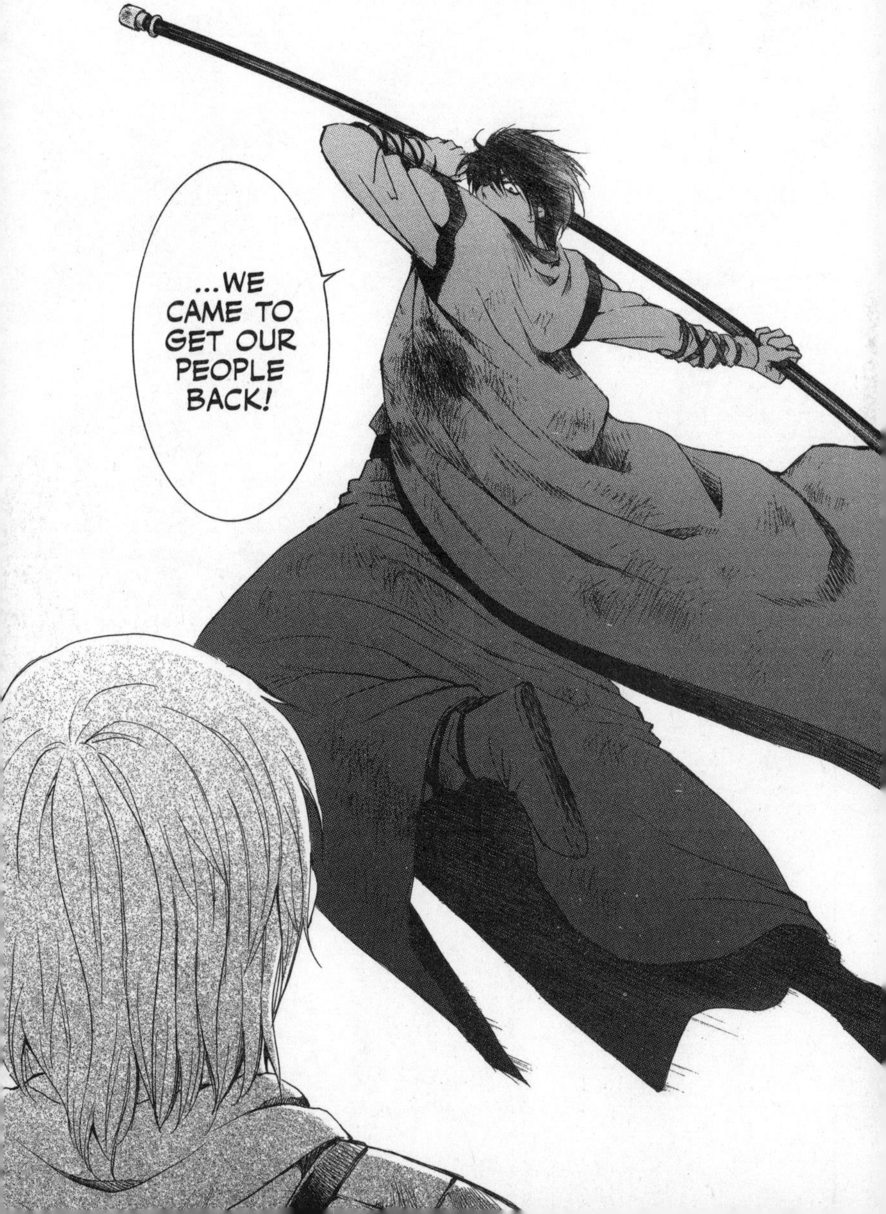
...WE CAME TO GET OUR PEOPLE BACK!

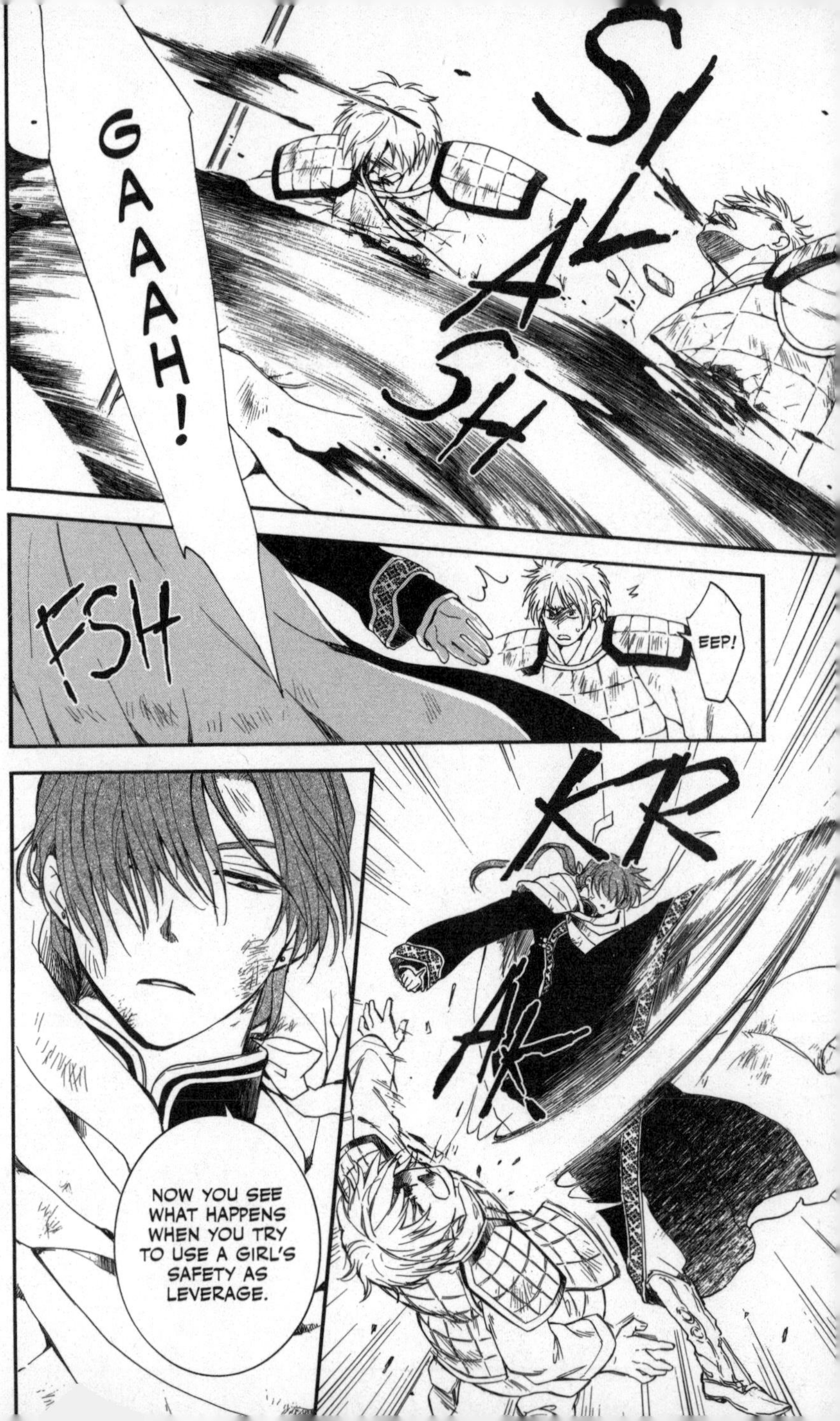
SLASH
GAAAH!
EEP!
FSH
KRAK
NOW YOU SEE WHAT HAPPENS WHEN YOU TRY TO USE A GIRL'S SAFETY AS LEVERAGE.

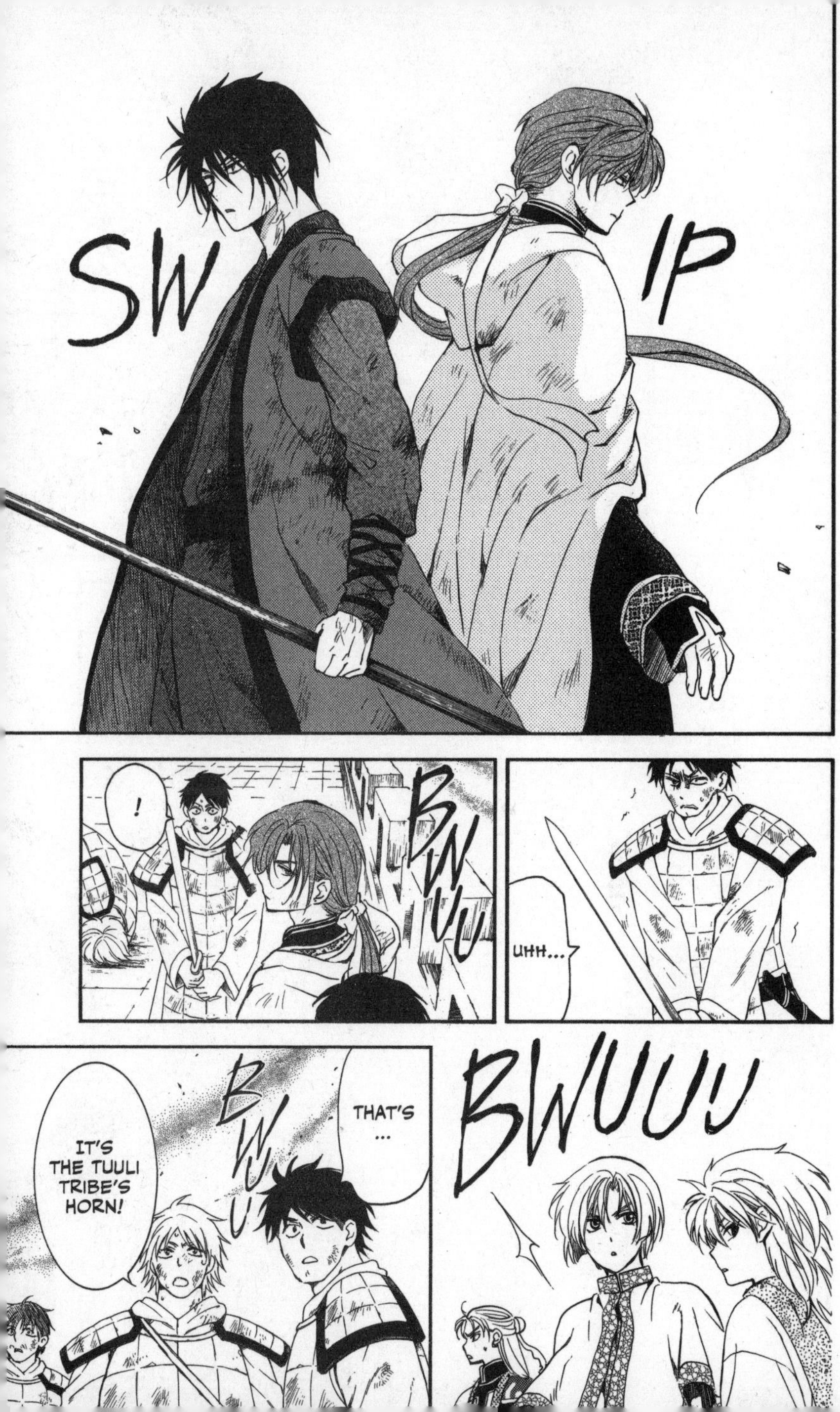
SWIP
UHH...
!
BWUU
BWUUU
THAT'S ...
BWU
IT'S THE TUULI TRIBE'S HORN!

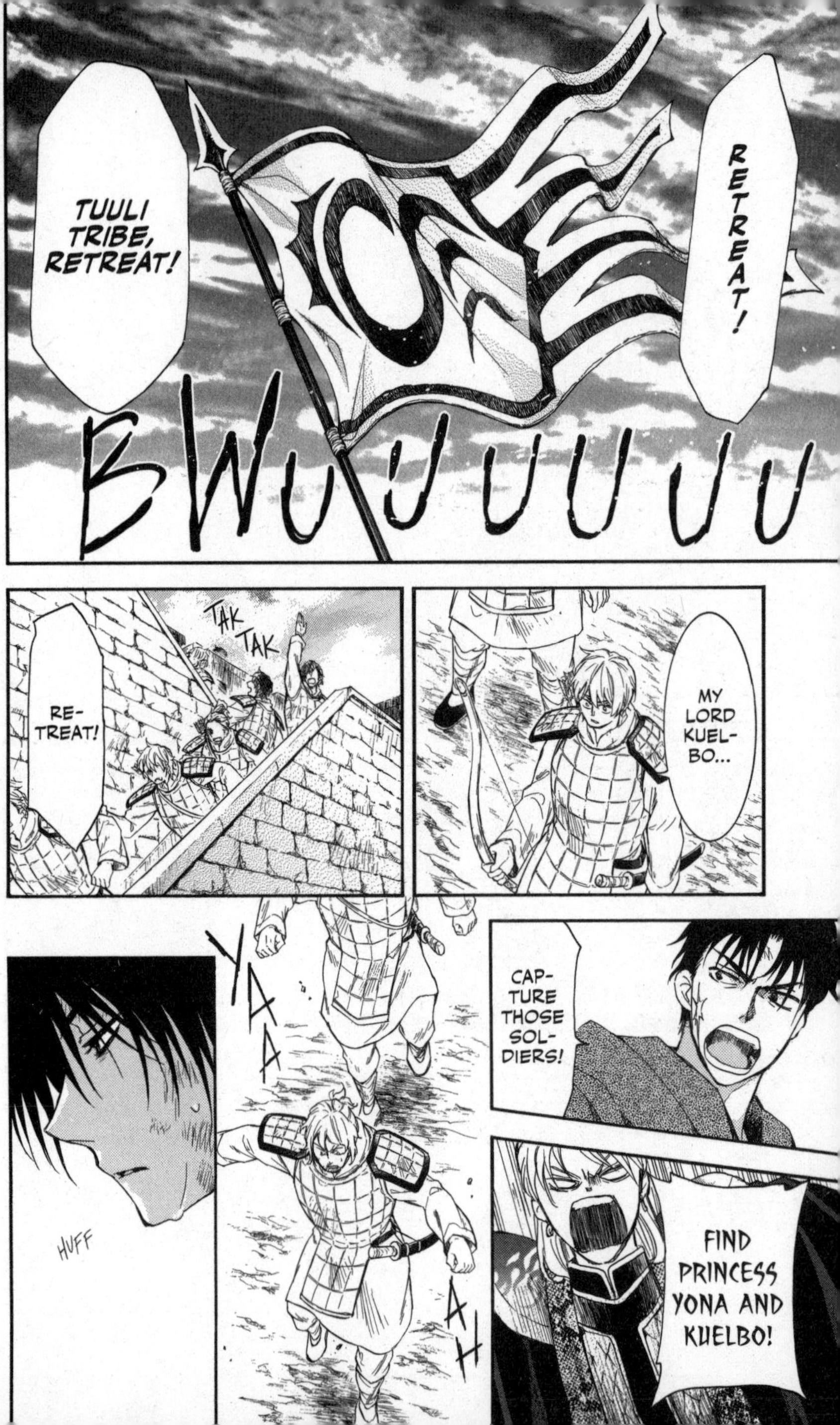
RETREAT!
TUULI TRIBE, RETREAT!
BWUUUUUU
MY LORD KUEL-BO...
TAK TAK
RE-TREAT!
CAP-TURE THOSE SOL-DIERS!
FIND PRINCESS YONA AND KUELBO!
YAAAH
HUFF

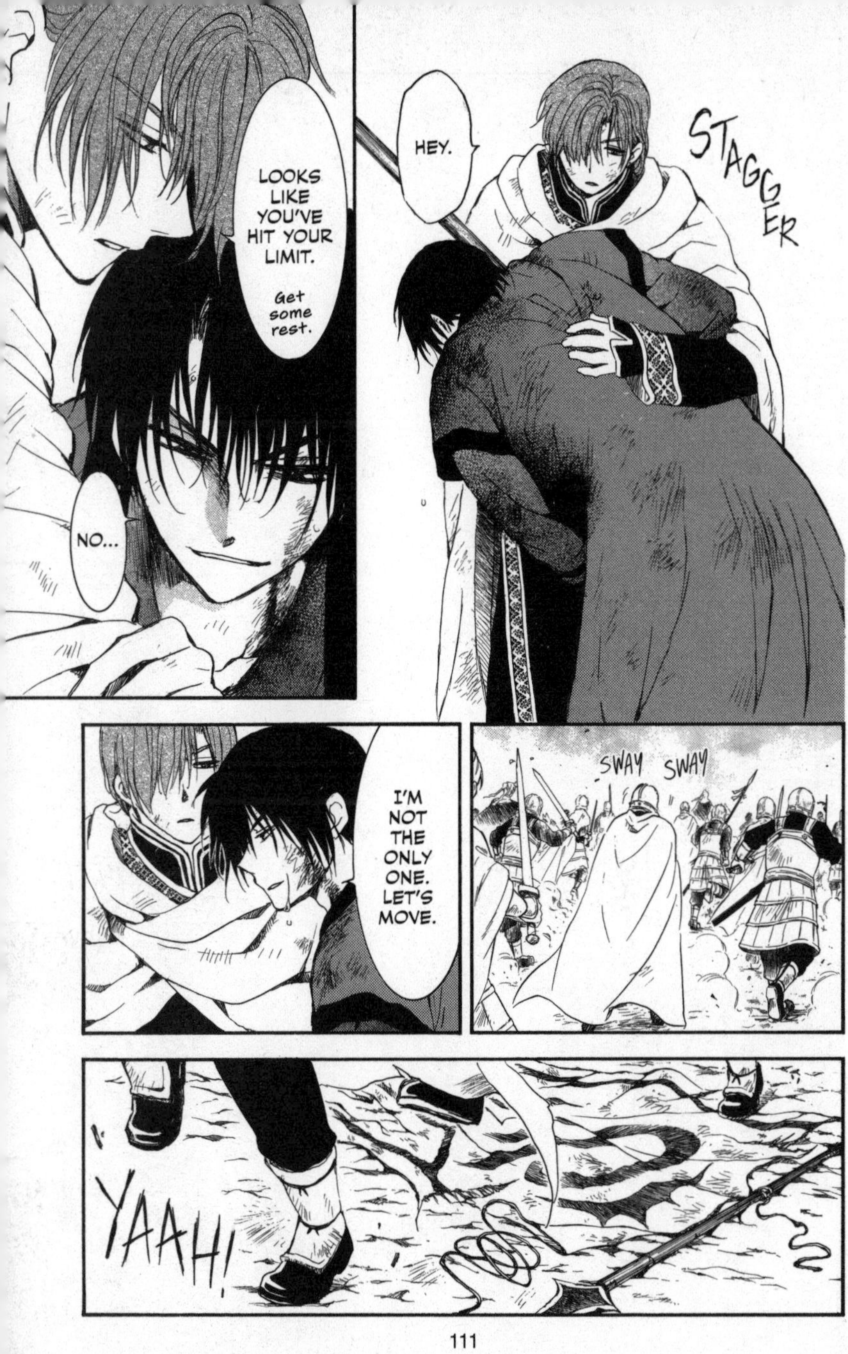
HEY.
STAGGER
LOOKS LIKE YOU'VE HIT YOUR LIMIT. Get some rest.
NO...
SWAY SWAY
I'M NOT THE ONLY ONE. LET'S MOVE.
YAAH!

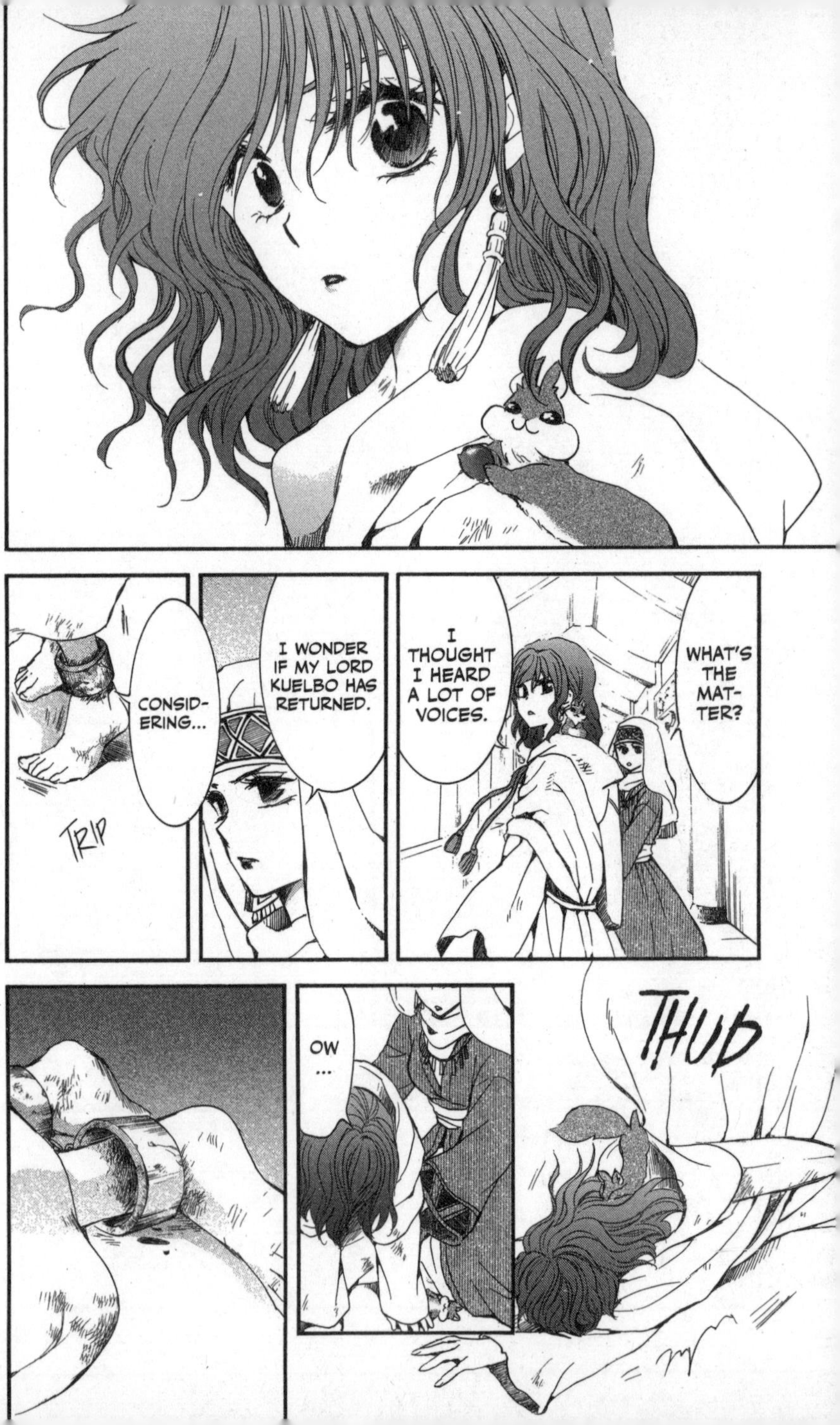
WHAT'S THE MAT-TER?
I THOUGHT I HEARD A LOT OF VOICES.
I WONDER IF MY LORD KUELBO HAS RETURNED.
CONSID-ERING...
TRIP
THUD
OW ...

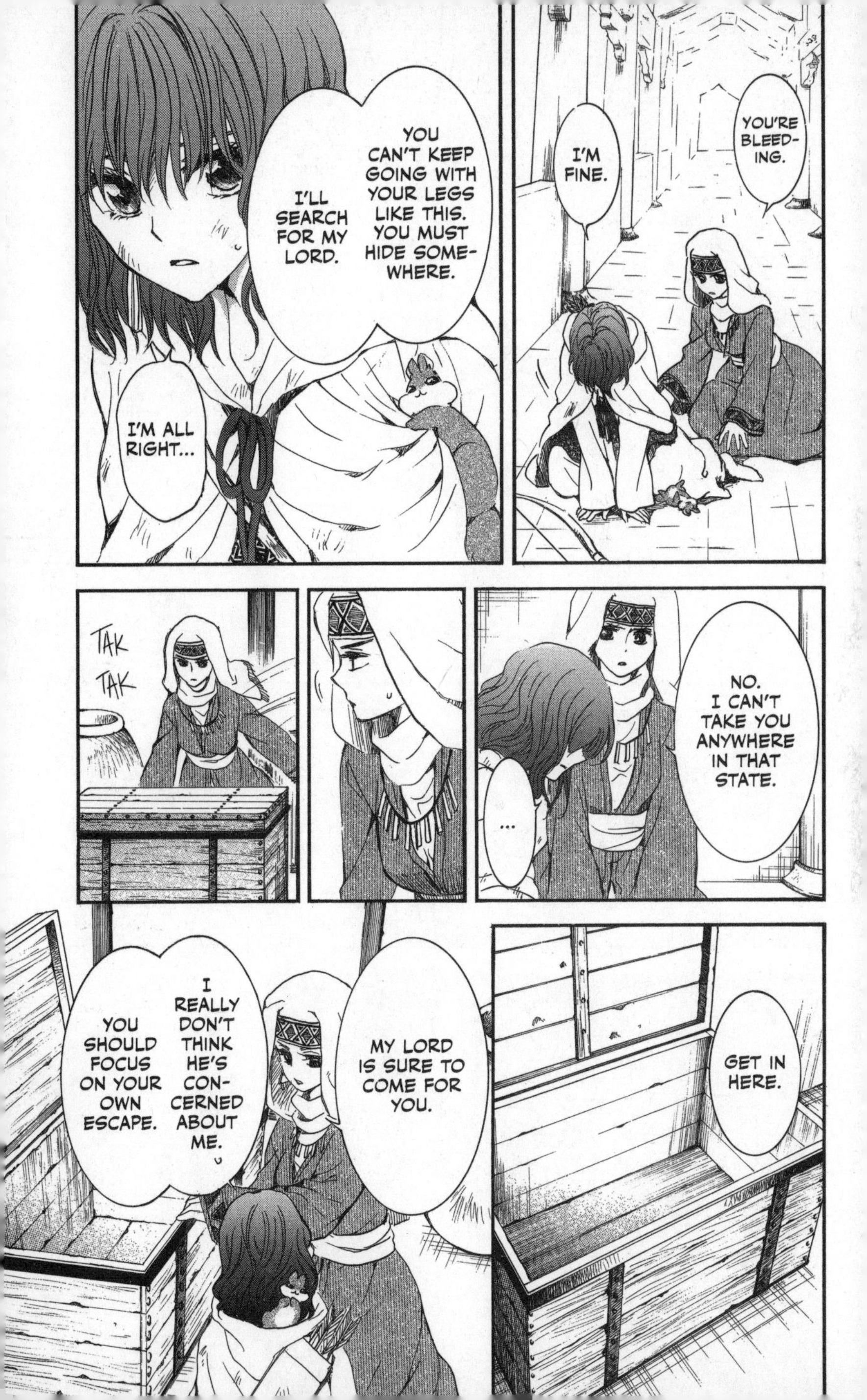
YOU'RE BLEEDING.
I'M FINE.
YOU CAN'T KEEP GOING WITH YOUR LEGS LIKE THIS. YOU MUST HIDE SOMEWHERE.
I'LL SEARCH FOR MY LORD.
I'M ALL RIGHT...
NO. I CAN'T TAKE YOU ANYWHERE IN THAT STATE.
...
TAK TAK
GET IN HERE.
MY LORD IS SURE TO COME FOR YOU.
I REALLY DON'T THINK HE'S CONCERNED ABOUT ME.
YOU SHOULD FOCUS ON YOUR OWN ESCAPE.

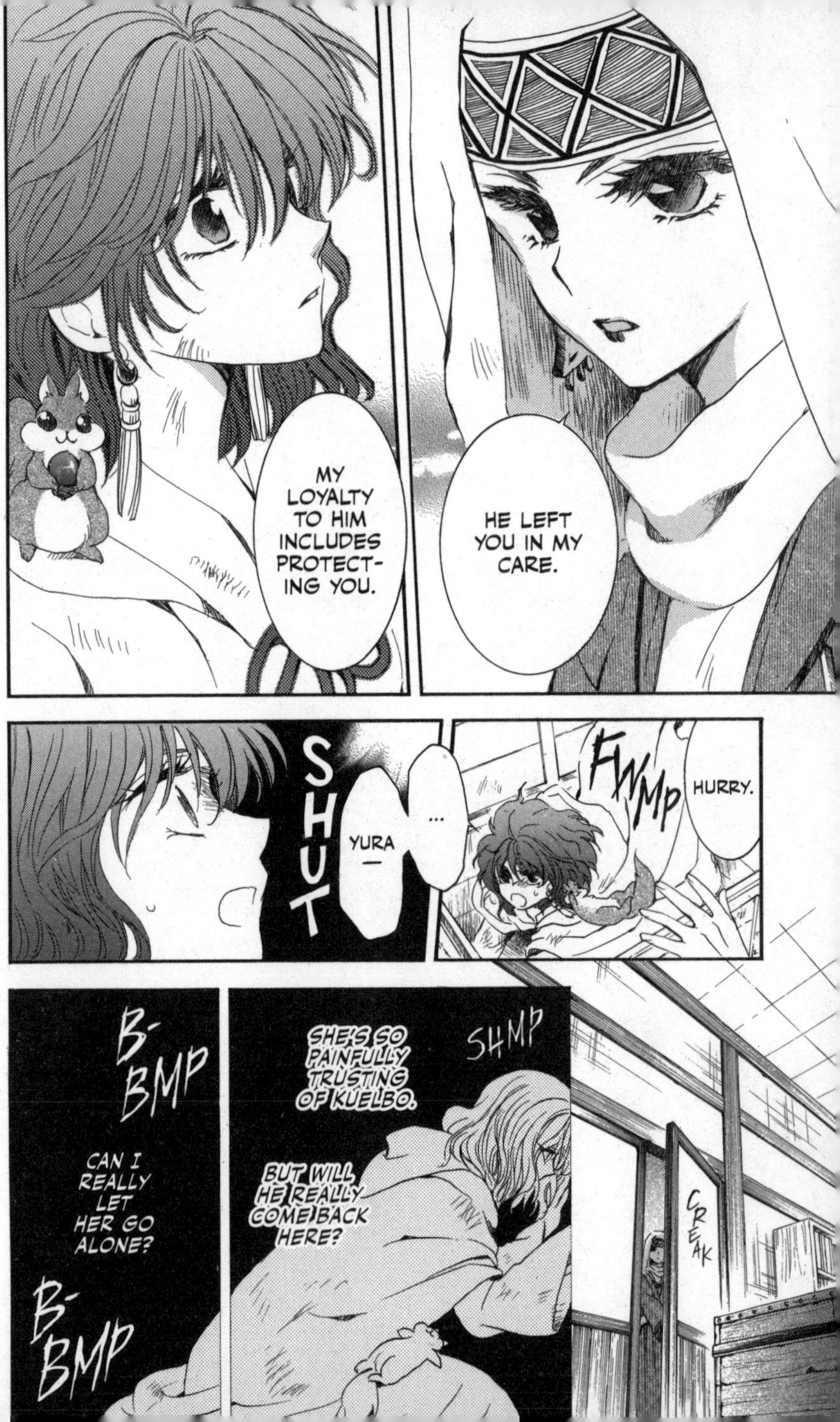
HE LEFT YOU IN MY CARE.
MY LOYALTY TO HIM INCLUDES PROTECT-ING YOU.
HURRY.
FWMP
...
YURA—
SHUT
CREAK
SHMP
SHE'S SO PAINFULLY TRUSTING OF KUELBO.
BUT WILL HE REALLY COME BACK HERE?
B-BMP
CAN I REALLY LET HER GO ALONE?
B-BMP

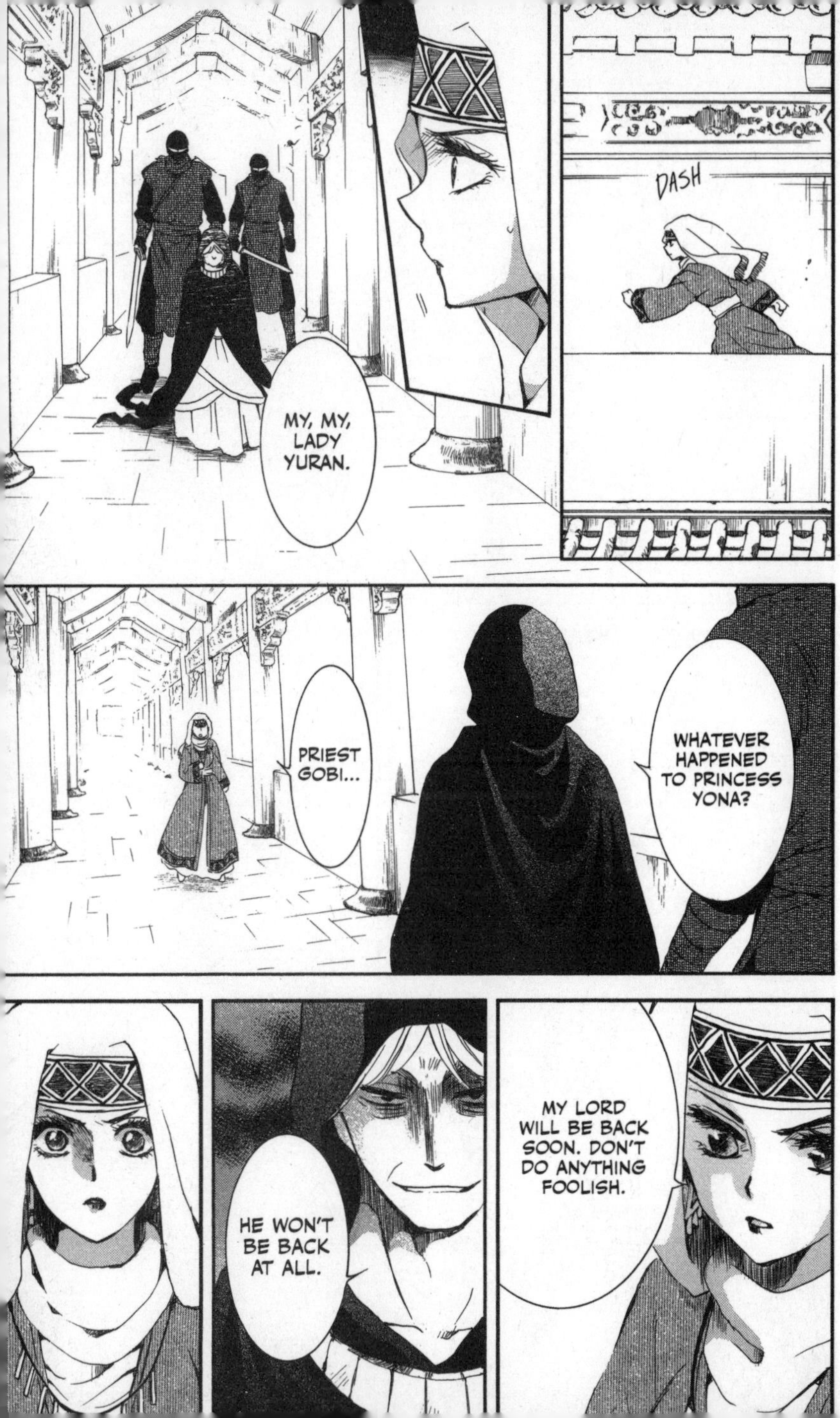
DASH
MY, MY, LADY YURAN.
WHATEVER HAPPENED TO PRINCESS YONA?
PRIEST GOBI...
MY LORD WILL BE BACK SOON. DON'T DO ANYTHING FOOLISH.
HE WON'T BE BACK AT ALL.

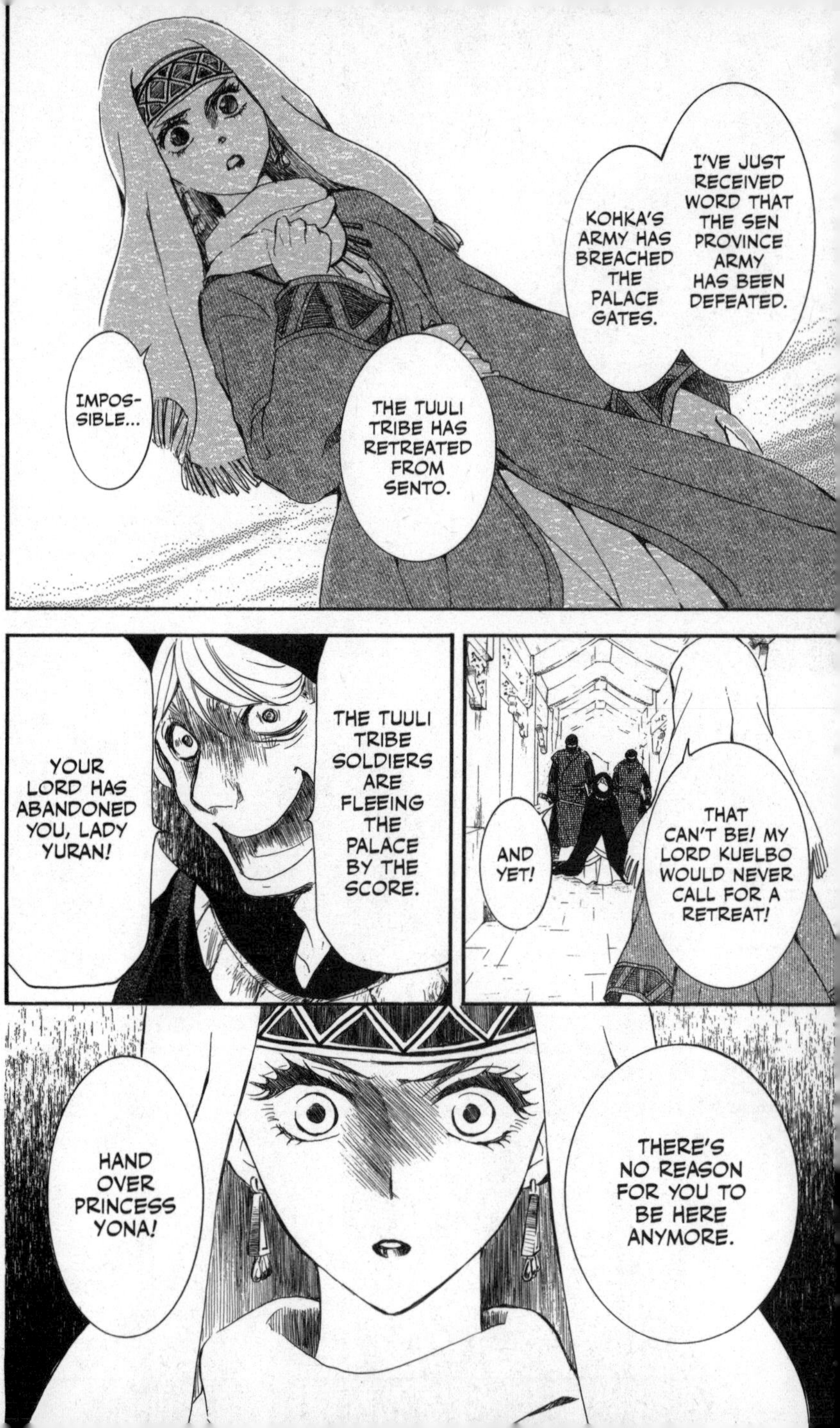
I'VE JUST RECEIVED WORD THAT THE SEN PROVINCE ARMY HAS BEEN DEFEATED.
KOHKA'S ARMY HAS BREACHED THE PALACE GATES.
THE TUULI TRIBE HAS RETREATED FROM SENTO.
IMPOS-SIBLE...
THAT CAN'T BE! MY LORD KUELBO WOULD NEVER CALL FOR A RETREAT!
AND YET!
THE TUULI TRIBE SOLDIERS ARE FLEEING THE PALACE BY THE SCORE.
YOUR LORD HAS ABANDONED YOU, LADY YURAN!
THERE'S NO REASON FOR YOU TO BE HERE ANYMORE.
HAND OVER PRINCESS YONA!

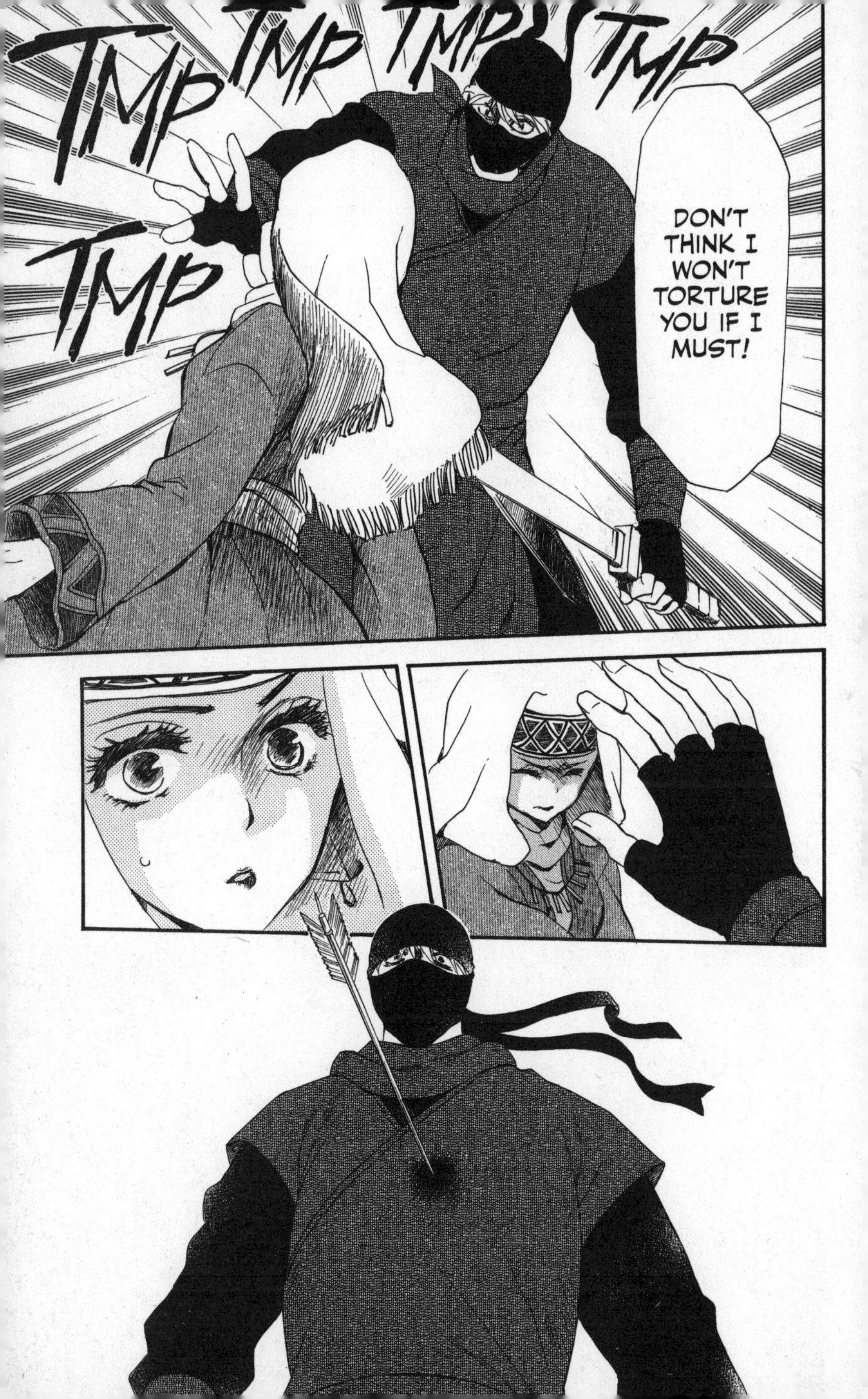
TMP TMP TMP STMP
TMP
DON'T THINK I WON'T TORTURE YOU IF I MUST!

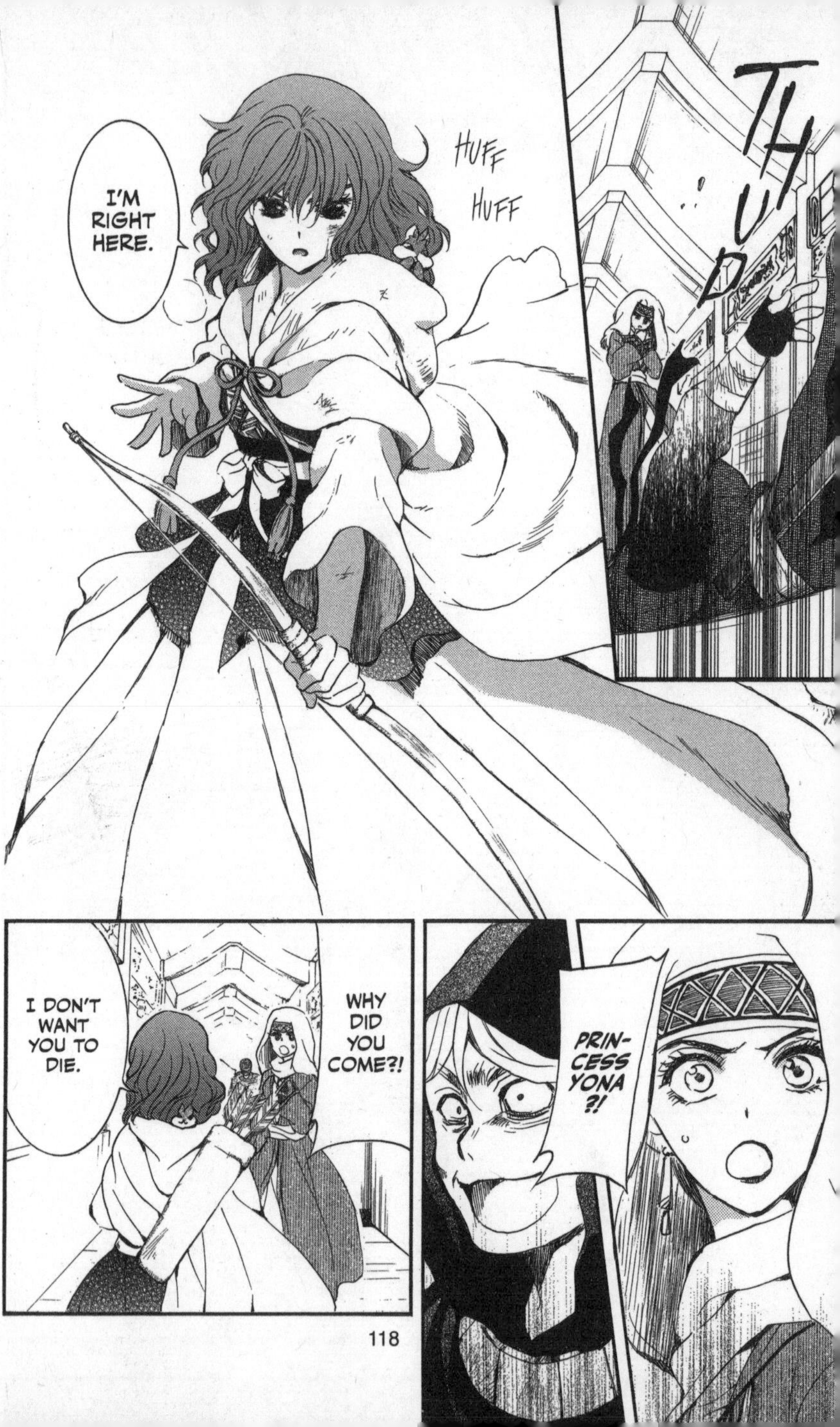
THUD
..!
I'M RIGHT HERE.
HUFF
HUFF
PRIN-CESS YONA ?!
WHY DID YOU COME?!
I DON'T WANT YOU TO DIE.

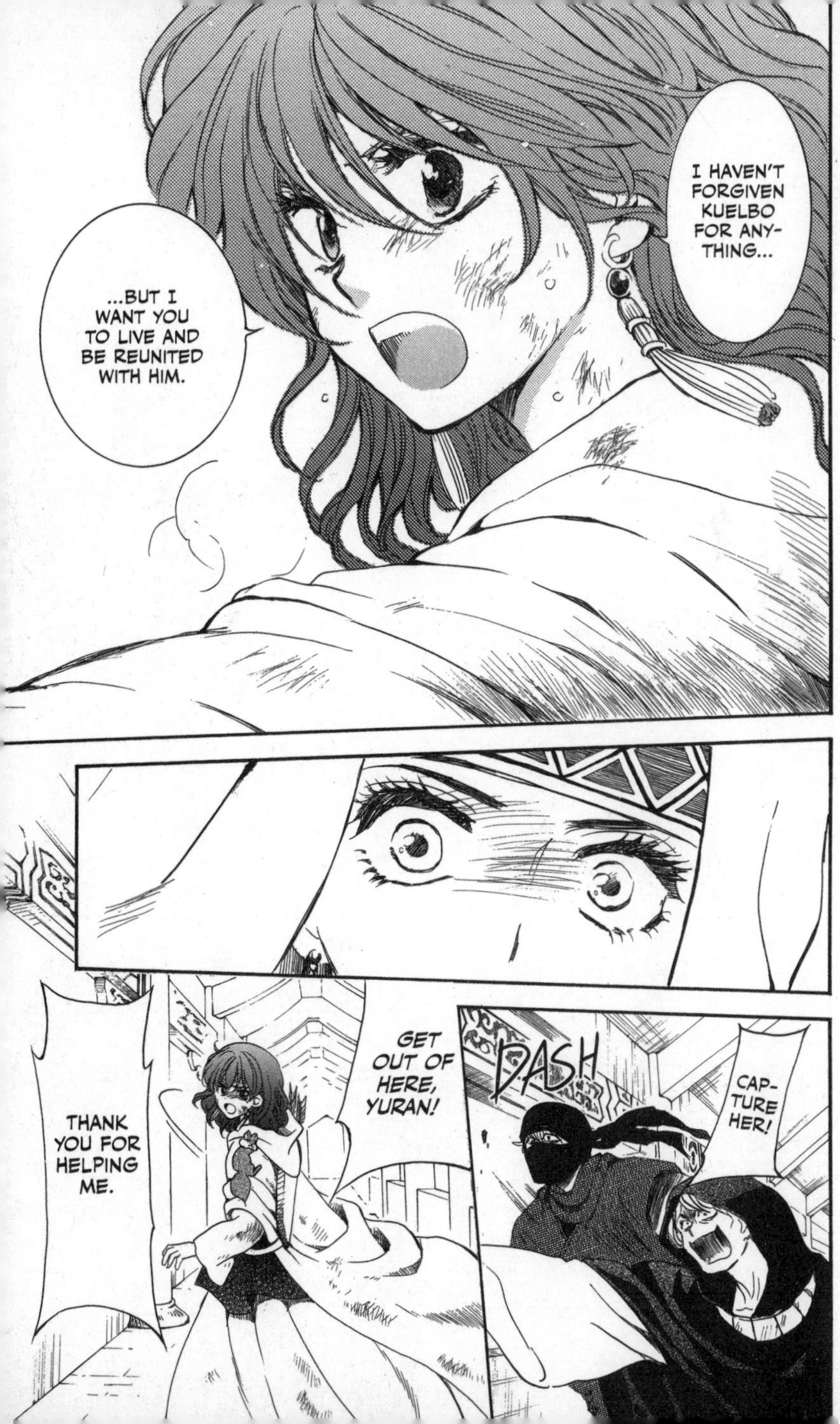
I HAVEN'T FORGIVEN KUELBO FOR ANY-THING...
...BUT I WANT YOU TO LIVE AND BE REUNITED WITH HIM.
CAP-TURE HER!
DASH
GET OUT OF HERE, YURAN!
THANK YOU FOR HELPING ME.

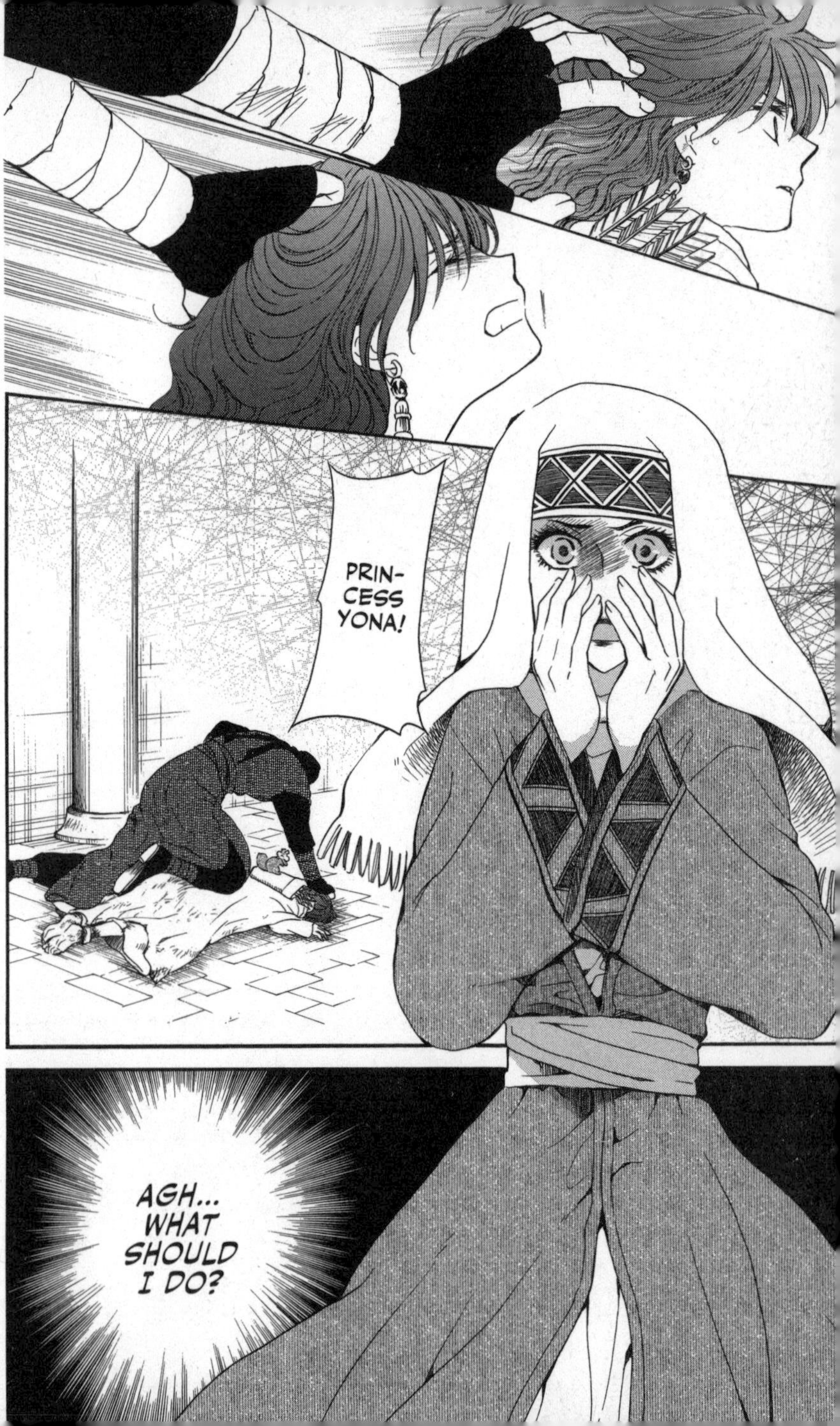
PRIN-
CESS
YONA!
AGH...
WHAT
SHOULD
I DO?

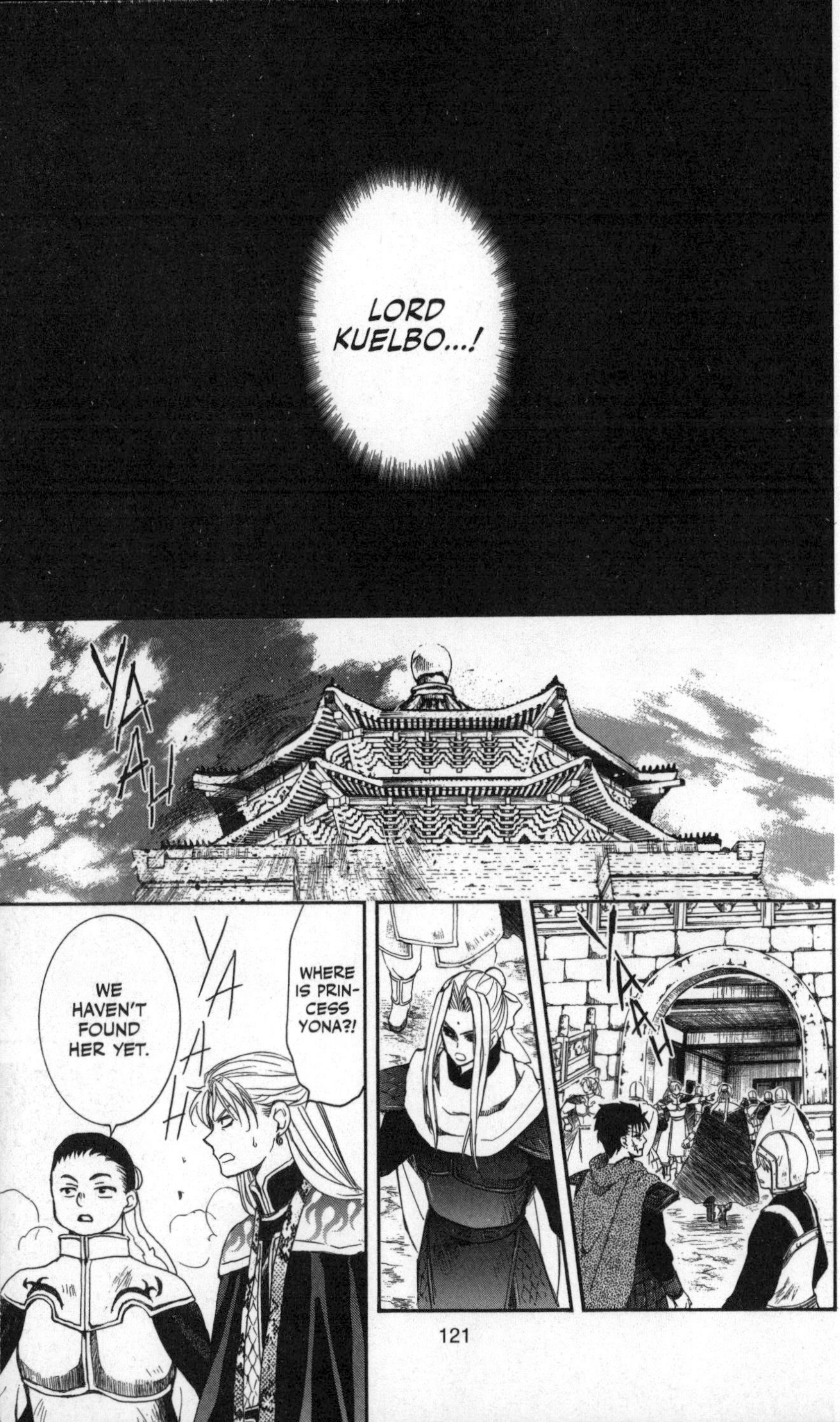
LORD KUELBO...!
YAAAH
YAAAH
WHERE IS PRIN-CESS YONA?!
YAAAAH
WE HAVEN'T FOUND HER YET.

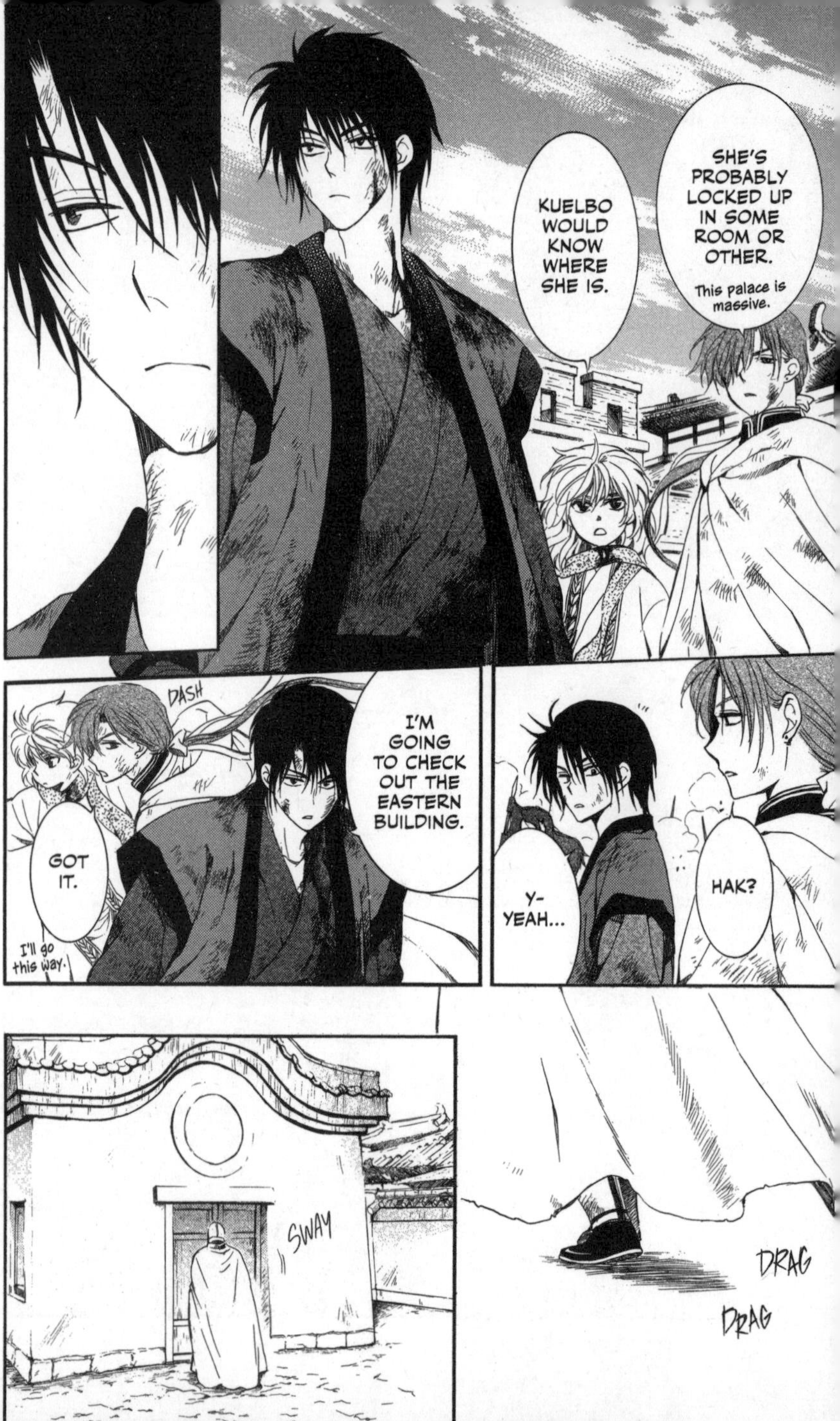
SHE'S PROBABLY LOCKED UP IN SOME ROOM OR OTHER.
This palace is massive.
KUELBO WOULD KNOW WHERE SHE IS.
HAK?
Y-YEAH...
I'M GOING TO CHECK OUT THE EASTERN BUILDING.
DASH
GOT IT.
I'll go this way.
DRAG
DRAG
SWAY

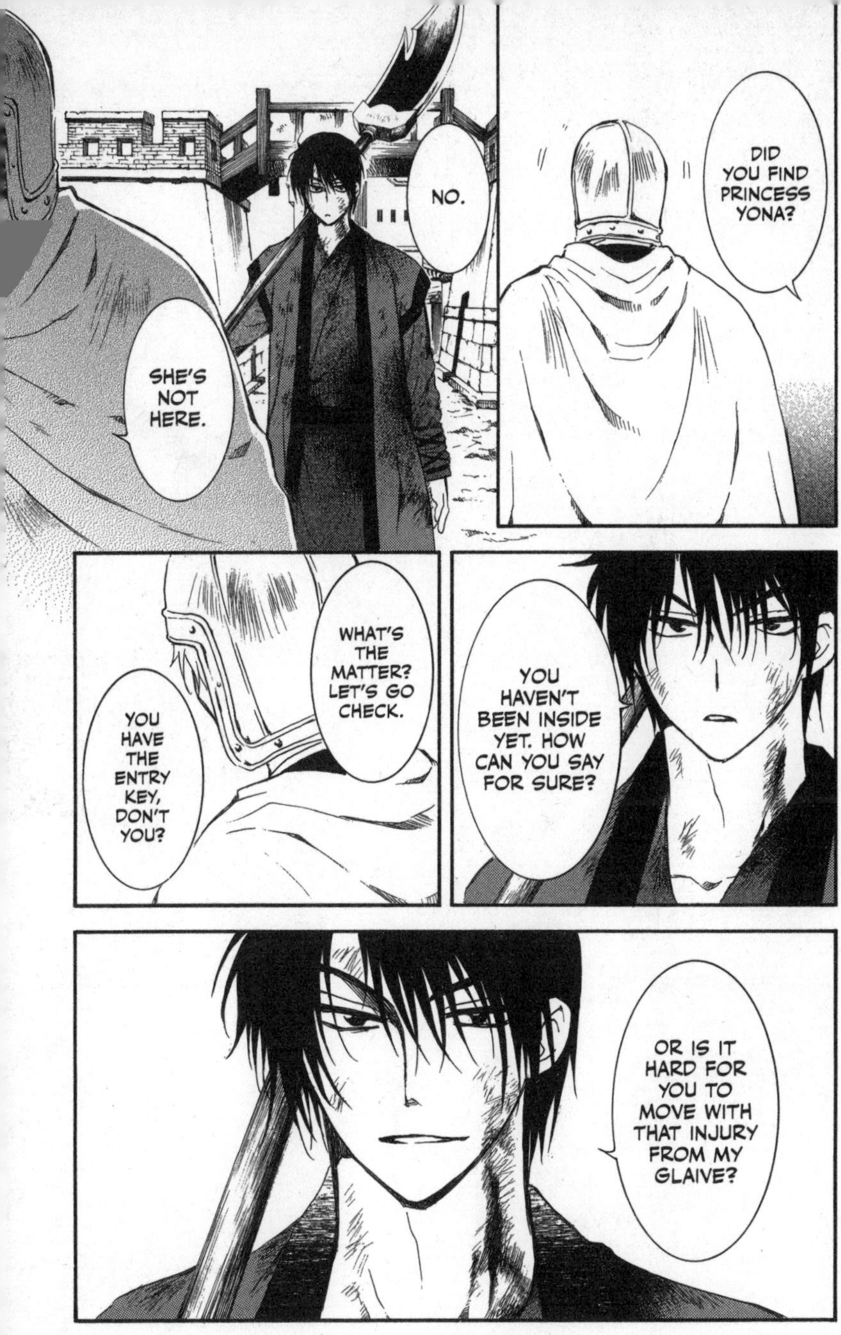
DID YOU FIND PRINCESS YONA?
NO.
SHE'S NOT HERE.
YOU HAVEN'T BEEN INSIDE YET. HOW CAN YOU SAY FOR SURE?
WHAT'S THE MATTER? LET'S GO CHECK.
YOU HAVE THE ENTRY KEY, DON'T YOU?
OR IS IT HARD FOR YOU TO MOVE WITH THAT INJURY FROM MY GLAIVE?

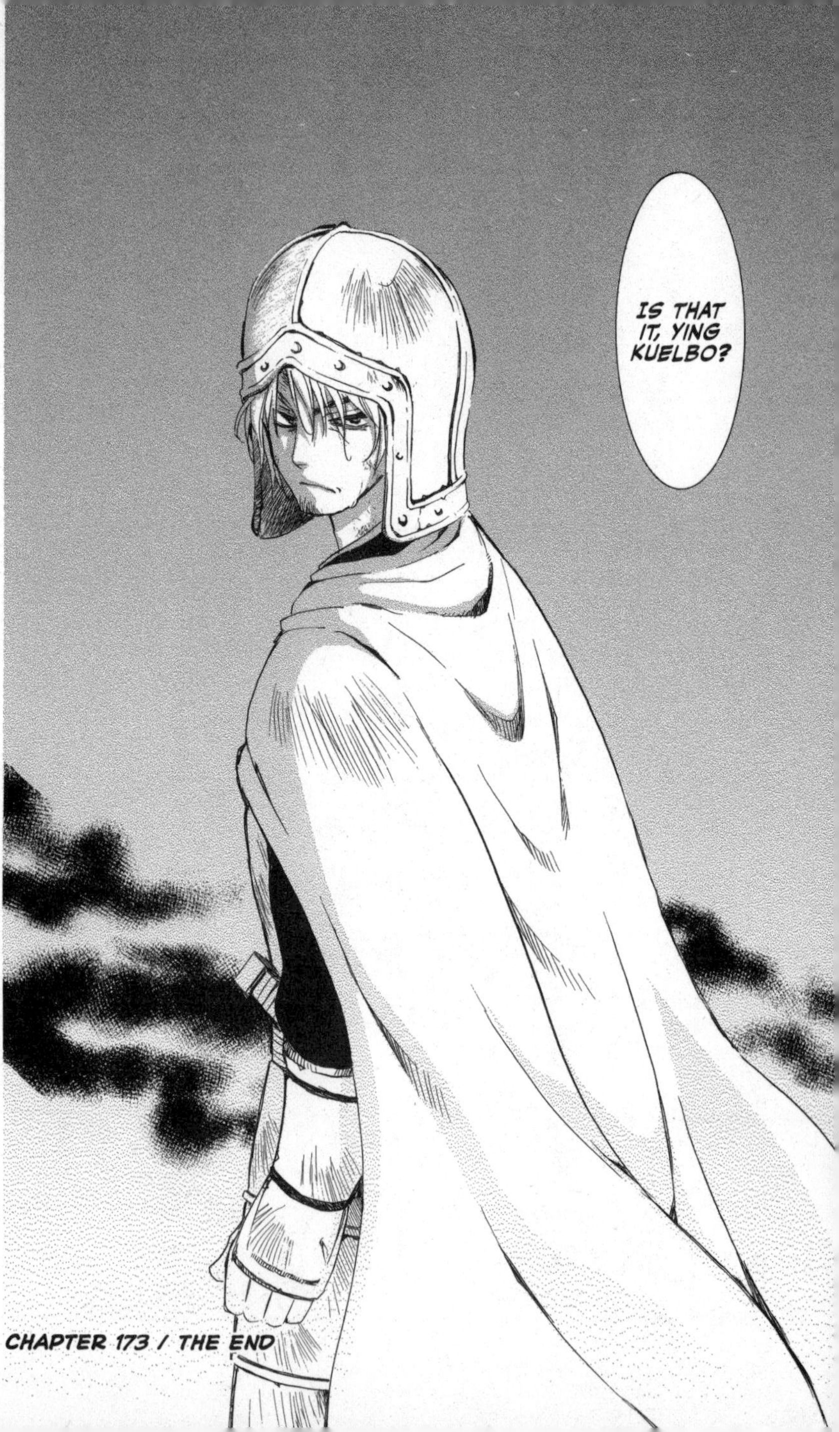
IS THAT IT, YING KUELBO?
CHAPTER 173 / THE END

LINE Creators' Stamps for Yona are on sale!
Check them out!

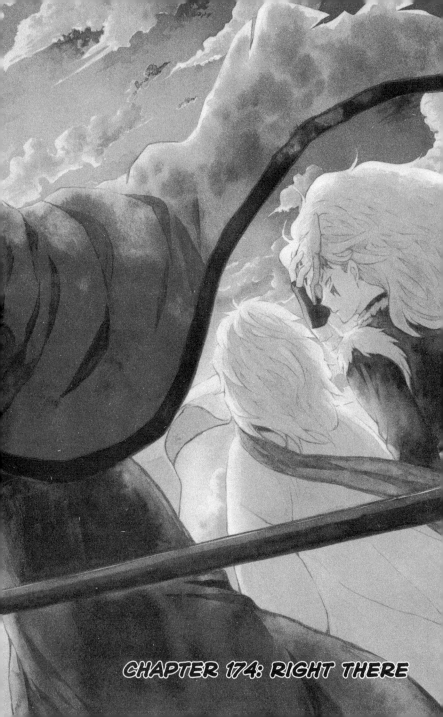

CHAPTER 174: RIGHT THERE

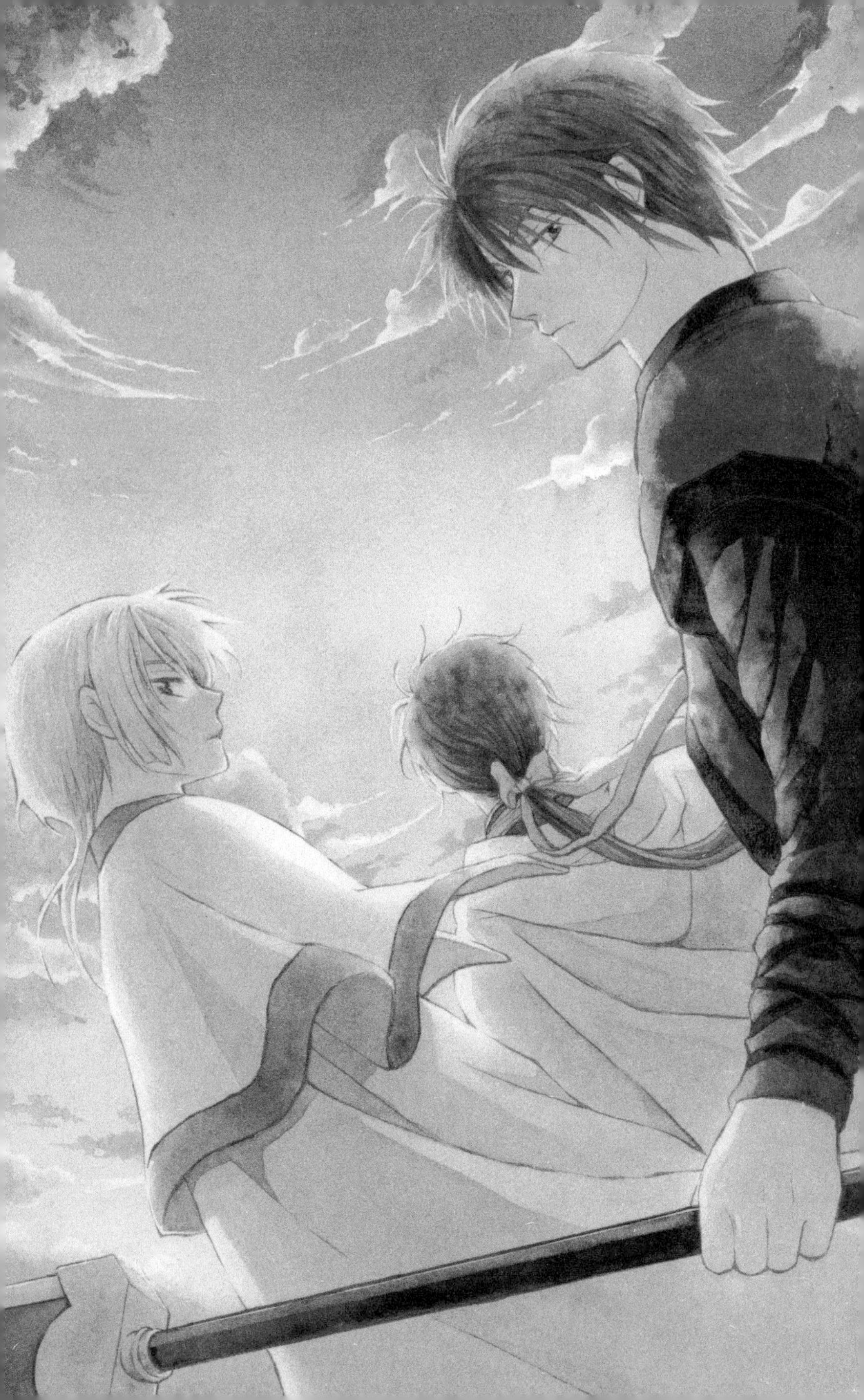

Jaeha, age 22
Hak, age 15

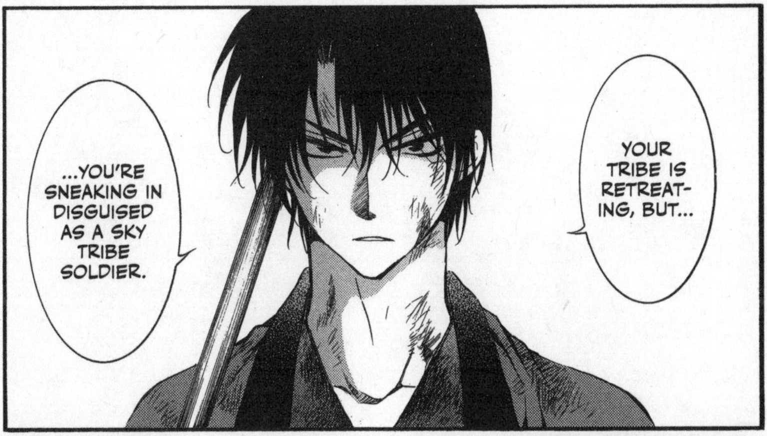
YOUR TRIBE IS RETREAT-ING, BUT...
...YOU'RE SNEAKING IN DISGUISED AS A SKY TRIBE SOLDIER.

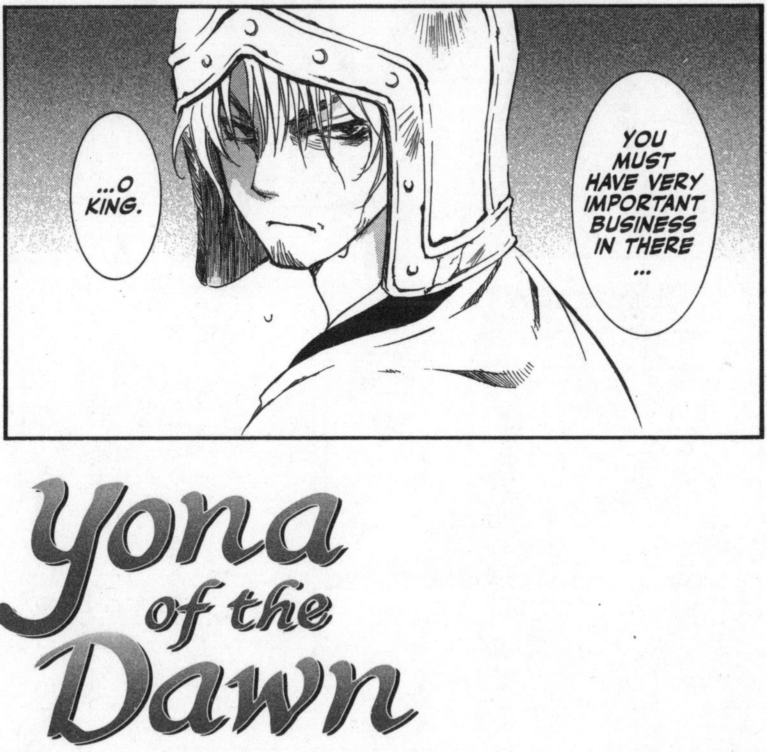
YOU MUST HAVE VERY IMPORTANT BUSINESS IN THERE ...
...O KING.

Yona of the Dawn

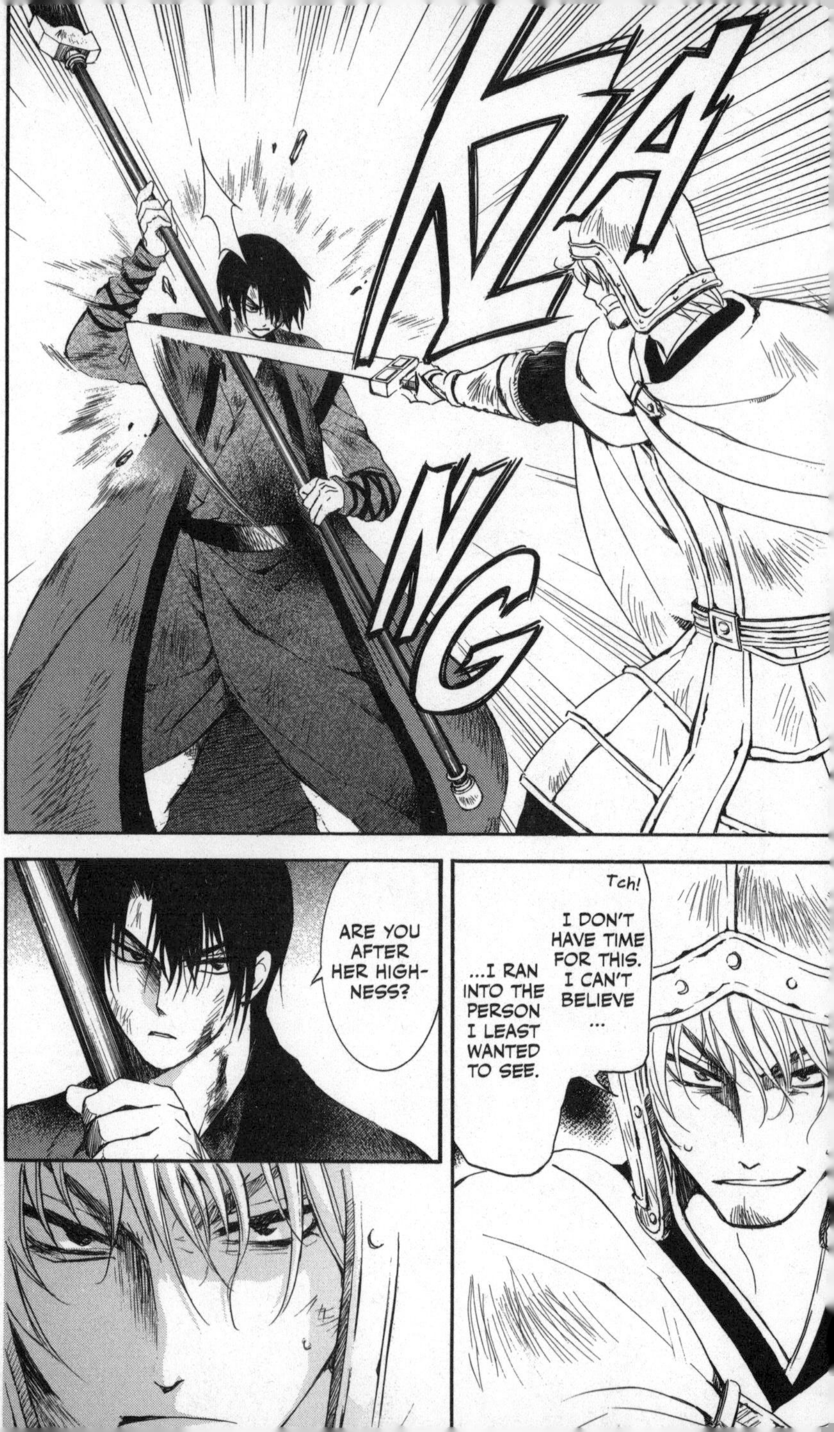
KANG
Tch!
I DON'T HAVE TIME FOR THIS. I CAN'T BELIEVE ...
...I RAN INTO THE PERSON I LEAST WANTED TO SEE.
ARE YOU AFTER HER HIGH-NESS?

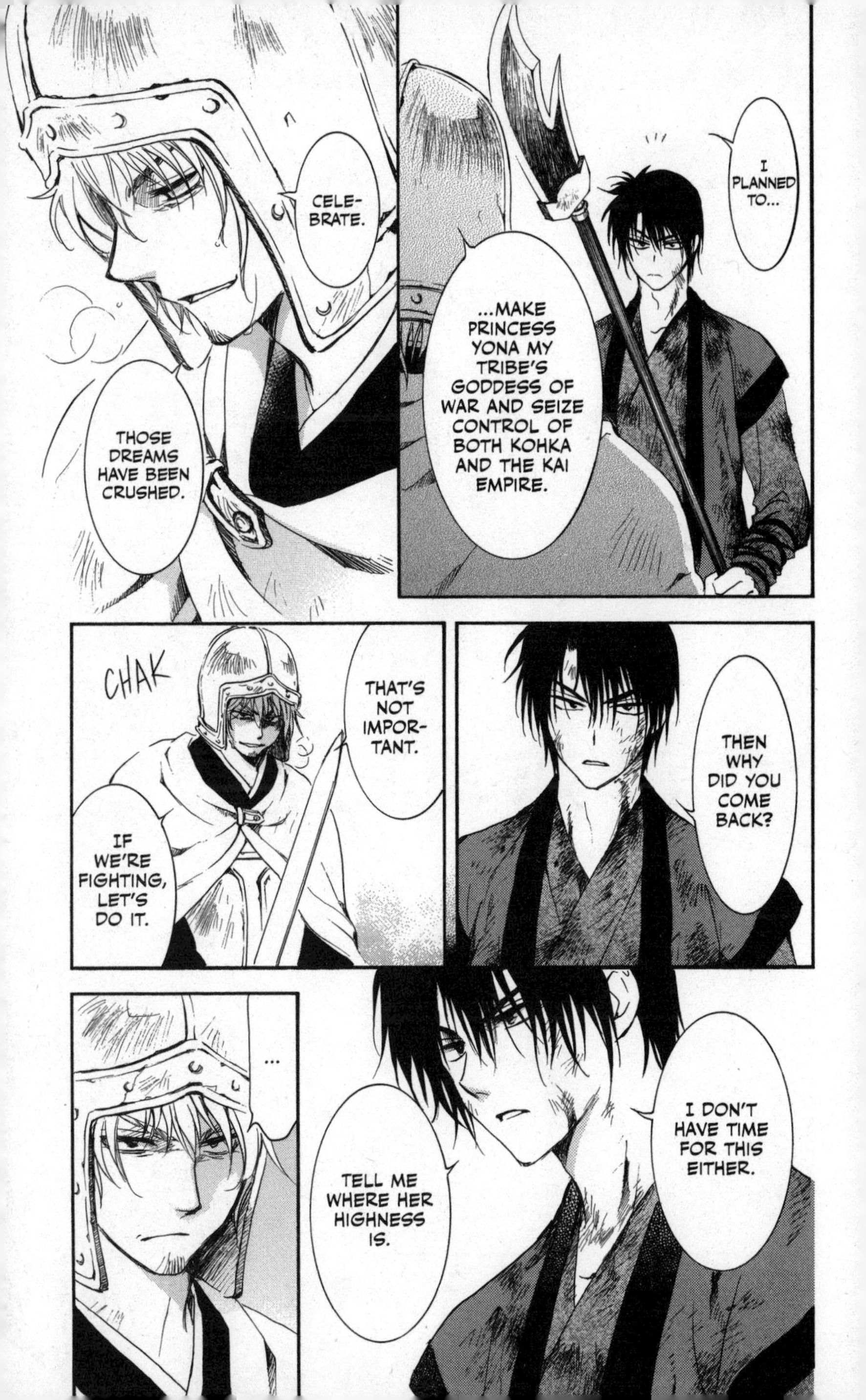
I PLANNED TO...
...MAKE PRINCESS YONA MY TRIBE'S GODDESS OF WAR AND SEIZE CONTROL OF BOTH KOHKA AND THE KAI EMPIRE.
CELE-BRATE.
THOSE DREAMS HAVE BEEN CRUSHED.
THEN WHY DID YOU COME BACK?
THAT'S NOT IMPOR-TANT.
CHAK
IF WE'RE FIGHTING, LET'S DO IT.
I DON'T HAVE TIME FOR THIS EITHER.
TELL ME WHERE HER HIGHNESS IS.
...

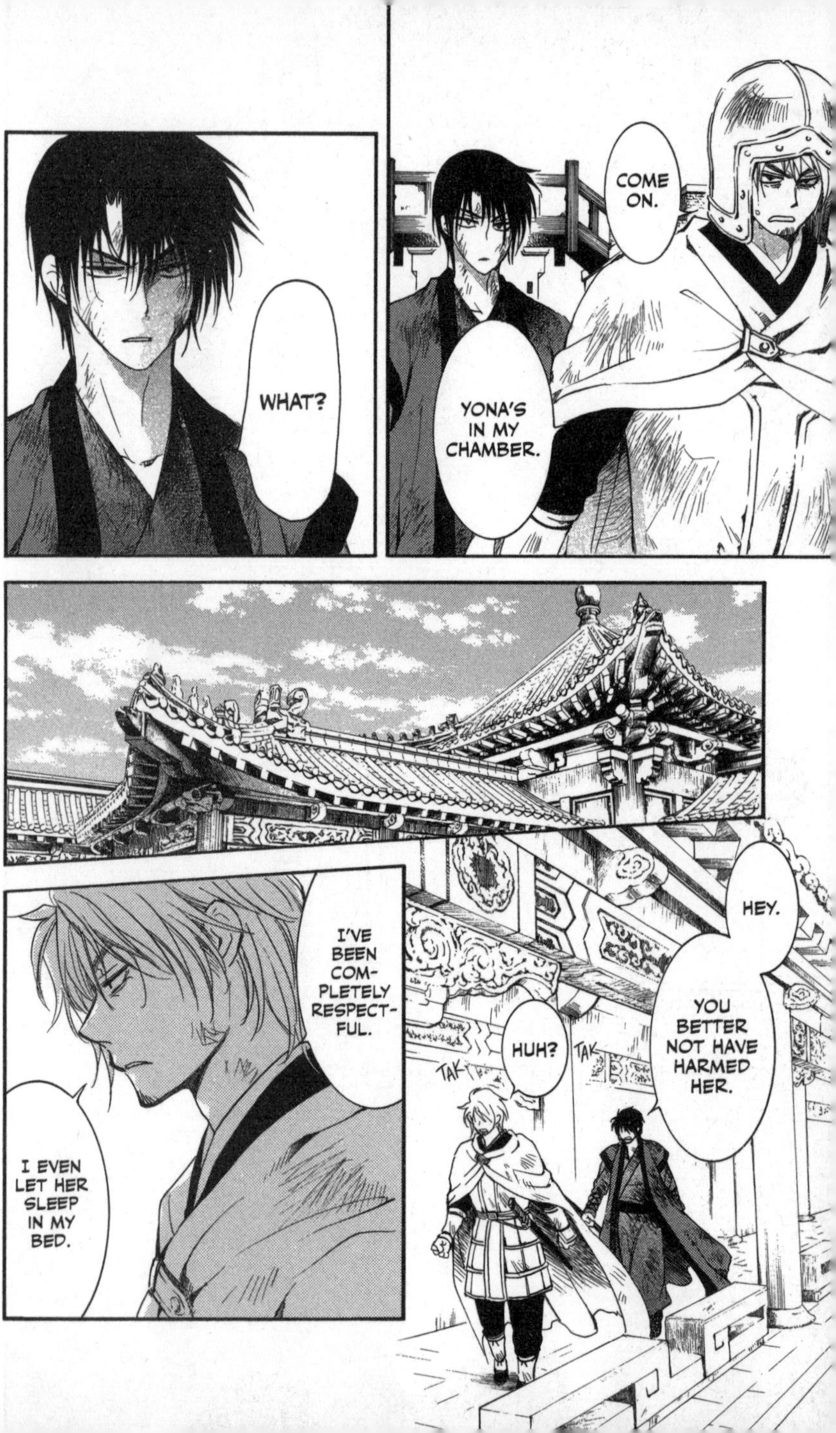
COME ON.
YONA'S IN MY CHAMBER.
WHAT?
HEY.
YOU BETTER NOT HAVE HARMED HER.
TAK
HUH?
TAK
I'VE BEEN COM- PLETELY RESPECT- FUL.
I EVEN LET HER SLEEP IN MY BED.

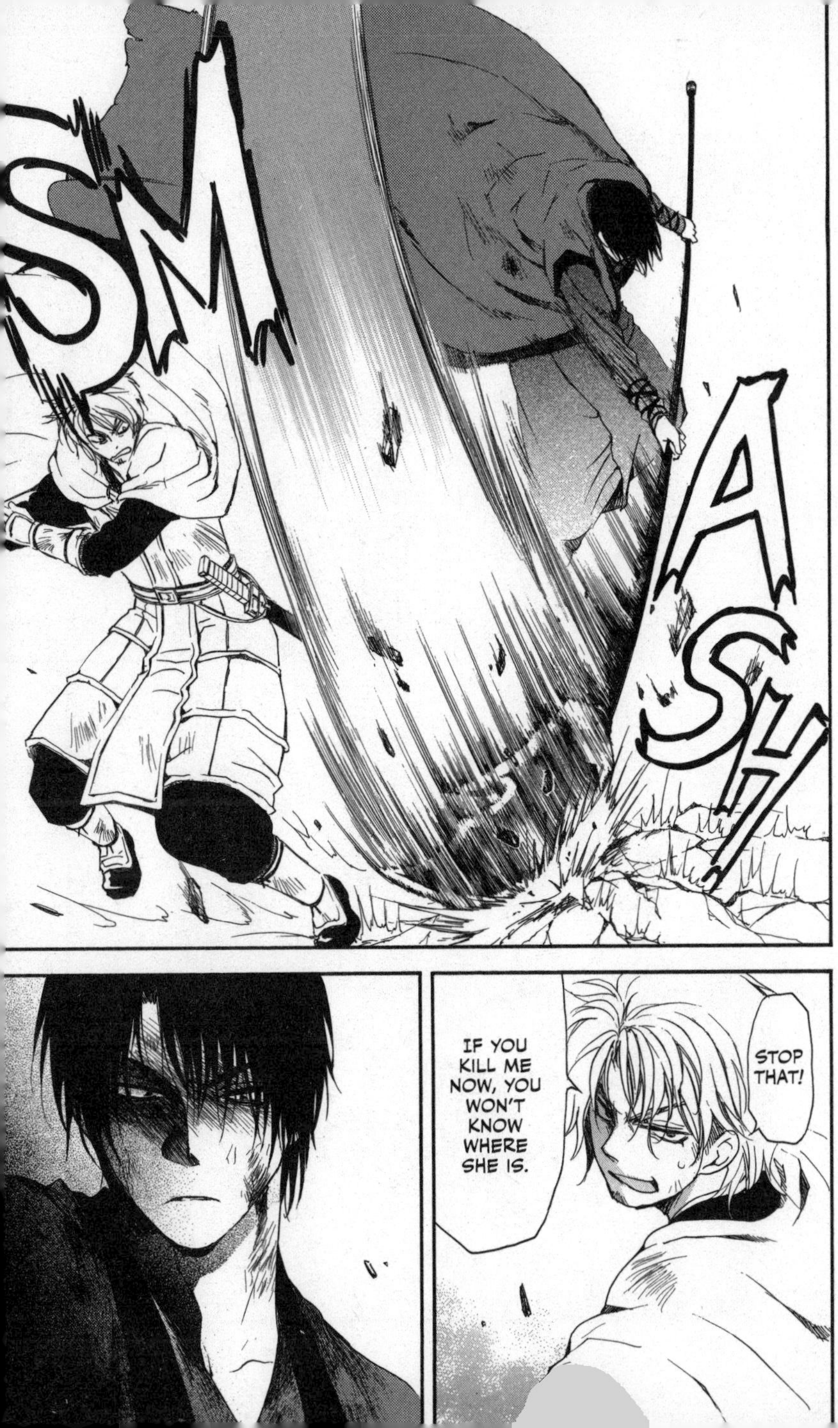
SMASH
STOP THAT!
IF YOU KILL ME NOW, YOU WON'T KNOW WHERE SHE IS.

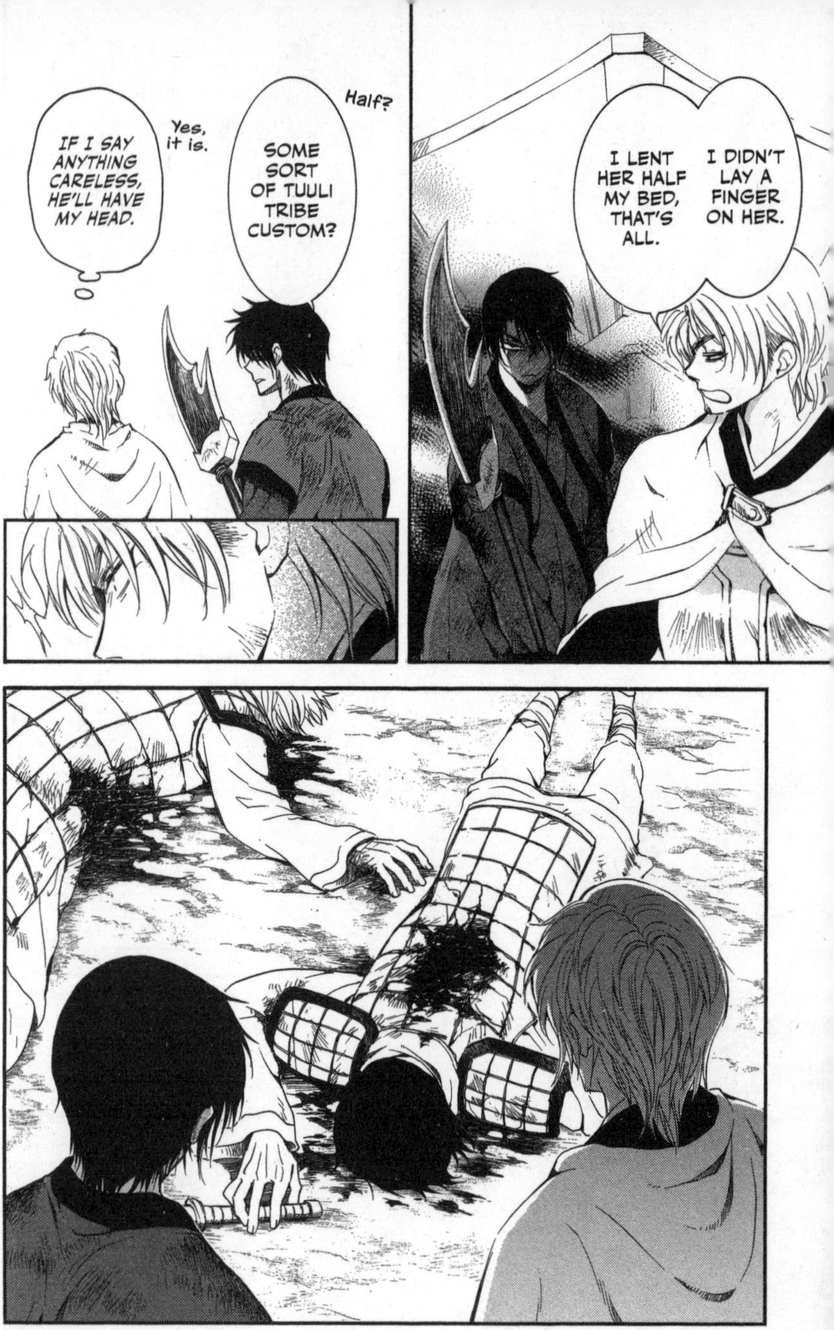
I DIDN'T LAY A FINGER ON HER.
I LENT HER HALF MY BED, THAT'S ALL.
Half?
SOME SORT OF TUULI TRIBE CUSTOM?
Yes, it is.
IF I SAY ANYTHING CARELESS, HE'LL HAVE MY HEAD.

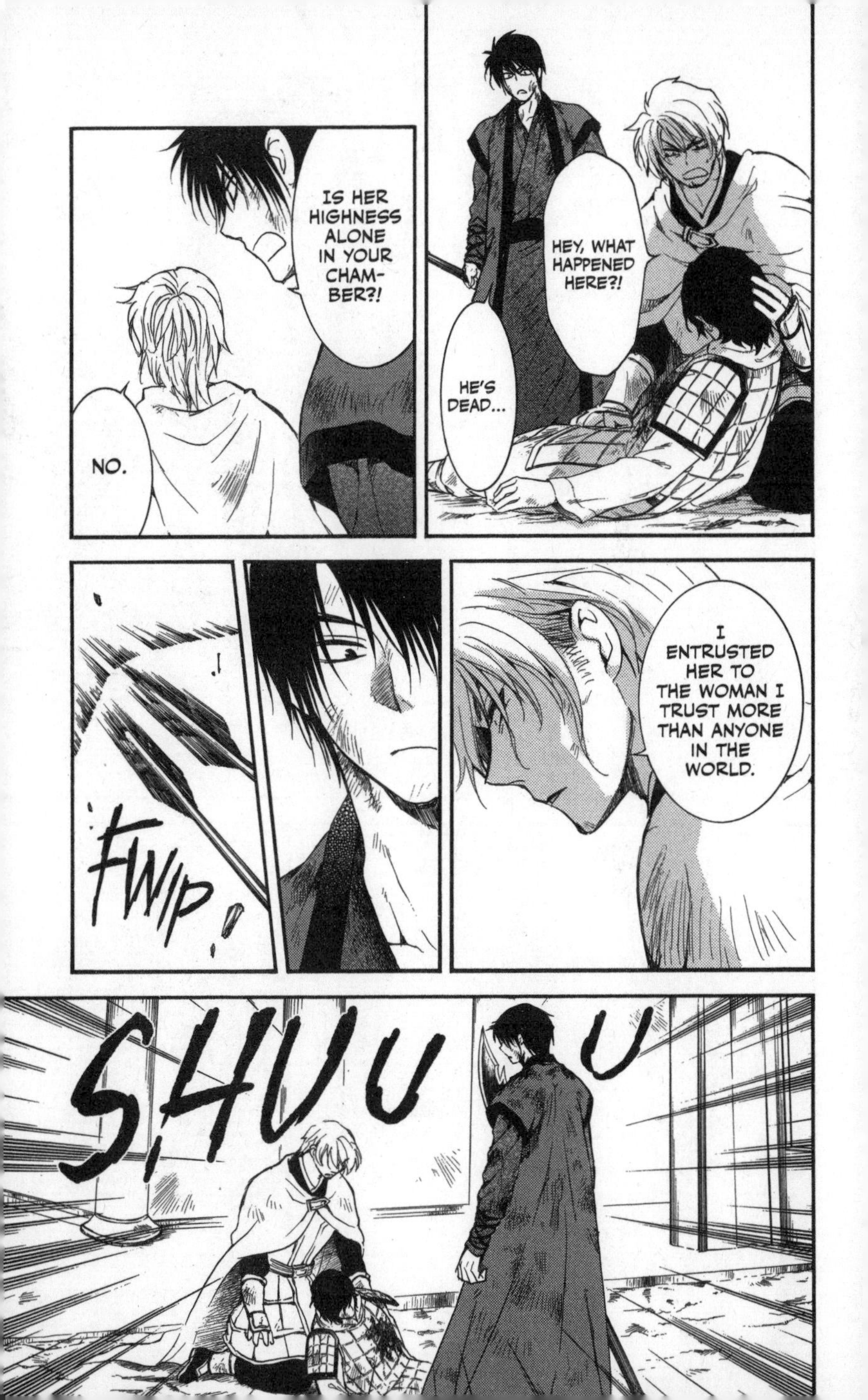
HEY, WHAT HAPPENED HERE?!
HE'S DEAD...
IS HER HIGHNESS ALONE IN YOUR CHAM-BER?!
NO.
I ENTRUSTED HER TO THE WOMAN I TRUST MORE THAN ANYONE IN THE WORLD.
FWIP
SHUU U

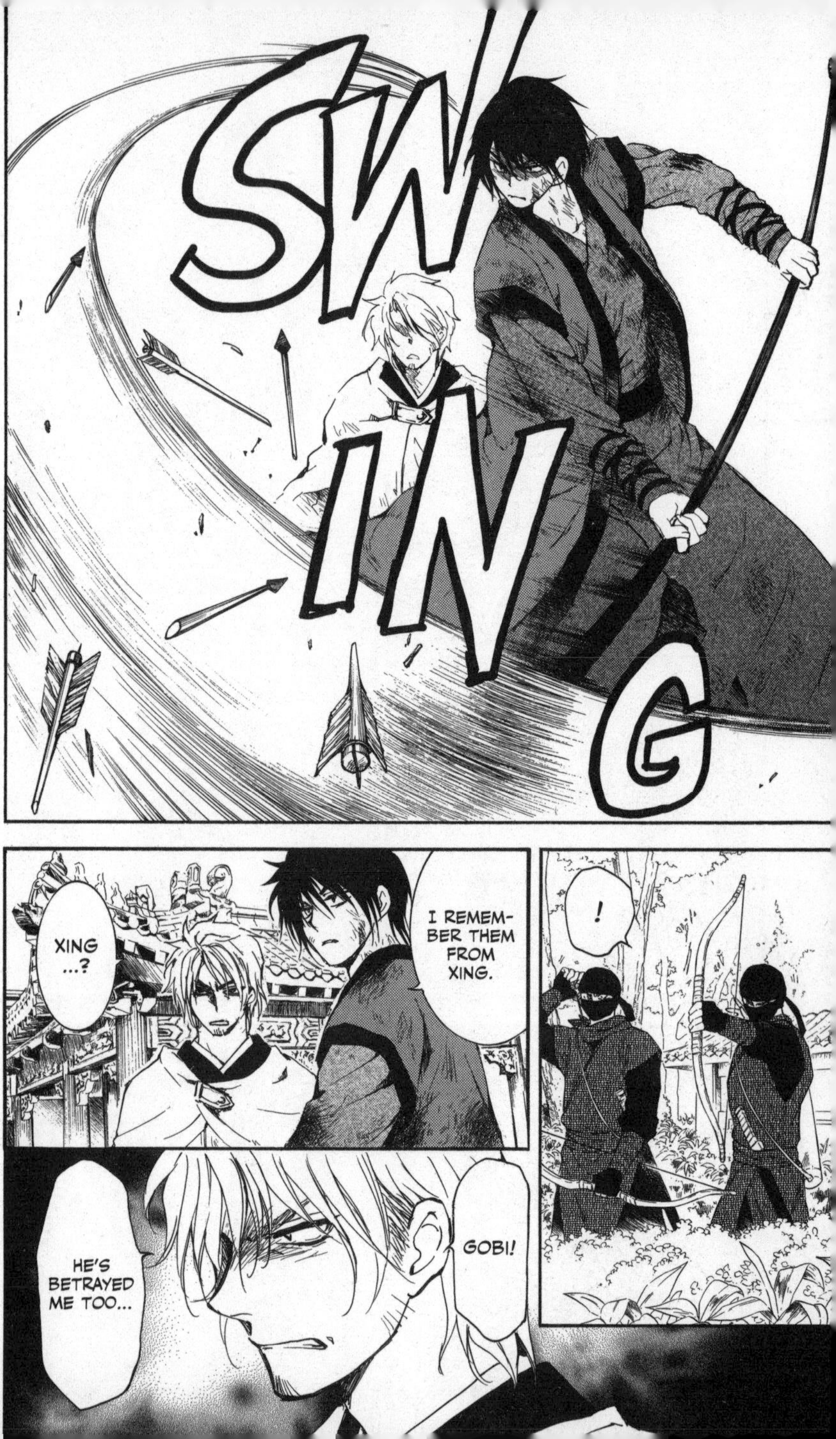
SWING
!
I REMEMBER THEM FROM XING.
XING ...?
GOBI!
HE'S BETRAYED ME TOO...

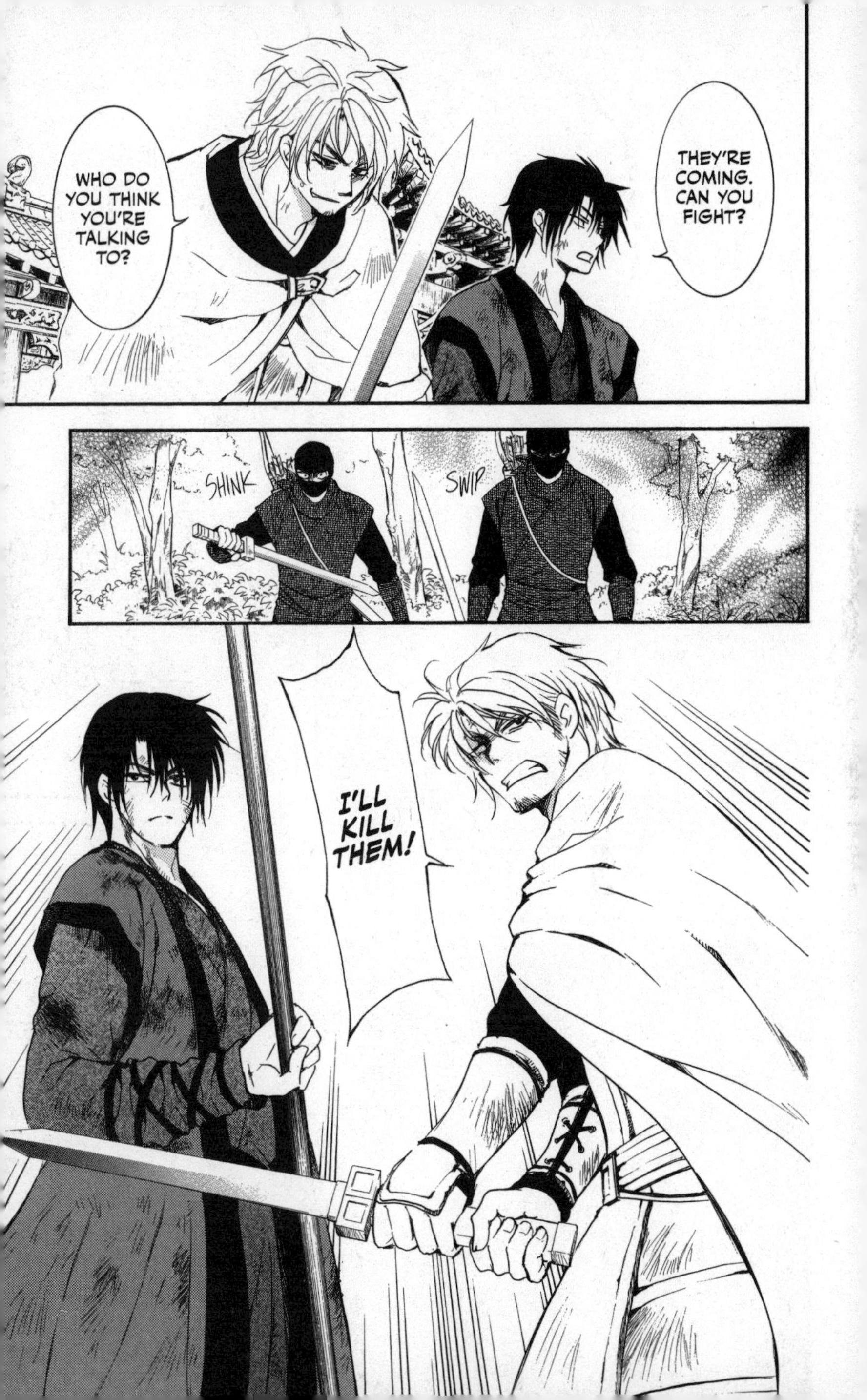
THEY'RE COMING. CAN YOU FIGHT?
WHO DO YOU THINK YOU'RE TALKING TO?
SWIP
SHINK
I'LL KILL THEM!

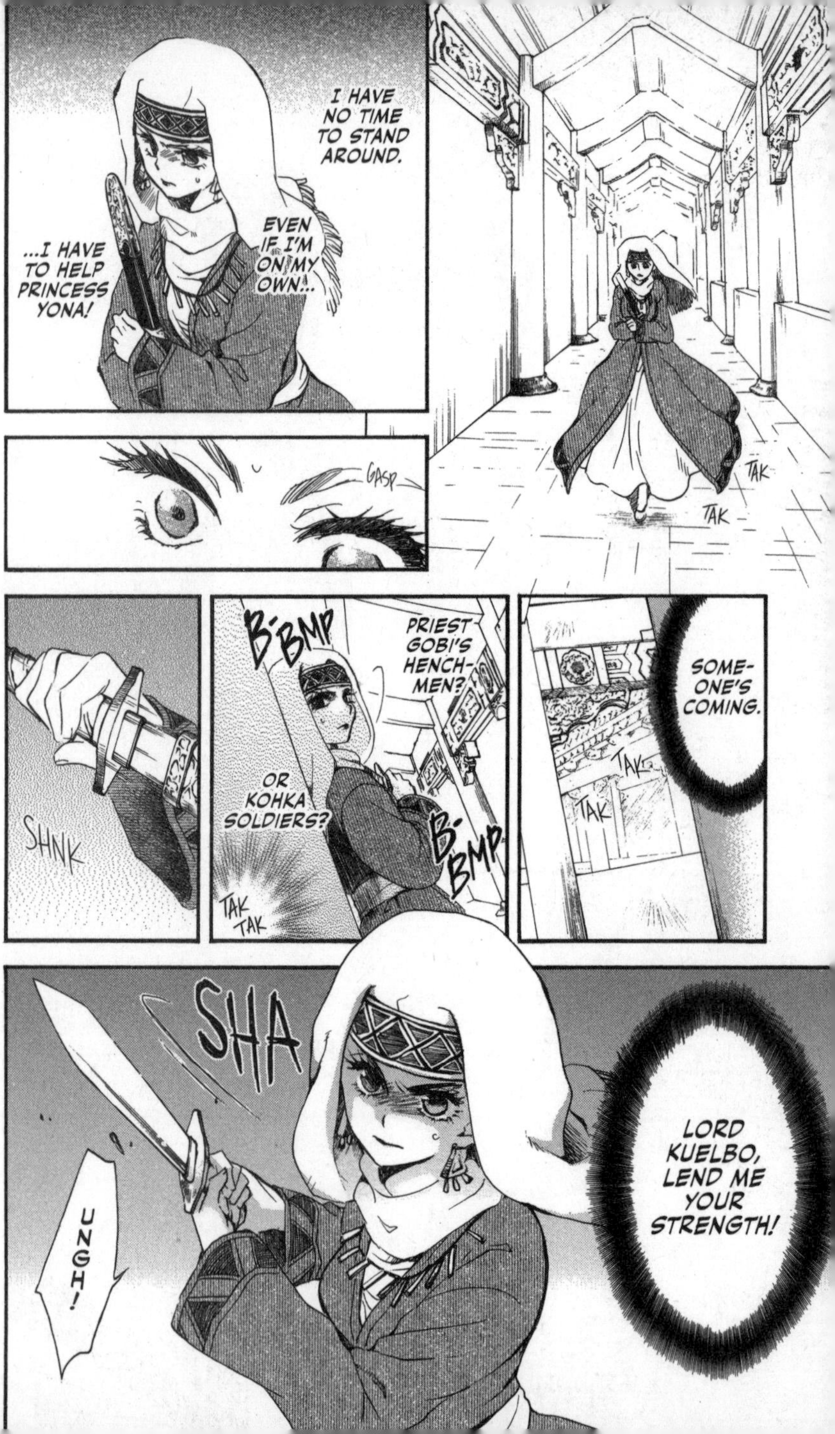
TAK
TAK
I HAVE NO TIME TO STAND AROUND.
EVEN IF I'M ON MY OWN...
...I HAVE TO HELP PRINCESS YONA!
GASP
SOME-ONE'S COMING.
TAK
TAK
PRIEST GOBI'S HENCH-MEN?
B-BMP
OR KOHKA SOLDIERS?
B-BMP
TAK TAK
SHNK
SHA
LORD KUELBO, LEND ME YOUR STRENGTH!
UNGH!

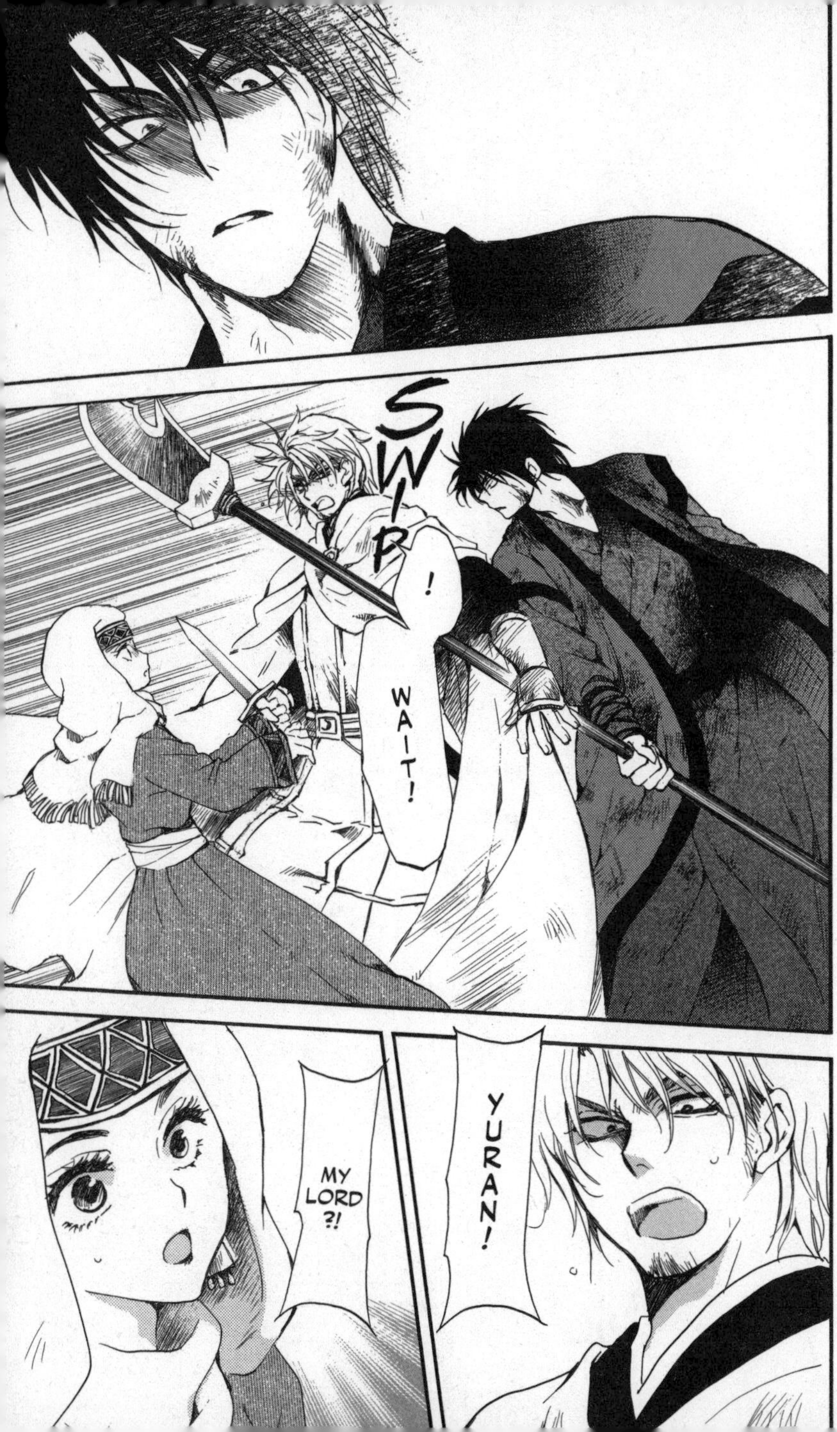
SWIP
!
WAIT!
YURAN!
MY LORD?!

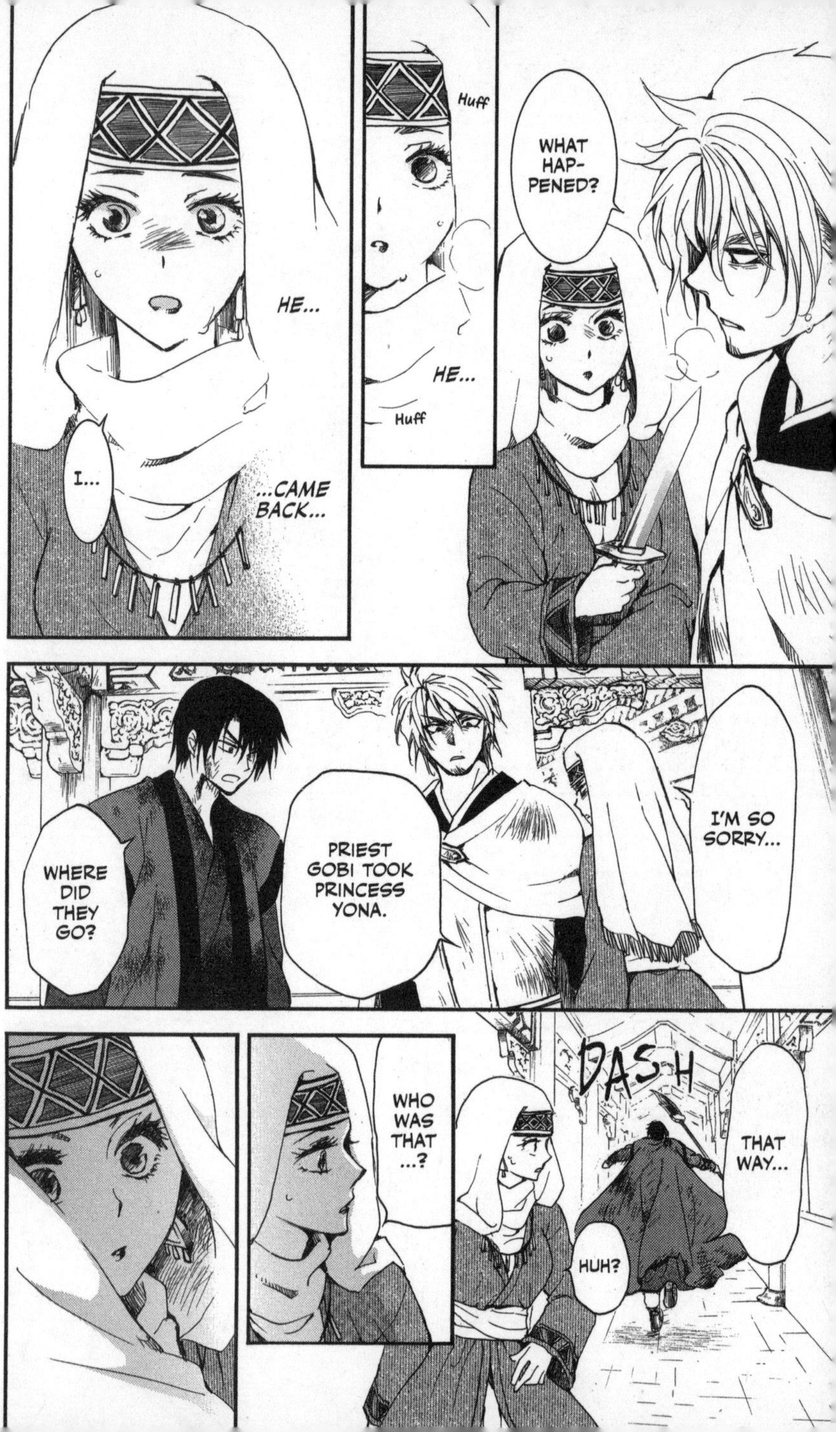
WHAT HAP-PENED?
Huff
HE...
Huff
HE...
I...
...CAME BACK...
I'M SO SORRY...
PRIEST GOBI TOOK PRINCESS YONA.
WHERE DID THEY GO?
THAT WAY...
DASH
HUH?
WHO WAS THAT ...?

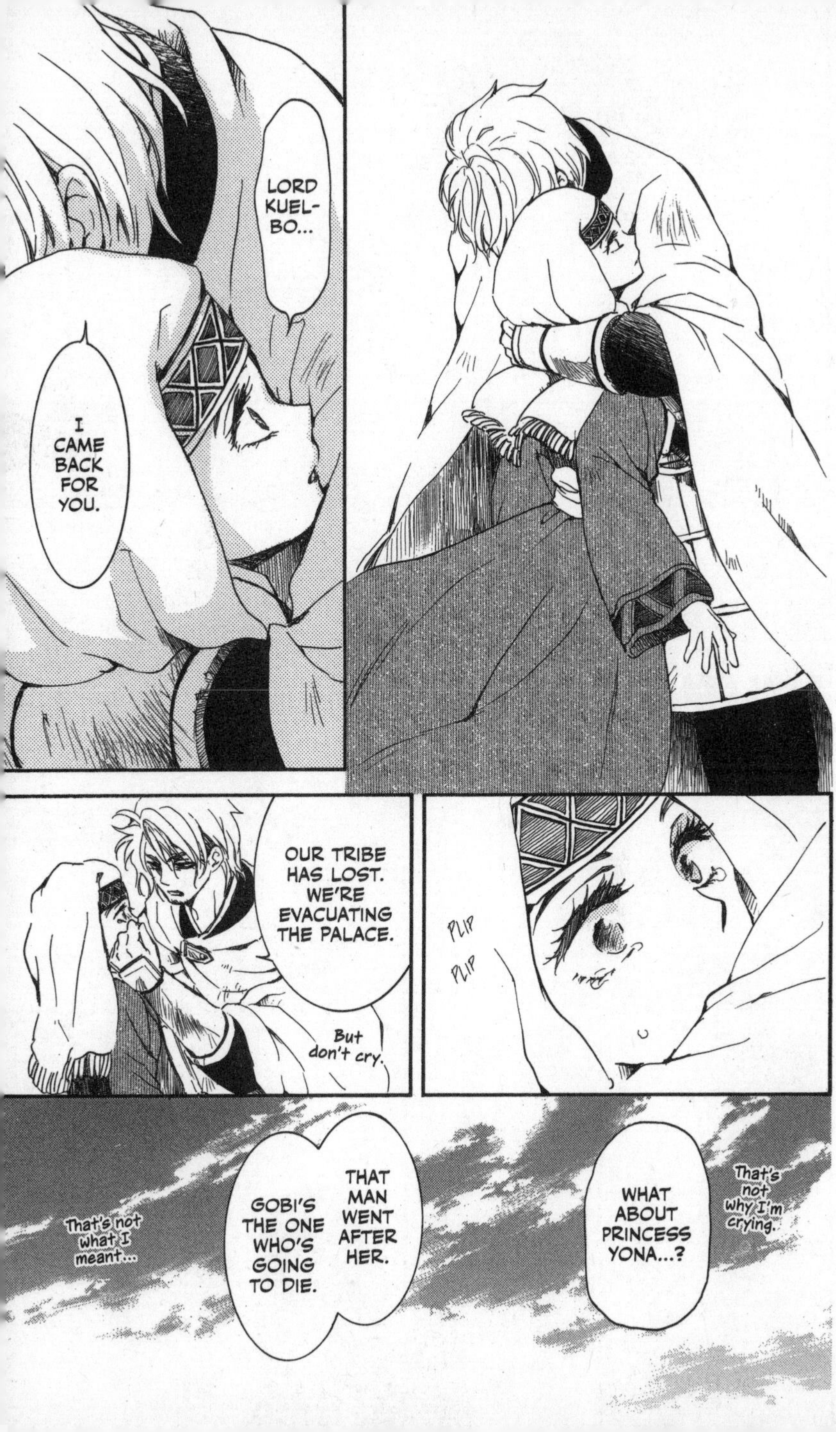
LORD KUEL-BO...
I CAME BACK FOR YOU.
PLIP
PLIP
OUR TRIBE HAS LOST. WE'RE EVACUATING THE PALACE.
But don't cry.
That's not why I'm crying.
WHAT ABOUT PRINCESS YONA...?
THAT MAN WENT AFTER HER.
GOBI'S THE ONE WHO'S GOING TO DIE.
That's not what I meant...

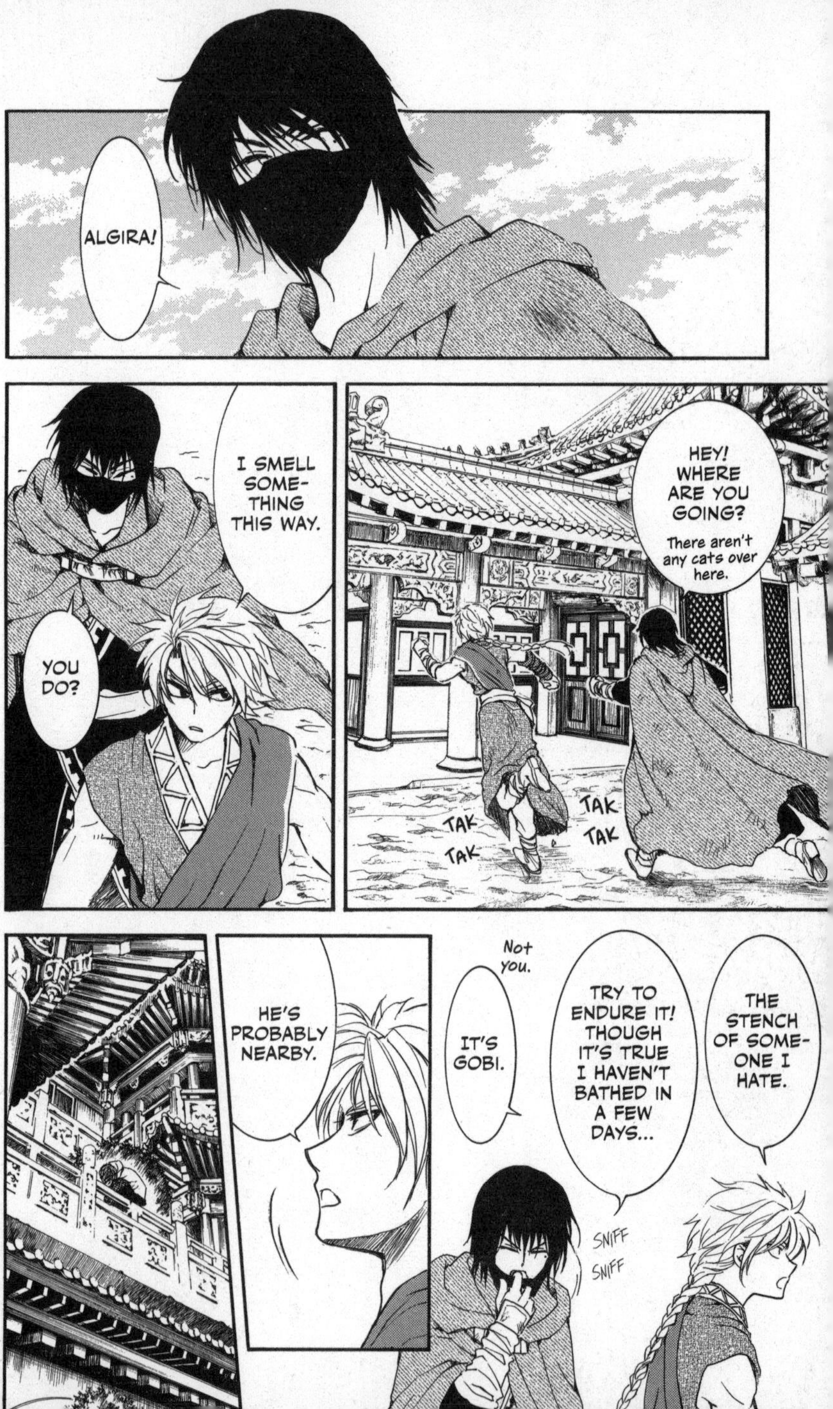
ALGIRA!
HEY! WHERE ARE YOU GOING?
There aren't any cats over here.
TAK TAK
TAK TAK
I SMELL SOME-THING THIS WAY.
YOU DO?
THE STENCH OF SOME-ONE I HATE.
TRY TO ENDURE IT! THOUGH IT'S TRUE I HAVEN'T BATHED IN A FEW DAYS...
SNIFF SNIFF
Not you.
IT'S GOBI.
HE'S PROBABLY NEARBY.

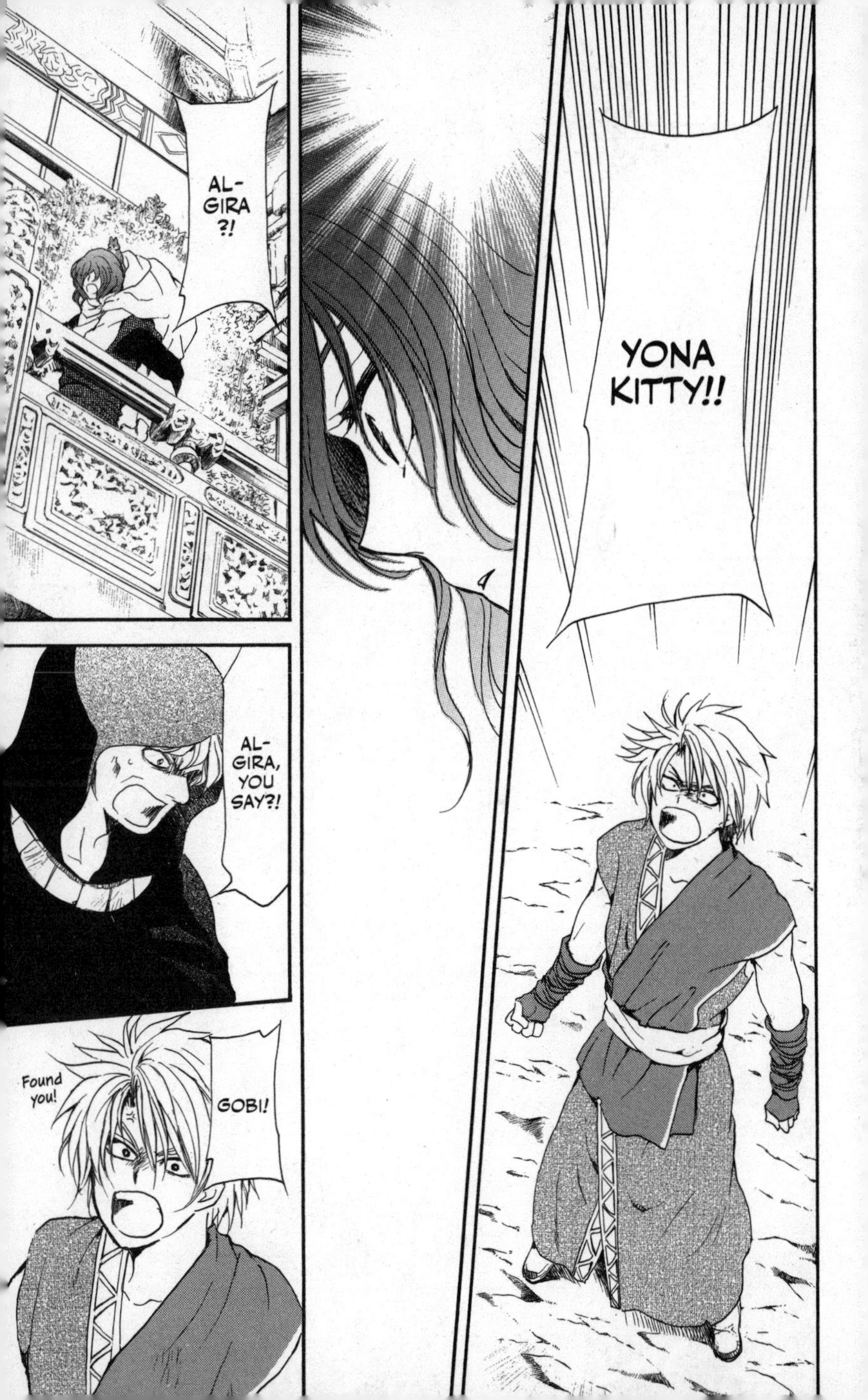
YONA KITTY!!
AL-GIRA?!
AL-GIRA, YOU SAY?!
GOBI!
Found you!

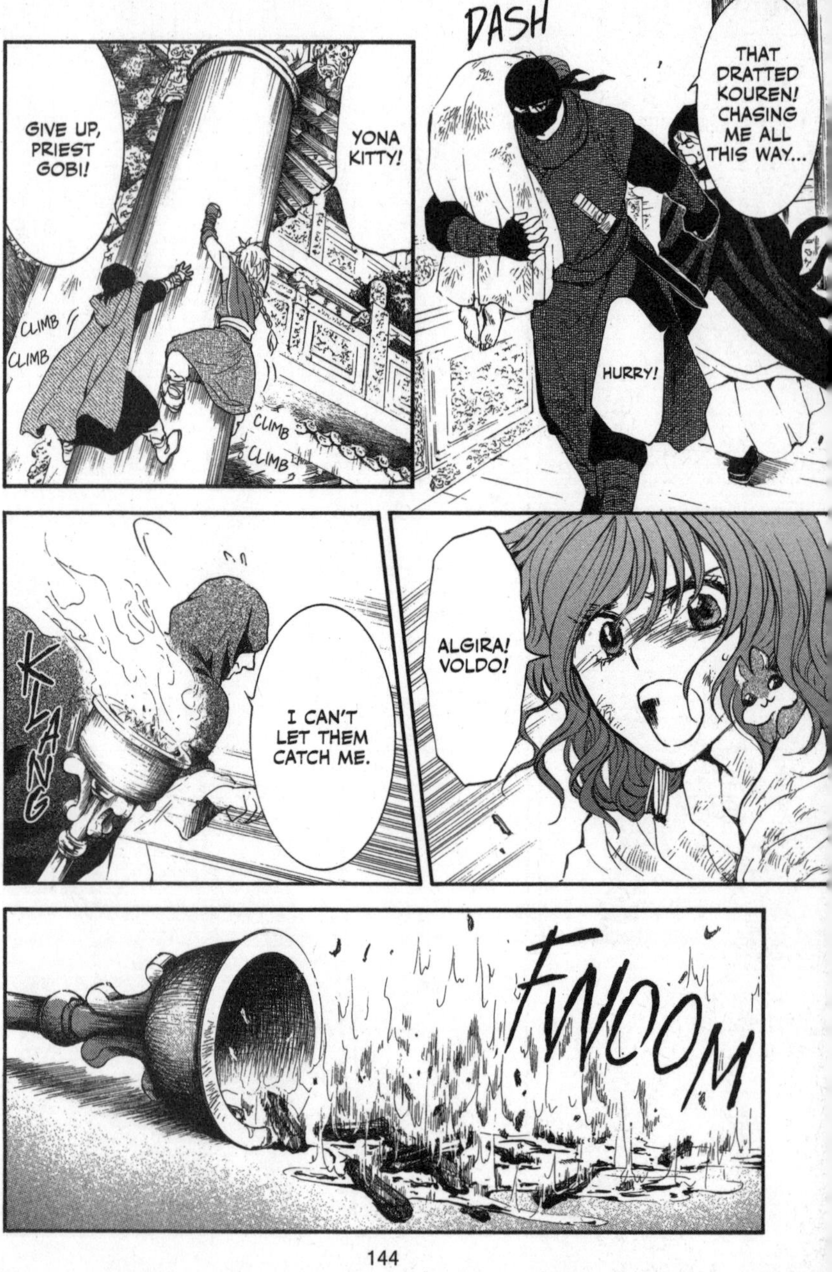
DASH
THAT DRATTED KOUREN! CHASING ME ALL THIS WAY...
HURRY!
YONA KITTY!
GIVE UP, PRIEST GOBI!
CLIMB
CLIMB
CLIMB
CLIMB
ALGIRA! VOLDO!
I CAN'T LET THEM CATCH ME.
KLANG
FWOOM

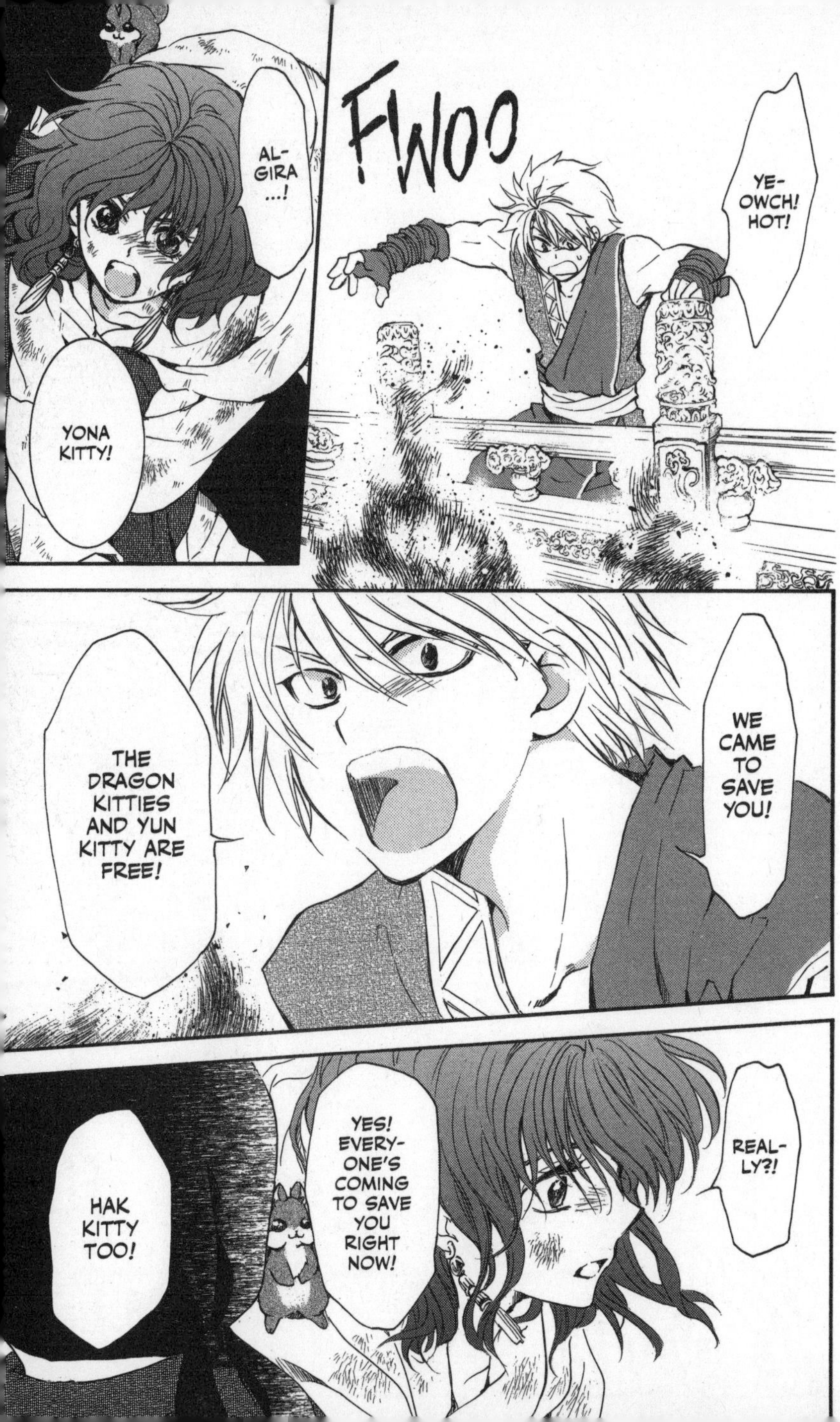
YE-OWCH! HOT!
FWOO
AL-GIRA ...!
YONA KITTY!
WE CAME TO SAVE YOU!
THE DRAGON KITTIES AND YUN KITTY ARE FREE!
REAL-LY?!
YES! EVERY-ONE'S COMING TO SAVE YOU RIGHT NOW!
HAK KITTY TOO!

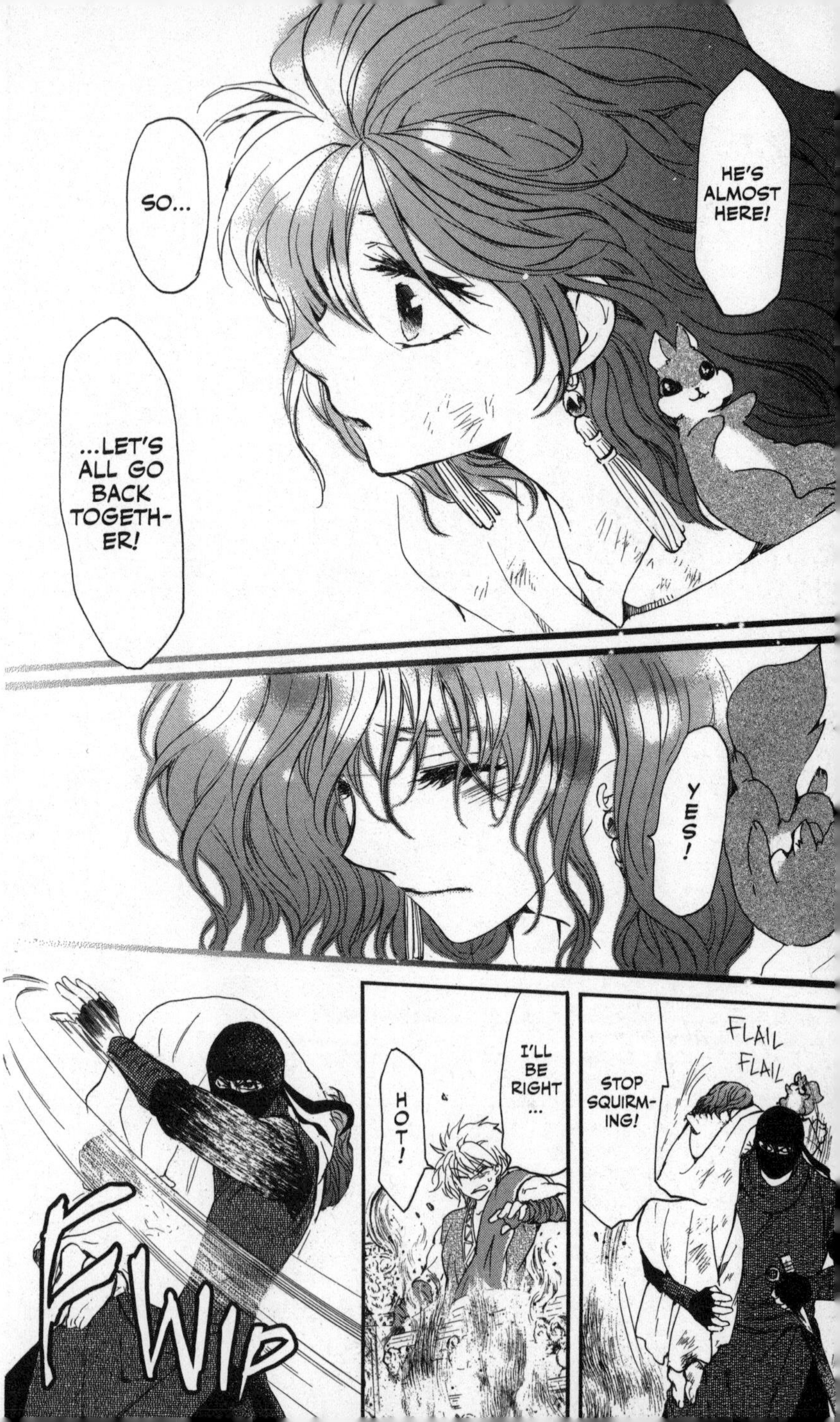
HE'S ALMOST HERE!
SO...
...LET'S ALL GO BACK TOGETH-ER!
YES!
FLAIL FLAIL
STOP SQUIRM-ING!
I'LL BE RIGHT ...
HOT!
FWIP

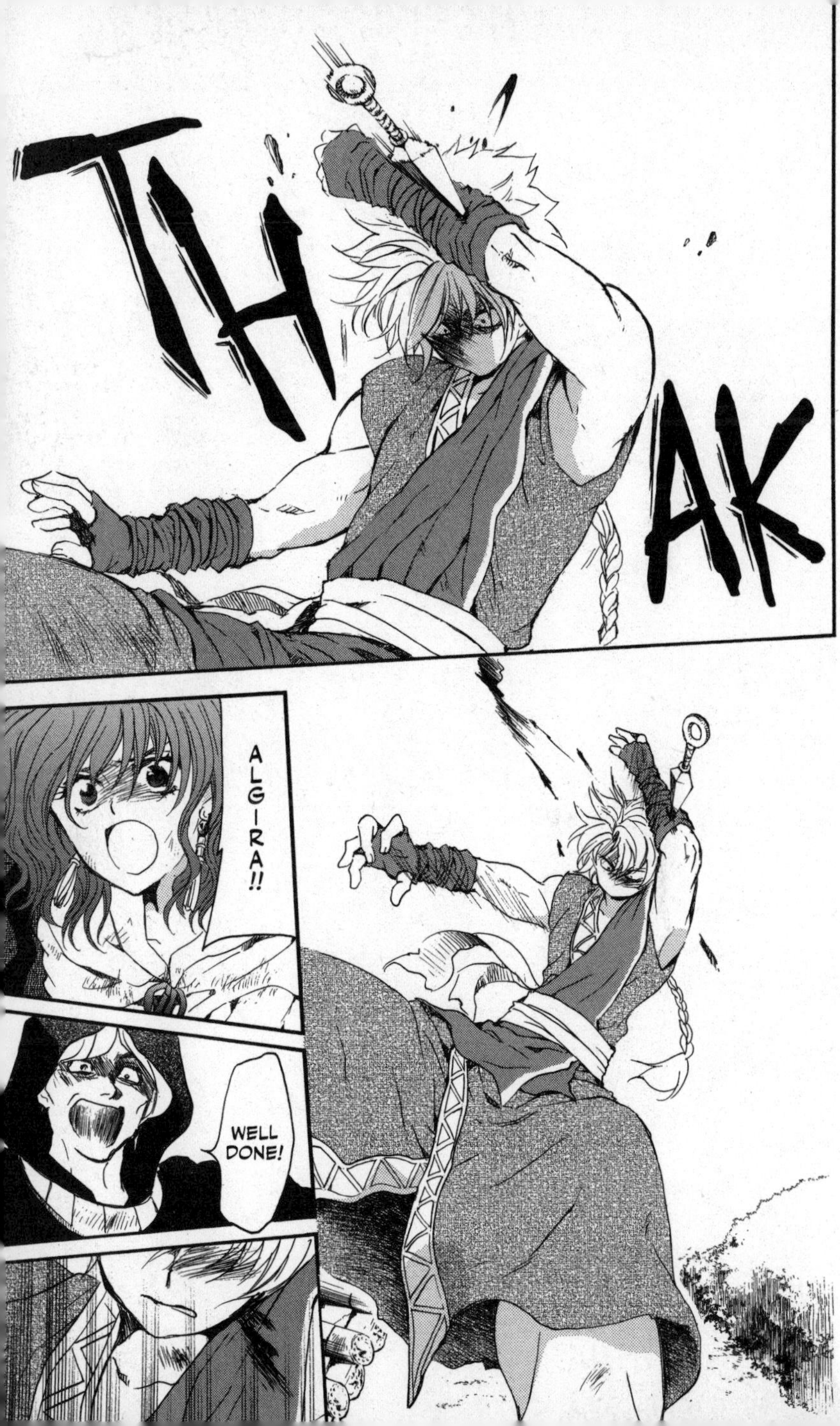
THWAK
ALGIRA!!
WELL DONE!

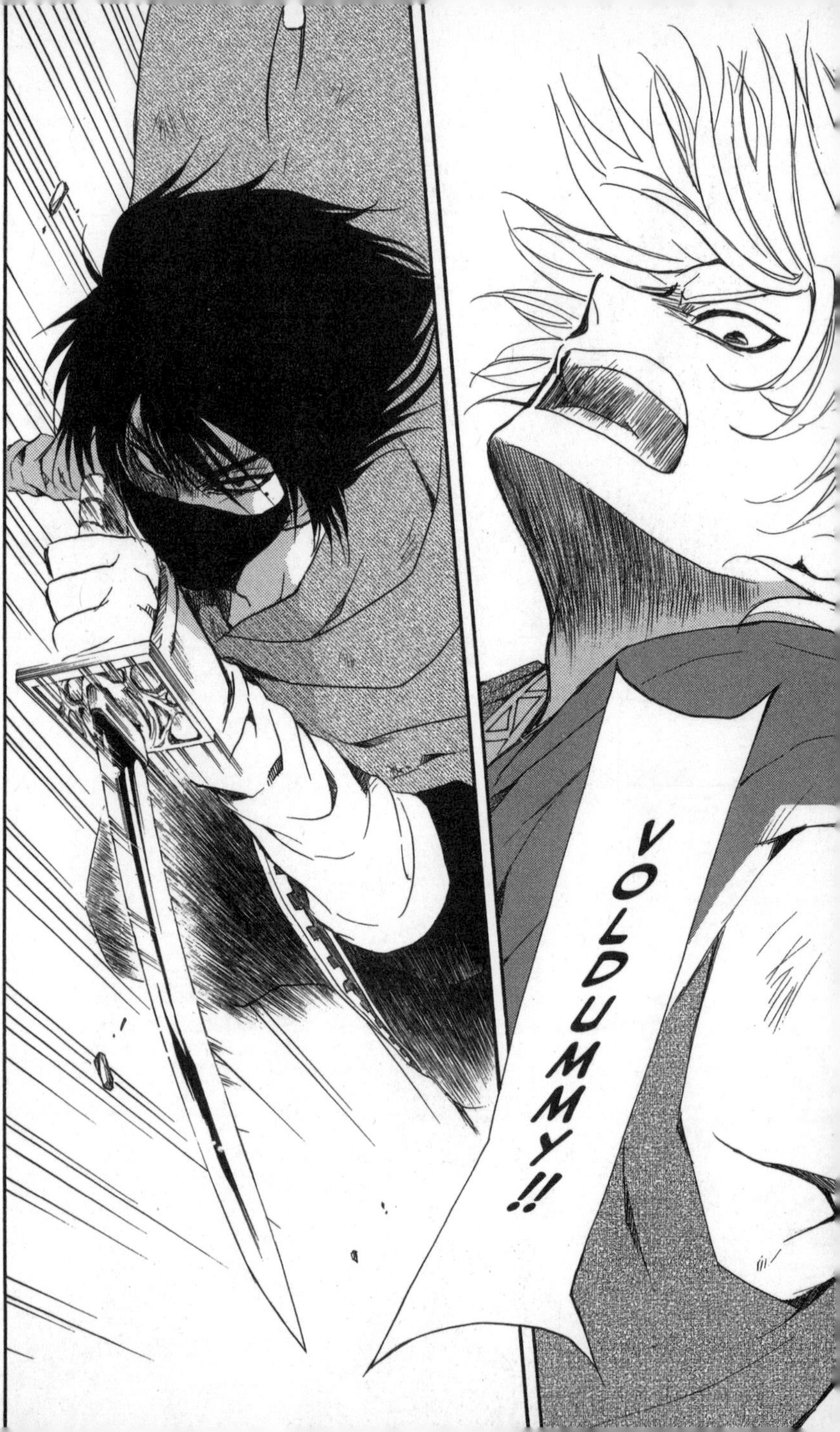
VOLDUMMY!!

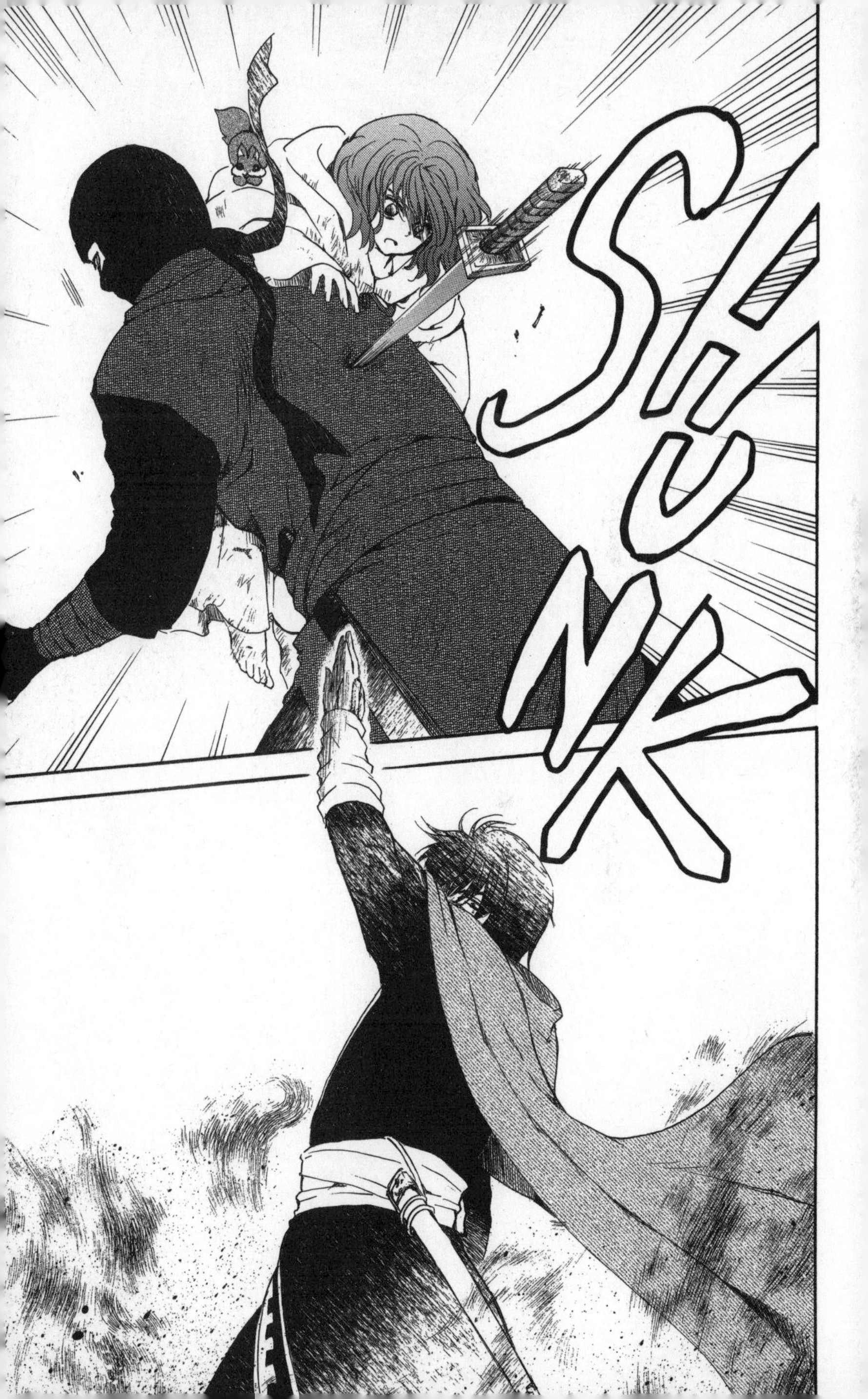
SHUNK

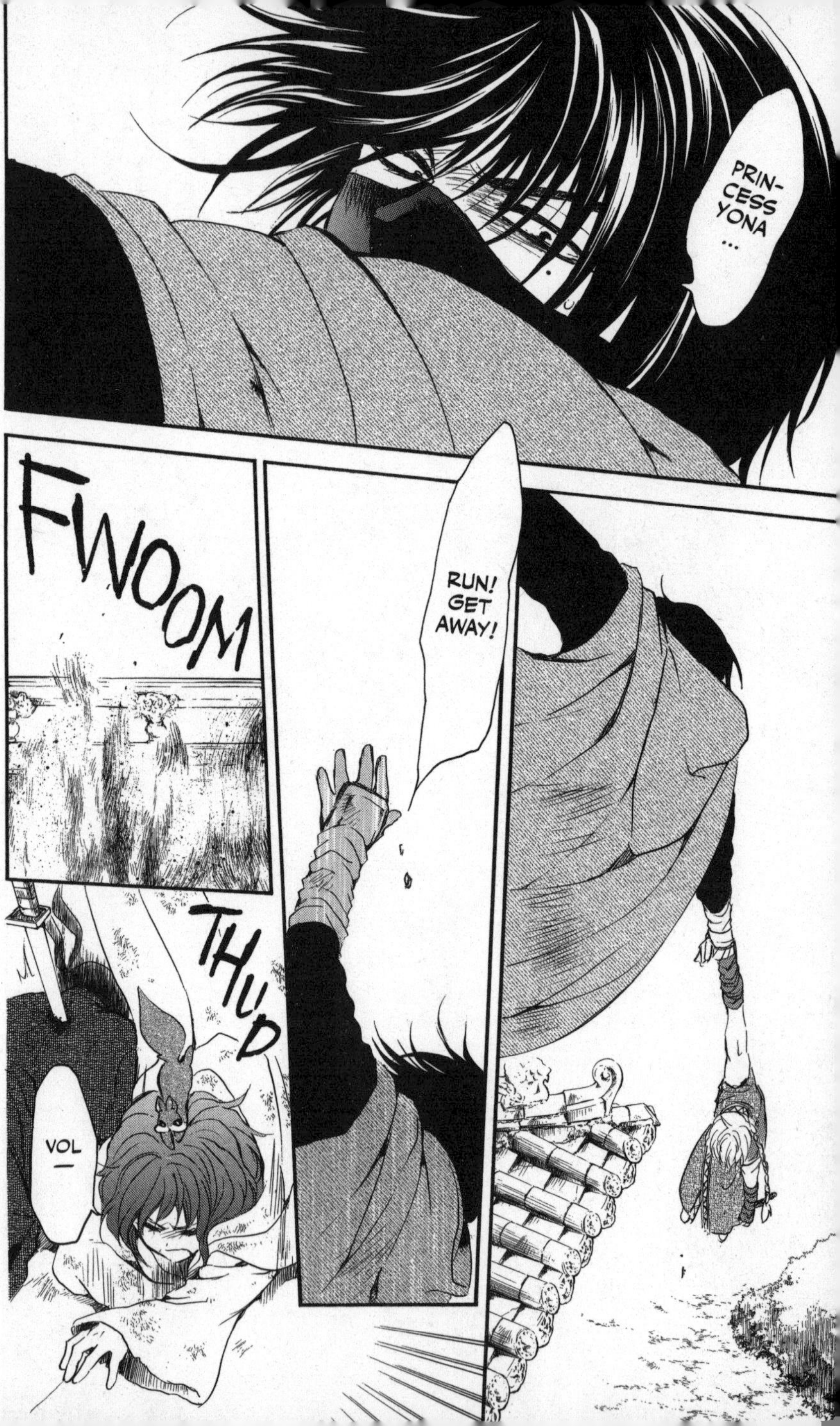
PRINCESS YONA...
RUN! GET AWAY!
FWOOM
THUD
VOL—

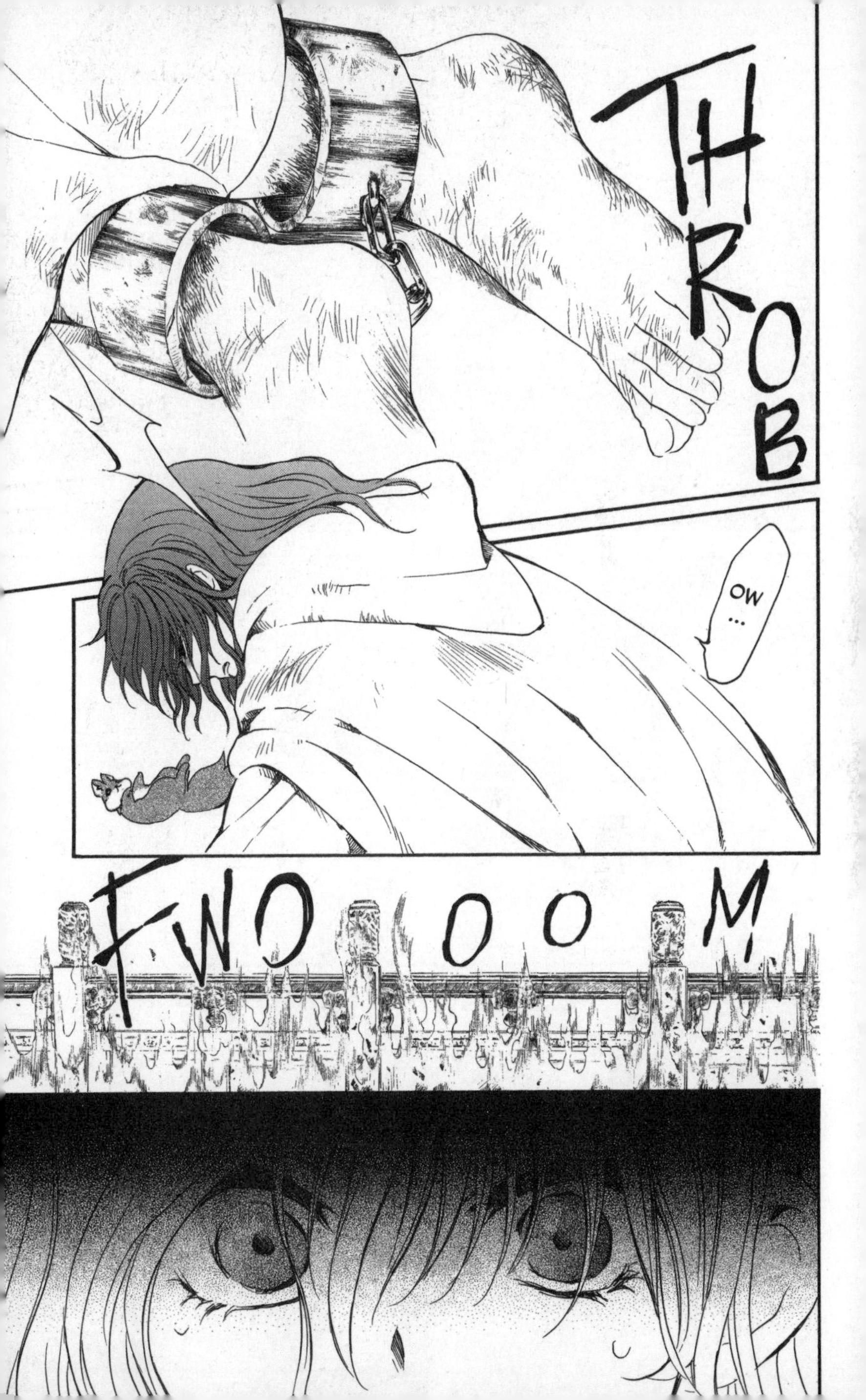
THROB
OW...
FWOOOM

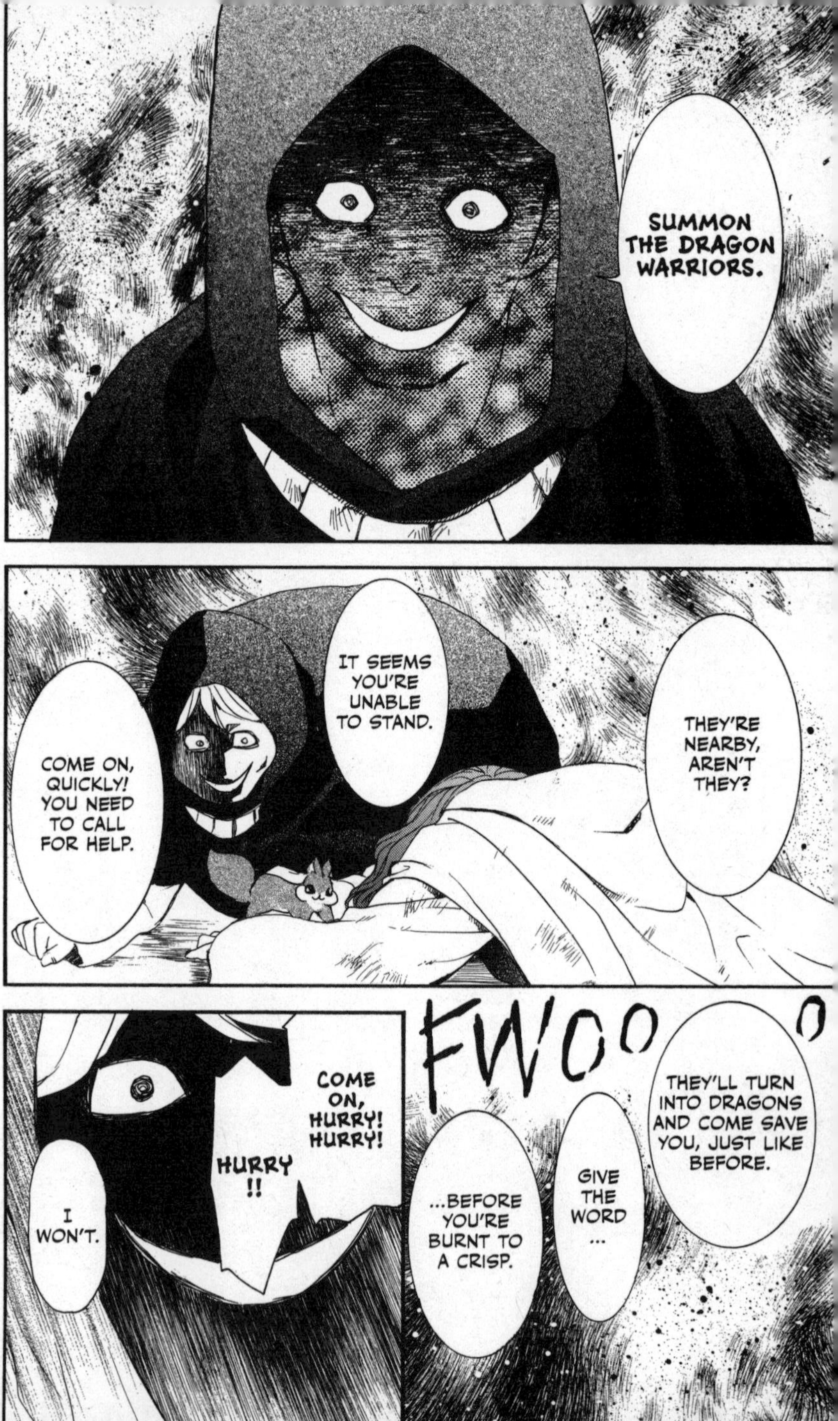
SUMMON THE DRAGON WARRIORS.
THEY'RE NEARBY, AREN'T THEY?
IT SEEMS YOU'RE UNABLE TO STAND.
COME ON, QUICKLY! YOU NEED TO CALL FOR HELP.
FWOOO
THEY'LL TURN INTO DRAGONS AND COME SAVE YOU, JUST LIKE BEFORE.
GIVE THE WORD ...
...BEFORE YOU'RE BURNT TO A CRISP.
COME ON, HURRY! HURRY!
HURRY !!
I WON'T.

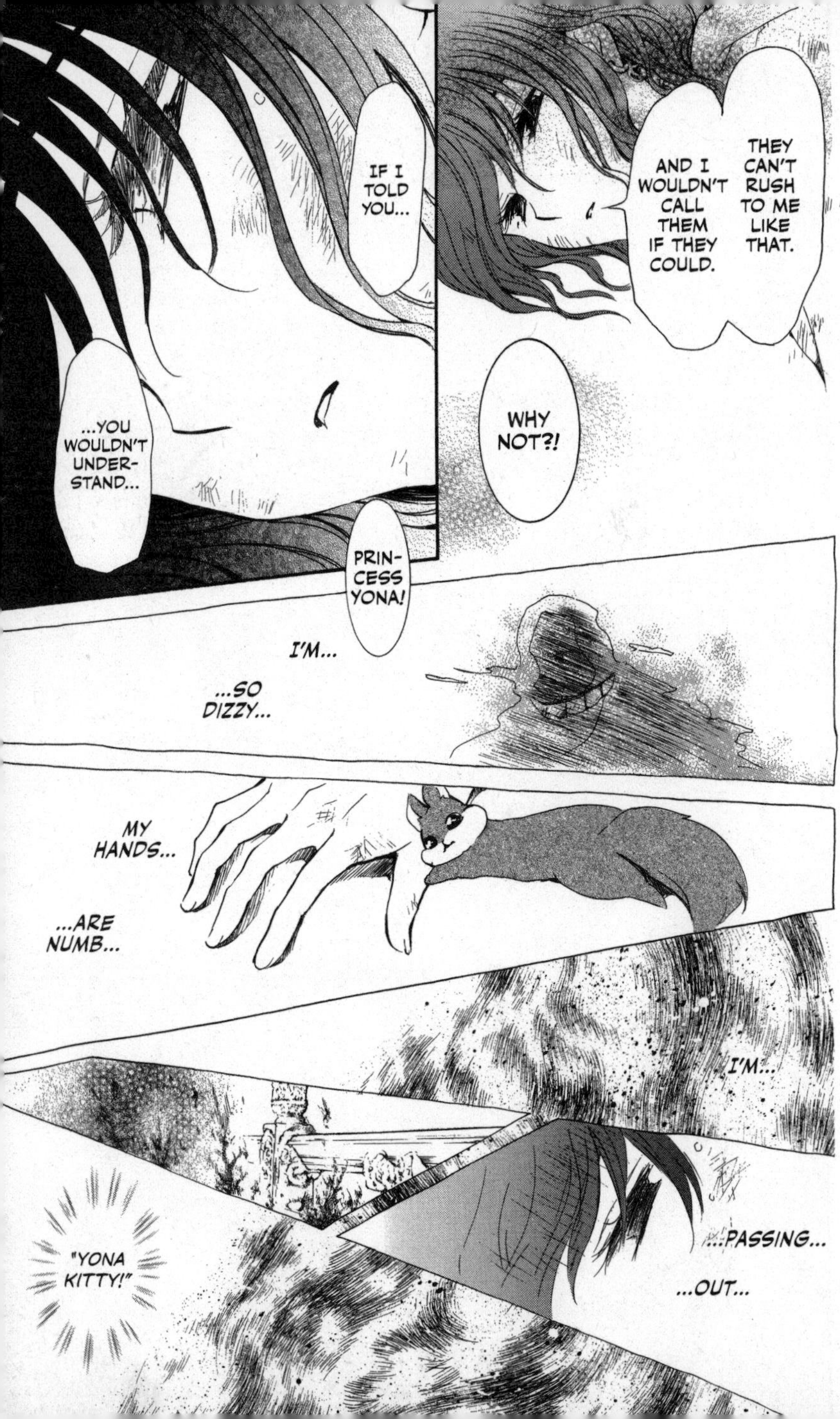
THEY CAN'T RUSH TO ME LIKE THAT.
AND I WOULDN'T CALL THEM IF THEY COULD.
WHY NOT?!
IF I TOLD YOU...
...YOU WOULDN'T UNDER-STAND...
PRIN-CESS YONA!
I'M...
...SO DIZZY...
MY HANDS...
...ARE NUMB...
I'M...
...PASSING...
...OUT...
"YONA KITTY!"

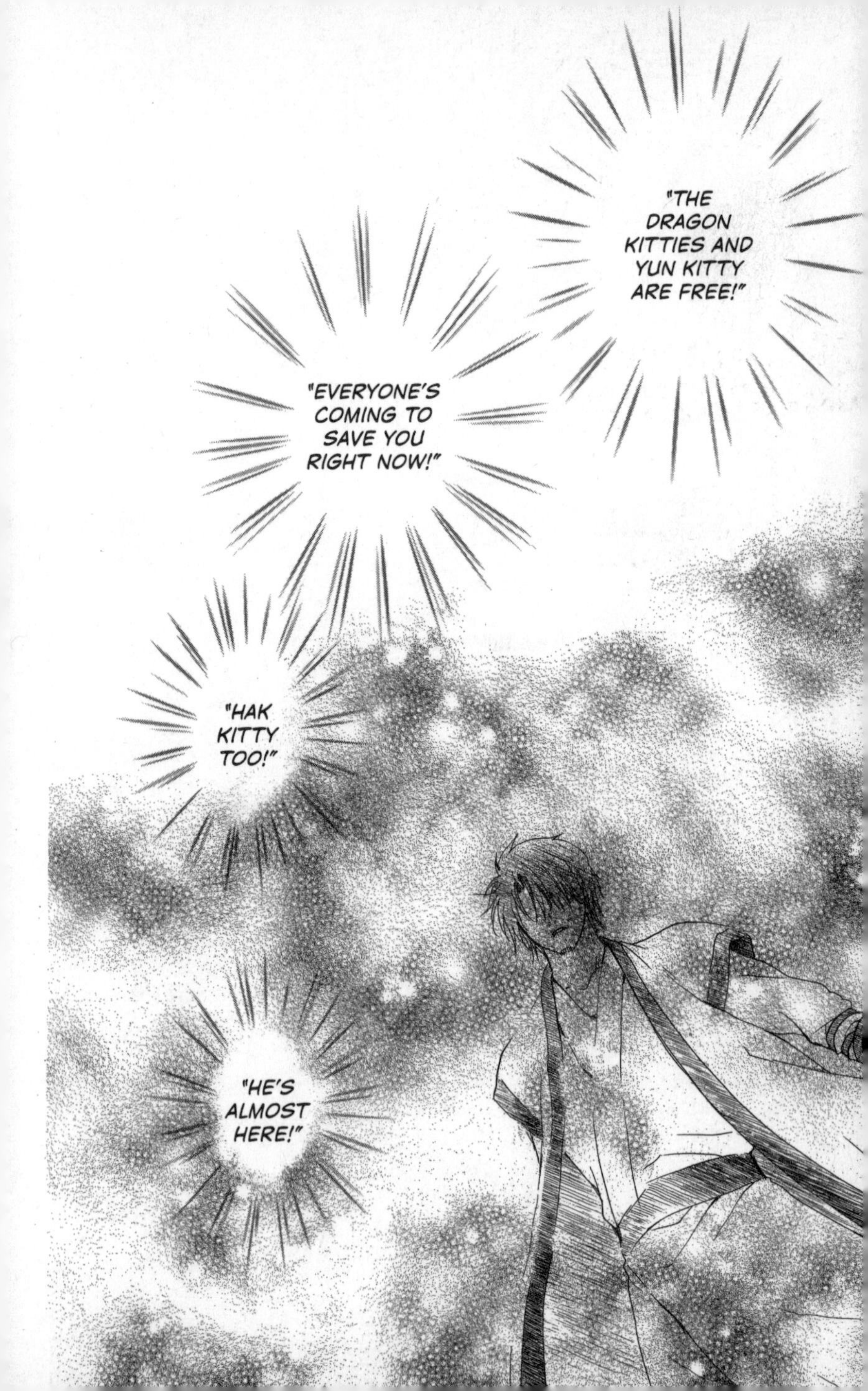
"THE DRAGON KITTIES AND YUN KITTY ARE FREE!"
"EVERYONE'S COMING TO SAVE YOU RIGHT NOW!"
"HAK KITTY TOO!"
"HE'S ALMOST HERE!"

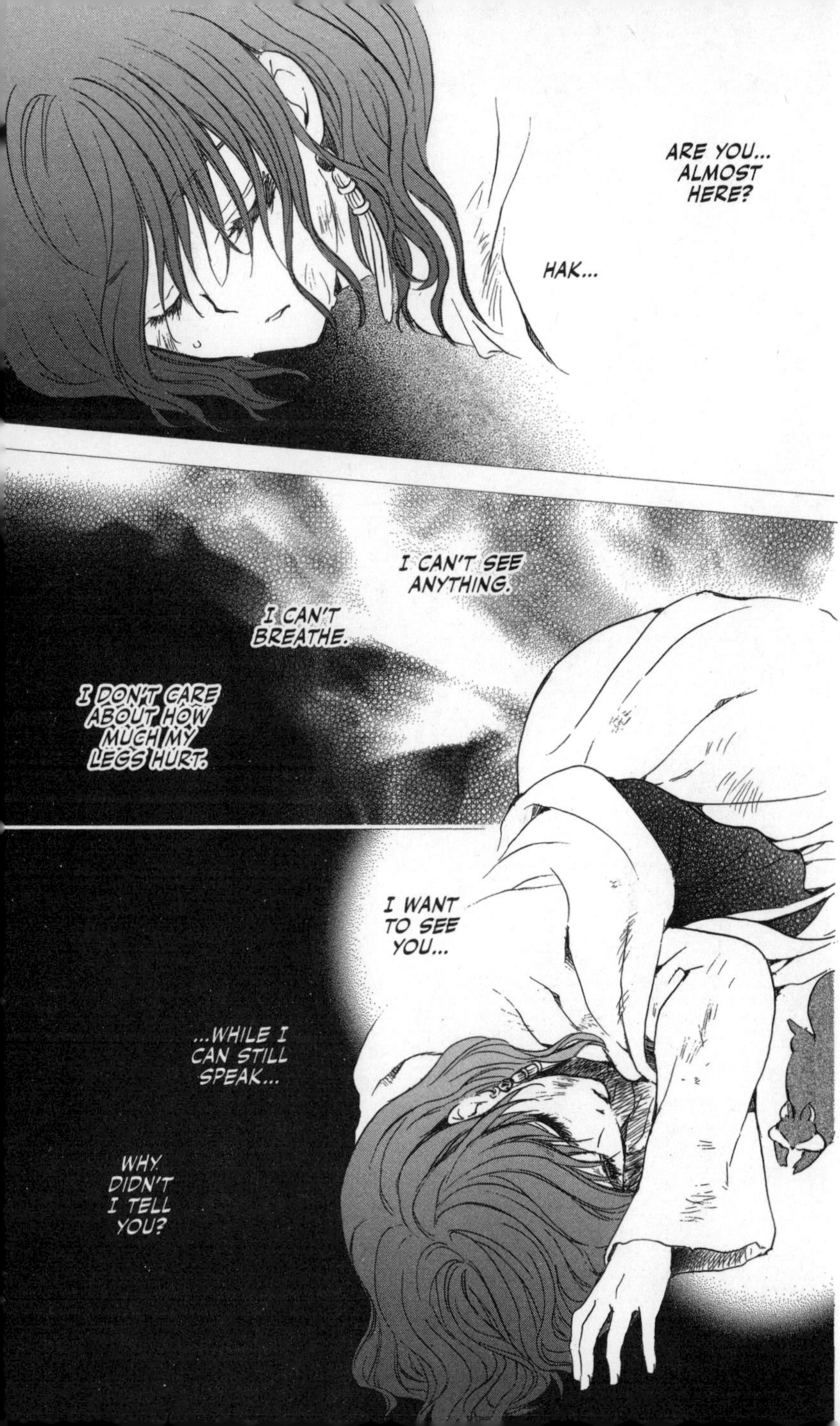
ARE YOU... ALMOST HERE?
HAK...
I CAN'T SEE ANYTHING.
I CAN'T BREATHE.
I DON'T CARE ABOUT HOW MUCH MY LEGS HURT.
I WANT TO SEE YOU...
...WHILE I CAN STILL SPEAK...
WHY DIDN'T I TELL YOU?

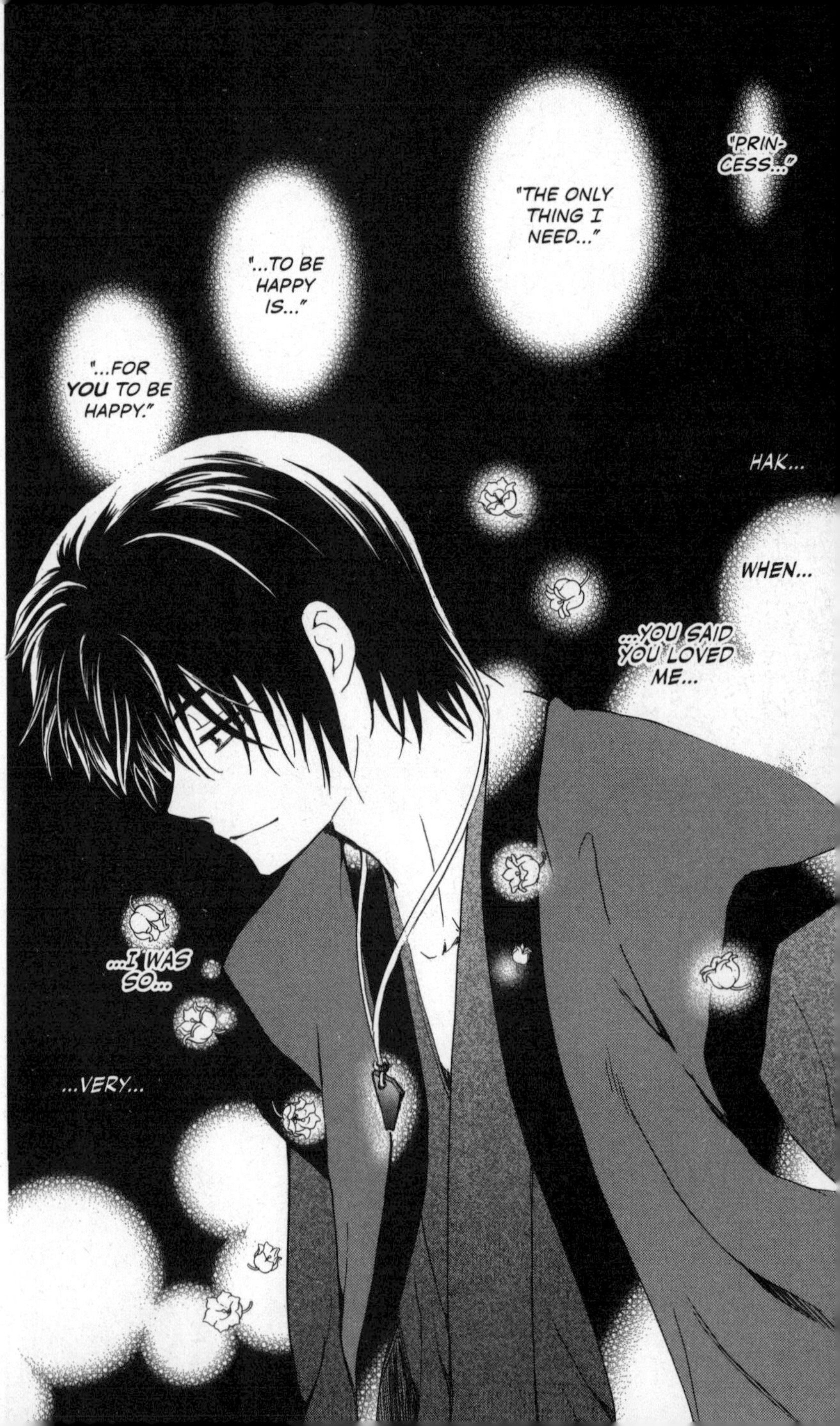
"PRIN-CESS..."
"THE ONLY THING I NEED..."
"...TO BE HAPPY IS..."
"...FOR YOU TO BE HAPPY."
HAK...
WHEN...
...YOU SAID YOU LOVED ME...
...I WAS SO...
...VERY...

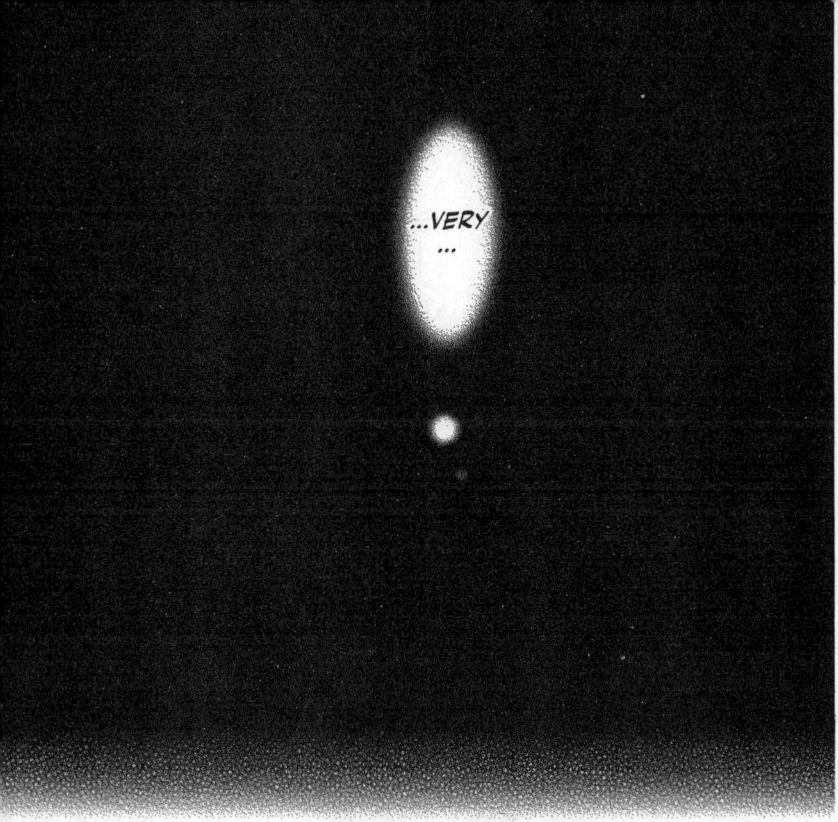
...VERY
...
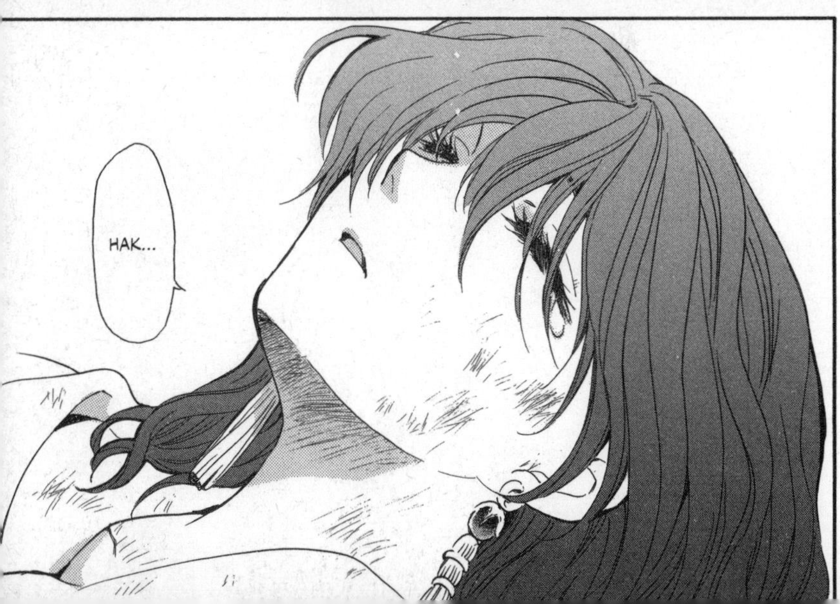
HAK...

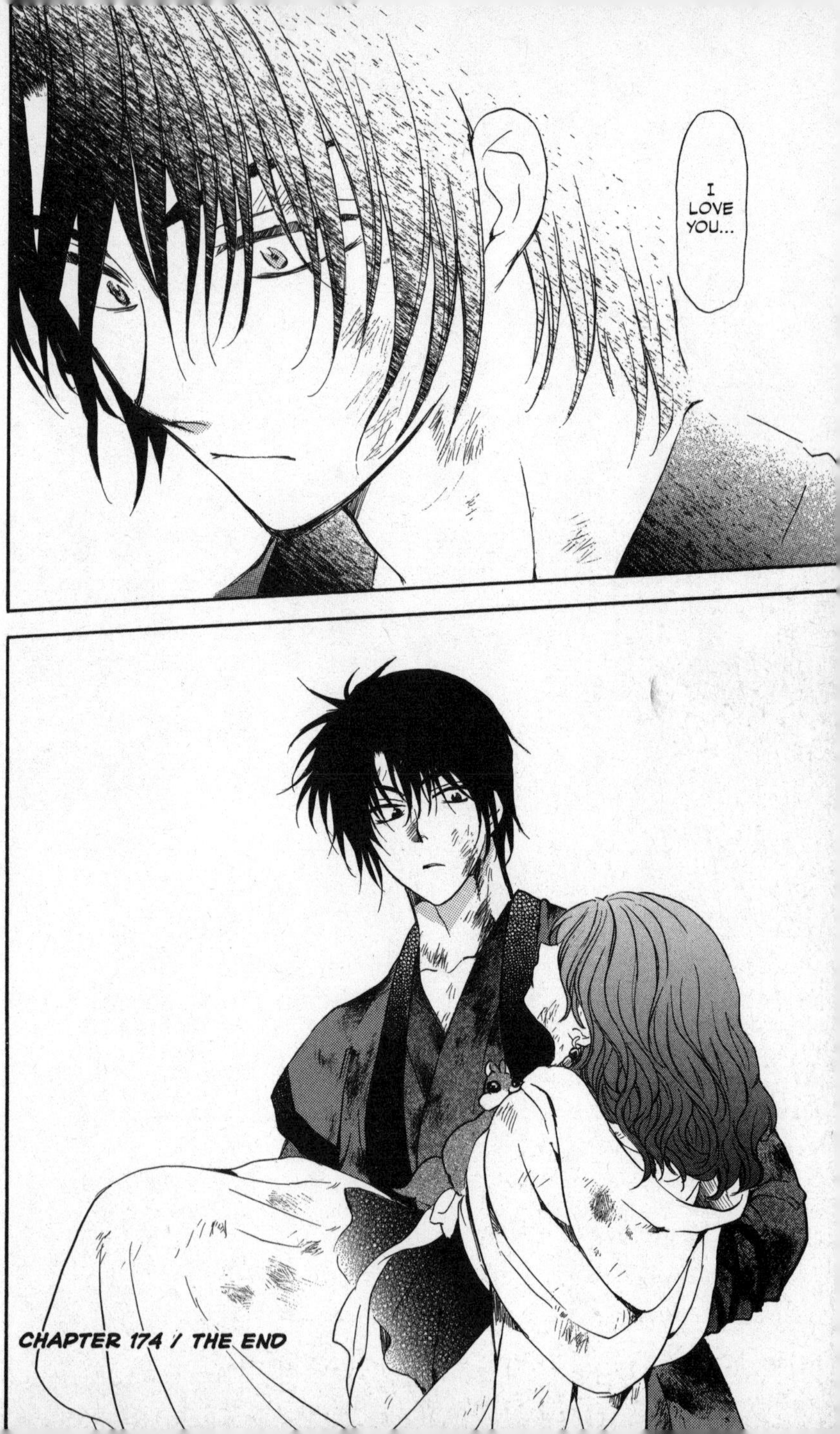
I LOVE YOU...
CHAPTER 174 / THE END

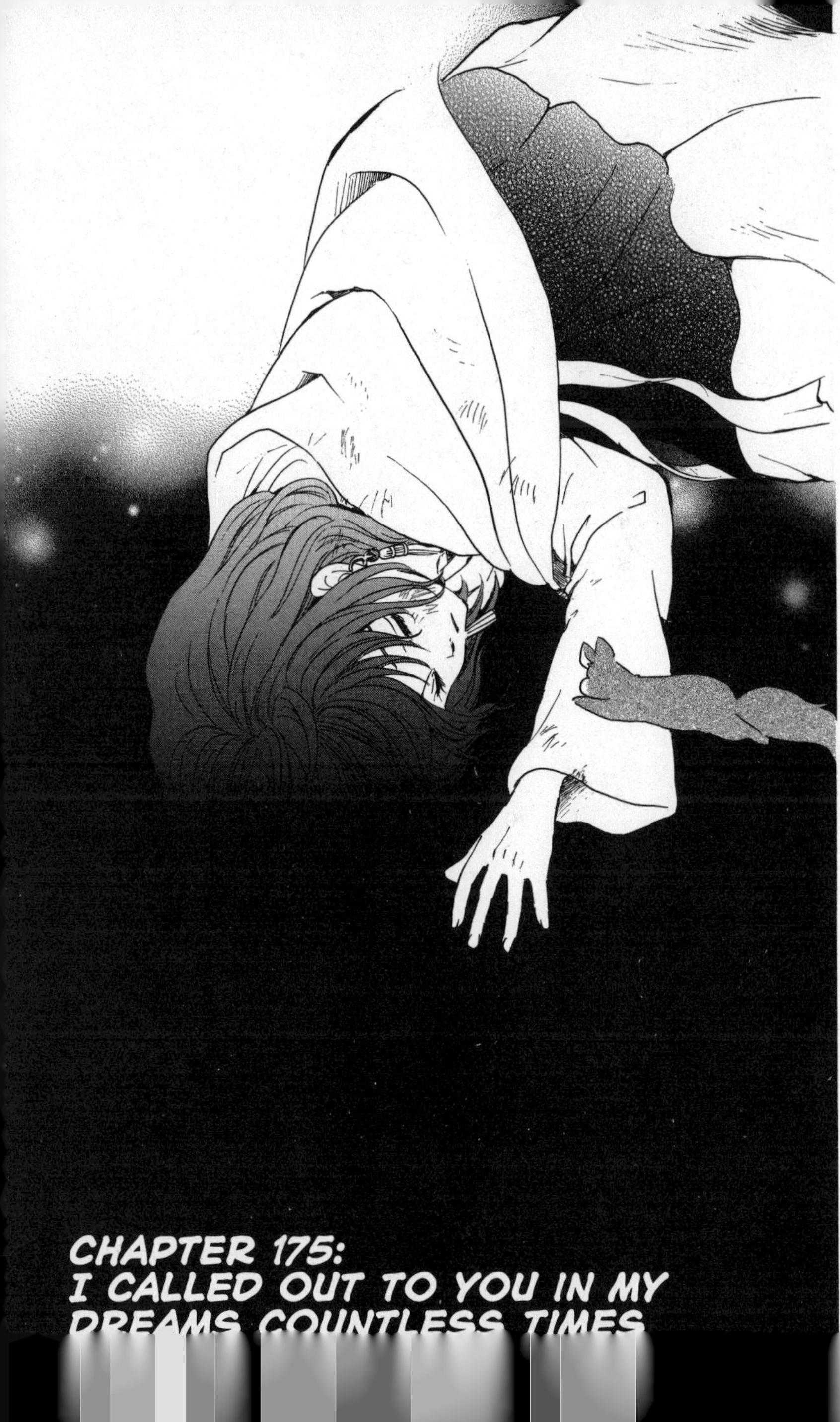
CHAPTER 175:
I CALLED OUT TO YOU IN MY
DREAMS COUNTLESS TIMES

PRIN-
CESS!
FOOM
Pu-
kyu!
!
Pu-
kyu!
FWOOM

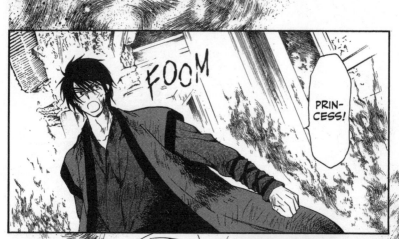

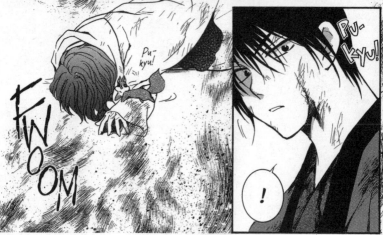

Yona of the Dawn

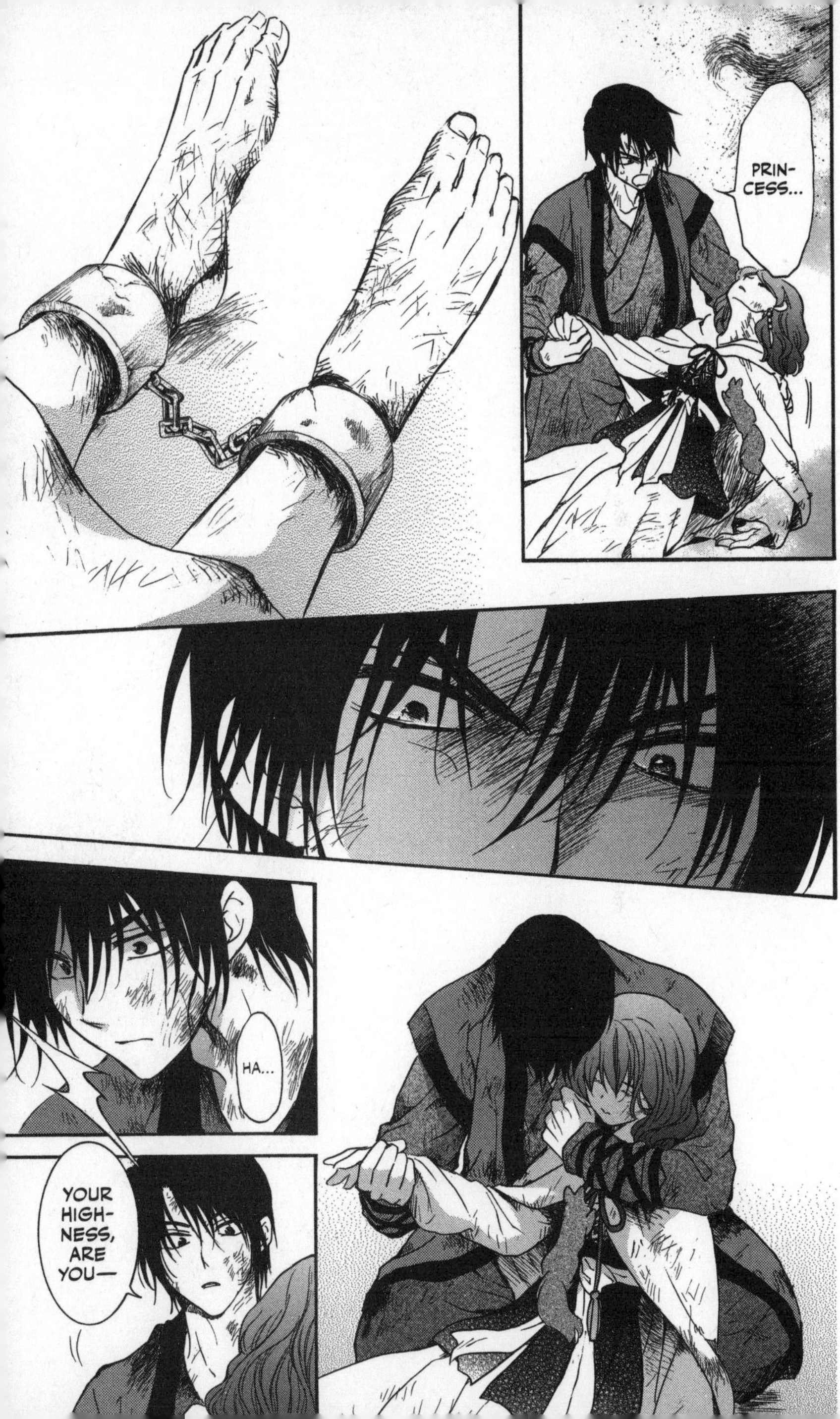
PRIN-CESS...
HA...
YOUR HIGH-NESS, ARE YOU—

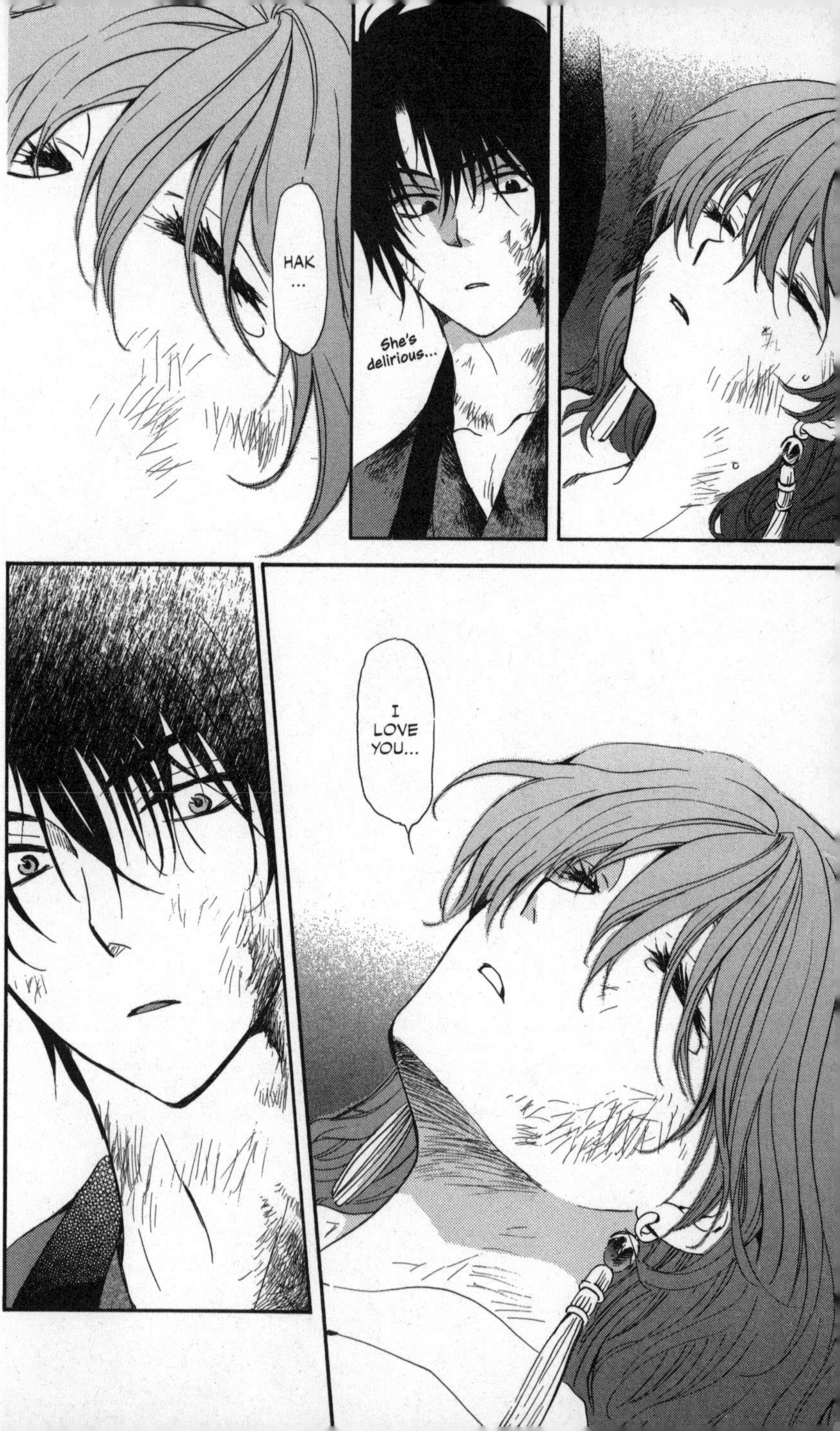
She's delirious...
HAK ...
I LOVE YOU...

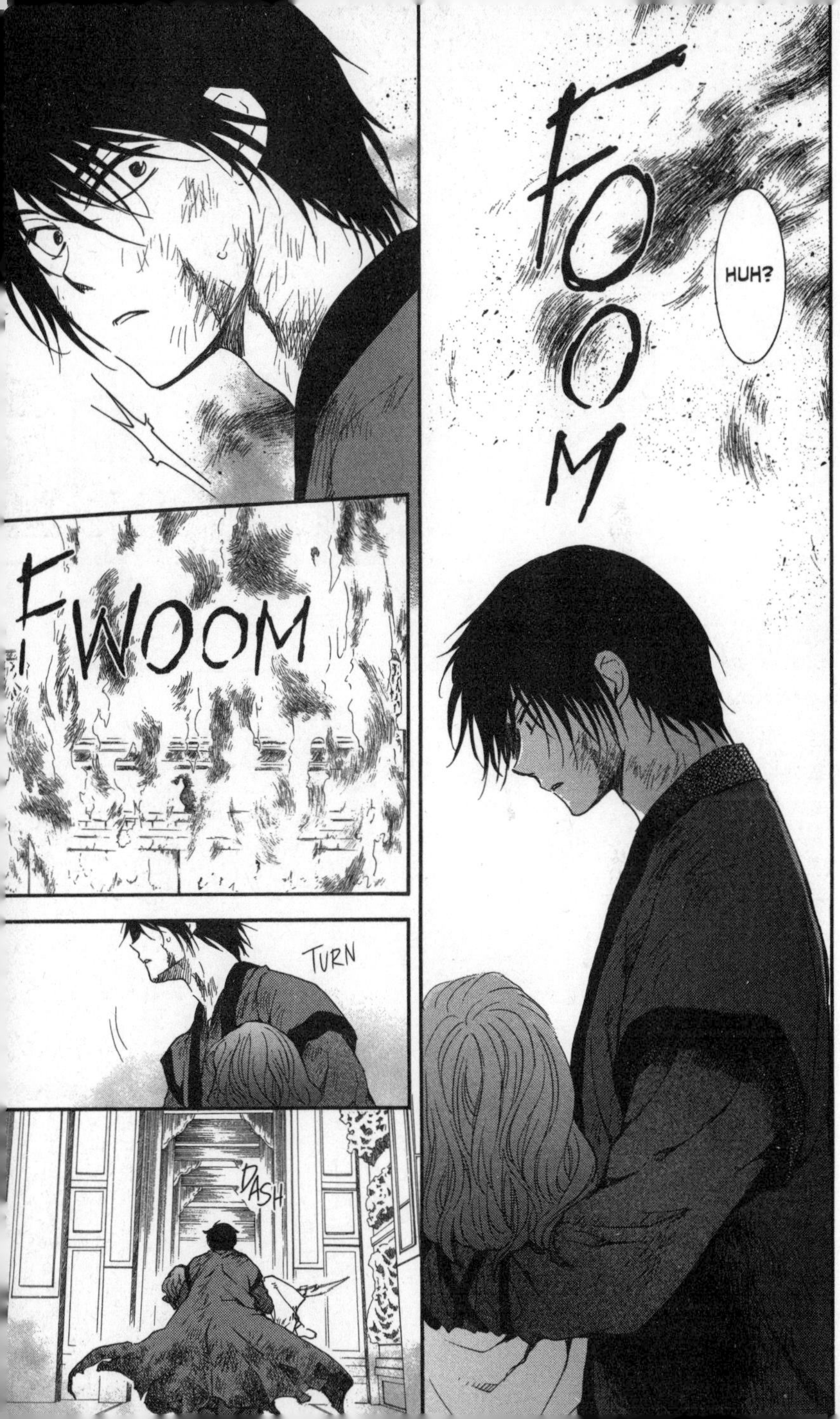
FOOM
HUH?
FWOOM
TURN
DASH

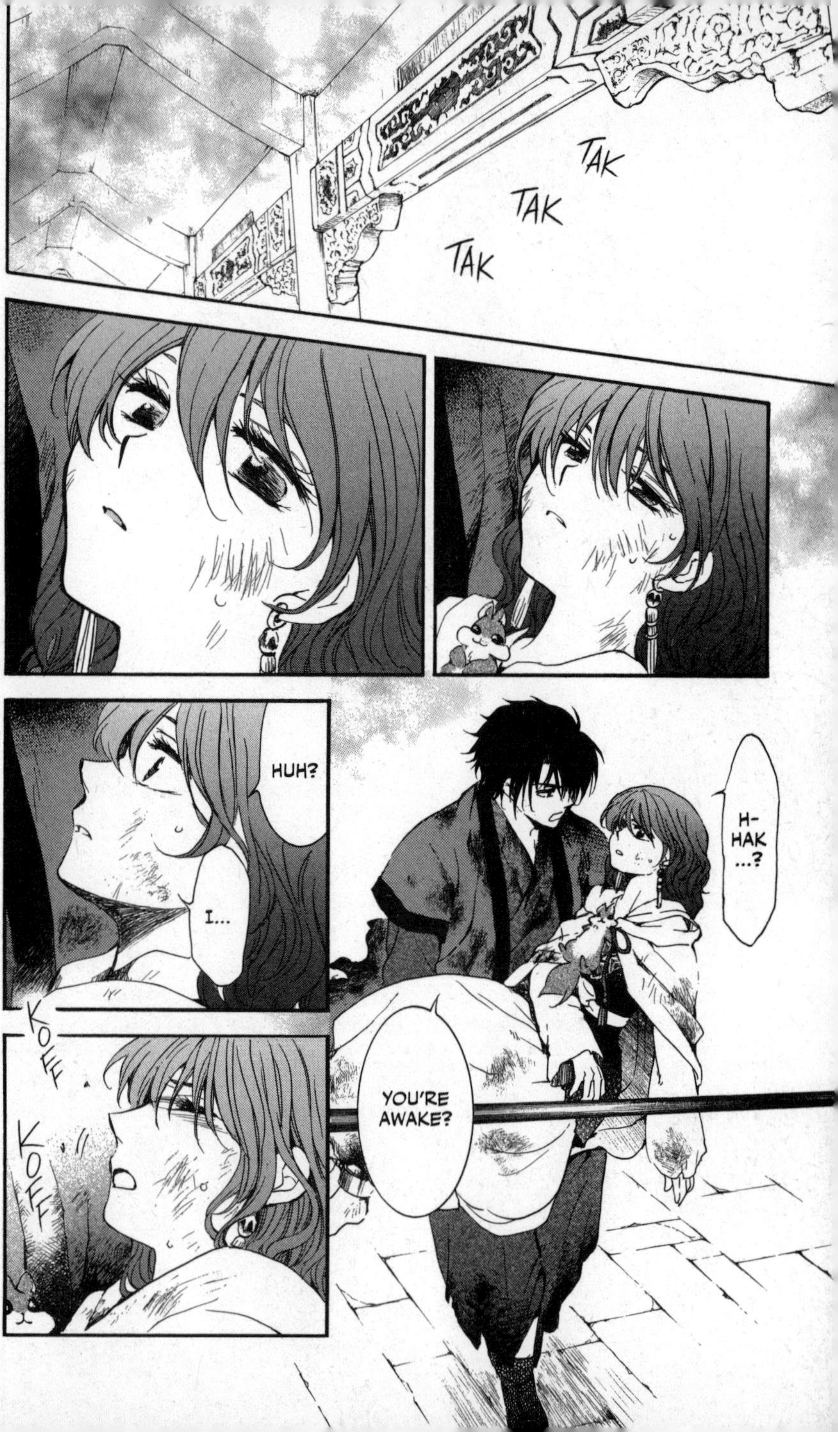
TAK
TAK
TAK
H-HAK ...?
YOU'RE AWAKE?
HUH?
I...
KOFF
KOFF

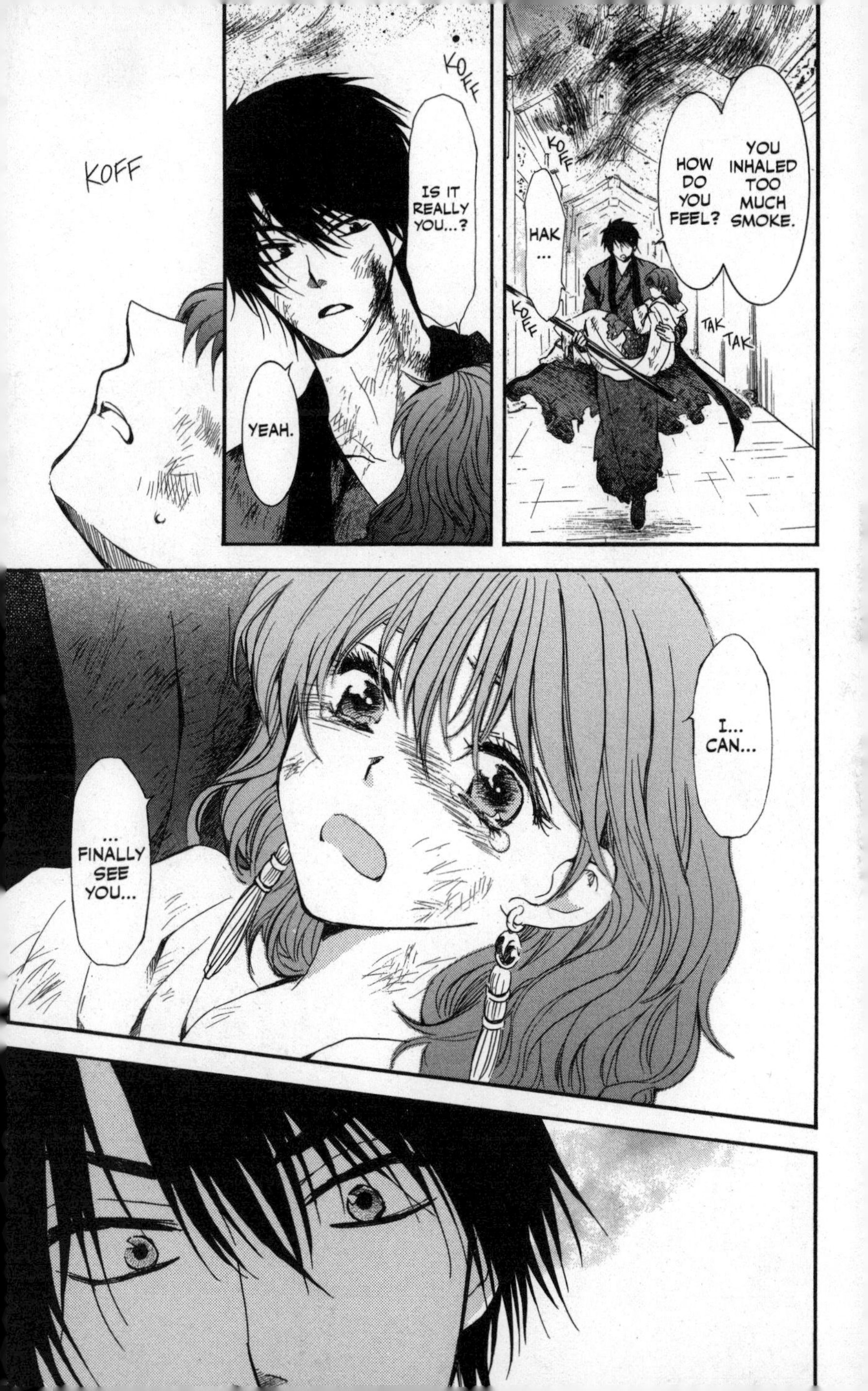
YOU INHALED TOO MUCH SMOKE.
HOW DO YOU FEEL?
KOFF
HAK...
TAK TAK
KOFF
KOFF
IS IT REALLY YOU...?
YEAH.
KOFF
I... CAN...
... FINALLY SEE YOU...

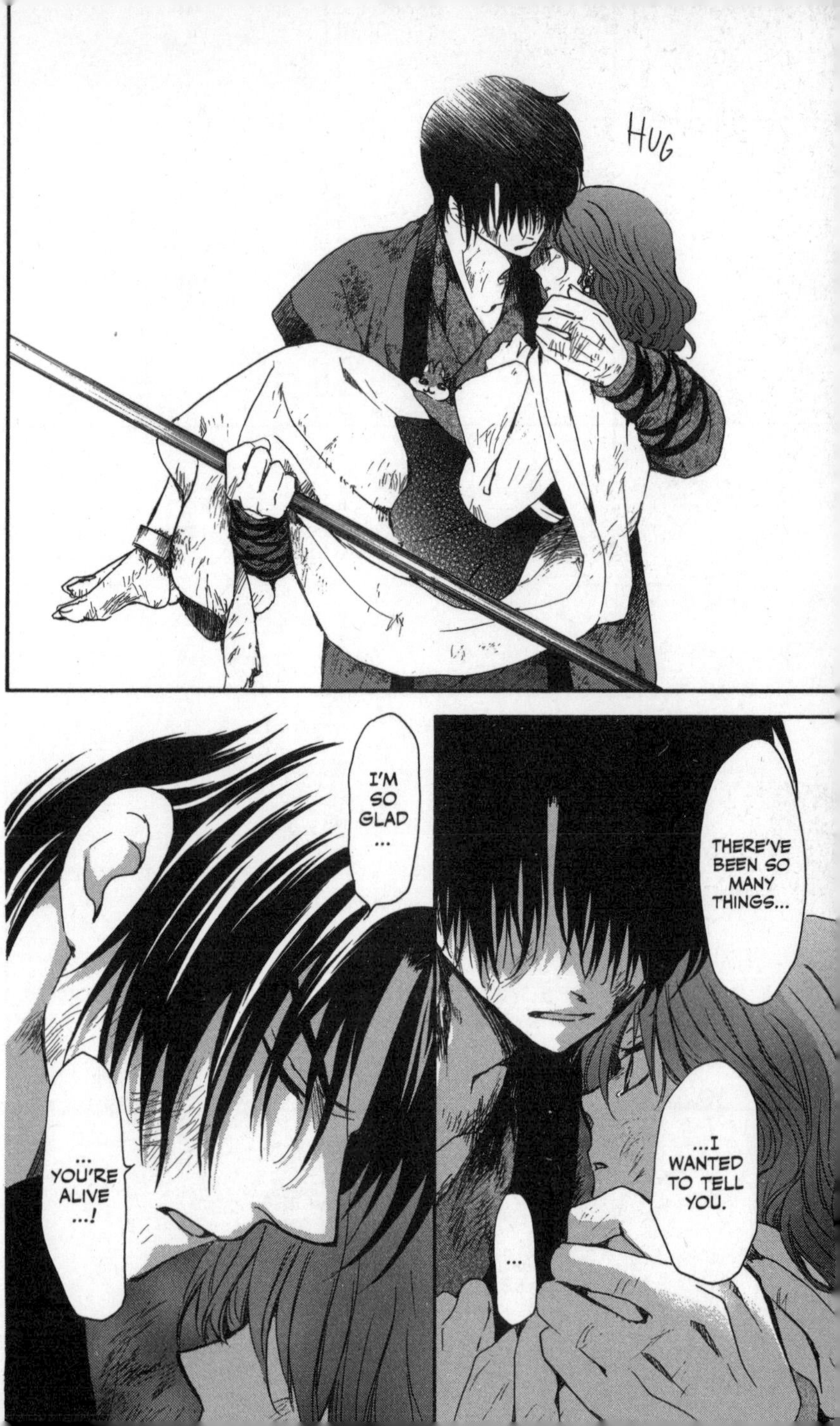
HUG
THERE'VE BEEN SO MANY THINGS...
...I WANTED TO TELL YOU.
...
I'M SO GLAD...
...YOU'RE ALIVE...!

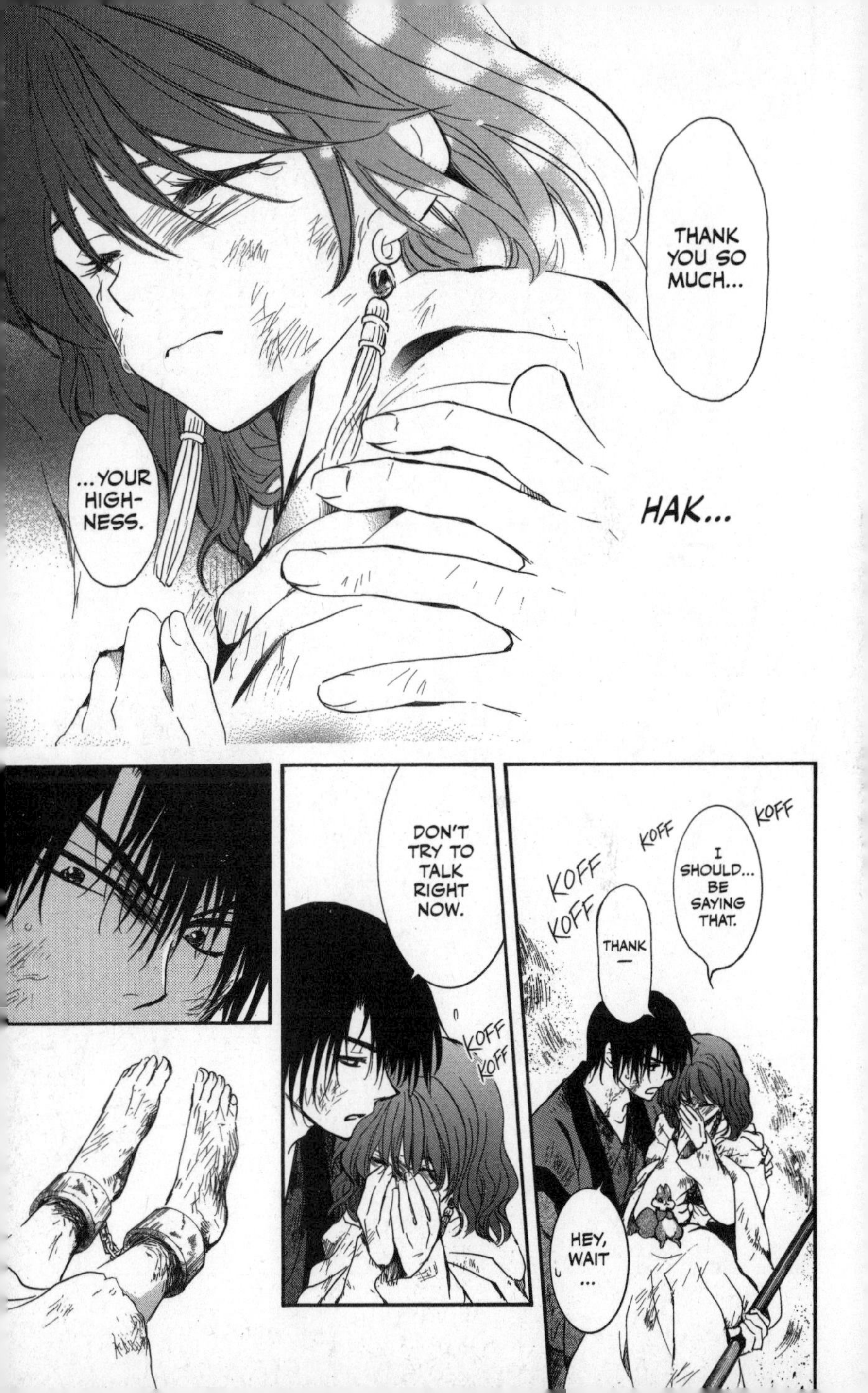
THANK YOU SO MUCH...
HAK...
...YOUR HIGHNESS.
KOFF
I SHOULD... BE SAYING THAT.
KOFF
KOFF KOFF
THANK—
HEY, WAIT...
DON'T TRY TO TALK RIGHT NOW.
KOFF KOFF

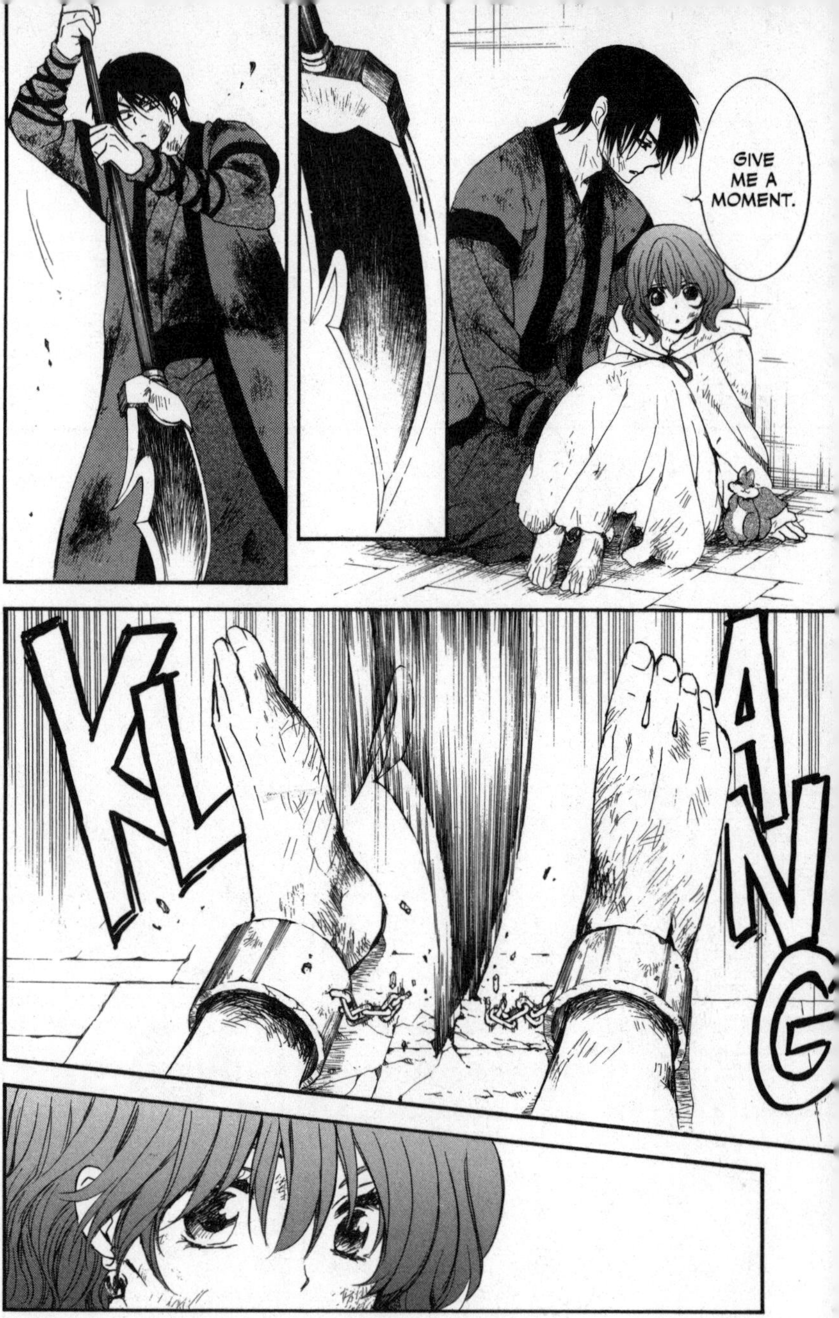
GIVE ME A MOMENT.
KLANG

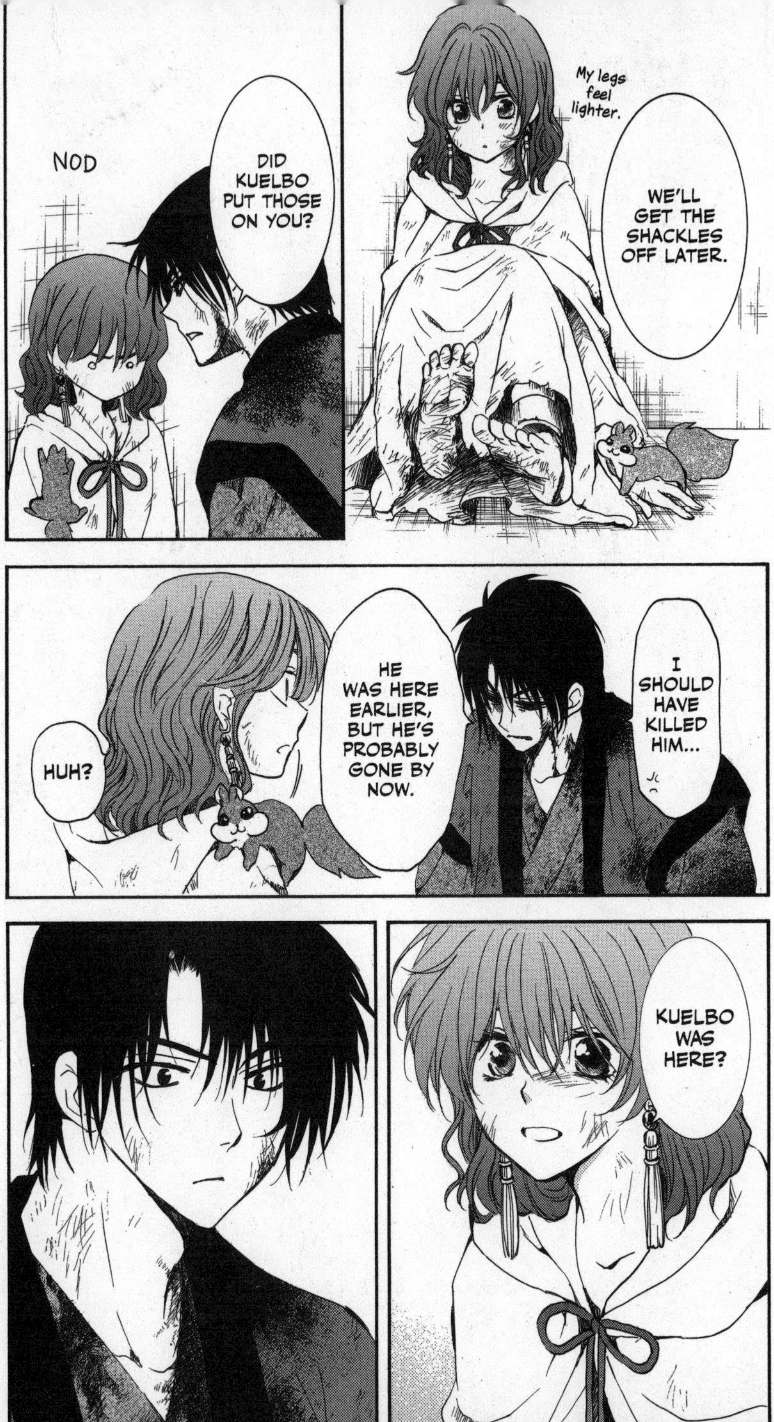
My legs feel lighter.
WE'LL GET THE SHACKLES OFF LATER.
DID KUELBO PUT THOSE ON YOU?
NOD
I SHOULD HAVE KILLED HIM...
HE WAS HERE EARLIER, BUT HE'S PROBABLY GONE BY NOW.
HUH?
KUELBO WAS HERE?

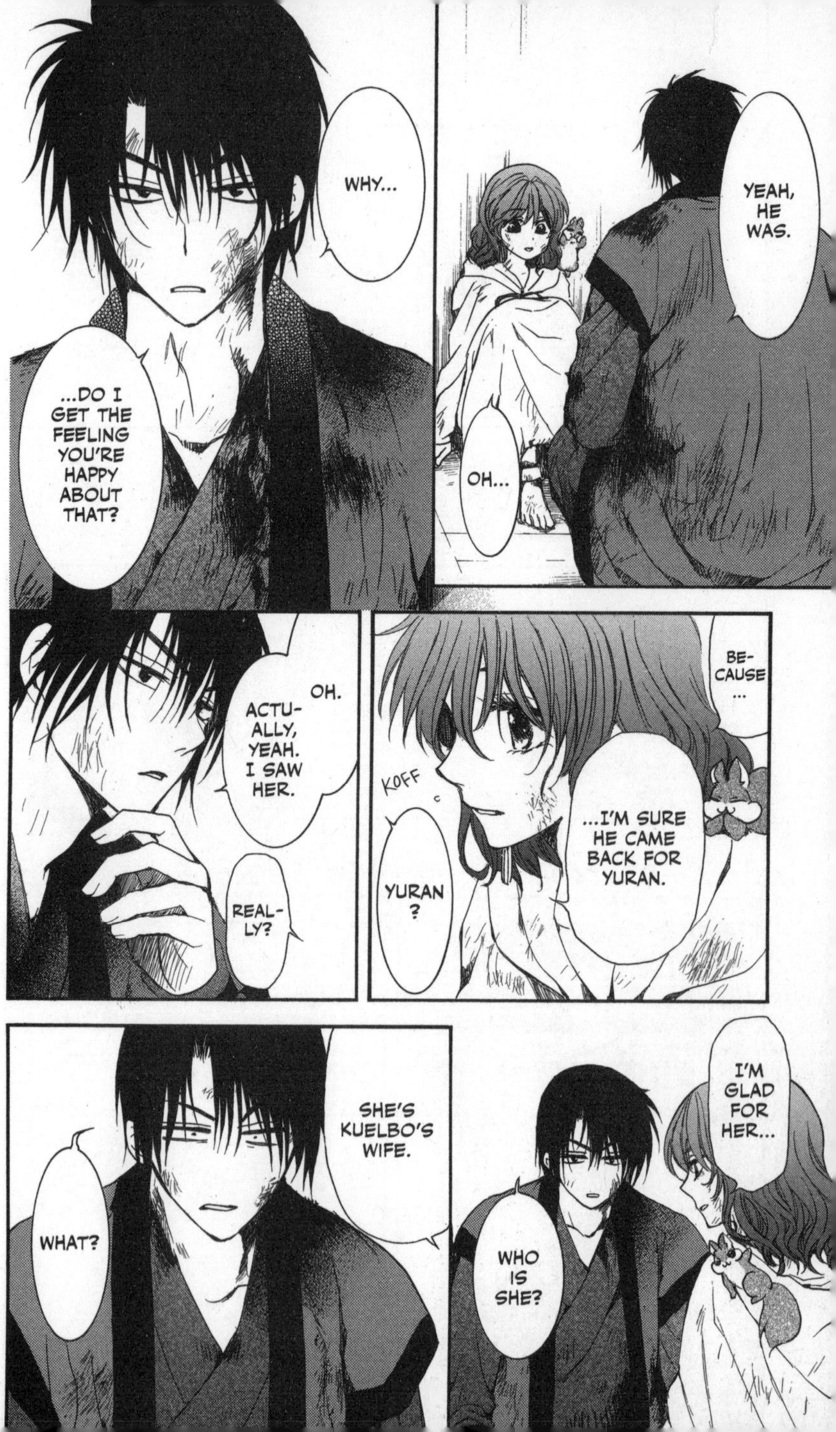
YEAH, HE WAS.
OH...
WHY...
...DO I GET THE FEELING YOU'RE HAPPY ABOUT THAT?
BE-CAUSE...
...I'M SURE HE CAME BACK FOR YURAN.
KOFF
YURAN?
OH. ACTU-ALLY, YEAH. I SAW HER.
REAL-LY?
I'M GLAD FOR HER...
WHO IS SHE?
SHE'S KUELBO'S WIFE.
WHAT?

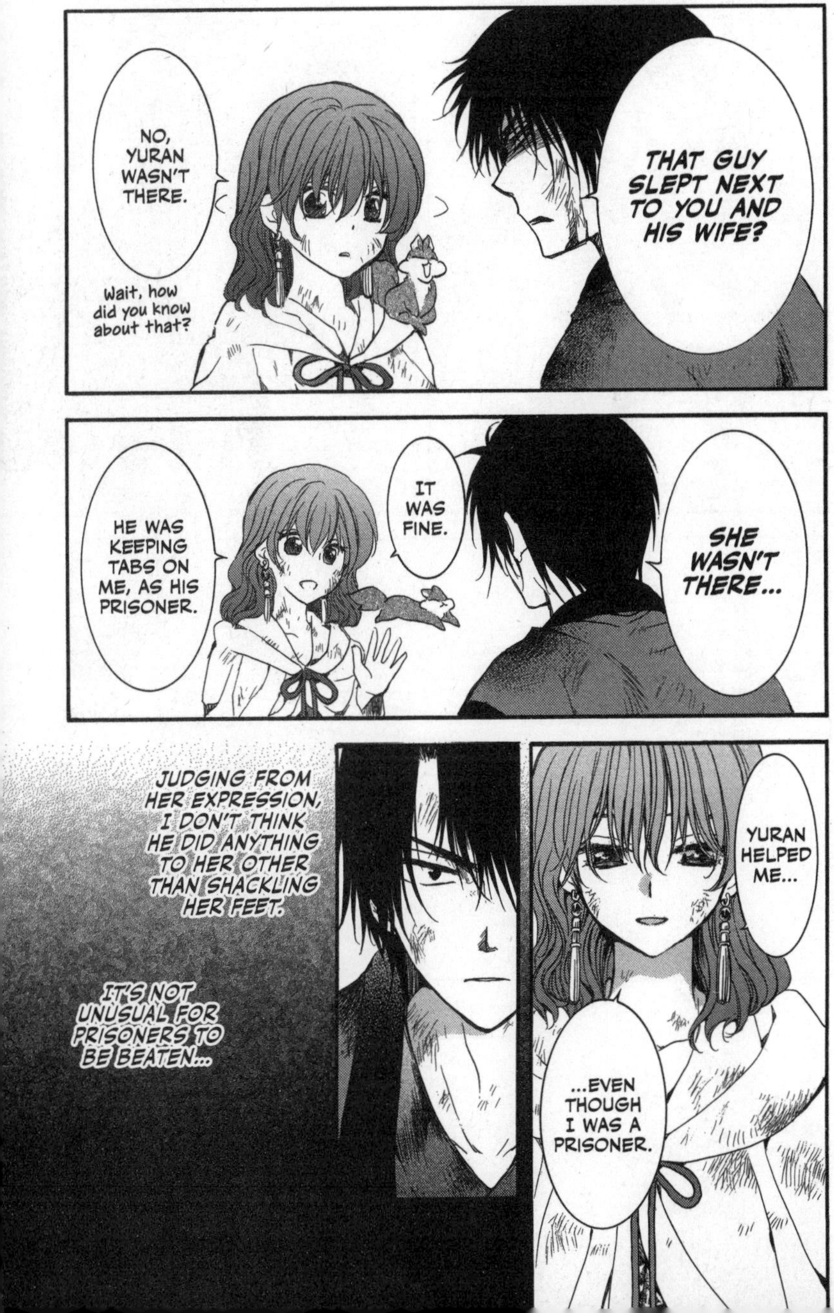
THAT GUY SLEPT NEXT TO YOU AND HIS WIFE?
NO, YURAN WASN'T THERE.
Wait, how did you know about that?
SHE WASN'T THERE...
IT WAS FINE.
HE WAS KEEPING TABS ON ME, AS HIS PRISONER.
YURAN HELPED ME...
...EVEN THOUGH I WAS A PRISONER.
JUDGING FROM HER EXPRESSION, I DON'T THINK HE DID ANYTHING TO HER OTHER THAN SHACKLING HER FEET.
IT'S NOT UNUSUAL FOR PRISONERS TO BE BEATEN...

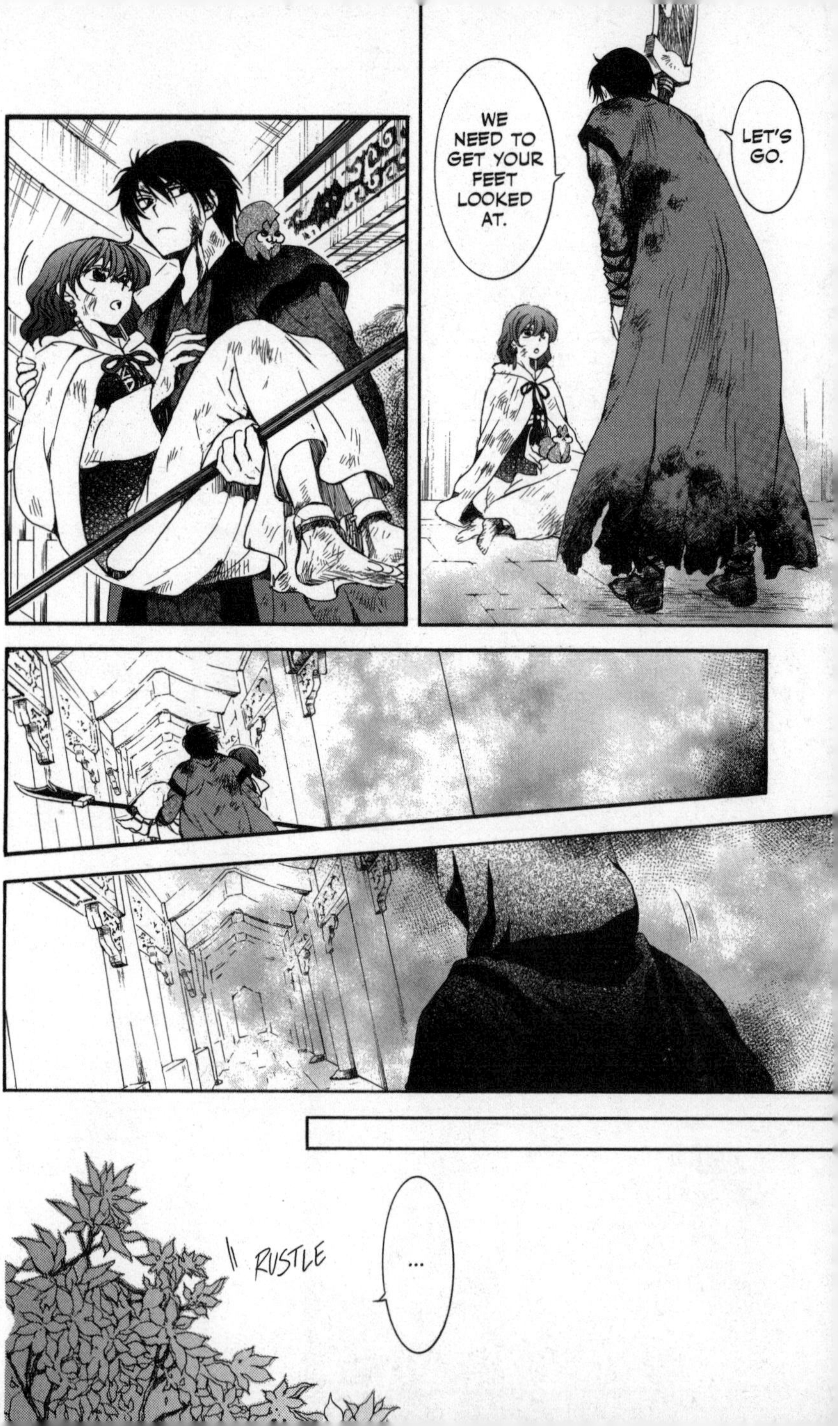
LET'S GO.
WE NEED TO GET YOUR FEET LOOKED AT.
...
RUSTLE

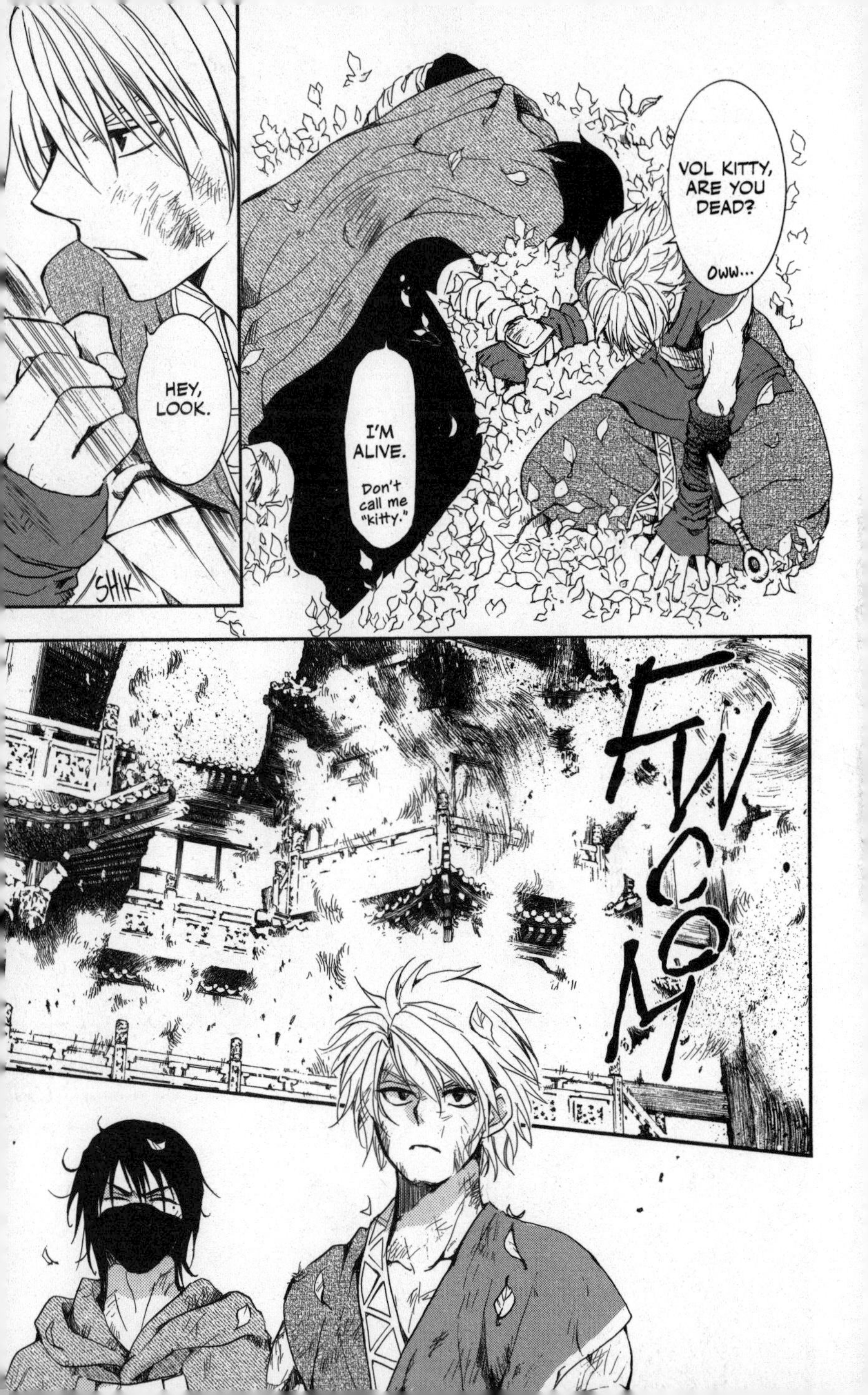
VOL KITTY, ARE YOU DEAD?
OWW...
I'M ALIVE.
Don't call me "kitty."
HEY, LOOK.
SHIK
FWOOM

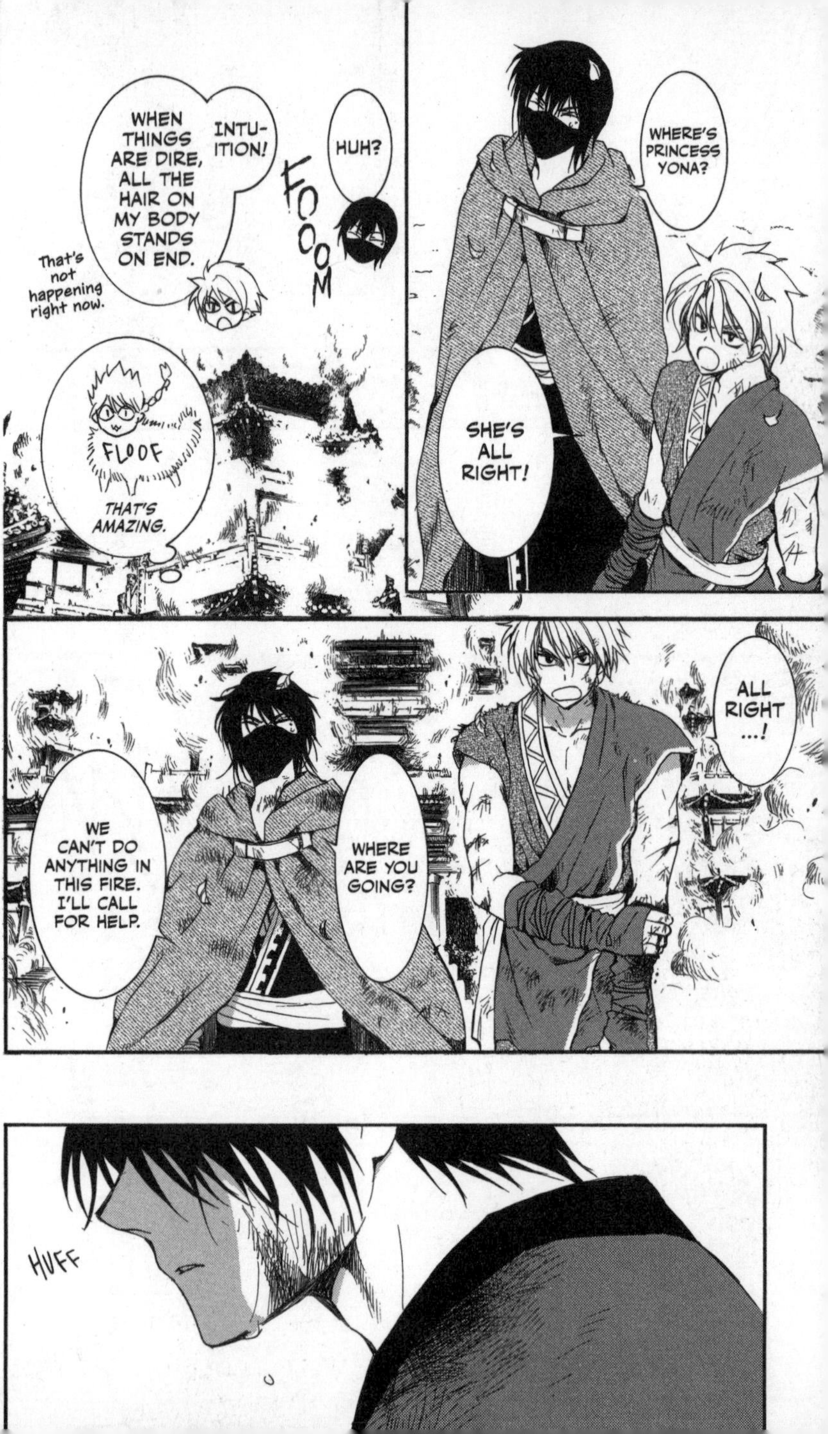
WHERE'S PRINCESS YONA?
SHE'S ALL RIGHT!
HUH?
FOOOM
INTUITION!
WHEN THINGS ARE DIRE, ALL THE HAIR ON MY BODY STANDS ON END.
That's not happening right now.
FLOOF
THAT'S AMAZING.
ALL RIGHT...!
WHERE ARE YOU GOING?
WE CAN'T DO ANYTHING IN THIS FIRE. I'LL CALL FOR HELP.
HUFF

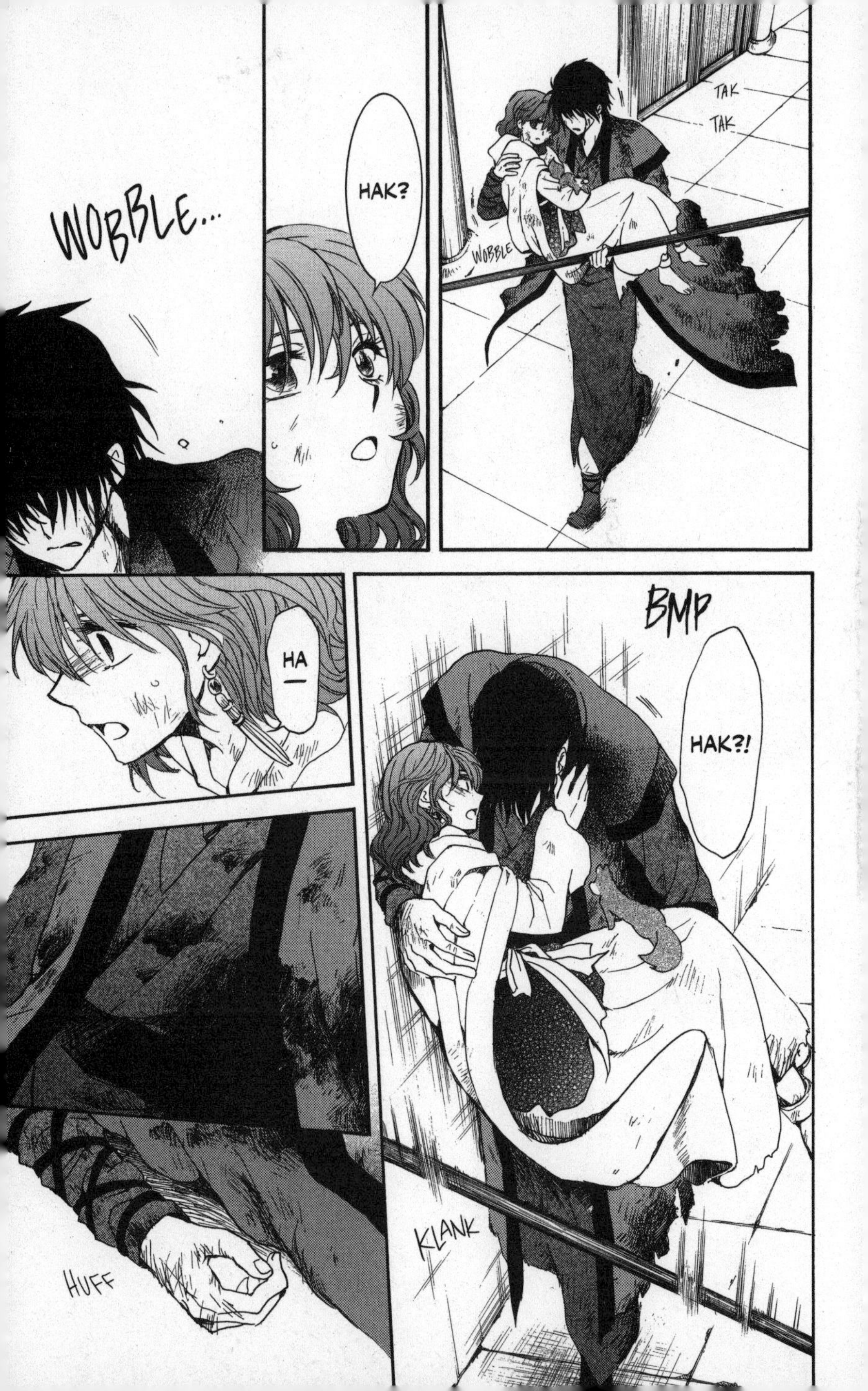
TAK
TAK
WOBBLE
HAK?
WOBBLE...
BMP
HAK?!
KLANK
HA—
HUFF

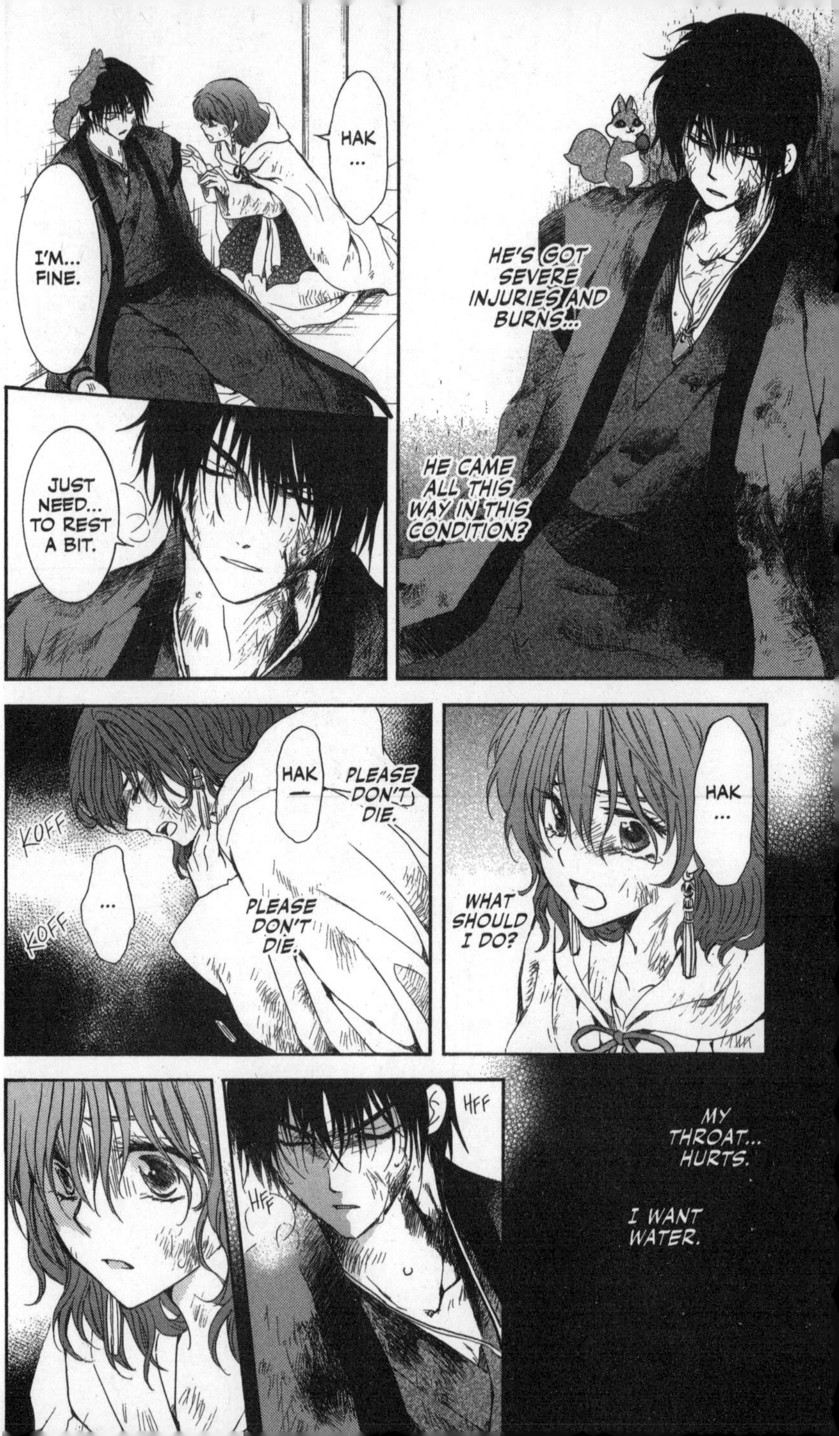
HE'S GOT SEVERE INJURIES AND BURNS...
HE CAME ALL THIS WAY IN THIS CONDITION?
HAK ...
I'M... FINE.
JUST NEED... TO REST A BIT.
HAK ...
WHAT SHOULD I DO?
HAK —
PLEASE DON'T DIE.
PLEASE DON'T DIE.
KOFF
...
KOFF
MY THROAT... HURTS.
I WANT WATER.
HFF
HFF

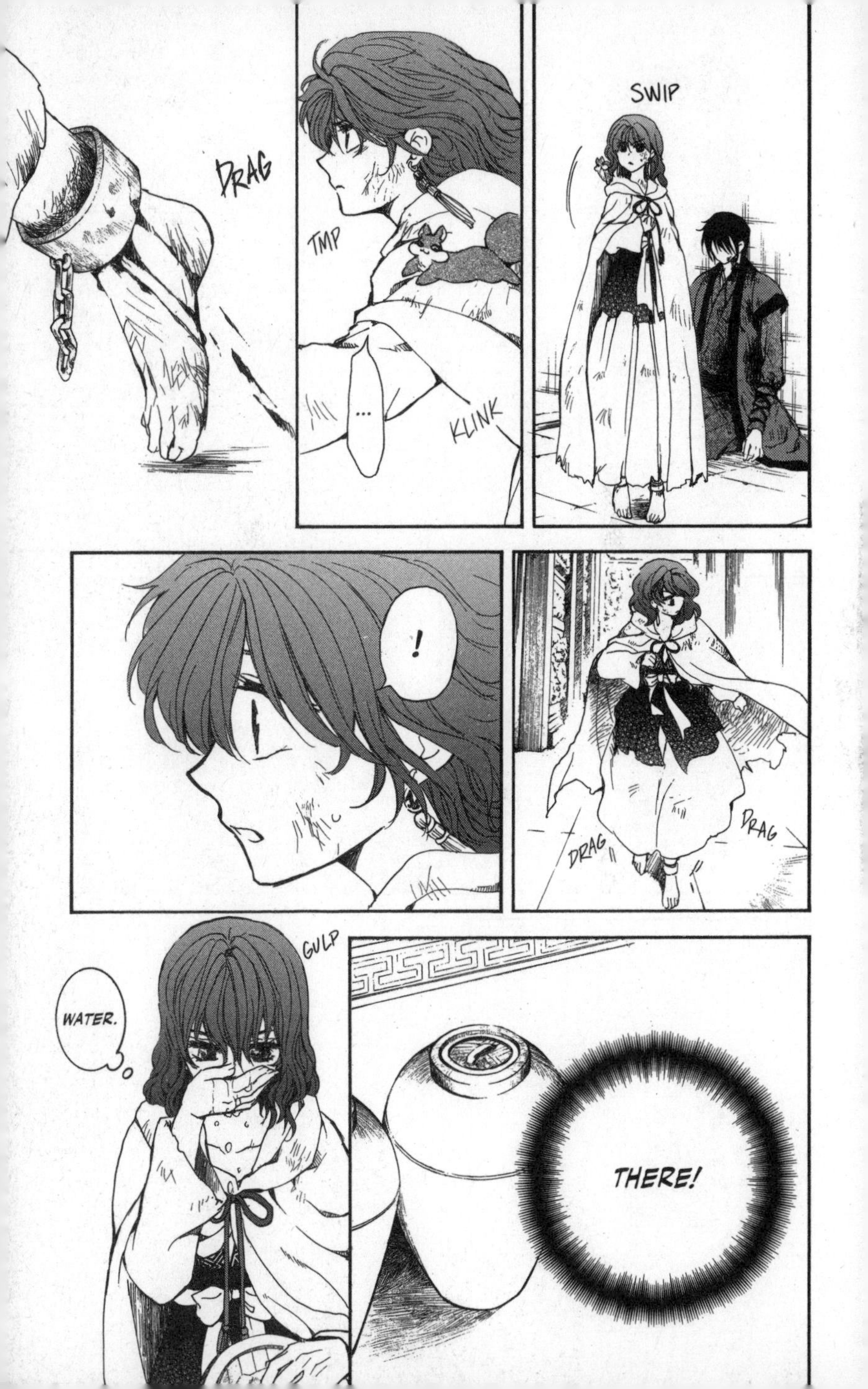
SWIP
TMP
...
KLINK
DRAG
DRAG
DRAG
!
THERE!
GULP
WATER.

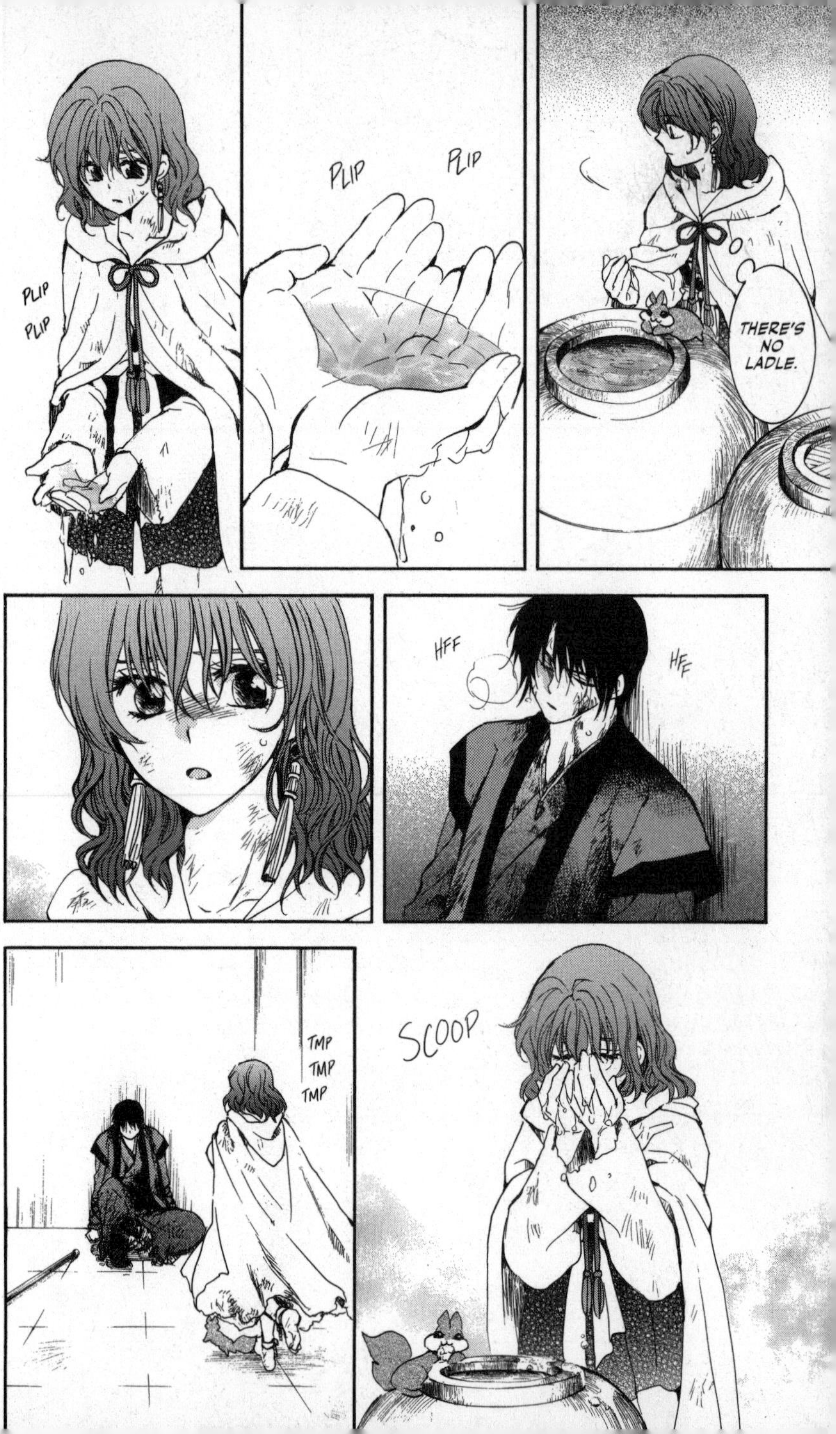
THERE'S NO LADLE.
PLIP
PLIP
PLIP
PLIP
HFF
HFF
SCOOP
TMP
TMP
TMP

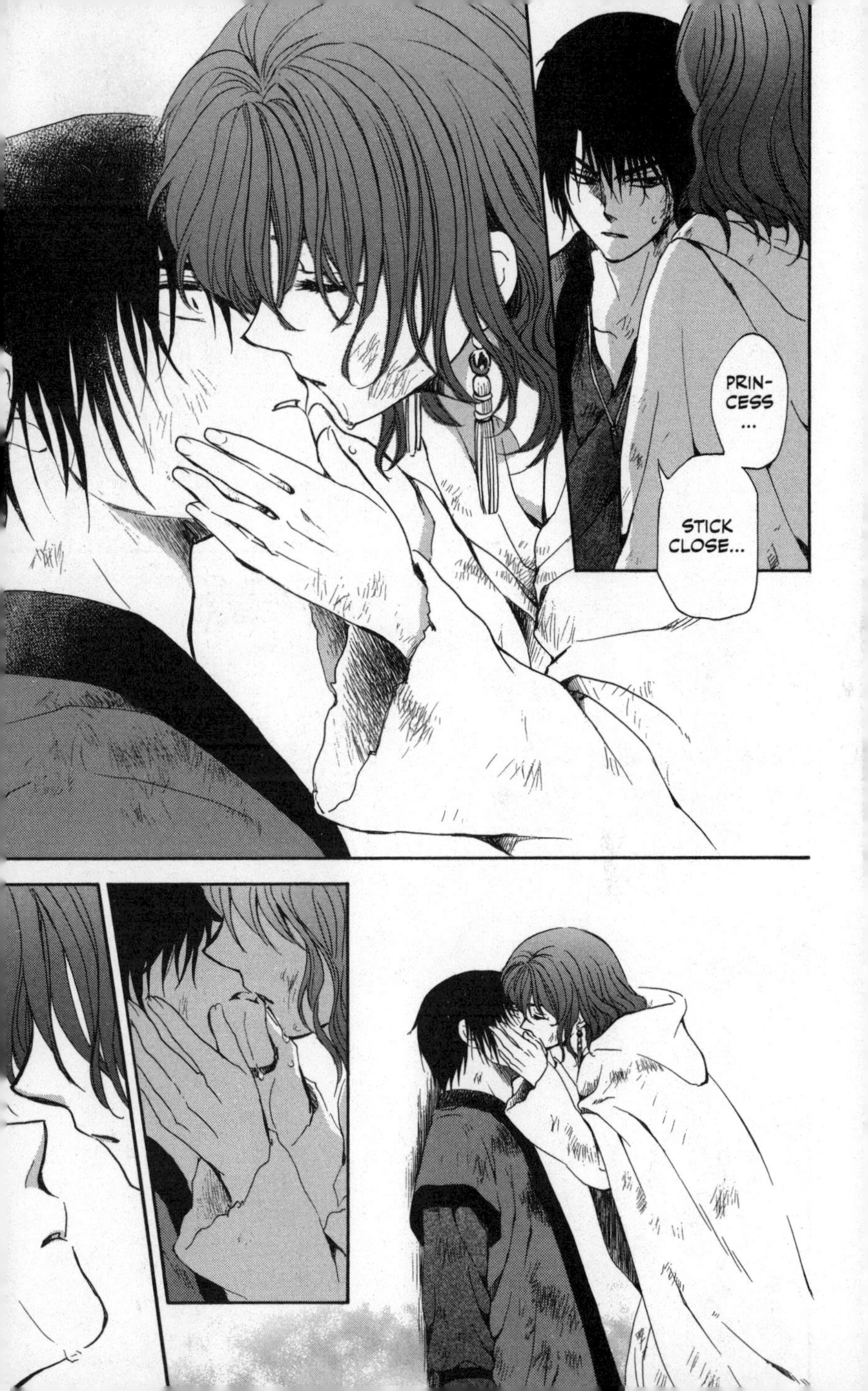
PRIN-
CESS
...
STICK
CLOSE...

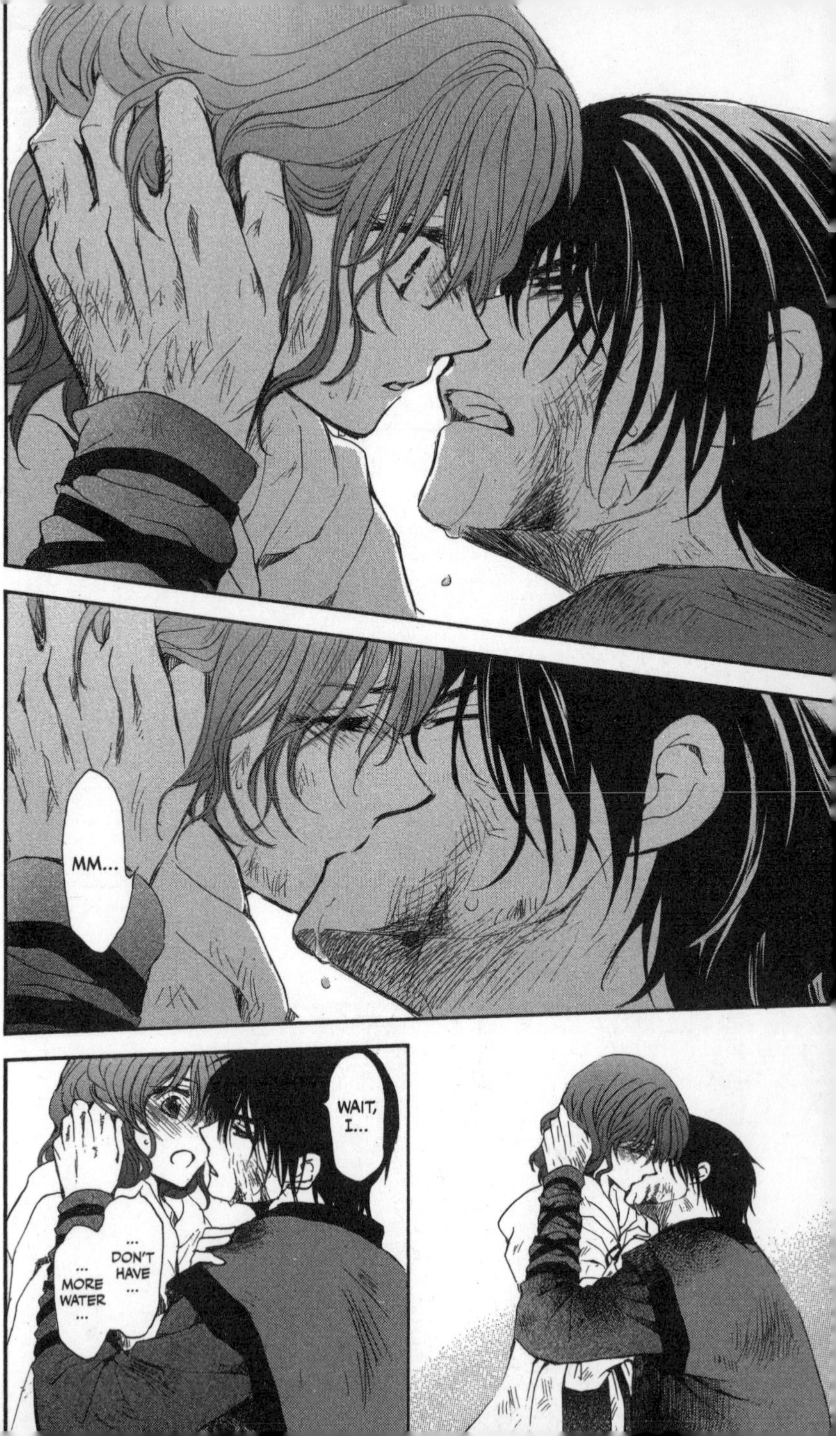
MM...
WAIT, I...
... DON'T HAVE ...
... MORE WATER ...

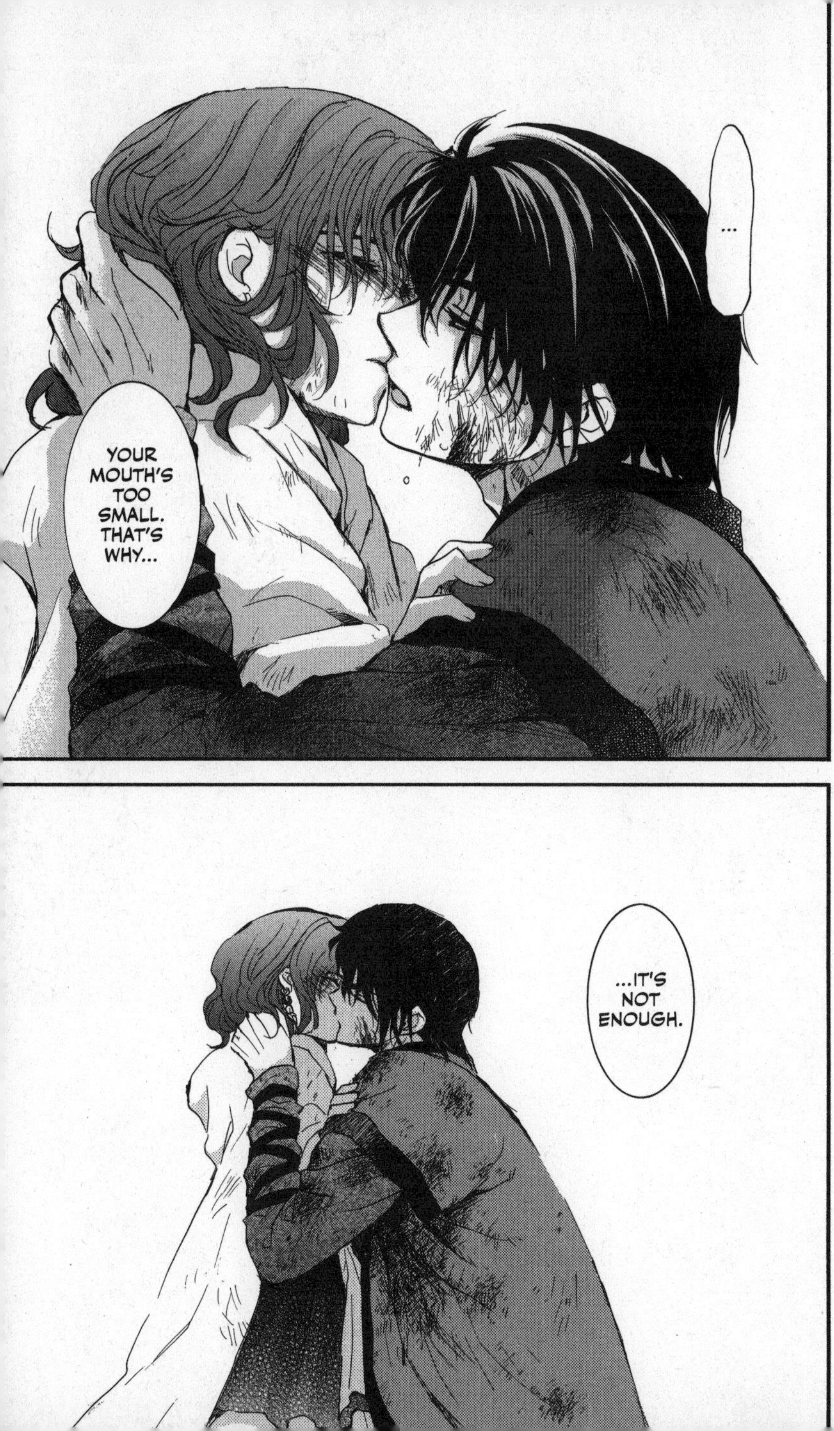
...
YOUR MOUTH'S TOO SMALL. THAT'S WHY...
...IT'S NOT ENOUGH.

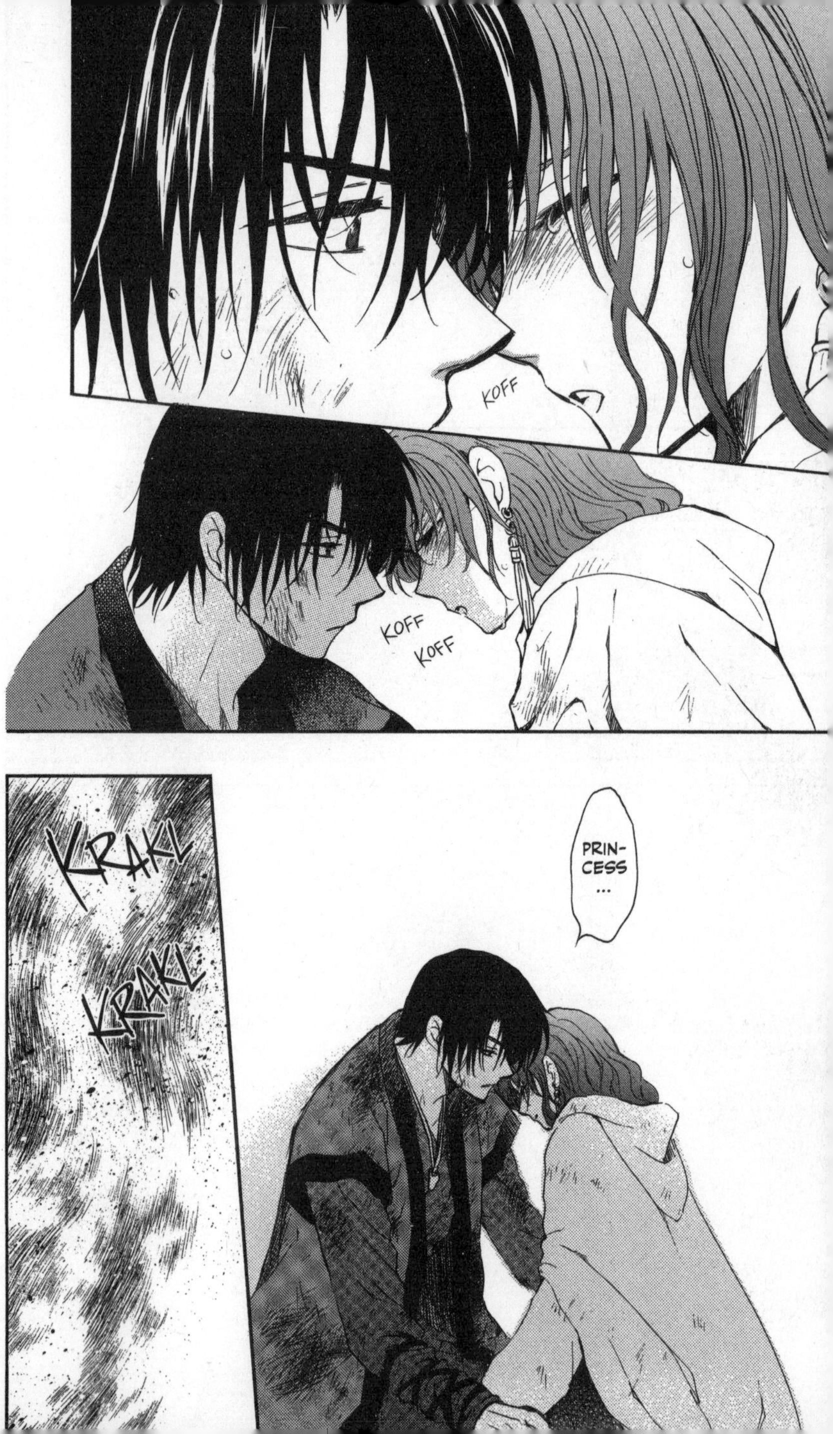
KOFF
KOFF
KOFF
PRIN-CESS...
KRAKL
KRAKL

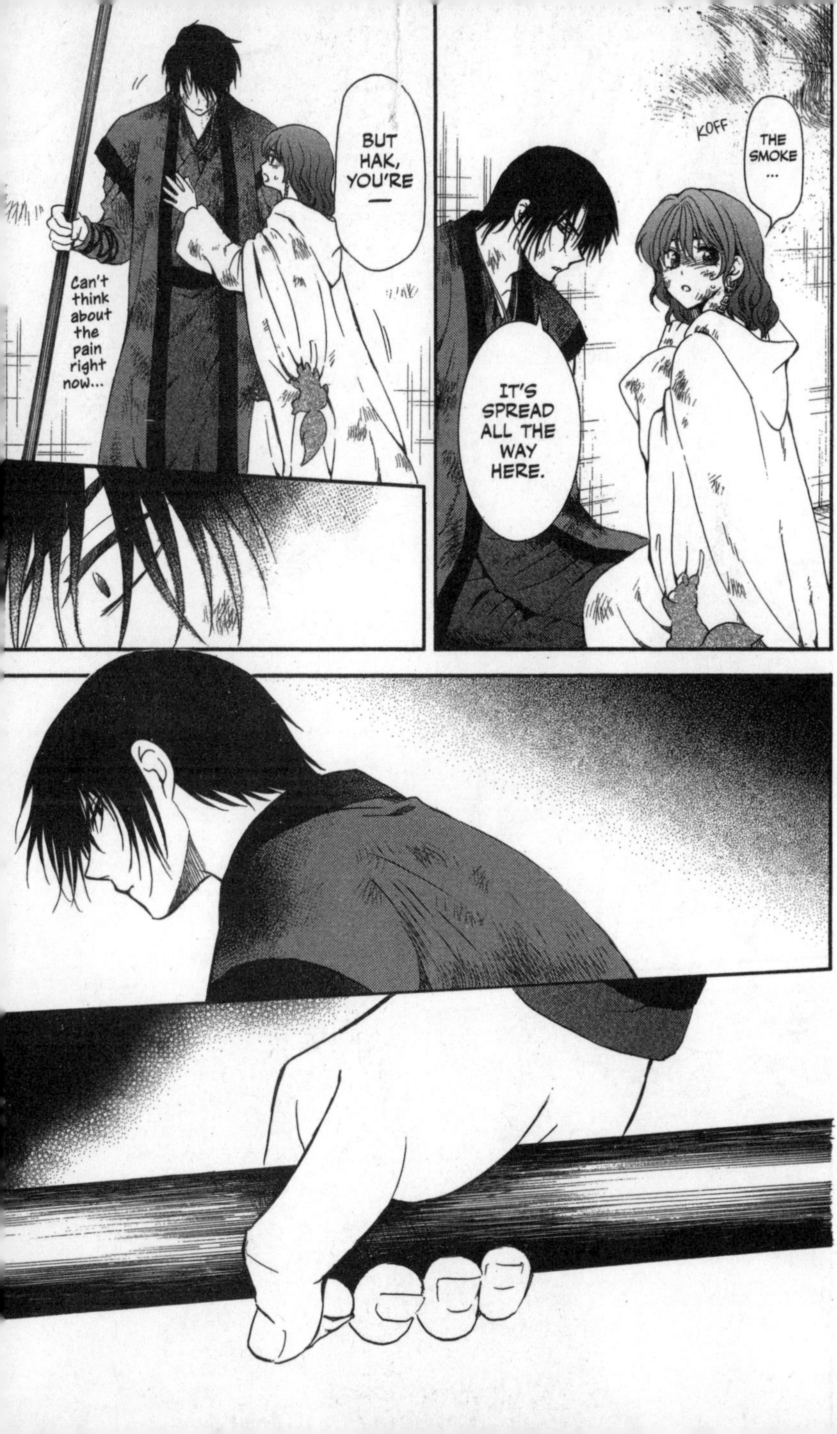
KOFF
THE SMOKE ...
IT'S SPREAD ALL THE WAY HERE.
BUT HAK, YOU'RE —
Can't think about the pain right now...

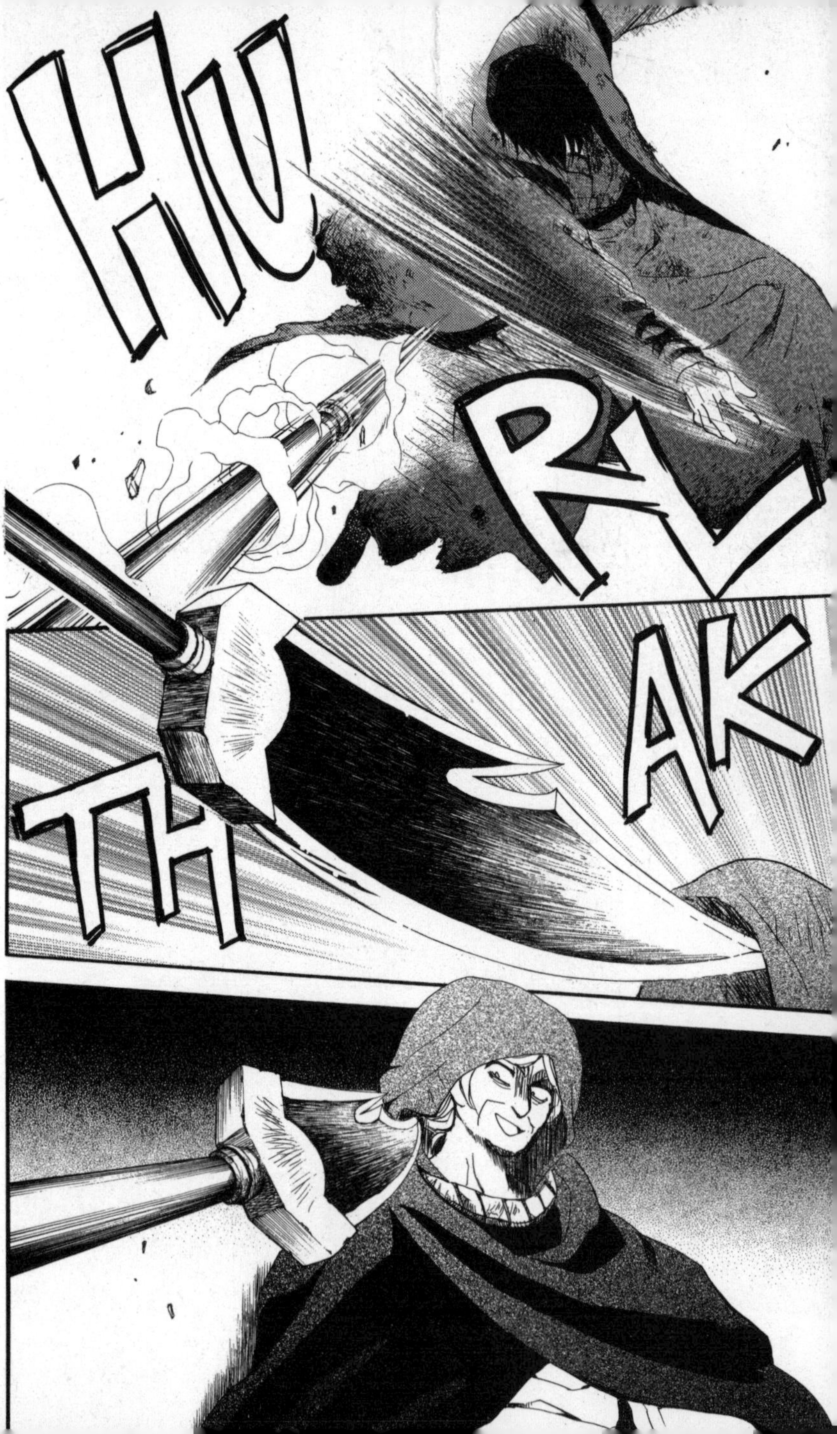
THAK

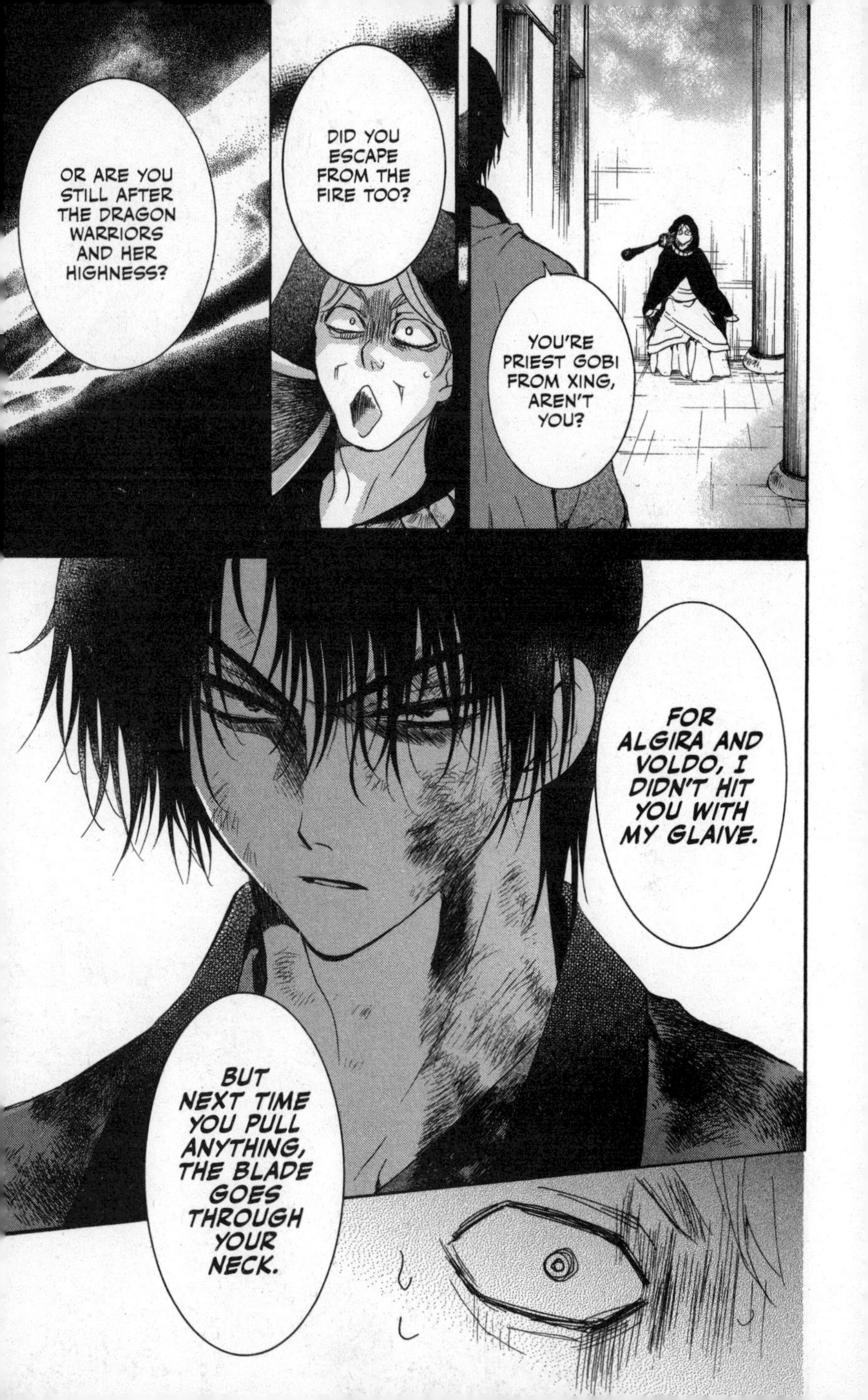
YOU'RE PRIEST GOBI FROM XING, AREN'T YOU?
DID YOU ESCAPE FROM THE FIRE TOO?
OR ARE YOU STILL AFTER THE DRAGON WARRIORS AND HER HIGHNESS?
FOR ALGIRA AND VOLDO, I DIDN'T HIT YOU WITH MY GLAIVE.
BUT NEXT TIME YOU PULL ANYTHING, THE BLADE GOES THROUGH YOUR NECK.

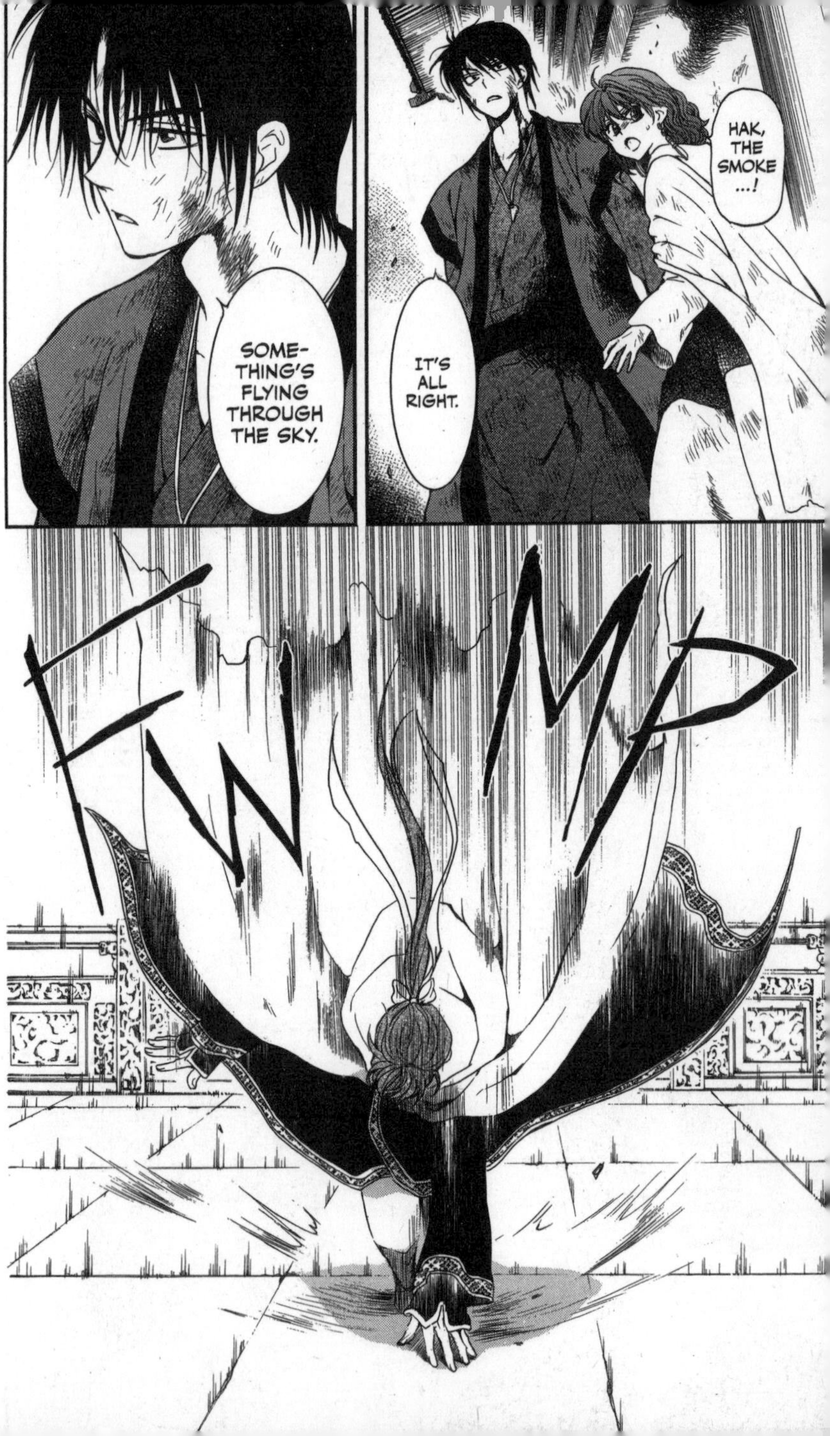
HAK, THE SMOKE ...!
IT'S ALL RIGHT.
SOME-THING'S FLYING THROUGH THE SKY.
FWMP

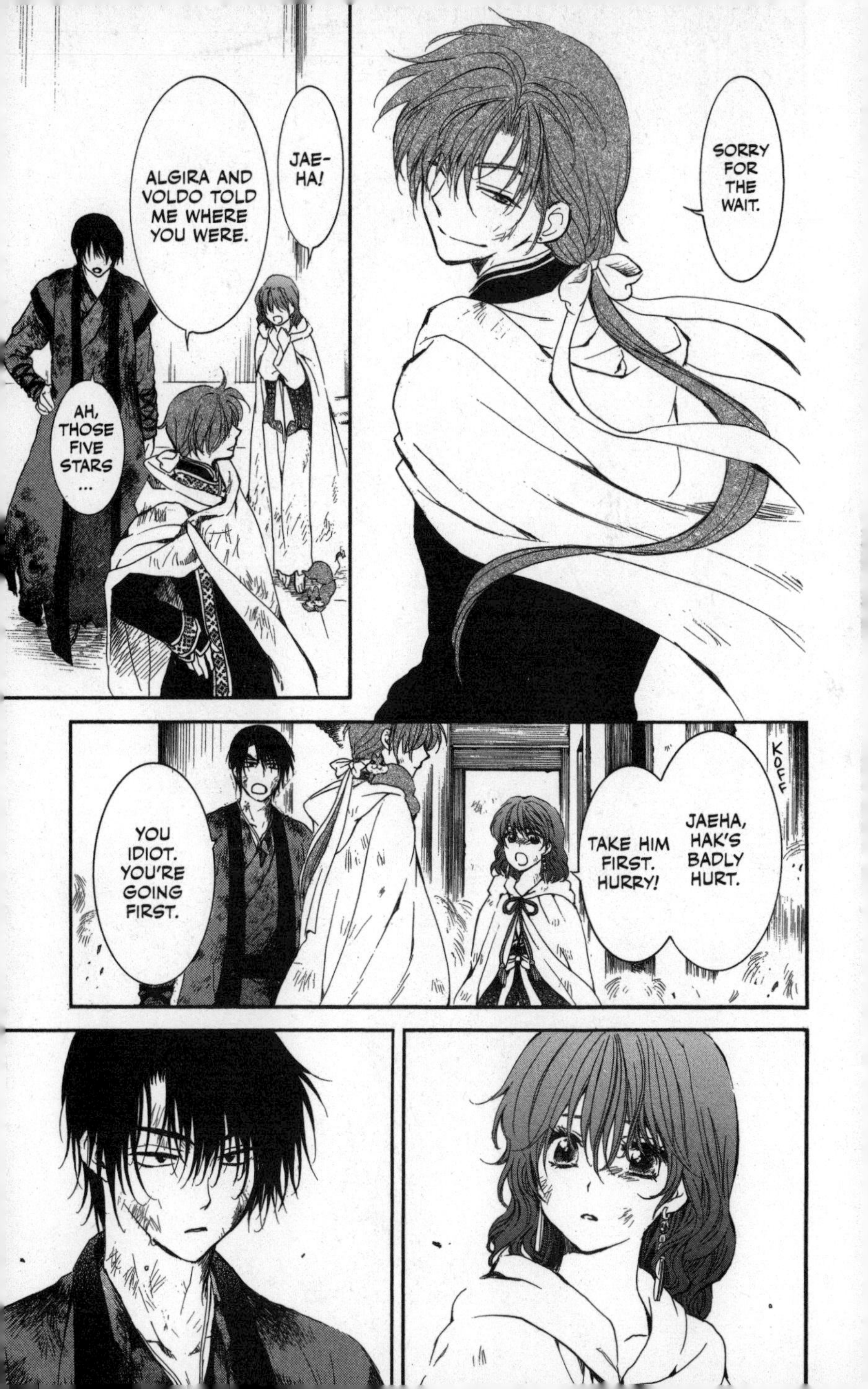
SORRY FOR THE WAIT.
JAE-HA!
ALGIRA AND VOLDO TOLD ME WHERE YOU WERE.
AH, THOSE FIVE STARS...
KOFF
JAEHA, HAK'S BADLY HURT.
TAKE HIM FIRST. HURRY!
YOU IDIOT. YOU'RE GOING FIRST.

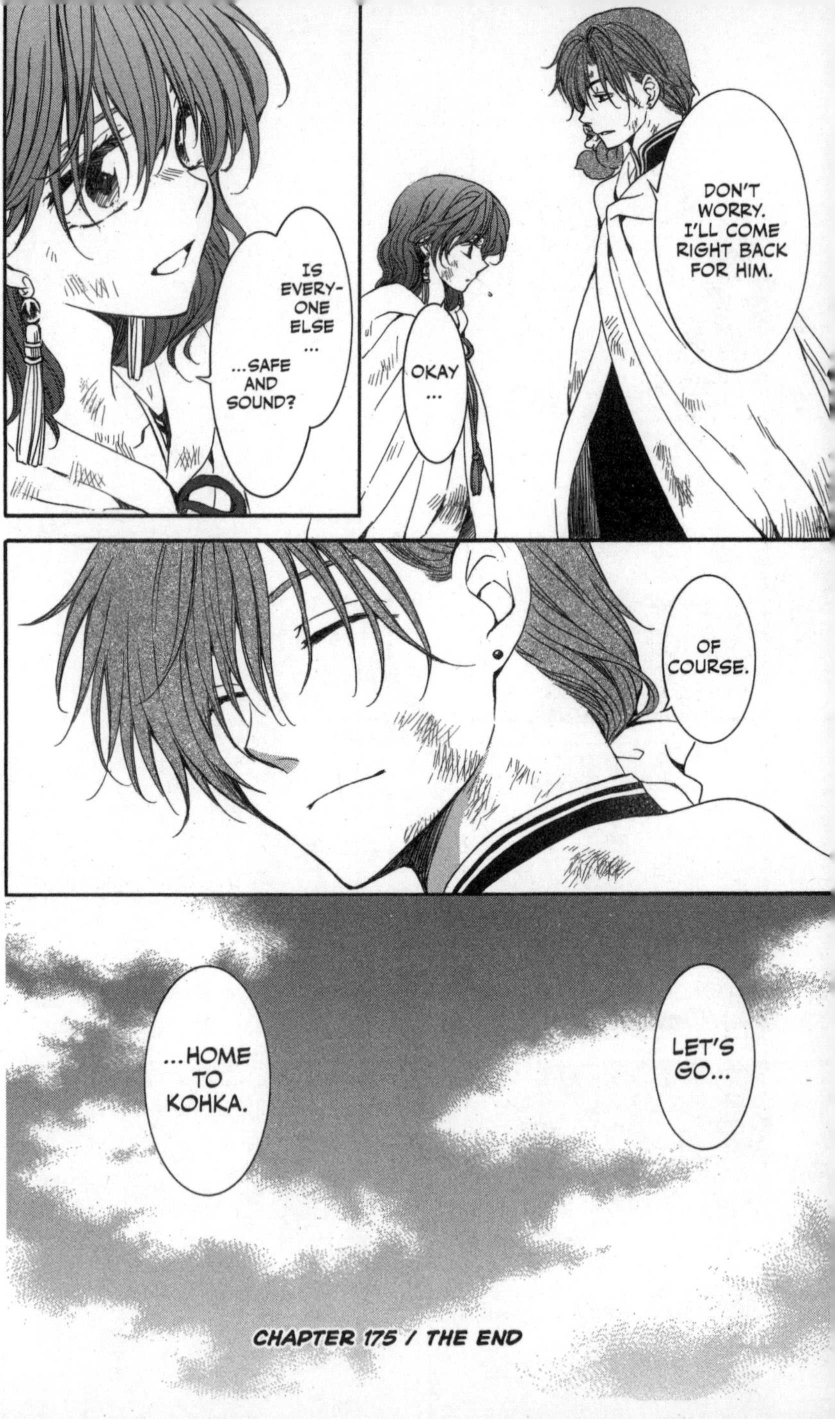
DON'T WORRY. I'LL COME RIGHT BACK FOR HIM.
OKAY...
IS EVERYONE ELSE...
...SAFE AND SOUND?
OF COURSE.
LET'S GO...
...HOME TO KOHKA.
CHAPTER 175 / THE END

Bonus Manga

The Five Stars Afterward

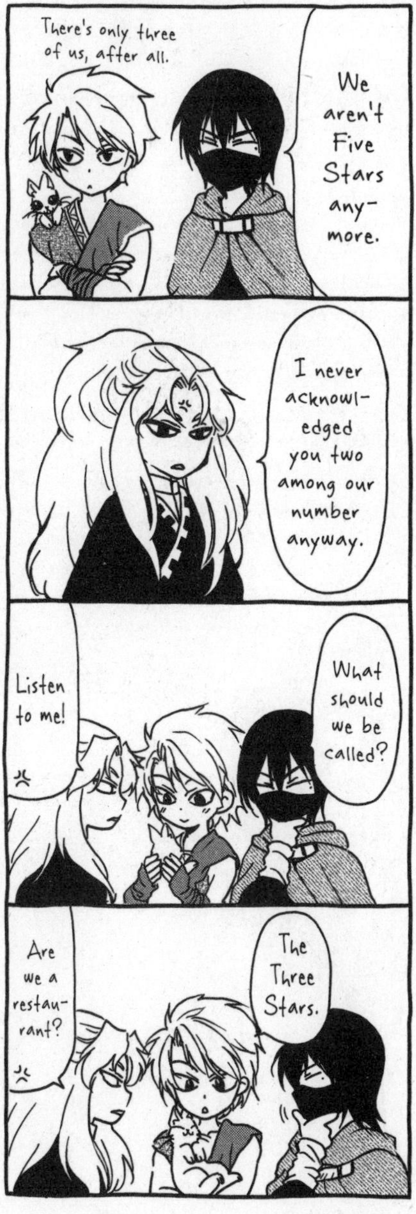
We aren't Five Stars anymore.
There's only three of us, after all.
I never acknowledged you two among our number anyway.
What should we be called?
Listen to me!
The Three Stars.
Are we a restaurant?

Afterword

Thank you very much for reading‼ I wanted to draw Yuran's hair, but I didn't have the opportunity, so I'm showing it here. I also wanted to give additional information on Kuelbo and the Tuuli tribe.

Kuelbo is 35 years old and 190 cm tall [about 6'3"]. (He's actually taller than Hak.)
Yuran is 25 years old.

Even though Yona was a prisoner, Kuelbo only shackled her legs for her defiance, so he felt he was being truthful when he said he treated her respectfully. Though the status of women in the Tuuli tribe improved after Kuelbo's older sister Titia became the goddess of war, men still hold most of the power. Because of his sister's influence, Kuelbo was never especially cruel toward women. Since the Tuuli tribe's nomadic days, it's been normal for the men to be the breadwinners and to take several wives. I think Kuelbo treated Yona like his sister rather than a potential wife. He might have eventually married her for political reasons though. He loved his sister and competed with her as the unifier of their tribe.

Drawing the battles for the Sen Province arc was difficult but fun. I wanted to spend a bit more time on them‼ There's just a little more in the next volume to wrap up this arc.

I'd like to thank my assistants for helping me with my tight deadlines, my editor and the Hana to Yume editorial office for all the trouble I put them through, everyone who's involved with selling Yona merchandise, and my readers for sticking with me for this long. I hope to see you in volume 31‼

Mizuho Kusanagi

Kuelbo
and
Yuran

It's finally volume 30! This series has been continuing for ten years now. Thank you so much to everyone who has been reading it!

—Mizuho Kusanagi

Born on February 3 in Kumamoto Prefecture in Japan, Mizuho Kusanagi began her professional manga career with *Yoiko no Kokoroe* (The Rules of a Good Child) in 2003. Her other works include *NG Life*, which was serialized in *Hana to Yume* and *The Hana to Yume* magazines and published by Hakusensha in Japan. *Yona of the Dawn* was adapted into an anime in 2014.

YONA OF THE DAWN
VOL.30
Shojo Beat Edition

STORY AND ART BY
MIZUHO KUSANAGI

English Adaptation/Ysabet Reinhardt MacFarlane
Translation/JN Productions
Touch-Up Art & Lettering/Lys Blakeslee
Design/Philana Chen
Editor/Amy Yu

Akatsuki no Yona by Mizuho Kusanagi
© Mizuho Kusanagi 2019
All rights reserved.
First published in Japan in 2019 by HAKUSENSHA, Inc., Tokyo.
English language translation rights arranged with
HAKUSENSHA, Inc., Tokyo.

The stories, characters and incidents mentioned in this publication
are entirely fictional.

Printed in the U.S.A.

Published by VIZ Media, LLC
P.O. Box 77010
San Francisco, CA 94107

10 9 8 7 6 5 4 3 2 1
First printing, June 2021

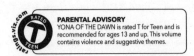

viz.com   shojobeat.com